TONAL INTELLIGENCE

———————
LITERATURE NOW

LITERATURE NOW

Matthew Hart, David James, and Rebecca L. Walkowitz, Series Editors

Literature Now offers a distinct vision of late-twentieth- and early-twenty-first-century literary culture. Addressing contemporary literature and the ways we understand its meaning, the series includes books that are comparative and transnational in scope as well as those that focus on national and regional literary cultures.

Caren Irr, *Toward the Geopolitical Novel: U.S. Fiction in the Twenty-First Century*

Heather Houser, *Ecosickness in Contemporary U.S. Fiction: Environment and Affect*

Mrinalini Chakravorty, *In Stereotype: South Asia in the Global Literary Imaginary*

Héctor Hoyos, *Beyond Bolaño: The Global Latin American Novel*

Rebecca L. Walkowitz, *Born Translated: The Contemporary Novel in an Age of World Literature*

Carol Jacobs, *Sebald's Vision*

Sarah Phillips Casteel, *Calypso Jews: Jewishness in the Caribbean Literary Imagination*

Jeremy Rosen, *Minor Characters Have Their Day: Genre and the Contemporary Literary Marketplace*

Jesse Matz, *Lasting Impressions: The Legacies of Impressionism in Contemporary Culture*

Ashley T. Shelden, *Unmaking Love: The Contemporary Novel and the Impossibility of Union*

Theodore Martin, *Contemporary Drift: Genre, Historicism, and the Problem of the Present*

Zara Dinnen, *The Digital Banal: New Media and American Literature and Culture*

Gloria Fisk, *Orhan Pamuk and the Good of World Literature*

Peter Morey, *Islamophobia and the Novel*

Sarah Chihaya, Merve Emre, Katherine Hill, and Jill Richards, *The Ferrante Letters: An Experiment in Collective Criticism*

Christy Wampole, *Degenerative Realism: Novel and Nation in Twenty-First-Century France*

Heather Houser, *Infowhelm: Environmental Art and Literature in an Age of Data*

Jessica Pressman, *Bookishness: Loving Books in a Digital Age*

Tonal Intelligence

THE AESTHETICS OF ASIAN INSCRUTABILITY DURING
THE LONG COLD WAR

Sunny Xiang

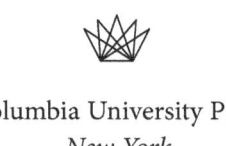

Columbia University Press
New York

Columbia University Press
Publishers Since 1893
New York   Chichester, West Sussex
cup.columbia.edu
Copyright © 2020 Columbia University Press
All rights reserved

Library of Congress Cataloging-in-Publication Data
Names: Xiang, Sunny, author.
Title: Tonal intelligence : the aesthetics of Asian inscrutability during the long cold war / Sunny Xiang.
Other titles: Temperament, temporality, and the American Cold War in Asia
Description: Book edition. | New York : Columbia University Press, [2020] | Includes bibliographical references and index.
Identifiers: LCCN 2020017168 | ISBN 9780231196963 (hardcover) | ISBN 9780231196970 (trade paperback) | ISBN 9780231551915 (ebook)
Subjects: LCSH: Asia—Foreign public opinion, American. | Pacific Area—Foreign public opinion, American. | Orientalism—United States—History—20th century. | Cold War—Secret service. | Asians in literature. | Asians in motion pictures. | Asian-American—Race identity. | Propaganda, American—Asia—History—20th century. | Propaganda, American—Pacific Area—History—20th century. | United States—Foreign relations—1945–1989.
Classification: LCC DS33.4.U6 X53 2020 | DDC 303.48/2507309045—dc23
LC record available at https://lccn.loc.gov/2020017168

Cover image: Charles Yuen, *Gook Mondrian*, 68 inches across, oil on canvas, wood, plaster, 1981
Cover design: Chang Jae Lee

CONTENTS

ACKNOWLEDGMENTS   vii

Introduction: Hardly War, Partly History   1

Chapter One
The Tone of Intelligence: Unconventional Warfare
and Its Archives   25

Chapter Two
The Tone of Rumors: Imperial Tours and Kazuo Ishiguro's
Critique of Japanese Exceptionalism   53

Chapter Three
The Tone of the Times: Historical Temperament in the Works
of Induk Pahk and Theresa Hak Kyung Cha   96

Chapter Four
The Tone of Documentation: Combating the Brainwashee's Drone
in Korean War "Testimonies" and "Confessions"   143

Chapter Five
The Tone of Intimacy: Imperial Brotherhood
and Trinh T. Minh-ha's Cinematic Interviews   189

Coda—The Tone of Commons: Solidarities Without a Solid   236

NOTES   263

BIBLIOGRAPHY   309

INDEX   335

ACKNOWLEDGMENTS

I remember once being charmed by Walter Benjamin's suggestion that people choose to write books because they "are dissatisfied with the books which they could buy but do not like." This seemed like a fine reason to write a book, and so I tucked the quote away. As it happens, my own experience as a writer has been the exact opposite of what Benjamin describes. The book you're reading is a testament to my deep and abiding admiration for those who came before me and came with me. I could never have finished (or started) this book without a long line of people who challenged and encouraged me at close range, who practically enabled a path forward, and who modeled how to meaningfully participate in a life of social, political, and cultural thought. The overwhelming gratitude that I feel for their wisdom, guidance, love, and example exceeds what the genre of the acknowledgment will allow me to express.

First and foremost, I must thank Colleen Lye, my dissertation adviser at UC Berkeley. I can hardly enumerate all the ways that Colleen has made me a better scholar, but I've benefited the most from her lessons in tenacity and generosity. More than anyone else, Colleen helped me recognize how introversion and tenderness can be powerful places from which to think, write, build, and connect. I'm honored to have had Sau-ling Wong in my corner since my first year at Berkeley. Sau-ling essentially taught me how to read Asian American literature and offered discerning feedback on my writing—and she did all this with remarkable compassion and wit, often over food and tea. I couldn't have written my dissertation without the shrewd guidance of Dorothy Hale. Dori had the canny ability to break down exactly what I needed to do and how I ought to go about doing it. On numerous occasions, Steven Lee has offered poignant advice that I carry with me to this day. Elizabeth Abel, Oliver Arnold, Sharon Chon, Alvin Henry, Jason Kim, Rosaline Kyo, Grave Lavery, Janey Lew, Sara Mousavi, Margaret Rhee, and Namwali Serpell also assisted my graduate studies and dissertation writing.

I wouldn't be who or where I am now without the friendships that began in Berkeley and that still nourish me. I strongly suspect that Colleen's dissertation group will forever remain my unsurpassable ideal of conviviality and collaboration. I've learned so much thinking alongside Christopher Fan, Trinh Luu, Paul Nadal, and Ragini Srinivasan over all these years. I'm fortunate to have entered graduate school with Juliana Chow, Seulghee Lee, Manya Lempert, Rosa Martinez, and Rasheed Tazudeen. Their brilliance, passion, humor, and sympathy (as well as their shared devotion to NBA basketball) continue to sustain me. I associate Jeehyun Choi and Xia Zhang with Berkeley, but their impact on me goes far beyond that. In their own special way, they have gifted me with their intellectual and emotional camaraderie and made it safe for me to open myself to them.

It's hard to imagine a time before the "aesthetic migrants." Which is to say, much of my intellectual life can be traced to the seminar "Migratory Aesthetics and Asian/American Studies," organized by the indomitable Tina Chen. An astounding number of official panels, seminars, special issues, and talks were set in motion by this week at Penn State in the summer of 2015. More important, Crystal Baik, Christopher Eng, Christopher Fan, Michelle Huang, Andrew Leong, Cheryl Naruse, Vinh Nguyen, Leland Tabares, and Hentyle Yapp have become the dearest of friends. While everyone listed here provided thoughts on some part of the book manuscript, I'm especially keen to thank Crystal, Chris E., Chris F., Cheryl, Vinh, and Hentyle, who accompanied me along multiple loops of my circular writing process, often reading drafts on short notice and in close succession. Tina herself has been at the very heart of so many aspects of this book. In 2017, at the Global Asias 4 Conference, Tina and Josephine Park organized a roundtable on "Forgetting Wars," which then became a special issue of *Verge: Studies in Global Asias*. Dialoguing with Tina and Jo—as well as with

ACKNOWLEDGMENTS

Jessica Nakamura, Xiaojue Wang, and We Jung Yi—ended up being formative to reshaping the project's conceptual frame. I should also note that my thinking has been enriched and enlarged by the various communities that Tina has spearheaded under the auspices of "Global Asias."

Tina once joked that Penn State was my summer vacation home. She's basically right. In 2018, I returned to State College for the First Book Institute, run by the Americanist dream team of Sean Goudie and Priscilla Wald. Sean, Priscilla, and a whole range of Penn State faculty answered questions I didn't even know I had about writing and publishing a book. They also created a genuine scholarly community. A huge and hearty thanks goes to my fellow FBI participants Ben Bascom, Jordan Carroll, Juliana Chow, Mary Kuhn, Christopher Perreira, Kathryn Walkiewicz, and Xine Yao. There's a corner of my shelf reserved for all of their first books.

I've had the good fortune and exceptional privilege of being supported by various organizations, centers, and libraries while working on this book. Thanks to the American Council of Learned Societies, UC Berkeley's Center for Race and Gender, Yale's MacMillan Center, Yale's Whitney Humanities Center, and Emory's Rose Library for funding my research and writing. The librarians and archivists at the Hoover Library, the Truman Library, the Rose Library, the UC Berkeley Ethnic Studies Library, the Berkeley Art Museum and Pacific Film Archive, the New York Public Library, and the U.S. National Archives helped make this project possible. Eric Van Slander at the National Archives at College Park and Stephanie Cannizzo at the BAM/PFA deserve special mention for going out of their way to facilitate my research.

This book was written in institutions that became intellectual homes. In Florida Atlantic University's English Department, Raphael Dalleo, Elena Machado Sáez, and Adam Spry provided guidance and fellowship. Eric Berlatsky was a chair whose door was always open. When I think about the people at Yale University who enabled this book's materialization, my mind immediately flies to Jane Bordiere and Erica Sayers, the wizards holding down LC 107. I'm humbled by their ability to be fully present—for me and for everyone—every single day of the week. As chairs of the English Department, Langdon Hammer, Ruth Yeazell, and Jessica Brantley often overextended themselves on my behalf. In ordinary and extraordinary ways, my life at Yale has been supported and transformed by Melissa Barton, Felisa Baynes-Ross, Daphne Brooks, Alicia Schmidt Camacho, Jill Campbell, Wai Chee Dimock, Anastasia Eccles, Marta Figlerowicz, Ben Glaser, Alanna

ACKNOWLEDGMENTS

Hickey, Denise Ho, Margaret Homans, Matthew Jacobson, Jill Jarvis, David Kastan, Greta LaFleur, Albert Laguna, Bill Landis, Naomi Levine, Annie Lin, Priyasha Mukhopadhyay, Joe North, Catherine Nicholson, John Peters, Stephen Pitti, Jill Richards, Emily Thornbury, and Quan Tran. I'm indebted to Joe Cleary, Jacqueline Goldsby, Amy Hungerford, Cajetan Iheka, Lisa Lowe, Mary Lui, Stephanie Newell, Rasheed Tazudeen, and John Williams for reading portions of the manuscript with probity and care. Anusha Alles, Yuni Chang, Madeleine Han, Janis Jin, Aanchal Saraf, Courtney Sato, Oriana Tang, Minh Vu, and Arthur Wang are among the many students who have imparted lasting wisdom.

Anne Cheng, Joseph Jeon, Crystal Parikh, Thy Phu, Dorothy Wang, and Jini Kim Watson fortified me during the writing of this book with their feedback and mentorship. At one point or another, Wesley Attewell, Long Bui, Douglas Ishii, Long Le-Khac, Marguerite Nguyen, and Amy Tang provided reading tips, timely texts and emails, and brilliant friendship. Sejal Amin, Jie Feng, Grace Huang, Daniel Hsu, Dorothy Jackson, Christina Kwauk, Tina Lam, Denny Lau, Kathy Lin, Eugene Oh, Jaime Quan, Tiffany Sakato, Aram Seo, April Simpson, Joy Woellhart, and Kathryn Yu have made the journey better. None of this would have been possible without my undergraduate adviser Jules Law. Thank you for teaching me to see the world and myself anew.

My appreciation for Philip Leventhal at Columbia University Press runs deep. As an editor, he did much more than shepherd; he also listened, read, critiqued, and advocated. Editorial assistant Monique Briones was a calming force and made the heavy lifting for this book seem easy. The series editors of Literature Now—Matthew Hart, David James, and Rebecca Walkowitz—gave me the courage to write. In particular, Matt's comments helped spur and shape my thinking at various stages. The two anonymous readers solicited by Columbia University Press offered some of the most useful and gratifying feedback for this book. Not only did they seriously engage my claims, but they tried to make the project better based on a genuine understanding of what it's trying to do. The production of this book coincided with the COVID-19 outbreak. For this reason, I'm all the more eager to thank Susan Pensak, Partha Chakrabartty, and Do Mi Stauber. Charles Yuen graciously allowed me to use *Gook Mondrian* (1981) for the cover art. I'm grateful to Margo Irvin at Stanford University Press for her unstinting attention and support. An earlier version of chapter 4 appeared in *Comparative Literature.*

I used to envy the Asian Americans who grew up on the two coasts. Now I take due pride in calling Alabama home. Part of this comes from being my mother's daughter. She's the fiercest and most determined woman I know. Not only did she raise me by herself in a strange country but—crucially—she made sure that I always had books on hand, allowed me to linger for hours at the public library, and, after a bit of cajoling, eventually relaxed the rule against reading at the dinner table. Whatever the circumstance, my father tends to respond by loving—and laughing—more deeply and expansively. I hope I've managed to learn this from him. Throughout the years, my sister has buoyed me with joy and light. She's my inspiration for living fully and fearlessly. I've often thought of my grandfather while writing. Because we could understand each other simply by sitting side by side holding hands, I have reason to believe that he can understand this book, and his importance to it, without my ever having told him. I haven't always been the best company during the writing of this book, and I've often prioritized my job over the people dearest to me. In spite of this, the Xiangs, Wangs, Voungs, and Lees have given me an abundance of love. But if there's anyone who has been here for me at every turn, who has graced me with presence and plenitude every step of the way, it's Jan. Thank you for this and more.

TONAL INTELLIGENCE

INTRODUCTION

Hardly War, Partly History

> It was hardly war, the hardliest of wars. Hardly, hardly.
>
> It was partly history.
>
> —DON MEE CHOI, *HARDLY WAR* (2016)

In many respects, this book is a study of the American Cold War in Asia. In others, it is about the methodological quandaries and insights introduced by this seemingly straightforward statement. "The American Cold War in Asia" appears to name both a period and a place, but can we put this war on a timeline or a map? And, just to be sure, are we talking about an American war *in* Asia, or do we mean an American war *against* Asia? Who fought whom exactly, and what does it even mean to fight—or win—a "cold" war?

This line of questioning presupposes a particular image of war. Wars are pegged to specific dates that make up the endpoints of a line. They possess a strong oppositional stance, an agonistic and moralized division between two sides. These facets are related: we can "peg" wars because they are explosive and climactic. That is, wars are seen as a discrete period because their exceptionality is so insistently troped as violence, because their heroic and destructive capacities produce eventfulness. And yet, to the extent that wars are triumphant and traumatic, they are also temporary. The exceptional violence of war can be brought into relief only by an abiding state of peace. Wars are cushioned by normalcy, by a *before* and *after*, a *prewar* and *postwar*. Of these, the postwar holds particular significance. For it is presumably from this newly enlightened vantage point that the devastations of war can be judiciously remembered, represented, studied, and redeemed. The postwar, a state of reason and healing, marks war's end.[1]

All wars can be understood through this rubric. Suffice to say, no war adheres to it. The American Cold War in Asia, however, foils this rubric so thoroughly that it all but commands us to transform *war* from a historical event into a historiographic problem. *Tonal Intelligence*, then, is less a straightforward study of the American Cold War in Asia than a methodological experiment in what it means to take this war up as an object of inquiry. As the title of my book suggests, such an experiment will entail reconceptualizing both the archive animated by the Cold War (an archive of *intelligence*) and the method for analyzing the racial aporias therein (a method guided by *tone*). I should say at the outset that this study's principal objective is not to unveil a new account of *tone*, a term that many readers have asked me to define; rather, it is to use an intuitive understanding of tone to provide an alternate account of *race* and *war*, terms that, due to their apparent self-evidence, no one has ever asked me to define.

With this latter aim in mind, let us begin by unsettling the term *Cold War*; let us call out its bluster and cut it down to size. Although used in France as early as the 1930s, the *Cold War*, as we now understand it, is commonly traced to British writer George Orwell's 1945 essay "You and the Atomic Bomb." The term was then ushered into the American consciousness by Walter Lippmann's articles in the *New York Herald Tribune* in 1947. During these years, terms such as "cold war" and "so-called cold war" still pervaded the vernacular. By the mid-1950s, such hesitant, conjectural expressions would give way to "'the Cold War' in capital letters," thereby converting "a number of disputable perspectives" into a single, "bipolar" confrontation.[2] This Manichaean conflict that we now know as the Cold War had global effects, but it is a distinctly American appellation and concept. The Soviets did not really take up the term until the late 1980s, during Mikhail Gorbachev's administration.[3] And in the "Third World," the Cold War between superpowers intermixed with civil wars, colonial wars, and guerrilla wars to create an array of deadly conflagrations and mundane practices that went by different names.

The Cold War, enclosed between 1945 and 1989, connotes a dyadic global order of "Soviet communism" and "American democracy." Based on this definition, the Korean War, the Bay of Pigs invasion, the overthrow of Iran's democratically elected prime minister, the suppression of the anti-imperial Hukbalahap movement in the Philippines, the nuclear tests at the Marshall Islands, and other U.S. interventions in the Third World

INTRODUCTION

can be comprehended as peacekeeping measures, noble efforts to *avoid war* with the Soviet Union. In this book, I set aside the *Cold War* for the more open-ended *cold war*, a typographical convention that I borrow from Heonik Kwon.[4] Where the Cold War is a historical event, the cold war is a historiographic problem. And if the Cold War is bipolar, then the cold war is irreducibly plural, gesturing toward the many proxy affairs that were indelibly accented, or forcibly imposed, by the Soviet–American standoff, but that do not live out the histories, subscribe to the politics, or bear forth the subjectivities proper to it. A lower-case cold war is what I think South Korean poet and translator Don Mee Choi has in mind when using the phrase "the hardliest of wars."[5] Fittingly, *hardly* can mean both "violently" and "barely."[6] The title of Choi's 2016 poetry collection, *Hardly War,* thus signifies in two ways. On the one hand, "hardly war" refers to a war that has hardened into a historical event with a proper name. It reflects the fact that the U.S. government sought to impress upon its citizens that "the world situation, which is called a *cold war,* is in fact a *real war.*"[7] On the other hand, "hardly war" describes a war that lacks recognizably warlike features. Gallup polls from 1955 reveal that many Americans could not define this thing called a "cold war." Phrases such as "war without actual fighting," "war without arms," and "bloodless war" evince a belief that the period following World War II was a "long peace."[8] Washington's attempts to regulate the meaning of the cold war (at once a "real war" and a "long peace") were closely related to its portrayal of the United States as a "benevolent" leader that oversaw "occupations," "trusteeships," "dependencies," and "unincorporated territories." This efflorescence of euphemisms reveals the cold war to be not only an imperial war that proliferated new structures of governmentality, but also an imperial poetics that operationalized diminution and occlusion.[9] The distinctiveness of such a war—indeed, the violence—lies in transforming the very concept of war. A "cold" war fought by a "benevolent" empire pioneered a style of warfare that was deemed unconventional, and it created an experience of wartime that is often quotidian and still ongoing.

Without denying the presence of real guns, real fire, real bombs, and real casualties across Asia and the Pacific, this book explores why the United States saw the Orient as a theater of "total war." Total war may include heavy artillery and deadly explosives, but these are not part of its strategic appeal. As President Dwight Eisenhower put it in 1953, total war was "a new kind of war," insofar as it called for "the dedication of the energies, the resources, and the imaginations of all peaceful nations."[10] Waged at the scale of norms and values, the cold war, as a total war, was an effort to defend, define, and disseminate "the American way of life"—to turn *war* into a whole arrangement of everyday habits, relationships, feelings, and institutions. A lowercase cold war therefore not only problematizes and pluralizes war, but also normalizes it. For all the ways that this war was fought *over* lives and *through* lives, it was above all a habituation of war as a *way of life*. *Tonal Intelligence* is especially interested in the range of "unconventional" methods inaugurated by a totalizing cold war.[11] Beginning in the 1940s and 1950s, *intelligence*—what was variously called cultural diplomacy, propaganda, psychological warfare, and political warfare—became the governing principle of U.S. foreign policy. Intelligence was just as central to fighting a "war of ideas" against communist enemies as it was to protecting a "way of life" among democratic allies. In other words, despite their diametrically opposed self-conceptions, both the cold war's hawkish and dovish programs converged on a shared understanding of reliable intelligence. In the name of "peace-fare," both were tasked with the creative manipulation of objective information, official news, and secret propaganda.[12]

In the mixed media collection *Hardly War*, Choi draws out the poetic dimension of intelligence. What she calls a "geopolitical poetics" fashions histrionic neologisms out of the weakest words and discloses the brutality of the most ordinary phrases. Such a poetics disperses cheerily innocuous ideas across posters, photos, jingles, and guidebooks. One work anthropomorphizes the colorful hydrangeas of the 1962 film *The Manchurian Candidate*. Another riffs on a BBC broadcast that "counter-counterly stressed nothing in particular" (12). In marshaling a geopolitical poetics, Choi portrays "hardly war" as "purely illustrative," "narrowly narrated," "naturally convincing," "barely consequently," "nevertheless necessary," and—my favorite—"partly history." These adverbial phrases sap the explanatory power from words that typically link cause and effect. The war that they describe appears as a prolonged non-activity rather than an action drama. By rendering the experience of war ordinary rather than exceptional, Choi shows how intelligence operations made the temporality of war distended rather than discrete:

It was hardly war, the hardliest of wars. Hardly, hardly. It occurred to me that this particular war was hardly war because of kids, more kids, those poor kids. The kids were hungry until we GIs fed them. We dusted them with DDT. Hardly done. Rehabilitation of Korea, that is. It needs chemical fertilizer from the States, power to build things like a country. In the end it was the hardiest of wars made up of bubble gum, which GIs had to show those kids how to chew. In no circumstance whatever can man be comfortable without art. They don't want everlasting charity and we are not giving it to them. We are just lending them a hand until they can stand on their own two feet. A novel idea. This is why it occurred to me that this particular war was hardly war, the hardiest of wars.

My father was hardly himself during the war, then I was born during the era that hardly existed, and, therefore, I hardly existed without DDT. Beauty is pleasure regarded as the quality of a thing. I prefer a paper closet with real paper dresses in it. To be born hardly, hardly after the hardiest of wars, is a matter of debate. Still going forward. We are, that is. (6–7)

Hardly war consists of fairy dust, bubble gum, and a helping hand. It involves using chemical weapons against invisible and unidentifiable enemies and distributing charity and clichés among "kids, more kids, those poor kids." The key distinguishing feature of this indistinct war, though, is a protean grammar of hardliness: "hardly done," "hardly himself," "hardly existed," "born hardly," "hardly after," "hardiest of wars," "hardly hardly." In all these instances, the modifier *hardly* strains for greater precision yet obscures action, agency, and accountability. Its ostentatious exhibition of inconspicuousness and powerlessness works to elongate the action of war, inducing a temporal disorientation: "To be born hardly, hardly after the hardiest of wars, is a matter of debate. Still going forward. We are, that is." This formulation thematizes war's lack of origin and resolution. More, the repetition of "hardly," alongside other qualifications, has a slowing, sputtering effect. Not only are we temporally dislocated—"hardly after the hardiest of wars"—but our central action of "still going forward" seems quiescent and protracted.

War, Mary Dudziak tells us, is frequently treated as a "passive periodizer" and an "abstract historical actor."[13] This is why we tend to feel history's impact when it is incarnated as war. History seems disruptive, traumatic, and melancholic, because we construe it as the byproduct of catastrophe, the imposition of a hurt. It is thanks to this habitual twinning of war and history, I suspect, that our efforts to historicize so often end up fetishizing crises, ruptures, and breaks. Choi's depiction of war as hardly intelligible rather than as spectacularly violent—as conventionalized through unconventional methods—prods us to rethink our approach to cold war historiography. Because the cold war in Asia was a highly mediated regulation of norms, a temperature-controlled feeling of normal, it requires us to engage "war" as a temperament rather than a timeline. To periodize a war whose temporality is derived from a pervasive temperament rather than a punctual event, *Tonal Intelligence* attempts two methodological innovations: it assembles an archive of intelligence, and it employs a reading practice centered on tone.

PERCEPTUAL CRUXES: "WAR" AND "RACE"

This book claims that taking a tonal approach to reading intelligence is particularly critical for understanding the cold war in East and Southeast Asia, a region where the dominant temperament of U.S. foreign policy was suspicion. Put another way, paying attention to an affective-aesthetic register of racial meaning can help us study a theater of operations where the temporal and temperamental ambiguity between a real war and a long peace was closely related to the racial ambiguity between Oriental enemies and Asian friends. In existing criticism on the transpacific cold war, the United States' expansion of military bases, demonstration of nuclear power, and development of cultural programs have received the most attention. There have also been trenchant discussions of the wars in Korea and Vietnam and their slow-burning memory effects. As a whole, this body of thought has acquainted us with the overlapping forces and ideologies—militarism, colonialism, imperialism, settler colonialism, transnational capitalism, racial liberalism, and humanitarianism—that have brought disparate parts of Asia, different sectors of Asian America, and the distinct islands and archipelagos of the Pacific into difficult and asymmetrical relations with each other.[14] In this book, I occasionally use the term "transpacific cold war" to describe this intricate brace of inter-imperial relations. However, I mostly use phrases such as "the American cold war in Asia" in order to honor the specificity of Native Pacific experiences and histories.[15] Although elaborate legal, social, cultural, and discursive regimes of U.S. militarism across "Asia" and "the Pacific" have securitized and standardized the link between these "areas" over the course of the twentieth century, my focus on cold war intelligence contributes to efforts to denaturalize this link. More precisely, my study shows how the masked Oriental of the Far East, in contrast to the naked primitive of the South Pacific, presented racially specific challenges to a war that placed a high premium on strategic information. Geopolitical developments exacerbated these challenges. In particular, the emergence of two Chinas, Koreas, and Vietnams—combined with Washington's confusion of anticolonial nationalism with global communism—established the Oriental as a perfect cross of the racial and ideological unknowns. While to most Americans the Soviet symbolized "the red scare" and the Negro "the race problem," the Oriental exemplified the blending of two kinds of color, one hidden in the heart and the other worn on the skin.[16] So even though U.S. cold war policy viewed numerous racial groups as suspect, the Oriental best shows how the cold war's *suspicious thinking*—motivated by dichotomies of surface and depth, transparency and concealment, visibility and invisibility—converges with the ingrained structures of *racial thinking*. To the extent that suspicion generated an acute anxiety about racial intelligibility, it also intensified the desire for racial intelligence.

In coupling "hardly war" with "partly history," the title of this introduction posits intelligence as both a militaristic strategy and an archival practice. Intelligence may operate at the conjunction of war and history, but it also profoundly destabilizes these terms. Because a temperament of suspicion filters what can be admissible as evidence, I frame all of this book's primary sources—interrogation reports, policy memos, field notes, memoirs, novels, documentaries, and mixed media art—as *racial intelligence*. In a sense, appropriating the category of intelligence reproduces the paranoid perspective of the U.S. cold war security state. Intelligence is both an estimative and an ethnographic genre: its constructions of the "enemy" are inseparable from its imaginings of "race." As a calculation of an enemy's capabilities, intelligence links cultural and psychological analyses with a form of speculative practice. My own interest in intelligence is more historiographic than estimative. Hence, whereas the U.S. state's militarized perspective evaluates racial intelligence based on its credibility and usability, my historiographic perspective repurposes the framework of intelligence to instill a broader awareness about how we perceive, process, and make evidentiary claims about race during periods of crushing uncertainty and staggering change. My turn to Choi's poetry in these opening pages signals a belief that aesthetic forms can provide a kind of intelligence that is especially useful for historiographic ends. This belief is indebted to Raymond Williams, whose writings have taught us that art's core value lies not in its distinctiveness, imaginativeness, or beauty but in its ability to foster informed hypotheses about the historical present.[17] So even as Choi's work critiques the American cold war in Asia, it also introduces questions about the status of this war in our own moment. In the notes to *Hardly War*, Choi explains that one poem includes lines from artworks displayed at a Seattle gallery (91). Another poem incorporates Choi's dreams (94). Choi's receptivity to these "poetic interventions" suggests that a geopolitical poetics is a highly permeable mode of historical documentation (91). Though trained on the past, it remains steeped in the present.

As a lesson in periodization, *Hardly War* helps shift our sights from the obviousness of ruptures to the hardliness of continuity: hardly war is only partly history because it cannot be contained in the past tense. In this book, I use the term *post–cold war* to describe not the cold war's end but its transformation. While this term lends provisional coherence to a bygone era, it also discloses the indecipherability and unnameability of an uncertain future. For me, the most crucial sign of the post–cold war is the geopolitical coinage "Pacific Rim." The Pacific Rim is an "imperialist imaginary" that projects the "dispersed area of Asia and the Pacific as a unified region."[18] From the late nineteenth century to the mid-twentieth century, this "imperialist imaginary" was indisputably a product of U.S. foreign policy. Since the 1980s, however, it has become increasingly uncertain whether the term "imperialist imaginary" refers to an American imaginary or an Asian one. At a post–cold war juncture, the Oriental remains exemplarily suspicious, but we must ask what archetypes of intelligence, evidence, and information are begotten by suspicion at a moment when Asian capitalist modernities have come to emblematize broader global shifts. *Hardly War* is a fascinating study of "wartime" because it dramatizes the centrality of language and media to the cold war in Asia while also showing how this militaristic arsenal has become newly available for critique in a post–cold war period when "Asia" stands for a hyperbolic and immoral variant of capitalist development. If Choi's work reads differently than Asian American and American Orientalist cold war classics such as Jade Snow Wong's *Fifth Chinese Daughter* (1950) and Graham Greene's *The Quiet American* (1955), it is because her post–cold war compositional style discloses how the absorption of late capitalist logics into the artistic process changes the meaning, function, and effect of "information."

INTRODUCTION

Tonal Intelligence uses case studies to compare cold war and post–cold war documentations of race. Its chapters juxtapose Asian subjects who are similar *in profile* but whose self-representations differ *in tone*. These include: a retiring emperor touring postwar reconstruction sites and a self-important citizen meandering down memory lane (chapter 2); an exuberant Christian speaker traveling the lecture circuit and a depersonalized literary speaker who taxonomizes communication systems (chapter 3); an actual POW who is virulently anticommunist and a fictional POW who is seemingly neutral (chapter 4); a CIA officer who exploits informal information gathering and an experimental artist who reappropriates the formal device of the interview (chapter 5). Collectively, these case studies feature personas, both real and fictional, who are caught up in unending wars and who can't keep up with overwhelming change, whose historical shortsightedness often manifests as a frenetic effort to work out and inhabit a new historical scene. Examining parallel Asian subjects allows us to delineate the continuities between American cold war hegemony and Asian economic modernity—to see the resemblance between the "Pacific Rim" that came into global visibility in the 1970s and 1980s and the "Great Crescent" that U.S. planners and policymakers dubbed an "economic defense perimeter" in the 1940s and 1950s.[19] At the same time, these parallel figures produced by U.S.–Asian inter-imperial relations also enable us to get a *tonal* read on the idiosyncrasies of historical *temperament*—to discern how ongoing American militaristic regimes and emergent Asian capitalist regimes have differently formatted the evidence of race.

To make sense of how self-representing Asian subjects test out, try on, and make legible mutating racial identities in the midst of geopolitical transitions, I've found it necessary to devise a manner of reading that's attuned to an aesthetic modality of hardliness—to what I've been calling *tone*. Tone is commonly glossed as disposition, stance, or attitude. I submit that, during the cold war, tone was an axis of analysis amplified by suspicion. This is implied in Christopher Castiglia's assertion that the formalist literary approaches developed during the cold war—approaches that professed to be unencumbered by ideology—"not only made their tone a signature feature of literary criticism but turned dispositions into a *sign* of politics."[20] Because *Tonal Intelligence* investigates the interface between cold war suspicion and cold war Orientalism, it engages tone as an index of not only politics but also race—that is, of not only ideological color but also racial color. A tonal approach to examining Asian self-representation is especially valuable in light of American cold war programs that championed geopolitical and cultural evaluations of race. These evaluative frameworks have bequeathed to us the impossible and frustrating binaries of agency/complicity and authenticity/artificiality. I believe that tone can clear space for other interpretative possibilities, especially when it comes to the Oriental, whose loyalty and reliability were constantly being questioned by multiple parties.[21] If suspicion contoured the cold war paradigm of evidence, then the inscrutable Oriental offers a unique opportunity to explore how racial perception informed the parameters of credible intelligence and the benchmarks for reliable friends. Tone, I am arguing, can function as a historiographic tool for studying a war predicated on racial suspicion, fought through racial intelligence, and preoccupied with racial intelligibility. Reading intelligence tonally will help us appreciate how the cold war's suspicious temperament structures efforts to identify the evidence of race and to extract meaningful truths from it.

To be clear, my contention is not that tone is a distinctive feature of cold war texts populated by Asian personas (all texts have a tone). Nor am I proposing that attending to tone is innately superior to other methods of reading. Tone is an analytical approach provoked by and tailored to the perceptual crux of Oriental inscrutability and the historiographic crux of hardly war. I take pains to emphasize this because race is so easily naturalized as an empirical fact, and war is so frequently assumed to be a historical event. My insistence on deriving a method from the particularities of an analytical object, however, is not intended to foreclose the usefulness of tone for other scholarly endeavors. Indeed, to the contrary, my hope is that the tonal readings in this book can move us to reimagine how we go about studying "race" and "war." Considered tonally, the figure of the cold war Oriental incites us to devote closer scrutiny to the distributions of imperial power that contextualize our perceptions and analyses of race. That is, through tone, we become capable of historicizing the pervasive and mundane workings of American hegemony by tracing how government personnel, professional readers, and everyday individuals made the interpretive leap from racial intelligibility to racial intelligence. Tone, I am suggesting, equips us with a critical language for articulating the continuity between temperament and temporality—one could say, between *cold* and *war*. In this capacity, I wager that tone can be broadly useful for studying race and empire during transitional moments—moments when the very meaning of race and empire are under intense pressure and in extreme flux, when the past becomes incoherent and the future unpredictable for everyone, but most urgently for racial and colonial subjects. Reading for tonal intelligence at these historical stress points will enable us to work out the relation between the vagaries of racial perception and the uncertainties of geopolitical transition. It will also push us to more fully recognize how the evidentiary paradigms of "race" become undone and get remade during the periods of unprecedented change that we call "war."

"FREE ASIANS" AND "ASIAN DIASPORANS"

There are two kinds of Asians that the American cold war brings into view for me. One is the "free Asian." Most literally, a free Asian is an Asian of the "free world." In this book, free Asian names someone who is specially invested in racial *self-representation* as a vehicle for expressing confidence in American cold war values. The free Asians that make up my case studies are the Japanese emperor Hirohito, Korean educator Induk Pahk, Chinese Korean War POW Wang Tsun-ming, and the Philippine humanitarian group Operation Brotherhood. These free Asians appear across multiple genres and media: rumors, memoirs, interrogation reports, speeches, memos, and field notes. All were sponsored by U.S. intelligence organizations, both overtly and covertly, directly and indirectly. As we will find, however, formal intelligence grades such as secret, top secret, confidential, and unclassified are relatively meaningless. The questions driving my analysis of intelligence have little to do with the fact, the extent, or the transparency of government sponsorship. Instead, I want to probe how the latent suspicion underwriting the American cold war in Asia came to inform the evaluation of evidence, and how even the most dubious evidence came to be fashioned into actionable intelligence. How did an explosion of irreconcilable rumors transform the Japanese emperor from a wartime enemy into a cold war ally? Why did Induk Pahk prefer numerical over narrative modes of self-representation in documenting her travels across the United States? What distinguishes a free Chinese "testimony" that is voluntarily given from a communist Chinese "confession" that is forcibly extracted? Why do intelligence reports of a Philippine medical corps in South Vietnam devote more attention to their role as folk entertainers than as medical practitioners? What these cases ultimately share is not the presence of a free Asian; it is that they all mobilize vehicles of racial information for which the source is unknown, unnamed, suspicious, or compromised. And what draws me to these case studies is neither their exemplariness nor their exceptionality; it is that they allow us to perceive how an overabundance of improvisational, redundant, conflicting, and ordinary self-representations came to be converted into geostrategic intelligence.

Each chapter of *Tonal Intelligence* examines a cold war–free Asian alongside a post–cold war subject that I call "Asian diasporan." For this latter group of writers, artists, and critics, self-representation offers a discursive structure for wrestling with the legacies of the American cold war. Kazuo Ishiguro, Theresa Hak Kyung Cha, Ha Jin, and Trinh T. Minh-ha are not representative of a particular aesthetic, discipline, politics, or region. And like the cold war–free Asians I've assembled, they do not fit the mold of discovery or recovery: all are fully canonical and have garnered attention and acclaim. I should also clarify that even though Asian American Studies has provided the most essential conceptual tools for this book, the category of "Asian American"—demographic, political, or disciplinary—isn't always appropriate for the artists in this study. If Ishiguro, Cha, Jin, and Trinh must exist as a collective formation, it is a cold war one. And if this formation must have a name, then I settle for "Asian diasporan," not because this term is the most accurate but because it is the most generic. In this book, "diaspora," a notoriously vague and nostalgic term, is not intended to be ethnically or even racially unifying. That is, "diaspora" denotes disaggregation, and it takes not "Asia" but "cold war" as an origin story and departure point. Uprooting Ishiguro, Cha, Jin, and Trinh from their established critical genealogies and relocating them in a cold war genealogy fundamentally alters our understanding of them. For example, Cha's work has spawned extremely generative accounts of American militarism and Japanese colonialism in Korea, but we have yet to ask what the informational aspect of her aesthetic can tell us about the imperial underpinnings of Pacific Rim racial forms and formations. And while Ishiguro's readers have focused on either his earlier, post–World War II "Japan" novels or his later, "post-Fordist" novels, this divide has prevented us from recognizing that "post-Fordism" was all but synonymous with "Toyotaism," and that it was enabled by U.S. cold war policies in Japan.

As these examples indicate, the post–cold war Asian diasporans in this book must be situated both in the historical context of a post–cold war Pacific Rim and in critical juxtaposition with cold war case studies of Asian self-representation. Such an approach does not aspire to comprehensiveness. *Tonal Intelligence* cannot systematically account for the lived experiences of free Asians and Asian diasporans. Nor can it do justice to specific genres or media. With respect to persons, places, events, and texts, this study cannot demonstrate the diversity and density of examples available. The structure of my book takes inspiration from Yến Lê Espiritu's claim that "critical juxtaposing" can elucidate "what would otherwise not be visible about the contours, contents, and afterlives of war and empire."[22] Juxtaposition disables strongly determinative or merely chronological connections between the cold war and the post–cold war while bringing alternate kinds of relationships and unexpected points of emphasis into view. By juxtaposing case studies from these periods, my aim is to explore how information became intelligent and how difference became intelligible at two distinct yet inseparable moments of U.S.–Asian relations.

The idea of critical juxtaposing reminds us that the prefix *post* is not just a temporal marker but also a methodological one. The term *post–cold war* thus shows how the effort to name a historical period doubles as a reevaluation of methodological priorities. Among cold war scholars who have critically juxtaposed cultural texts and policy instruments, I've found Jodi Kim's study especially instructive. In exploring how "the U.S. governmental archive and Asian American cultural texts both produce knowledge, albeit different kinds of knowledge, about the Cold War," Kim makes a case for "the critical strength of Asian American critique and cultural politics."[23] My post–cold war case studies also perform the dual tasks of periodization and critique, but they use aesthetic techniques that are more akin to Choi's poetics of hardliness. Though lacking "critical strength," this minimalist aesthetic is not guilty of critical weakness. Rather, I suggest that an inexpressive and impersonal aesthetic can be read as a critique of the Pax Americana from the perspective of the Pacific Rim. In other words, a post–cold war aesthetic produces "parallax visions," a term that Bruce Cumings uses to describe a "perceptual turnaround" and a "reversal of optics" in U.S.–East Asian relations.[24] Cumings has geopolitics in mind. But if this visual metaphor of a parallax denotes a different and perhaps deceptive way of seeing the world, then it is surely also relevant to racial perception—to a post–cold war variant of inscrutability. While this post–cold war inscrutability qualifies as a "politics of refusal," a weak and inscrutable aesthetic cannot be a desirable end in and of itself.[25] In this study, I treat practices of perceiving race as historically situated acts, such that the significance of inscrutable representations lies neither in their false content nor in their immanent indeterminacy but in their delineation of the pathways and transfer points between difference and evidence, intelligibility and intelligence. Whether it's Ishiguro's decorously narrated novels, Cha's taxonomic conceptual art, Jin's documentary memoirs, or Trinh's interruptive cinematic techniques, a post–cold war aesthetic critically engages the consequences of the American cold war in Asia while also diagnosing the shifting registers of racial intelligibility in light of post–cold war geopolitical rearrangements. As a mode of *political critique*, this strangely depersonalized aesthetic disrupts the modes of racial legibility enshrined by U.S. cold war attempts to combat suspicion through intelligence. Aestheticizing the evidence of race produces an "intelligence" that is forgettable, parenthetical, unverifiable, and nonactionable. As a working *historical diagnosis*, a post–cold war aesthetic documents the decomposition of liberal personhood wrought by global changes for which Asian capitalist modernity has been a controversial flashpoint. By turning self-representation into different kinds of self-effacement, this aesthetic reveals a convergence between the affective profiles of post-Fordism and Orientalism—that is, between the cool, ugly, ordinary, and underperformative on the one hand, and the inscrutably withdrawn, cruelly disinterested, and inhumanly desensitized on the other.[26]

It may initially seem that cold war–free Asians are self-Orientalizing and ethnographic in their approach to self-representation, whereas post–cold war Asian diasporans are political and resistant. In *Tonal Intelligence*, I try to avoid presenting a political progress narrative that leads from the complicit informant to the critical activist, for such a narrative disavows the agency of cold war–free Asians (i.e., they could do no more than yield to social, geopolitical, and ideological forces) and obscures the historicity of post–cold war Asian diasporans (i.e., they have shed false consciousness entirely and can offer critiques from a position outside of history). At both cold war and post–cold war moments, Asians representing themselves as "Asian" indicate and transform the conditions of domination. Through self-representation, these historical actors dynamically participate in—they activate, interpret, shape, critique, and redraw—rather than outright refuse articulations of power. My objective in this book, then, is neither to demystify the inscrutable in search of clarifying truths nor to overstate its capacity for political recompense but to ask what the mercurial evidence of race can tell us about a world that remains caught up in new and ongoing wars.

UNBOUND OBJECTS

By designating this study's central protagonists as "free Asians" and "Asian diasporans," I am opting to avoid more familiar and more stable disciplinary denominations ("Overseas Chinese," "Asian American," etc.). That said, "free Asian" and "Asian diasporan" are not exactly new terms; they are more forthrightly catachrestic versions of existing terms. *Tonal Intelligence*, like many studies before it, shows that studying the transpacific cold war requires us to occupy the cross-section between Asian American Studies, Asian Studies, and transnational American Studies, as well as between literary studies, cultural studies, and critical historiography. Yet my appeal to catachresis in lieu of disciplinarity also registers some dissatisfaction with the knowledge structures and vocabularies that are on offer. To start, I should note that this book comes from a belief that maintaining the barrier between Asian Studies and Asian American Studies—two fields that share an other-marked object yet understand this object in very different ways—would only serve to perpetuate cold war epistemologies. In *Asia as Method*, Kuan-Hsing Chen uses the term "de–cold war" to describe the endeavor to end the cold war on epistemological terms. Toward this endeavor, Chen asks, "Can an imagined universality be separated from knowledge produced during the cold-war era?"[27] Cold war epistemologies bury the fact that the American war in Southeast Asia galvanized Asian Studies as much as it did Asian American Studies.[28] These same epistemologies have also made the cold war "something of a black hole for ethnic studies scholars," who until recently have focused on either the pre-1952 era of "Asian exclusion" or the post-1965 era of "civil rights movement activism."[29]

To the extent that cold war geopolitics conditioned the formation of Asian and Asian American Studies as contradistinct fields with antithetical worldviews, a de–cold war perspective is beginning to bring these fields onto common ground. This common ground is animated by an "imagined universality," which bridges, exceeds, stretches, and dismantles existing disciplinary rationales. I'm grateful to have this undisciplined ground to stand on. In proceeding from here, *Tonal Intelligence* is ultimately inspired less by either Asian or Asian American Studies per se than by intellectual formations—critical refugee studies, comparative colonialisms, everyday militarisms, critical archival studies—that facilitate more relational lines of inquiry. In particular, my work has been fortified by an interdiscipline that might be called "de–cold war studies." Through de–cold war scholars, I've learned to conceive of the cold war transpacific as an inter-imperial formation structured by institutionalized, normalized, unredressable, and ongoing violences—a formation within which Asians, Asian Americans, and Pacific Islanders are neither passive victims nor complicit perpetrators but, above all, historical subjects who have been participating in the making of imperial modernity and responding to the untenable circumstances it has wrought.[30] Efforts within de–cold war studies to critically recuperate the cold war's militaristic, juridical, and cultural genealogies have also facilitated a transformative relation to the past in ways that allow us to move beyond the Orientalist Manichaeanism of an "East–West" schism. Such efforts have illumined, for example, the intra-Asian racial hierarchies exacerbated by cold war governance and the solidification of Asian settler power in the American Pacific under the auspices of cold war multiculturalism. *Tonal Intelligence* does have a stake in this conversation about inter-imperial relations. It negotiates an epistemological location inclusive of the "free Asian" and "Asian diasporan" in order to engage a parallax view of the Pax Americana and the Pacific Rim, neither of which can exist as such without the other.[31] Although the archives studied in *Tonal Intelligence* cannot countenance a sustained critique of Asian imperialism, they also do not avail a monolithic critique of American imperialism. By simulating a kind of parallax through critical juxtapositions, my hope is to employ U.S.–Asian inter-imperial relations as a motivating context for investigating the forms of racial evidence that the inscrutable Oriental brings to bear.

Tonal Intelligence's more central contribution to de–cold war studies lies in foregrounding questions of archive and method. Such an approach constitutes a strong rebuff of the cold war valorization of "applied knowledge." According to this cold war logic, Asian and Asian American Studies are built on the application of disciplinary methods to an already existing empirical object. Pheng Cheah writes: "Regardless of how interdisciplinary or theoretically sophisticated Asian studies are or have become, it is always concerned with a bound object. Generally, its focus is information retrieval and not theoretical reflection and speculation that pertain to the whole of humanity."[32] It is, however, not only the "universal" perspective that consigns the study of areas, cultures, and races to bounded particularity. I agree with Sylvia Yanagisako's assessment that Asian American Studies often ends up predicating its political desires on the preservation of a bound object: "The constitution of Asian American studies as an interdisciplinary field of study with its distinctive subjects and social and cultural processes affirms the distinctiveness of 'Asian American' space from 'Asian' space, thus reaffirming the typology of geopoliticocultural spaces of area studies." Yanagisako defines "Asian exclusion acts" as "the acts of exclusion through which scholars in Asian studies and Asian American studies have constructed and maintained the boundary between their respective fields of study."[33] By invoking the name of American exclusion laws, Yanagisako insinuates that denying the porosity between the objects claimed by Asian Studies and Asian American Studies enacts a kind of racial self-surveillance.

In *Tonal Intelligence*, I experiment with alternate historicisms and alternate empiricisms in the hope of sparking more methodological curiosity in ethnic studies, area studies, and other fields founded on, delimited by, and named after their object of study. This is less of an injunction to course-correct than an expression of appreciation for scholars who have challenged me to investigate why empires have an archival impulse and emboldened me to read imperial archives for something other than the empirical fact of race or the melancholic absence of race.[34] In reading for race in the American cold war archive, then, my guiding question is not so much how intelligence documents have captured, surveilled, and excluded the racial other, but rather how the Oriental has informed the methods, models, temperaments, and *tones* that allow one to resolve problems of racial intelligibility and to produce documents of racial intelligence. In being indeterminate rather than given, porous rather than bounded, the inscrutable Oriental obliges us to better recognize how an object of analysis can reshape the methods that we bring to it. Less of a doing than an undoing, *method* in this book refers neither to broadly applicable procedures nor to cherished disciplinary orthodoxies but to a condition of historically mindful and aesthetically attuned questioning.

When tasked with studying an inscrutable object and an imperceptible war—when faced with an inability to corroborate ostensibly self-evident facts and events—a methodological turn to tone will allow us to dwell in a critical encounter and to be surprised and transformed by an analytical object.

Of course, the inscrutable Oriental is not the only racial object to possess a tenacious yet generative opacity.[35] In fact, I credit the misprisions of a whole range of other racial objects for impressing upon me the critical power of what Robyn Wiegman calls "object lessons." Instead of assuming that a disciplinary field is circumscribed by its bound object, Wiegman encourages us to ask how objects beget particular "field imaginaries," a term that includes both interpretive practices and political ideals.[36] I think of *Tonal Intelligence* as an effort to draw out such object lessons; it is not an effort to document a valorized subjectivity or to write this subjectivity into being. Given this methodological orientation, I am rather undiscriminating in my usage of the terms *object* and *subject*, as well as *Oriental* and *Asian*. I let this oscillation overrun the page in order to register the epistemological effects of a dissembling, disruptive, and unbound object, which we must be careful to distinguish from both a given object and an achieved subject. In centering a tonal analysis, I am endeavoring to engage these epistemological effects toward historiographic ends. Unlike actual intelligence analysts, I rely on tone not to target the racial enemy but to heed and honor the recondite racial object. This method of racial analysis is an inducement to tarry with our perceptions and misperceptions—to hold off on accepting, correcting, or denying these perceptions and to instead ask how "race" and "war" came to be such historically interesting and politically fraught *problems* of perception.[37] Although tone will do little to clarify the objects and events under examination, I believe that it can be an unusual resource—maybe our best resource—for historicizing the inscrutability of the Oriental and the hardliness of the cold war.

EXPERIMENTS IN TONE

The racial objects of this study are known to undermine the frames of reference that have been applied to them—by intelligence analysts, state officials, everyday citizens, academic scholars, and all kinds of "readers" from both sides of the Pacific, including myself. The chapters to follow can be seen as an effort to track the ways in which these objects exceed the explanatory scope of existing epistemological and evidentiary schemes. This project of tracking takes the form of exploratory case studies, each of which features experiments in tone. The chapters in this book are not intended to be chronological, but they do have a temporal arc, moving from the enormously successful intelligence operations in Japan that grew out of U.S. wartime policy to the last flicker of optimism in the short-lived U.S.-backed nation of South Vietnam. There is also a spatial arc, as the case studies move from the heart of Pacific Rim discourse—U.S.–Japan relations—to the more distant and less miraculous cases of Mainland China and postsocialist Vietnam. By reading for the tone of intelligence—whether in a classified record or a literary text, and in both cold war and post-cold war contexts—we will be able to discern the relation between an inscrutable other and an epistemological style, a problematic object of knowledge and an improvisational way of knowing.

The most satisfying account of how all this plays out will come in the case studies in chapters 2–5. Before proceeding there, chapter 1, "The Tone of Intelligence: Unconventional Warfare and Its Archives," will offer a fuller elaboration of the book's key concepts—tone and intelligence—in relation to the long cold war. I discuss here how U.S. cold war policy made archival practice part and parcel of unconventional warfare through the innovation of its intelligence apparatuses. Most fundamentally, this process involved creating separate domains for overt and covert information. We will discover, though, that the cold war Oriental, as prospective ally yet probable enemy, unsettled these neat divisions. In doing so, this inscrutable figure exerted a shaping force on cold war archives and conditioned the forms of evidence delivered by these archives. How do we go about reading for inscrutability in the cold war archives? I make two propositions. First, I suggest that the Oriental's ideological and racial inscrutability requires us to understand cold war Asian self-representation as a problem of *intelligence* rather than an expression of *culture*. Second, in order to track but not parse inscrutability, I advocate shifting our focus from the archive's expressed/repressed content to its formal logics and affective tones. This chapter takes an inductive approach to explaining what exactly I mean by tone. Key to this endeavor is the CIA's internal journal *Studies in Intelligence*. By following the charged debate within this journal on the role of *qualifiers* in intelligence writing, I will show how tone became a vital intelligence resource during the cold war, insofar as it could relay the temperaments of suspicion and uncertainty provoked by the racial unknown. To conclude, this chapter considers how tone can help us periodize the post–cold war, a term that—I cannot emphasize enough—describes not a decisive end to the cold war but an especially charged instance of instability within this war.

My first case study explores a most unreliable source of intelligence: rumors. Chapter 2, "The Tone of Rumors: Imperial Tours and Kazuo Ishiguro's Critique of Japanese Exceptionalism," shows how during the U.S. Occupation of Japan, this anonymous and disreputable vehicle of communication indirectly helped remake the Japanese emperor Hirohito from a divine ruler into a friendly "human emperor." The part of this democratization project that inspired the most intense public speculation was a series of "inspection tours" across Japan's prefectures. Although U.S. officials often dismissed the prodigious, outlandish, and contradictory rumors that accompanied the touring emperor, I contend that these rumors in fact helped calibrate the political and emotional atmosphere of regime change. Specifically, the tone of rumors, a quality that has to do with their quantity rather than their content, had the effect of binding the harmless, hapless, and merely human emperor to the everyday Japanese citizenry, rendering both innocent bystanders to Japanese militarism. This account of the emperor's tours as an occasion for affective norming sets up my discussion of Kazuo Ishiguro, a Japanese-born British writer who has been far more interested in the everyday processing of national forgetting than the traumatic witnessing of war. *An Artist of the Floating World* (1986) presents a "tour" of postwar Japan that parallels the emperor's outings. As narrator Masuji Ono wanders across sites of national reconstruction, he recalls not so much memories but rumors, all of which serve to substantiate his reputation as a wartime propaganda artist. Strangely, over the course of this novelistic journey, Ono's ritualistic championing of Japanese militarism evolves into unthinking tributes to American democracy. Examining Ono alongside Hirohito allows us to make sense of this about-face. Where Occupation-era rumors gave Hirohito a "human" shape, Ishiguro's dialogic approach to characterization stages his protagonist's disappearance into a circuit of hearsay. I suggest that the narrative economy of rumors formalizes a post-Fordist information economy. If a cold war tone has the ability to restore a sentiment of innocence during Japan's rebirth as a democratic nation in the 1940s and 1950s, then a post–cold war tone gives expression to the busy buzz of indistinguishable characters whose rumors have turned "identity" into a kind of knowledge work during Japan's economic resurgence in the 1970s and 1980s.

The fact that U.S. cold war priorities in Asia and the Pacific indefinitely delayed the adjudication of Japanese war crimes in this region has led Lisa Yoneyama to coin the term *transwar*.[38] Such a war remains unresolved precisely because it confuses the ideological agendas of separate conflicts and commingles American and Japanese imperial desires. A transwar produces a dilemma for racial intelligence not only because good Asians and bad Asians were indistinguishable but also because the geopoliticized criteria for "good" and "bad" were being rapidly reworked as former enemies became indispensable allies. Chapter 3, "The Tone of the Times: Historical Temperament in the Works of Induk Pahk and Theresa Hak Kyung Cha," examines how the transwar was experienced in South Korea, a place where the residual legacies of Japanese colonialism and the surging demands of American militarism came to a head. This chapter focuses on two Korean American writers whose documentations of their transitional present may at first seem blatantly ahistorical. One is Christian educator Induk Pahk, whose three English-language memoirs, published between 1951 and 1976, detail her extensive travels as a U.S.-sponsored speaker. Pahk's memoirs employ rhetorical devices—numbers and aphorisms—that cast modern progress as a product of scientific reason and divine will. These modern facts and moral truths contribute to a tone of excessive haste: the teetering present that Pahk occupies is always too rapidly sliding into a triumphal future. I propose that Pahk's disproportionate hurry is specific to a transwar moment when U.S. cold war priorities required Koreans to move on from the crimes of their Japanese colonizers. Even though Pahk largely avoids addressing politics or geopolitics, her memoirs nonetheless tonally convey the urgency of overcoming the anticolonial nationalism of World War II and securing the anticommunist nationalism of a free-world future. I juxtapose Pahk's self-representations with those of Theresa Hak Kyung Cha, a conceptual artist working in the 1970s and 1980s. Whereas Korea's colonial history seems mostly inconsequential for Pahk, it is exceptionally traumatic for Cha. This difference exemplifies David Scott's observation that modernity's transitional moments can inspire tonally different interpretations. The "mood of [a] historical drama" (in our case, a drama of war and colonialism) differs depending on whether it's interpreted as revolutionary heroism or tragic suffering. If periods of transition give rise to "a new darkened atmosphere" or "a new tone" that is subject to historically differentiated interpretations, then we might view the euphoric breathlessness of Pahk's narrative and the traumatic suspension of Cha's as tonal interpretations of the era in which they are writing.[39] Moving away from characterizations of Cha as a melancholic historian of Korea's tragic past, I explore her aestheticization of communication systems in relation to Korea's unprecedented economic ascent. This interpretation does not deny the significance of Japanese formal colonialism or American military occupation; rather, it emphasizes that these neocolonial relations have surfaced in new ways at a post–cold war moment when Korea's economic success is entangled with Japan's economic resurgence and with America's war in Vietnam.

In Ishiguro's novels and Pahk's memoirs, we encounter figures who blatantly lack historical insight or foresight: in their frenetic attempts to catch up with their own historical moment, these enthusiastically presentist subjects paradoxically end up seeming very dated very fast. In chapter 4, "The Tone of Documentation: Combatting the Brainwashee's Drone in Korean War 'Testimonies' and 'Confessions,'" we meet a different kind of narrative persona: a POW who touts his singular ability to rise above ideological suasion and, in turn, above historical contingency. This persona appears in both Ha Jin's novelized Korean War memoir *War Trash* (2005) and a U.S. intelligence report entitled *Wang Tsun-ming, Anti-Communist: An Autobiographical Account of Chinese Communist Thought Reform* (1954). Where Jin's fictional protagonist Yu Yuan maintains a political and tonal neutrality in order to demonstrate his resilience to indoctrination, Wang suggests that it is the tenacity of his anticommunism that has steeled him against political and psychological manipulation. To understand the tonal difference between Wang's cold war anticommunism and Yu's post–cold war anticommunism, I situate their first-person accounts in relation to U.S. psychological warfare campaigns during the Korean War. I'm especially interested in the United States' characterizations of Chinese communist "brainwashing" as not only a strategy of indoctrination but also a technique of inscription. Against the eerie tonality of the "brainwashee," whose mind has been rewired and rewritten, Wang infuses his anticommunist declarations with embodied fervor. His narrative and political reliability, in other words, depends on suturing mind and body. By contrast, Yu's crafts a professedly neutral account by extinguishing the heat of ideological speech. In a move that literalizes what he calls a "documentary manner," Yu restricts his narrative presence to a dispassionate and disembodied hand manipulating documents. For Jin, this documentary realism bespeaks a conviction in the ability of literary fiction to countermand the distortive propaganda of the Chinese party-state. While this post-Tiananmen stance against censorship tends to position Jin's work as a testimony or exposé, I analyze his documentary technique of reproducing "notes and files" in relation to the PRC's rise as a pirate nation—that is, as a premier violator of intellectual property laws. Through this alternate framing, we can come to view *War Trash*'s tone of documentation as both distinctly literary (in view of Jin's critique of actual Korean War memoirs) and disconcertingly literal (in view of Jin's alleged plagiarism of these same memoirs).

Of course, racial self-representation is never merely individualistic; it is often intended as or interpreted as representative of some social group. This was especially the case during the cold war when ideological and geopolitical schisms made it imperative to certify political legitimacy through cultural authenticity. It was by portraying communism as anathema to traditional values that free China, free Korea, and free Vietnam attempted to claim both political and cultural authority. My last case study explores what happens when self-representation serves to secure intimacy bonds within an imagined political collective. Chapter 5, "The Tone of Intimacy: Imperial Brotherhood and Trinh T. Minh-ha's Cinematic Interviews," juxtaposes two disreputable intimacy-making devices that have been disparaged as a trick of ventriloquism. The first is the *brother*, which was "invented" by CIA officer Edward Lansdale in the wake of the 1954–1956 Vietnamese refugee migration. The second is the *interview*, which came into prominence during the post-1975 Vietnamese refugee migration and which filmmaker Trinh Minh-ha exploits for alternative ends in the experimental documentary *Surname Viet, Given Name Nam* (1989). The first part of chapter 5 reads Lansdale's documentations of Operation Brotherhood, a Philippine humanitarian group that arrived in South Vietnam following the partition in 1954. Keying in on Lansdale's representations of Operation Brotherhood's female volunteers, I show how an informal tone helped naturalize the "brother's" informal labors. This tonal analysis serves two ends: first, to disclose the foundational role of racialized and gendered labor in the making of an imperial brotherhood and second, to depict American intelligence officers, rather than Third World Asians, as susceptible to myth and in need of help. I compare the informal tones of intimacy enabled by the counterinsurgency strategy of the brother with Trinh's formal evocation of intimacy through the cinematic strategy of the interview. In *Surname*, Trinh's literalization of the "inter-view" as an interruptive view forecloses the communication between—and the intimacy between—a refugee interviewee and a listener-viewer. More significantly, this self-representational strategy, by emptying out the interview frame, gives tonal expression to the diasporic filmmaker's love for her subjects. The interview, in Trinh's rendering, displaces the sentimental intimacy of a face-to-face dialogue with the tonal intimacy of frame-to-frame encounters. Caught together in the net of representation, filmmaker and subject thus transform self-representation into a kind of co-habitation.

Chapter 5's discussion of tonal intimacy raises the question of what an engagement of race through *tone* rather than *identity* bodes for political forms and formations. Although this question in some sense guides the entire book, I take it up most explicitly in my coda, "The Tone of Commons: Solidarities Without a Solid." In this coda, I think alongside contemporary writers Myung Mi Kim, Ed Park, Eugene Lim, and Pamela Lu, whose works have produced ambient, parasitic, and vaporous manifestations of political collectivity. I pay special attention to Lim's *Dear Cyborgs* (2017) and Lu's *Ambient Parking Lot* (2011). These novels imagine narcoleptic, anemic, indecisive, unmotivated, and underemployed characters in a precarious place between background and foreground, absence and presence. In depicting post–cold war subjects whose coherence as a distinct person is under strain and erasure, Lim and Lu attune us to the tonal profile of a political solidarity that is so contingent yet so overwhelming, so incremental yet so fantastical, so unintelligible yet so common, that I call it a "solidarity without a solid."

Chapter One

THE TONE OF INTELLIGENCE

Unconventional Warfare and Its Archives

> The dissemination of truth is not enough.
>
> —JACKSON COMMITTEE, "THE PRESIDENT'S COMMITTEE
> ON INTERNATIONAL INFORMATION ACTIVITIES" (1953)

"What is in a rim?" This is the question that Arif Dirlik poses in the title of the widely cited critical anthology, *What Is in a Rim? Critical Perspectives on the Pacific Region Idea* (1995).[1] There is a mock earnestness to Dirlik's question, which simultaneously points out and deflates the wonder of "the Pacific Region idea." Dirlik phrases it in a way that preempts the possibility of defining "a rim;" instead, he enjoins the reader to ponder the void *in* this rim. To the extent that this flickering rim/void converges with speculative definitions of archipelago as both "arc" and "abyss," it can be said to function as "a prime metaphor within the structuring grammar of colonial modernity."[2] The crux of the question seems to be: What can fill in a rim and round out a real? Or: How does a rim seduce us with its puffed-up promise of boundlessness? What "ideas"—observations, hypotheses, visions, epistemologies—are borne out by this seduction? Concisely: How does a rim "manifest" destiny?

Insofar as the United States has persistently denied its settler origins and zealously domesticized new frontiers, it has long imagined "empire" as a distant "rim." Initially, overseas exploits, which began with the annexation of the Midway Islands in 1867, were seen as incompatible with American republicanism. However, after acquiring Hawaiʻi, Guam, the Philippines, Puerto Rico, and Cuba in 1898, the United States began to tout the benevolence of American governance over the cruelties of European colonialism. This archipelagic rim, in charting the antipodes of empire, allowed Americans to glimpse the outlines of a transcendent future, to imagine the world's outermost horizons as available for the taking. At the same time, these geographically and culturally removed outposts, some appearing as mere dots on the map, abstracted the very concept of empire, rendering it *merely* imaginary, beyond the realm of the here-and-now. Dirlik, of course, is writing with regard to the "Pacific Rim," which is of a more contemporary vintage. Late twentieth-century "Rimspeak" features a different (geographically and geopolitically "bigger") set of islands[3]— Japan, Hong Kong, South Korea, Singapore, and Taiwan. But this discourse, too, is suffused with fantasy, discovery, and illusion. As scholars have reiterated, neologisms such as "Pacific Rim," "Pacific Basin," and "Asia-Pacific" do not refer to an actual region but are a trick mirror, a screen "reflecting the contradictions of capitalism itself."[4] Because of this mirage-like quality, Wendy Chun has compared Asiatic rim worlds to cyberspace: both these high-tech, late capitalist dreamscapes are distinguished by "navigability" and afflicted with "epistemophilia."[5] The hallucinatory mapping of a late twentieth-century rim, like the buoyant pursuit of a late nineteenth-century rim, at its base evidences a *temporal* disorientation. Christopher Connery writes, "The Pacific Rim, being the new, the future, the space of temporality, and not coincidentally arising in the 'information age,' is constructed around an anxiety over knowledge."[6] The rim induces the historical whiplash of the future encroaching too rapidly upon the present. This combination of fantastical possibility and radical unknowing is why it arouses epistemophilia.

The two *fin de siècle* "rim" moments discussed above are linked by imperialism and empiricism—a delirious desire to imagine the rim of empire and a studious attempt to see, describe, analyze, and comprehend this rim's interior. The cold war context of my study leads me to understand this epistemophilia in the more specific terms of "racial intelligence." Throughout the long twentieth century, the specter of a receding rim repeatedly transformed the object of military intelligence (the enemy) into a problem of racial knowledge (the Oriental). The Philippine–American War offers a compelling starting point for our considerations of this phenomenon. This war, the first to be significantly fought outside of the United States, created a new hunger for foreign intelligence and endowed the recently established Military Information Division with purpose and force.⁷ Another potential starting point would be the early republic's "Indian Wars." The language, methods, and spirit of these frontier battles would time and again animate U.S. counterinsurgency campaigns, from the Vietnam War to the "War on Terror." As we are beginning to see, the American genealogy of racial intelligence is more about recursivity than origins. It is this recursivity that prompts me to view the American cold war in Asia not as an offshoot of a more central Soviet–American standoff but as a part of a long-running, self-renewing imperial project of manifest destiny.

In this chapter, I will home in on the 1940s and 1950s, the decades when "peripheral" wars in the Third World created a militarized rim and when the suspicious Oriental of these wars emerged as a paradigmatic object of U.S. intelligence. These years are responsible for multiple intelligence origin stories. Japan's surprise attack on Pearl Harbor, in spurring the reorganization and expansion of intelligence operations, was said to be "the original spring from which secrecy flowed."⁸ In ensuing decades, "the name Pearl Harbor" persisted as "a symbol of our disastrous failure to read rightly the many omens." A.R. Northridge attributes this intelligence failure to a "faulty stereotype," which resulted in the "miscalculation of an adversary's capability and intent."⁹ Similar concerns dogged the Korean War, which recast the larger cold war conflict in terms of "conventional behavioral paradigms rather than a battle of ideas." According to Ron Robin, the Korean War normalized the partnership between military and academic personnel, not only in the analysis of but also in the very *making* of the Oriental enemy.¹⁰ Even in the 1970s, after nearly a century of wars against the Filipinos, Japanese, Koreans, and Chinese, U.S. intelligence officers—and the American public too—still pondered if the war in Southeast Asia was being lost due to irresolvable cultural misunderstandings.¹¹ If the 1940s and 1950s were responsible for the most dramatic transformations in U.S. intelligence, then we might note that many of these transformations were provoked by confrontations with an Oriental enemy. Such an enemy elevated the importance of "psychological" and "cultural" intelligence, areas previously seen as secondary to more expressly military calculations. As a sign of unconquerable civilizational difference and a threat of Western annihilation, this enemy brought a whole range of new methods, ideas, and specialists into the world of intelligence. More discreetly, it also shuffled in new standards of evidence and honed new instincts of evaluation.

U.S. cold war intelligence operated from within a fog of suspicion. This heightened milieu articulated security to credibility and, accordingly, made information mastery a byword for diverse causes. In a "real war" that was a "long peace," stockpiling strategic information came to be both a way of expanding military options and a way of avoiding "conventional warfare." And yet, the uncertainty of whether intelligence ensured security *through* war or *from* war forced incommensurable emotions to coexist uneasily. For example, both authority and anxiety, transparency and evasiveness, are on full display in former CIA director Allen Dulles's *The Craft of Intelligence* (1963). Written for an American public newly captivated by espionage, intrigue, and conspiracy, Dulles's volume opens by pairing a quotation from Sun Tzu with one from a 1955 American taskforce: "Both statements, widely separated as they are in time, have in common the emphasis on the practical use of advance information in its relation to action." By invoking a fifth-century Chinese philosopher whose "book is a favorite of Mao Tse-tung and is required reading for Chinese Communist tacticians," Dulles sets up his case that "the East" has long been more sophisticated in intelligence and advocates that the United States steps up its covert practices to catch up. Should these covert practices reassure American citizens or worry them? Even as Dulles performs a kind of showy unveiling, his efforts to steer readers through the intricacies of the intelligence machinery nonetheless draw attention to the potential unsavoriness of hiding and hoarding information. Apologetic yet defensive, Dulles repeatedly addresses skeptics "who regret the necessity" for "secret intelligence operations" and belabors the point that "the dangers we face in the Cold War . . . cannot all be met by the usual tools of open diplomacy."[12]

Dulles portrays U.S. cold war intelligence as an effort to achieve the perfect balance between secrecy and openness. It was toward this end that the U.S. government created distinct realms for overt and covert intelligence. The Central Intelligence Agency, the "peacetime" organization that succeeded the Office of Strategic Services in 1947, was to be responsible for "covert" or "black" intelligence. These included espionage, wiretaps, coups, paramilitary forces, and other subversive activities that ought not be traceable to the U.S. government. Meanwhile, the U.S. Information Agency (USIA), founded in 1953, was to oversee "overt" or "white" intelligence. These included cultural, educational, and news programming that bore the official stamp of the U.S. state.[13] Together, these distinct infrastructures of information helped launch both a "global imaginary of containment" and a "global imaginary of integration." Global containment, Christina Klein writes, "imagined the Cold War as a crusade against communism." Its covert tactics were "aimed at ferreting out enemies and subversives," a way of doing psychological battle. By contrast, global integration imagined the cold war as not a battle but "an opportunity to forge intellectual and emotional bonds with the people of Asia and Africa."[14] Civic duty, social pedagogy, and democratic sympathy were stimulated through aesthetic and cultural apparatuses. Containment and integration represented different ideals of global governance, one of hawkish defense and another of democratic citizenship. Both, however, involved collecting, manipulating, and circulating information. In principle, Washington preached secret operations against enemies and open diplomacy among allies. In practice, such distinctions rarely abided. According to a 1956 board of consultants, USIA programs were "almost indistinguishable in their operational aspects from programs of the Central Intelligence Agency—and vice versa."[15]

One touchstone for the racializing of cold war intelligence is George F. Kennan's well-known formulation of "containment." In the "Long Telegram," Kennan's envisioning of containment as a means of psychological rather than military conquest was predicated on his Orientalist view of the Soviet bloc: this bloc was "Asiatic" to the extent that it was weak and feminine.[16] The Orientalism of Kennan's telegram anticipates how assumptions about Asian psychology—or, as it was frequently termed, "the Oriental mind"—would come to function as a proxy for broader concerns about a world vulnerable to communist indoctrination.[17] On the psychological dimension of containment, John Lewis Gaddis writes, "The idea, in all of this, was that, confronted by Western firmness, Stalin would see Western patience as the more desirable alternative." Kennan's Orientalist prognosis of Western firmness and Eastern tractability accounts for the incredible fact that in September 1946, American intelligence experts were still able to "hope that [the Soviets] will change their minds."[18] But of course, the Soviets would not "change their minds." The idea of "western firmness" thus became redirected towards the Third World in the form of both public diplomacy and clandestine operations. The official propaganda painted the United States as a heroic "liberator" of Japan's and Europe's former colonies and a stalwart protector of these newly independent nations from imminent Soviet penetration. For example, U.S. leaflets, magazines, and newspapers routinely advertised its anticolonial record by trumpeting its past triumph over chattel slavery and its present indignation over Soviet slavery. Sometimes, past and present were even placed side by side. A *Life* article proclaimed: "The system of chattel slavery . . . was shameful and abhorrent, but it was a capital investment: the slave owner fed, clothed, and cared for his slaves; it was against his economic interests to work them to death. In Communist-dominated countries, however, the state owns all the slaves and doesn't mind working them to death in the least."[19] In a more sentimental vein, U.S. propaganda also drew lessons from nineteenth-century abolitionism. This sentimental propaganda was so central to U.S. consensus-building that in the newly established Republic of Korea, Abraham Lincoln and the Civil War became dependable rhetorical conventions for evidencing the harmony between anticommunism and anticolonialism.[20] When we turn to the internal communication among U.S. officials, however, we find a very different picture. In closed chambers, policy and intelligence experts worried that decolonization would lead not to political autonomy but to political chaos, a condition eminently susceptible to communist influence. For cultural and racial reasons, "Oriental minds" were deemed particularly at risk. A 1949 National Security Council report expressed alarm about the "Far Eastern situation" due to the fact that "Asiatic peoples . . . are traditionally submissive to power when effectively applied and habituated to authoritarian government and the suppression of the individual."[21] With Vietnam in mind, Secretary of State Dean Acheson declared in 1949 that "all Stalinists in colonial areas are nationalists." In achieving independence, "their objective necessarily becomes subordination state to Commie purposes."[22] In 1955, Arthur Radford of the Joint Chiefs of Staff argued against normalizing trade relations with China because "the stoic temperament of the peoples of Asia would cause them to seek an accommodation with the Communists."[23]

The contradictions between official pronouncements and classified reports show that the United States' support for anticolonial and antiracial programs was selective and self-interested. Hence, the settler colony of Hawai'i was pegged for statehood under the banner of racial integration and anticolonialism, even though a similar path was never on the table for the United States' other "territories."[24] To be sure, the United States was not the only world power to strategically shun colonial oppression during the

1940s and 1950s. From this book's standpoint, the distinguishing feature of the cold war is not the epochal battle between communism and democracy but the fact that the United States, the Soviet Union, and even the People's Republic of China all pitched their ideological platforms as singularly hospitable to anticolonialism and antiracism. In other words, what makes the cold war historically unique is the widespread use of racial intelligence to refashion empire in an image counter to the European colonial powers of a prior era.[25]

THE ARCHIVAL PRESENCE—THE ARCHIVAL PLENITUDE—OF THE COLD WAR ORIENTAL

Because the most crucial renovations in U.S. intelligence were precipitated by concerns about colonial and postcolonial regions, Andrew Rubin portrays the cold war as a biopolitical version of Edward Said's relatively innocuous "textual Orientalism." In *Archives of Authority*, Rubin shows how the cold war converted "the field of human social activities into a zone of military conquest."[26] While I share Rubin's interest in how military operations relate to archival practices, I'm less convinced that state authority smoothly links up with archival authority. The cold war no doubt occasioned the founding of the "human sciences," "behavioral sciences," "area studies," and "modernization theory." But even as these modes of knowledge production testify to the state's overreaches, they also disclose its vulnerabilities. In characterizing the U.S. National Archives as archives of *in*security rather than archives of authority, I am following the lead of scholars who have shown that colonial archives may not represent pristine order or contain meaningful truths after all. For example, Lisa Lowe's lateral probe of the British national archives locates not only the "intimacies between four continents" but also the "territories of failure" and eruptions of "colonial uncertainty" in the archives themselves.[27] In a more explicit articulation, Ann Laura Stoler describes archives "not as repositories of state power but as unquiet movements in a field of force, as restless realignments and readjustments of people and the beliefs to which they were tethered."[28] Stoler's examination of the Dutch colonial record reveals racial unknowability to be an especially fraught site of epistemic rupture and documentary surplus. For the *Inlandsche kinderen*, an amorphous category used in the Indies that included both poor whites and mixed bloods, the uncertainties of racial identification produced an excess of convoluted documentation that concealed a shortage of evidence.

Stoler's suggestion that racial indecipherability surfaces as documentary excess raises the question of what archival logics, forms, styles, and tones are conjured forth by the inscrutable Oriental. Scholars of transatlantic slavery and queer studies have portrayed official archives as brutally suppressing the presence of disenfranchised subjects, who can then only appear to us as spectral traces.[29] In the context of queer studies, Anjali Arondekar has shown how an epistemology of foreclosure, deferral, and irretrievability establishes a parallel between the homosexual closet and the archival trove: both are premised on an "open secret" of ineluctable loss yet perpetuate the utopian promise of future disclosure. As an alternative to this "melancholic historicism," Arondekar argues that treating the archive as a site of "radical abundance" can make room for histories of sexuality that are more "quotidian" and "ordinary."[30] In Black studies, the preferred metaphor for the archive has been a tomb. This figuration has begotten an even more melancholic strain of hauntological inquiry. Saidiya Hartman writes, "the archive of slavery rests upon a founding violence," which "determines, regulates and organizes the kinds of statements that can be made about slavery." Such an archive can yield "no exhaustive account of the girl's life" and instead "catalogues the statements that licensed her death."[31] Inspired by both Hartman and Arondekar, I characterize the archival presence of the cold war Oriental as resting upon a *founding suspicion*, and I contend that this suspicious temperament yielded a *radical abundance* of racial hypotheses that gradually recalibrated the quotidian rhythms of "wartime." The most appropriate metaphor for this archive of cold war intelligence is neither a closed closet nor a sealed crypt but a veiled enemy.

It is because of this veiled enemy that the cold war temperament of suspicion produced a fetish for secrecy. Secrecy is intrinsically related to power, but with the cold war's intelligence revolution, it became more precisely a precondition of security. Hence, whereas Max Weber calls the "official secret" the province of *all* bureaucracies, Wesley Wark distinguishes secrecy as the "organizational mentality" that separates intelligence services "from other, more mundane bureaucracies."[32] Fittingly, it was in the United States during the 1940s that the generically bureaucratic term "classified" evolved into a specific descriptor of secret intelligence.[33] To further exploit this term's double meaning, I suggest that the act of *classifying* the cold war enemy entailed both concealing knowledge in the name of power and applying rough grids of social intelligibility that cover over the lack of knowledge. When the enemy's presence is certain but their identity unknown—when the potential enemy persists indefinitely—intelligence relies at once on confidently guarded classified secrets and anxiously provisional forms of classification.

For the Oriental enemy, classified intelligence was motivated by the interlinked concerns of racial and ideological classification. Because the Oriental rendered race and ideology inextricable from yet irreducible to each other, "American propaganda in Asia, more so than in any other part of the world, prioritized expressly anticommunist themes."[34] As classified subjects of suspicion, cold war Orientals fueled the desire for ever more intelligence and ushered in a new archival dispensation. Certainly, the archive of intelligence wrought by suspicion is, more often than not, racist, biased, contradictory, unfounded, and blatantly wrong. But what I'm after is not so much the truth of the cold war Oriental than the manners of thought that the problem of racial decipherment activated. As we will find, the inscrutable Oriental enhanced the belief that secrecy guarantees security, that enemy intelligence is related to racial intelligibility, and that a deeper meaning lies beyond the surface deception of masks, covers, and veils. The paradox, though, is that the U.S. intelligence establishment's scripts of knowing and exhibits of unveiling transformed an "unreadable enemy" into an "overdetermined" enemy. In *The Naked Communist*, Roland Végső adapts the Marxist concept of overdetermination to describe a cold war enemy that cannot be understood through ideology alone. For Végső, overdetermination means that the vital need "to determine the enemy inevitably leads to an excess of determinations." Moreover, any "attempt to ground this enmity in a discourse external to the actual antagonism (capitalism vs. Communism) produces inconsistences."[35] In this rendering, "overdetermination" not only allows for the multiple forces that make up a historical situation, but also indexes the historical complexity of multiple racial and cultural hypotheses. So while the Oriental may have structured any number of "East–West" encounters, this figure became overdetermined during the cold war in the specific sense that it produced a glut of conjectural thinking and truth claims based on the competing exigencies of ideological affiliation and racial filiation. Contrary to the closet or the tomb, an archive structured by the "open secret" or "official secret" of the inscrutable enemy houses not a lost subject but a profusion of subjects, a permutation of all possible enemies.

FREE ASIANS: ALLIES OR ALIENS?

Of course, not all Asians and Asian Americans were seen as enemies. Many were cultivated as sources and championed as friends. In fact, the cold war personalities that will preoccupy me are "free Asians"—the native informants, junior partners, and little brown brothers who were intended as countermeasures to the overdetermined Oriental enemy. Free Asians inhabit a gray zone in the world of intelligence. Unlike *white propaganda*, which is openly backed by the United States government, and *black propaganda*, which is made to appear as emanating from an enemy source, Asian self-representation functions as a species of *gray propaganda*. Designed to bolster the United States' global image, gray intelligence demands a kind of ventriloquism: it draws its power from "putting praise of the United States or, at least, a reasonably stated understanding of U.S. positions, in the mouths of those whom the world at large would not identify as U.S. spokesmen."[36] The need for gray intelligence, in both foreign policy and public culture, gave rise to an unprecedented outpouring of Asian self-representation in the 1940s. It is worth underlining that this was not a resurgence of racial visibility but its first instance.[37] These newfound opportunities for Asians to represent themselves as "Asian" bear out what scholars have termed "American Orientalism" and "post-Orientalism."[38] Saidian Orientalism, let us recall, positioned the racial Other as "central to *European self-representation* in the eighteenth and nineteenth centuries." By contrast, American Orientalism made *Asian self-representation* equally important. During the cold war, Melani McAlister writes, the United States' "collective self-identity was not an unambiguous antithesis to the projected distant others" since the self-identity of those minority others was necessary for integrating and legitimizing a U.S.-led free world.[39]

As a response to empire by invitation, Asian self-representation in some ways exemplify what Rey Chow calls "coercive mimeticism," a process by which minorities "replicate the very banal preconceptions that have been appended to them."[40] By this account, self-representation is tantamount to self-Orientalization. Criticism on cold war Asian self-representation often highlights this Foucauldian instability between the obligation to confess and the freedom to speak truth to power. For example, Josephine Park views the multiple alliances pursued by the Asian friend as "potential sources of self-definition." Similarly, Cindy Cheng notes how "state-generated narratives on the benefits of the American way of life provided Asian Americans a discourse through which to articulate their own self-conception."[41] From some angles, this new pathway to "self-definition" and "self-conception" seems more cultural than political. This is because, in a region where ideological divisions licensed the formation of new national entities, cultural authenticity became the language of geopolitical legitimation. San Francisco Chinatown thereby emerged as the privileged locus of Chinese *cultural tradition* in contradistinction to Mainland China, which represented a corrupt site of Chinese *cultural revolution*. In this cold war milieu, Asian Americans became empowered to assert that their "ancestries endowed them with innate cultural expertise that qualified them to serve as the United States' most natural ambassadors to the Far East."[42] The celebration of cultural difference also functioned as a remedy for resolving America's "race problem" on a global stage. On goodwill tours across the Orient, free Asians such as writer Jade Snow Wong, swimmer Sammy Lee, and painter Dong Kingman recounted their ethnic credentials *and* flaunted their professional successes. The autoethnographic bent of their messages served to provide living proof that American democracy valued racial inclusion in the specific form of cultural preservation.[43]

These free Asians illustrate, in a pronounced way, how the cross-pollination of anthropological and aesthetic notions of the term *culture* contributed to establishing the cold war as "a way of life."[44] Yet, cold war geopolitics so officiously commanded the "duty of self-resemblance" that, in the endeavor to effect an "ideal correspondence between the self and its representations," free Asian cultural productions tended to pursue "what might be called a *panic of reduction*."[45] Put more bluntly, because of the pressures of authenticity, free Asian self-representations often took the form of crude propaganda. In a cold war context, culture's tendency to create forked paths—between unvarnished truth and garish caricature, plucky swagger and abject puppetry—is what ultimately makes me turn away from it. I don't deny that culture is indispensable to understanding how cold war racial "ambassadors" performed a kind of public relations work. However, my book's interest in how free Asians troubled the distinction between aliens and allies leads me to conceive of their self-representations as intelligence, a term that is more often reserved for covert operations.[46]

Treating self-representation as a source of strategic information rather than cultural expertise unlocks interpretive possibilities beyond self-Orientalization. For one, the category of intelligence reminds us that overtly expressive Asian friends were at times even more suspicious than stealthy Oriental communists. "While the Asiatic enemy was entirely recognizable," Josephine Park writes, "the friend presented an acute crisis of representation."[47] For example, Jade Snow Wong, though probably the best-known free Asian in the United States, was actually seen as exceedingly unreliable. After her USIA-sponsored tour, officials deemed Wong "only a qualified success" due to "personality traits we unfortunately did not anticipate."[48] Wong's 1975 memoir *No Chinese Stranger* further complicates her reputation as a self-Orientalizing "model minority." By offering her cultural services to both the United States and the People's Republic of China—and by heaping a staggering amount of praise on the latter—Wong ends up seeming more like a double agent than a racial ambassador. The mixed responses to Wong's ambassadorship show that even though Asian self-representation was intended as an antidote to Oriental inscrutability, it in effect further entrenched the belief that all Orientals look and behave the same. The most confounding intelligence concern of the cold war, therefore, was neither containing Oriental enemies nor promoting Asian friends but distinguishing one from the other. In a 1970 article on "America's setbacks in the Far East," Stanley Karnow unearthed "two elements" in the "delusion of our policy makers." One is the misplaced "conviction that there must be measurable facts in Asia because, regarding ourselves as rational, we had to operate on the basis of facts." The other is the habit of "rely[ing] on Asian allies who spoke our language and imitated our mannerisms, even though we were never quite sure whether they shared our values." The impossibility of securing "measurable facts" is related to the impossibility of identifying intelligible friends. Both have resulted in the tendency "to miscalculate our enemies" and the inability "to estimate their response to force or diplomacy."[49] Karnow's distrust of the Asian ally who has only superficially adopted the American way reveals the limits of global integration. Asians of the free world were apparent friends who always remained potential enemies.

The likes of Wong have received no shortage of scholarly attention, but free Asians were not just famed luminaries. A shift from culture to intelligence thus also directs our attention beyond the proverbial stage. As unidentified translators and anonymous clerks, free Asians worked the foreign posts and back channels of the cold war bureaucracy. As undercover agents, local informants, secret lovers, and escapees with false names, they supplied the field knowledge and "raw intelligence" that "officers"—white American men—processed into analyses, estimations, and recommendations.[50] Some free Asians indeed took advantage of their situation. Others, though, did not self-consciously serve as "ambassadors" and did not view their everyday actions or life decisions in the context of international relations. In blurring the ambassadorial and the quotidian, cold war Asian self-representation contributed to an unconventional war fought across multiple social sectors.[51] As Eisenhower once declared, "psychological warfare can be anything from the singing of a beautiful hymn up to the most extraordinary kind of physical sabotage."[52] Intelligence operations certainly made up a spectrum, but they also destroyed it, rendering beautiful hymns and physical sabotage (so to speak) virtually indistinguishable from each other. In military, social, cultural, and political contexts, self-representing Asians troubled the boundary between overt and covert information in ways that remade the textures, rhythms, and norms of everyday life. For example, rehabilitating post-WWII Japan to solidify U.S. influence in Asia and the Pacific required contriving new interfaces between the emperor and his people. As we will see in chapter 2, Emperor Hirohito's tours across Japan manipulated the overt optics of an Asian ally's public image, even as these tours were being managed by the covert hand of the occupying U.S. regime. The interplay between the overt and covert is also at play in a Philippine humanitarian group that I examine in chapter 5. The brotherliness of Operation Brotherhood depended on concealing its relationship to the CIA and making its self-representations seem genuinely friendly and voluntary. As these examples show, self-representation often mediated people-to-people interactions rather than government-to-government relations. In occluding where individual intent ends and state influence begins, free Asian self-representation made intelligence operations indistinguishable from daily routines.

TONE: A RACIAL-AESTHETIC TENSION

Overdetermined and ordinary, the cold war Oriental possesses too many representations rather than not enough. Accordingly, *Tonal Intelligence* seeks not to recover new subjectivities nor to renounce existing ones, but to theorize the archival presence of the cold war Oriental. To theorize this presence in relation to intelligence is to treat Asian self-representation as a problem of evidence rather than a source of expertise. Hence, even though the free Asians under consideration in the succeeding chapters may appear to be offering cultural guidance, my concern will be how these free Asians in fact withhold the indicative features of credibility. This focus on the problem of evidence—specifically, how empirical evidence fails to substantiate "the fact of race"—prompts me to center a *tonal* analysis. I believe that reading for impressionistic tones, in addition to hard facts, can open us to less deterministic and more oblique patterns of racial referencing and inspire a historicism that is more alive to incipience, inchoateness, and flux.

To many, terms such as "race," "facts," and "evidence" may seem synonymous. Racial perception, after all, tends to recruit an uncompromising empiricism. As Mark Jerng puts it, "Race is either seen at the level of a 'smoking gun' or it is not seen at all."[53] This zero-sum situation prioritizes visual and corporeal traits. Consequently, in the United States, the "race problem" has been the most historically salient when the evidence of race (often muddied by sex) is the most nebulous, mutable, and contested. The history of the "one-drop rule" for African Americans, the questionable whiteness of "swarthy" Europeans, the exemption of Native Americans from antimiscegenation laws, the cases of Asians petitioning for citizenship as Caucasian—such flashpoints in American history have adjudicated the meaning of race precisely because the visual indices of difference were not obvious. In this book, the unreliable, distorted, attenuated, and *inevident* presence of race has to do with the inscrutable Oriental. Inscrutability, as I've been discussing it, conveys a faithless relationship between surface phenomena and inner truths. Scaled up, it also links referential uncertainty to civilizational crisis. This scalar move from inscrutable Oriental to yellow peril underpins Colleen Lye's conceptualization of "Asiatic racial form": "the 'yellow peril' denotes a radical dissolution of boundaries between inside and outside, friend and enemy: Asiatics can look just like friends, and enemy aliens have already taken up residence within."[54] Construed as an imperilment of national boundaries, the inscrutable Oriental is not just an individual enemy but the threat of a mass takeover and the harbinger of apocalyptic change. During the cold war, American Orientalism's "horizonlike" imagery—floods, waves, wheat, and germs—became a premonition of falling dominoes, a fear of the Third World's inevitable submission to communism.[55]

In its warping of visual evidence and embodiment of historical unpredictability, the figure of the cold war Oriental provides an occasion to search out alternate empiricisms and alternate historicisms. Key to both these tasks, I argue, is tonal intelligence. As I have been suggesting, during the cold war, the racialized indistinction between enemy and ally was closely related to the temporal indistinction between war and peace. Tone enables an approach to cold war historiography that allows us to take stock of these perceptual difficulties. Given my attention to rethinking seemingly unambiguous terms such as *war* and *race*, it may surprise the reader that I do not intend to provide a firm definition of the exceedingly amorphous term *tone*. One reason is that I want to accommodate tone's polyvalence. However, the decision to largely preserve the intuitive meanings of tone, while actively defamiliarizing war and race, also emerges from a worry that the critical valorization of ambiguity, indeterminacy, instability, and illegibility (value judgments associated with terms such as *tone*) is symptomatic of the tendency to treat *war* as a discrete event and *race* as an empirical truth. In other words, whereas war and race so routinely appear as fast and fusty facts that obviate the need for definition, the aesthetic-affective term tone immediately calls for fuller conceptualization. What draws me to tone ultimately is that this term possesses both racial and aesthetic connotations. Tone, I think, can help us talk about racial perception and aesthetic perception in ways that invalidate the bifurcation between a stolidly mundane (racial) fact and a critically salutary (aesthetic) ambiguity.

In aesthetic disciplines, "the concept of the tone has always enjoyed both an abstraction and a certain materiality."[56] For example, in sound studies, tone can refer to the abstract system of ratios and notations as well as to the materiality of an individual's voice. It can span both ends of the sound quality spectrum, sometimes signifying pure sound and, at other times, white noise.[57] There is also an uncertainty as to where tone falls with respect to the human and the inhuman. Most frequently, tone extends from intonation, such that it is the distinguishing imprint, the pre-linguistic cadence, of the human voice. Yet in other instances, tone is extrapolated from dial tones or ring tones, the synthesized sounds of the long-distance telephonic voice.[58] Literary accounts of tone similarly negotiate the material and the abstract. In 1929, I.A. Richards, in an effort to empiricize literary response, defined tone as the objectified relation between a literary speaker and an implied receiver.[59] Despite this definition's staying power, the formal logicians known as the New Critics actually tended to use tone as shorthand for the ineffable and unnameable. Monroe Beardsley, for example, offers a familiarly formalist definition of tone as "the speaker's attitude toward the receiver" before immediately adding "there is no special reason to restrict it so." The paragraph concludes: "Tone is a regional quality which we may perceive clearly . . . without being able to describe it well."[60] Contrary to our expectations, these mid-twentieth-century explications of tone are often consonant with attempts to update the term. Note the echo between Beardsley's definition above and Sianne Ngai's influential characterization of tone as a text's "global or organizing affect, its general disposition or orientation toward its audience and the world."[61] Whether as impersonal form or prepersonal affect, literary tone is productively paradoxical, designating something that is diffuse and atmospheric yet also emotional, intersubjective, and attitudinal.

When adjoined to race, the term tone loses these vertiginous, paradoxical properties: a racial tone evokes the literal and indexical. In its most common interpretation as skin color or speech quality, tone provides the informatics of race. Hue, pigment, timbre, and accent all corral sight and sound toward the production of anthropomorphic certitude. Described this way, tone is what makes difference perceptible. This racialized notion of tone is unsurprising, given that "race" has long stood for what can be reliably perceived. That is, the legibility of race has historically depended on the verifiability of sensory information, such as where a sound comes from or how to distinguish between white and light brown. Because of this history, some of the most powerful efforts to challenge the unequivocal empiricism of racial perception have critiqued in tandem the naturalness of biological difference and the naturalness of sensory experience. For instance, by interpreting speech tones not as an innate feature of a speaker's constitution but as a multisensory performance, Nina Sun Eidsheim casts race not as a piece of information lodged in people's throats but as a "*structural choreography* adopted by or imposed upon them."[62] Additionally,

Anne Cheng, Michelle Stephens, and Krista Thompson have thoroughly refurbished our understanding of skin, calling attention to its opacity and tactility. In their studies, the tone of skin has both a corporeal and metallic quality, referring not so much to epidermal color but to a refractive shine, a technological surface, a costume or prop.[63] Rey Chow synthesizes these accounts of color and accent by attending to both "visual and audial significations of the word *tones*." With skin whitening and accent norming as key examples, Chow conceives of tone as a prosthetic. It is an "external graft," something that can be wielded through a process called "languaging."[64]

Aesthetic tone is complexly paradoxical; racial tone is self-evidently literal. Yet even in my brief account, we can see how these ostensibly divergent meanings of tone can overlap. In particular, studies that have contested the immutability of difference by engaging race as choreography, performance, prosthesis, and technique show that the racial and aesthetic dimensions of tone can be difficult to parse. My own understanding of tone proceeds in a similar spirit. This book's stake in historiographic method, however, leads me to focus on the seeing, reading, and perceiving of race rather than on a subject's racial project of self-making. Because racial perception and aesthetic perception can infringe upon each other in surprising ways, it seems worthwhile to highlight the etymological relation between *tone* and *tension*. Tone as tension conveys friction but not bipolarity or incommensurability. It is a stretching that facilitates a holding position, a holding together.[65] A critical method that holds the racial and the aesthetic in tension allows us to stretch the standard interpretations of these terms.[66] In this book, aesthetic perception is less exceptional and less exclusive than professional aesthetes would like, and racial perception is less empirical and less natural than conventional wisdom tells us. This means that I will treat the aesthetic not as a specialized judgment of the beautiful, the sublime, or the imaginary but as a general perceptual mode attentive to rhetorical, stylistic, sensory, and affective details. Reading for tone will therefore be as pertinent to an intelligence report as to a literary novel. My engagement of tone also reworks the terms of racial perception. I'm especially interested in how tone suggests a relation between perception and conception or, as I've been phrasing it, between intelligibility and intelligence. My turn to tone arises from a belief that racial forms and formations require us to remain open to different manners of reading and styles of knowing. Tone, then, is neither some sort of moral imperative nor a one-size-fits-all formula. This book, it follows, is neither an effort to proselytize tone's intrinsic value nor a call to institute Critical Tone Studies. It'd be more apt to think of tone as a conjoined mode of racial-aesthetic attunement that can help bring historical contingency into focus. As a method for studying race during times of war, it is an improvisation pursued in the absence of sounder footing and when the headwinds of change are still awhirl. Without endorsing tone's broad applicability or belittling its historical perspicacity, I take up this concept-term in order to forge a critical practice that is adequate to studying the temporal ambiguity of the cold war and the racialized inscrutability of the Oriental.

WHAT KIND OF INTELLIGENCE IS TONAL INTELLIGENCE?

Although the tension between racial and aesthetic perception is most apparent in self-consciously aesthetic works, my interest in how geopolitical pressures shape perception and intensify suspicion makes the genre of intelligence a more revealing starting place. While all state documents possess a tone, intelligence documents are a special case, insofar as some mix of arrogance and anxiety, openness and intimacy, underlies nearly every hypothesis. To put a finer point on it, bureaucratic classifications that gauge "confidentiality" and "sensitivity" can also be tonal expressions.[67] For example, John Lewis Gaddis has noted that what's "most striking about NSC-68 was its rhetorical tone," for, despite its classification as "top secret," this report sounded as if it were intended for a "conspicuous public platform." Gaddis writes, "it was only the details of NSC-68 that were sensitive." The report's conclusions were "widely publicized" but "without attribution to their source."[68] Classifications are intended to measure the damage of unauthorized exposure, but a security grade can also be viewed as an affective gradient. Which is to say, classifications can pronounce the intelligence community's level of confidence about the credibility of a source, its desire for security given the sensitivity of a document's content, and its faith in free, open, and truthful expression. One could make a related case about descriptors of evidence, such as "white," "black," "gray," "overt," "covert," "hard," and "soft." These are supposed to be based on objective evaluations of a document's source, but, as in the case of Gaddis's observations about NSC-68, the displaying or withholding of a source can affect whether an intelligence document's tone seems more official and open or more guarded and secretive.

Scholars typically credit Eisenhower's presidency with expanding the use of "unattributed propaganda." This tactic of informational warfare was the emphatic recommendation of the Committee on International Information Activities, also known as the Jackson Committee. In a 1953 report, this committee decreed: "As a general rule, information and propaganda should only be attributed to the United States when such attribution is an asset. A much greater percentage of the information program should be unattributed." To be unattributed is not simply to leave a name off a document. The Jackson Committee's varied propositions for avoiding attribution include: "the utilization abroad of personnel other than American"; "the utilization of numerous private American organizations active abroad"; the deployment of "exchange of persons in influencing the attitude of important local individuals"; and the provision of U.S. "advice and assistance" to film, radio, and publishing industries across the free world.[69] We will encounter many of these modes of "unattributed" intelligence in chapters 2–5. For instance, Korean educator Induk Pahk participated in "exchange of persons" programs, and the CIA cover organization Operation Brotherhood was publicly funded via private American foundations. In anticipation of these case studies, the two points that I want to press are these: first, an indirect consequence of obscuring and manipulating "attribution" is that tone became a principal determinant of whether a text is "dependable, convincing, and truthful";[70] and second, the problem of attribution—of locating and evaluating the source of free-floating information—was particularly fraught and vexing in the case of an enemy racialized as inscrutable.

To comprehend the significance of tone for intelligence involving an inscrutable enemy, we must look specifically at the task of estimation. The need to systematize an estimative language stirred lively debates within the intelligence community during the cold war years. These debates began with Yale history professor and intelligence pioneer Sherman Kent. In *Strategic Intelligence* (1949), Kent defines intelligence as the synthetic knowledge about an enemy nation's historical developments, current happenings, and future actions. Communicating this knowledge requires three rhetorical modes: description, reportage, and speculation.[71] In all three areas, intelligence is to be factual and objective. The difficulty, however, is attaining scientific precision "not merely in the area of description but more importantly in the area of prognosis."[72] The work of prognosis, called estimation, forms the bedrock of intelligence. In fact, the method, style, and language of estimation so consumed Kent that he ended up founding the CIA's in-house journal. In a memo to the CIA Director of Training, Kent expressed "outrage at the infantile imprecision of the language of intelligence" and, as a solution, recommended a "systematic literature" for the profession.[73] Two years later, in 1955, Kent introduced *Studies in Intelligence* as a venue for intelligence professionals to work out a mission, a method, and *"a definition of terms."*[74]

Intelligence, Kent believed, must scrupulously guard its lexicon from both casual colloquialisms and ornate verbiage. Like steady and sober "mathematicians," analysts must "get firm meaning out of impressions" by employing an "air-tight vocabulary of estimative expressions."[75] The intelligence ranks, unfortunately, were overrun by loose-lipped and silver-tongued "poets." Poets provide "the flavor of odds" without detailing the actual mathematical odds. For Kent, the poetic element lies in a certain adverbial flair—a "may *well*" and "*distinctly* possible." To eliminate such distortions, he attempted to chart the correlations between words, feelings, and odds. This chart being unenforceable among "the aesthetic opposition," Kent sought to lay down a yet more fundamental grammatical law: "The word 'possible' (and its cognates) must not be modified."[76]

Thanks to Kent, matters of terminology became one of the most polemical topics in *Studies in Intelligence* between the 1950s and 1970s.[77] This discussion often came down to the problem of "modifiers" and "qualifiers." Kent, we now know, saw these locutions as skewing any objective rendering of probability. Other intelligence experts, however, deemed them indispensable for effective intelligence. Burney Bennett, despite sharing Kent's disquiet about "literary" language, contends that modifiers are absolutely essential for providing "indications of the degree of certainty." To wit, "an estimate is useful only to the extent that it is precisely qualified."[78] A deeper disagreement with Kent concerned what belongs in an intelligence report and, for that matter, what counts as intelligence. Whereas Kent denounced "the flavor of odds" as unscientific, others believed that "flavor" could relay an analyst's confidence in an estimate. Modifiers, they insisted, provide the "feeling," "instinct," and "impression"— the tone—that must accompany the hard evidence.[79] Communicating through tone seems especially valuable when an estimate must reckon with the unknowable. These are the scenarios that breed qualification and equivocation. Wayne Jackson writes, "The intelligence estimator feels instinctively that he should state what he believes true, qualifying the estimate to indicate his qualms about its validity." Estimates "clothed with caveats and qualifications" may be "annoying to the reader who craves certainty." But it is still "better to over-warn the U.S. policy maker than to engender any degree of complacency."[80] Taken to an extreme, tone can even carry more weight and offer more intelligence than what a report actually says. It is thus possible for a paper to be "basically correct even though it had a great many statements which proved incorrect." Abbott Smith writes, "The validity of such papers depends only partly upon the accuracy of each particular statement in them. It must also be judged by the impact and tone of the document as a whole."[81] We might conclude, then, that the habit of modification has the effect of shifting attention from estimable probability to aesthetic-affective tone. Often manifesting as a note of qualification, tone can be meaningful even if it offers no concrete facts or recommendations and even if a document's calculations and assessments are wrong.

What can the U.S. intelligence profession's wrangling over qualifiers tell us about a war that is distinguished by its hardliness? The fact that minute grammatical embellishments received such disproportionate attention among cold war analysts surely gives added significance to Don Mee Choi's "geopolitical poetics," which, as we saw in this book's introduction, likewise explores the outsized effects of adverbial accretion. By employing a poetics that literally hides the verbs, Choi's *Hardly War* demonstrates how an anarchy of adverbs weakens causality, delays action, and dilutes connections. Lacking antagonism and motive, "war" slows down to hardly anything at all. That the activity of war appears negligible is both the rub and the point. Reading Choi's *Hardly War* alongside *Studies in Intelligence*, we have cause to posit that the adverb gives grammatical form to an imperial hegemony that furtively exerts pressures through modification and modulation while openly abjuring outright domination. Considered together, the intelligence journal and the poetry collection position us to see that the force of "hardly war" lies in the regulation of intensity and impact—in the faint tones of "hardly" rather than in the fiery event of "war."

If one payoff of a geopolitical poetics is the debunking of "war" as a singular event, the other is the repudiation of "race" as a staid fact. Choi's privileging of a textural tone, often at the expense of textual content, is thus particularly important for considerations of *racial* intelligence. Indeed, Choi herself implies that factoring race into intelligence is one way that a geopolitics becomes a geopoetics: "I am trying to fold race into geopolitics and geopolitics into poetry. Hence, geopolitical poetics" (4). What Choi's geopolitical poetics of hardliness shares with Kent's estimative idiom of poetic modifiers is not only a proclivity for adverbial qualification. Rather, this grammar of uncontrollable wavering signals their mutual preoccupation with a racial object. A geopolitical poetics, like an intelligence poetics, is racial in tone rather than content. This quiet drama of tone shows that race, far from being an empirically observable fact, incites suspicion and eludes corroboration. Put another way, an inscrutable enemy augments the consequentiality of tone for intelligence analysis because it introduces race as an unresolvable conundrum, as that which exceeds the domain of probability and knowability. In eliciting a need to qualify and modify, this inscrutable object of intelligence turns an estimative language into a geopolitical poetics.

For the overdetermined enemy whose ideological and racial colors bleed together, an aesthetic-racial tone binds probability to perception: an estimation of probable enemy activity depends on the interpretation of perceivable racial difference. In Anthony Marc Lewis's 1973 article, "Re-examining Our Perceptions on Vietnam," the conversation about estimation changes from the approximation of probability to the perception of difference. Where Kent had used a mathematical chart to codify a vocabulary of probability, Lewis presents a behavioral chart to address the "intercultural or psychological dimension" of intelligence. Lewis asserts that "the main task of the analysts is to point up the differences between the American readers' culture . . . and the relevant foreign culture." Estimations fail not only if they miscalculate probability but also if they "rest on certain assumptions about the state of mind of large numbers of Vietnamese." Again, the problem of estimation centrally concerns language, although it is racial difference rather than mathematical probability that proves difficult to describe. The estimator who is "misled by mirror images reflecting his own preconceptions" makes "repeated use of terms such as 'subversion,' 'infiltration,' 'terrorism,' 'rooting out' Communists."[82] Lewis does not mention tone or any of its analogues. But if the credibility of intelligence conventionally depends on source evaluation, then the masked Oriental seems to throw the location, character, and quality of a source into serious doubt. Lacking any certifiable knowledge about the racial other, Lewis's hypothetical analyst can only resort to a culturally reductive language that produces a "mirror image" of the analyst's own insecurities rather than an objective picture of the enemy.

Tone, I conjecture, becomes an important register of race when the source of intelligence cannot be verified and when the method of intelligence cannot hold. Even Kent, the paramount "mathematician," indirectly admits that the inscrutable Oriental undermines the scientific method that he so avidly endorses. In a demonstration of this method, Kent contrives two imaginary scenarios involving Oriental art objects. These serve not to showcase the fail-proof accuracy of Western reason but to remind the reader that "the destruction of an interesting hypothesis is often as important a part of our trade as its confirmation."[83] By exhibiting the "death of a hypothesis," Kent frames the scientific method as a principled endeavor; it merits our confidence even when our hypotheses are wrong. Yet dancing at the edge of Kent's perception is the possibility that the artfulness of an Oriental object may kill our hypotheses with unusually high frequency. When the inscrutable Oriental is the object of scrutiny, does intelligence become less than a science? While the practice of estimation assumes the unassailability of logic and reason, are these useless against an enemy known for rash and unpredictable actions?[84] Kent, ever the proponent of method as law, would maintain that "what you do when you do not know" is fall back on a set repertoire of techniques.[85] If one puts "every effort into being well-girded for contingencies," then "nothing that happens can have been unexpected."[86]

I'd submit that the Oriental's invalidation of a method that is "scientific" directs us toward a method that is tonal. Contra Kent, tone is not a universal method that asserts the inviolability of laws, scientific or otherwise; it is a method that allows us to entertain rather than extinguish contingencies. Tone, I propose, can help develop a mode of analysis that can account for the heterogeneity of racial perception (so that race is not always a smoking gun) and the uncertainty of historical transitions (so that war is not always distinguished by exceptional violence). In arriving at this proposition through a survey of intelligence literature, my aim has been to show that tone may be especially instructive for historicizing the recalcitrance of the inscrutable Oriental. The potential conflict between tone and content observed by cold war intelligence analysts should intrigue us, therefore, not because it affects our interpretation of credibility, but because it indicates that tone may know something about the temper of a historical period—especially a period identified as a "cold" war—that cannot yet find explicit articulation at the level of content. That a document's tone can be historically revelatory while its content remains blindsided is similar to the point that Christopher Castiglia makes about mid-century literary criticism. While it is not uncommon to portray cold war criticism as "reproducing the *epistemological dispositions* of the Cold War state," what is more "surprising is that criticism . . . sustains an identification with the same state whose *ideological positions* that criticism, in its content, frequently opposes."[87] The historical significance of this contradiction between epistemological disposition (tone) and ideological position (content) becomes clearer through an example. In a review of Raymond Williams's *The Long Revolution* (1961), E.P. Thompson praises Williams for having "maintained his independence from the attractive poles of cold war ideology." Yet he remarks that Williams's "tone has been conditioned by a particular social context," and this tone "haunts Mr. Williams" whenever he mentions the "whole way of life."[88] Thompson's stipulation is that for all of Williams's expressed leftism, he sounds a lot like T.S. Eliot and practices a kind of cold war criticism after all.

What's funny about Thompson's tonal reading of Williams is that Williams himself has made the most compelling case for the historicity of tone. For this reason, my own reliance on a racial-aesthetic tone is very much indebted to Williams, specifically his concept of "structures of feeling." At their most useful, structures of feeling, the qualities of art that evidence emergent beliefs and sentiments, fulfill a periodizing function: they furnish a record of "the true social present." For Williams, a true *social present* extends from a true *embodied presence*. Structures of feeling are easy to dismiss because they are "taken to be private, idiosyncratic, and even isolating"—merely personal rather than truly social or recognizably historical.[89] In some sense, the "tension of tone" is a similarly paradoxical formulation: tone draws together the racially particular and aesthetically universal; the specificity of stance, attitude, and intonation and the ubiquity of atmosphere and mood; the concretely empirical and the abstractly immaterial. But compared to Williams's attempt to redeem the social value of experience, feeling, and presence, I view tone less as an individual expression of subjectivity and more as a historical expression of temperature and temperament.[90] This distinction is crucial given the vitalist bias of racial perception, which tends to locate difference in embodied particulars and emotional expressivity.[91] How might we embark upon "a field of investigation that lies beyond the metaphysics of presence, the view of the object"—in this case, the racial object—"as replete and fully (although indescribably) meaningful"?[92] That is, how might tone provide an idiom for talking about race when it is present but not adducible, when it is available at the level of hovering tension rather than that of pinpoint accuracy? And how might this tonal intelligence help us think anew about war, in particular a war whose temporality is bound up with its temperament?

WHAT KIND OF WAR IS THE POST-COLD WAR?

The following chapters will explore these questions through specific case studies. Although intelligence will seem most native to the context of mid-twentieth-century U.S. foreign policy, it will also inform my readings of contemporary Asian diasporic aesthetic texts. An aesthetic archive offers a valuable resource for periodizing the long cold war. Typically, archive-based studies, especially of intelligence, privilege access. As a result, it may appear that cold war scholarship matured in the late 1990s on the heels of the CIA's "openness" initiative, a widely publicized release of documents concerning U.S. clandestine operations. According to many within the intelligence community, this push for "openness" was facilitated by the end of the cold war. David D. Gries, Director of the CIA's Center for the Study of Intelligence, writes that with "the decline in direct threats to national security, the need for secrecy has been reduced."[93] The implication is that the United States, normally a free society, pursued secrecy only in self-defense and under extenuating circumstances. Yet historians "grew increasingly dissatisfied with the pace of the openness program" and charged that documents were "edited often in ways that rendered them useless." Some inferred that "secret information is accumulating . . . far quicker than it is being declassified."[94] The fact that parallel initiatives were taking place in the other "bloc" also gave pause. In the early 1990s, the new Russian government released the Communist Party's documents and even allowed television crews to tour the KGB.[95] Although this competitive truth-letting campaign purported to headline a new era, it seems uncannily reminiscent of propaganda efforts such as Harry Truman's "Campaign of Truth." Have we indeed moved beyond a cold war temperament of suspicion if the meaning of information is still structured by the dichotomy of secrecy and openness and the attendant drama of disclosure?

Tonal Intelligence is also interested in a geopolitical shift in the 1990s, but it does not treat this period as a clarifying moment when the cold war's newly blazed documentary trail suddenly makes history available for the telling. My usage of the term "post–cold war" proceeds from a conviction that we need more purposeful models for understanding why the cold war "exceeds and outlives its historical eventness."[96] A post–cold war period is hardly a "thaw," a natural and inevitable process of evaporating tensions. Rather, the period called *post–cold war* has an undecided and erratic quality—a sense of being caught up in change yet unable to interpret it or even name it. The prefix "post-," then, is more a "horizon of transition" than a point of terminus—if you'd like, a hyphen rather than a period.[97] I find that an aesthetic archive is particularly well suited for studying a historical moment that has yet to settle into a finished state. This is because art provides us a form of historical evidence that indicates rather than ratifies and refracts rather than reflects. The aesthetic case studies assembled here will not permit us to move from cold war secrecy to post–cold war disclosure or from false Oriental stereotypes to true Asian subjects. In delivering another kind of inscrutability, the self-representational works of Kazuo Ishiguro, Theresa Hak Kyung Cha, Ha Jin, and Trinh T. Minh-ha call for a juxtapositional structure of comparison and a tonal method of reading. By juxtaposing cold war and post–cold war Asian self-representations, we will be able to glimpse the elusive pattern of continuity and change without sensationalizing the break between past and present.

Like many scholars before me, I associate Asia's post–cold war horizon with the 1980s and 1990s. Lisa Yoneyama, for example, uses the term "post-Cold War" to describe a "historicized historical moment" in the 1990s during which "political and epistemic shifts" allowed for the coalescing of various legal redress movements across Asia.[98] Rob Wilson offers a different synopsis of a similar period, focusing on economic aspirations rather than war reparations: "*Homo Pacificus* will negotiate transpacific infinitude with Apple microcomputer and Sony Walkman interfaced, retracing the voyages of Balboa and Magellan to reclaim possession of El Mar Pacificó [*sic*]."[99] My book attempts these simultaneous gestures of looking backward toward unresolved wars and forward toward unimaginable futures. In the first decades of the new millennium, U.S. intelligence operations have most dramatically targeted the greater Middle East, a region whose complex histories of Orientalism I cannot properly address here.[100] And, because my inquiry is delimited by the American cold war in East and Southeast Asia, I end up focusing on the transitional decades of the 1980s and the 1990s, when the cold war was ratcheting up in some corners and evolving new social forms in others. Even within the relatively limited scope of this book, however, dates cannot synchronize disparate geographies. Vietnam, Cambodia, and Laos may have been experiencing the brunt of the cold war in the 1970s, but this decade also saw Japan inhabit a new geopolitical role and initiate appreciable geopolitical changes. The post–cold war, I stress, is not based on a concrete date, and my references to it are always contextual. But if this term has any utility within an ongoing war, it is to disarticulate the continuation of the cold war from the continuation of American empire.

In undertaking such a task, I wish to account for one of the most significant, if least acknowledged, monuments to the cold war's perpetuation: the "Pacific Rim." Many scholars, including the ones cited in the opening of this chapter, have argued that this "rim" is an already existing periphery to an American core, a consequence of U.S. cold war efforts to administer the flow of human and economic capital. As we will see, U.S. economic and cultural influences on nations such as Japan and South Korea are undeniable. But while this story of continuing American hegemony has led many to assume that the United States "won" the cold war, Giovanni Arrighi all but names the Pacific Rim nations as the true victor: "Japan and the four 'little tigers' were the main beneficiaries of the escalation of the Cold War between the United States and the USSR, and lately China has been emerging as the real winner of the U.S. War on Terror."[101] According to Arrighi, this growing split between American militaristic might and Asian economic power is unprecedented in the history of capitalism. For our purposes, this split means that in a post–cold war Pacific Century, information derives its most dominant meanings not from militaristic regimes but economic ones. As the case studies to follow will more fully address, tone holds another kind of relevance for a post–cold war period— that is, a period in which variations of "affect" (e.g., communication, language, performance, personality) were becoming increasingly integrated into the production process.[102]

While there is no shortage of studies on the Pacific Rim that consider its relation to cold war *geopolitics*, my book tries to understand this economic formation through its relation to cold war *temperaments*. Why did the fervent tones of "free Asia" begin flattening out in the late twentieth century? If the cold war tone of ideological commitment evidences the demands that American hegemony placed on free Asians, then the post–cold war tone of capitalist ennui that we find in Asian diasporic self-representations arises from the historical coincidence of Asian miracle discourse and late capitalist discourse. Or, to offer a more forceful articulation, I hazard that the recentering of the global economy around select Asian nations has informed and inflected Euro-American theorizations of a new hegemonic norm of labor within capitalist production. In the forthcoming chapters, we will see that the specific tensions crystallized by a racial-aesthetic tone—the tensions between individual flexibility and total interchangeability, informational labor and affective labor, intellectual property rights and political rights—also happen to strike upon the defining tendencies of late twentieth-century economic transformations. In exploring how the globalization of immaterial labor intersects with the arrival of Asian capitalist modernities, we will encounter the different ways in which an "Asian" tone has come to register the intensification of capitalism's vicissitudes.

Chapter Two

THE TONE OF RUMORS

Imperial Tours and Kazuo Ishiguro's Critique of Japanese Exceptionalism

If leaflets, newspapers, or radio broadcasts are likened to bullets, then rumor must be likened to a torpedo; for, once launched, it travels of its own power.

—ROBERT H. KNAPP, *"A PSYCHOLOGY OF RUMOR"* (1944)

Recently we have had such conversations over and over.

—KAZUO ISHIGURO, *AN ARTIST OF THE FLOATING WORLD* (1982)

They "spread swiftly." They are "virtually self-propelling." They "must be likened to a torpedo." They allow "people to *personify* the forces of evil." They present "a menace which had to be dealt with by careful study and analysis." They "became a problem of grave national concern in the frenzied years 1942 and 1943."[1]

Mysterious yet powerful, pernicious and even malevolent, "they" appear to be an extraordinary, superhuman life force. This force, of course, is rumor—a genre of communication that begins harmlessly enough, in the mouth of one individual, and yet gains momentum exponentially, consuming and destroying everything in its path. These characterizations of rumor come from American social scientists writing in the incipient field of rumor studies in the 1940s. Their alarmist imaginings of rumors as "evil," "menace," and "torpedo" alert us to the fact that rumor studies was forged in the fires of war. Specifically, it was "the appearance of the Second World War" that caused attention to be "forcibly drawn to this subject." Scholars of these tumultuous years saw their field's work as serving the war cause through "rumor control." Rumor analysis was said to help gauge morale, stamp out subversion, and combat enemy propaganda. Some researchers actively assisted "rumor clinics"—weekly newspaper columns and radio programs that worked toward the "reduction of rumor-belief."[2] Others devised a rumor circulation formula based on the ratio between the importance of a topic and the ambiguity of available information about it.³ Even rumor specialists who were not necessarily interested in war could not help encountering it in their rumor samples. For example, among the 1,089 rumors collected by the Massachusetts Committee on Public Safety and *Reader's Digest* for the month of September 1942 were the following:

The British are using only colonial troops, not men from England.
The Jews are evading the draft.
The Japanese do not have enough oil to last six months.
There will be a revolution in Germany.
The entire Pacific Fleet was destroyed at Pearl Harbor.
Crab meat packed by the Japanese contains ground glass.⁴

In surveying these samples, Robert H. Knapp would have us "note . . . the striking concentration of rumors on a very few themes."⁵ Clearly, rumors fed on the wartime temperament of suspicion and circulated themes of stealth and subversion. A mode of prognostic knowledge that embroidered fact with speculation, rumors served as vernacular theories about the typology and behavior of foreign elements—usually, enemies. In this way, rumors might be viewed as a kind of intelligence. The most obvious difference between intelligence and rumors is that the former seems reasonably reliable and the latter patently untrue. This apparent divergence in credibility presumably comes down to the origin of information: rumors are sourced from the mindless talk of the ignorant masses whereas intelligence is sourced from the scrupulous judgments of government analysts.

Notwithstanding these distinctions, it is significant that during the cold war years rumor studies reached their high point of influence, and intelligence operations renovated their tactics of evaluation.⁶ These simultaneous and related developments provide the context for "the transformation of rumor and gossip into legitimate sources of information within the decision-making apparatus of the loyalty-security state."⁷ With this claim, Jessica Wang implies that the admission of unsubstantiated rumors into the tight-lipped chambers of U.S. intelligence paradoxically resulted from heightened worries about loyalty and security. Two points follow from this insight. First, the prevalence of rumors within the intelligence establishment raises the possibility that this conjectural mode of information can exert material pressures and yield useful insights, even when the message itself is unfounded or untrue. While wartime researchers such as Knapp operated on the assumption of a rumor's improbability—for example, by calculating "distortion" and identifying "rumor symptoms"—Ron Robin analyzes rumors based not on their credibility but on their productivity. For Robin, rumors are productive in that they enable the "making of the cold war enemy." Unhinged from fact yet bearing the force of truth, rumors have the ability to transform "a distant adversary into a clear and present danger" and "a speculative version of the enemy into a powerful working hypothesis." What Robin calls the "enemy-as-rumor" may not offer "intelligence" about any actual enemy. Instead, the "enemy-as-rumor" provides a temperamental profile of the intelligence community, whose makings of the enemy "represented an attempt to resolve uncertainty, compensate for crucial information voids, and reframe a chaotic world in familiar forms."[8] The second implication of encountering rumors within U.S. statecraft is that we become able to view them as a middle ground between classified intelligence and official news. Can there be such a thing as a *classified rumor*? Rumors travel widely under the cover of secrecy yet also hide in plain sight. But whether whispered in hushed tones or trumpeted as breaking news, they are known for their spread, not their containment. This basic fact about rumors—the fact of their inevitable but often surreptitious transmission—makes them a unique transfer point between state secrets and popular discourse. Hence, Alan Nadel in effect credits rumors for helping create a "containment culture" in the United States. Containment culture is a geopolitically motivated public discourse animated by suspicions about unseen dangers and unscrupulous characters. In contrast to personal narratives, the "cultural narratives" of containment "are echoed and reiterated—in the forms of national narratives, religious dogma, class signifiers, courtship rituals—with a contagion that resembles viral epidemics."[9] In reading Nadel alongside Wang and Robin, we might conceptualize rumors as the traffic between "intelligence" and "culture." This inter-discursive (or inter-dialogic) traffic, which was particularly copious when the enemy was inscrutable, slackened the division between the reckless manufacturers of speculation and the dignified envoys of truth: the more suspicious the enemy, the more profuse and the more seductive the rumors. Robin's formulation of the "rumor-as-enemy" is instructive for showing how the medium and the subject of suspicion can become confused. To return to this chapter's opening paragraph, it is easy to see how the sensationalist language used to describe the spread of rumors borrows from the equally lurid language used to describe the onslaught of enemy forces. The indeterminate enemy gave fuel to rumors and assumed the dim, vaporous shape of rumors. "They" are the enemy.

Whether public or classified, reasonable or outlandish, rumors are neither social pathology, nor innocuous chitchat, nor factual truth. A more useful characterization is that "all rumors, regardless of their manifest content, may be regarded as expressions of underlying anxiety." According to Knapp, rumors can articulate "wish or aggression" at the surface, yet they are "motivated more deeply by fear."[10] In describing rumors as an expression of anxiety and a defense against fear, Knapp implies that they can provide us with tonal intelligence—with a documentation of affect, temperament, attitude, and psyche. In this capacity, it matters little if rumors appear to be dubious or prove to be erroneous. In fact, my case studies in this chapter will show that rumors are geopolitically productive and historically revealing, precisely when they are outrageously wrong, uncontrollably infectious, and diffusely abundant. Scholars have shown that rumors feed on social and colonial unrest, whether one calls it war, revolution, insurgency, or regime change.[11] But rumors are not simply the product of a period; rumors can also *produce* a period. That is, they can generate a historical mood and an ideological surround, something that operates "just below the surface of public awareness."[12] Tracking the rhythm of rumors can thus allow us to diagnose—to take the temperature of and to monitor the pulse of—historical periods that are marked, racked, fractured, and ultimately undermined by geopolitical instability.

My focus in this chapter will be rumors that, at two different periods, had the broader effect of substantiating Japanese exceptionalism. One case study involves the U.S. Occupation's rehabilitation of Japanese national identity during the cold war, and the other involves Japan-born British novelist Kazuo Ishiguro's representation of Japanese national identity during the U.S.-Japan trade war. In the first scenario of the 1940s and 1950s, rumors helped justify U.S. efforts to reinstate Japan as an economic power and anticommunist hub in Asia and the Pacific. During the 1970s and 1980s, meanwhile, another surge of rumors in the United States and Western Europe postulated Japan's economic miracle as the portent of a Pacific Century. In feeling out the throb and throng of rumors at these two historical scenes, I am suggesting that a viral liveliness finds expression in a peculiar tonal quality. A surplus of heterogeneous conjectures cannot cohere into a synthetic account or a verifiable truth—but it can convey the surface tension stretched taut across placid calm, the darkening cloud of gathering unease, and the snowballing weight of deadening dread. As I discussed in chapter 1, U.S. analysts prioritized source evaluation in determining the credibility of intelligence content. In reading rumors for tonal intelligence, we will not need to trouble ourselves with locating their source or even appraising their content, for it is ultimately the unruly *quantity* of rumors that has the most direct bearing on tone. By taking a tonal approach to investigating wars that evolve as they recur, I seek to reframe the basic problem of America's cold war friendship with Japan and its trade war competition with Japan. This problem can be summed up as a perceived lack of knowledge about the enemy. Numerous wartime studies tried to fill this lack, most famously Ruth Benedict's *The Chrysanthemum and the Sword* (1946), a methodologically innovative ethnography commissioned by the Office of War Information (innovative because Benedict could not conduct fieldwork in the traditional sense and thus relied on Japanese Americans as informants).[13] By taking rumors as my archive, I am suggesting that suppositional information about "Japan" can actually be more historically perceptive than ethnographic texts that strive for cultural authenticity. Reading for the ambient tone of rumors rather than the cultural truth of identity at the crisis points of U.S.–Japan geopolitics also takes the explanatory load off individual Japanese representatives, who were inevitably shoved into the spotlight and pried for native information when war amplified the enemy's murkiness. Though it may seem counterintuitive, we must resist the impulse to excavate, clarify, and verify racial facts and historical truths under such conditions of uncertainty and insecurity. Setting aside more proper genres of strategic intelligence and cultural knowledge, I argue that the tone of rumors can be more conducive to studying historical junctures when the operative terms of racial and national identity are being actively and conjecturally rethought.

The biological colloquialisms that accord rumors a life of their own—often as untraceable, invisible, self-propelling, and highly contagious viruses—throw light on the relative incapacity of the people caught up in them. Although scholars have treated rumors as mediums of communication in their own right, one might just as easily view not rumors but their participants as the vessel. This power dynamic is particularly acute when rumors concern a foreign adversary—that is, when otherwise "rational"

American individuals find themselves analyzing, fighting, and *making* an increasingly powerful enemy-as-rumor or rumor-as-enemy. The Japanese enemy presents a special case of inscrutability because the United States and its European Allies had long looked favorably upon Japan: it was a civilizational exception to Asian barbarism, a fact evidenced by its extensive colonial acquisitions. In the waning days of World War II, this assumption of Japanese exceptionalism began to guide U.S. military calculations. Take, for example, the propaganda film *Know Your Enemy—Japan*. Intended as "indoctrination" training for U.S. soldiers, this film was scripted in June 1942 but not released until August 9, 1945, the day that Nagasaki was bombed. This delay, John Dower surmises, was "derived in considerable part from uncertainty and controversy about who the enemy in Japan really was."[14] Screenwriter Irving Wallace recalls, "Some felt that the only good Jap was a dead Jap. . . . Others felt the enemy was the Emperor. Still others believed Tojo and the military clique were the real enemy."[15] Three weeks after its release and two weeks after Japan's surrender, *Know Your Enemy* was withdrawn. This, too, was motivated by confusion about the enemy. A telegram from General Douglas MacArthur's headquarters had apparently halted the film's release "due to change in policy governing occupation of Japan."[16] Though not specified, this policy change likely concerns the fact that the United States needed their World War II enemy to be a cold war friend, especially since China appeared to be cozying up to the Soviet Union. And the "indoctrination" question thus became not how to know your enemy, or even how to know your enemy from your friend, but how to transform your enemy of yesterday's war into your friend of tomorrow's war.

During the 1940s and the 1950s, U.S.–Japan relations were informed by the dictates of seemingly opposed wars. One was the conclusion of the decidedly "hot" Pacific War in which Japan and the United States were nuclear enemies. The other was the start of a nominally cold war in which the two nations were friendly allies. Lisa Yoneyama has introduced the term "transwar" to describe "the transferability of violence between the two imperial powers," the United States and Japan.[17] This transferrable violence refers not so much to the transfer *of* violence from one empire to another but rather to Washington's material support for reinstating Japan's economic and political dominance in its former territories. One key component of U.S. transwar policy was the "democratization" of Japan's emperor institution. This involved transforming His Majesty from a Shinto deity into a "human emperor" (*ningen tenno*) and, accordingly, from the premier wartime enemy into the democratic face of free Asia. In the following pages, I will show how this makeover was catalyzed by a series of staged encounters between the emperor Hirohito and his subjects that took place throughout Japan with varying intensity between 1946 and 1951. It is difficult to convey the significance and the strangeness of these "inspection tours." The previously cloistered emperor was facing his subjects for the first time. Without horse, regalia, or ceremony, he was asked to merely mingle among his people—a task for which neither side had been sufficiently prepared. If the uncertainties of war breed rumors, and these rumors assume the shape of the enemy, then what about the rumors appearing in war's aftermath— especially if a war's end yields not peace but another war? What shape do rumors take then?

To answer this question, I track the spread of rumors that accompanied the emperor's tours across the prefectures. Whether celebratory or critical in sentiment, Japanese or American in origin, these rumors ran the gamut from assassination attempts to impersonation attempts, casting Hirohito as "fat," "short-sighted," "good-natured," "stoop-shouldered," and "very happy." The official organs of the U.S. occupying forces collected and analyzed the everyday people's reactions to the emperor as he passed through their towns.[18] Although many officials dismissed the import of these reactions (they could not provide usable intelligence), I find that the wildly discrepant rumors about Hirohito enabled his democratic socialization by way of tone. This tone is best encapsulated by the touring emperor's cryptic refrain of "ah so." Was this feeble utterance a sign of shame, complacency, incompetence, or indifference? I show that, despite their inconsistency, the viral rumors traveling alongside and circling around Hirohito helped "humanize" and "democratize" him by keying in on his nervousness and awkwardness—a stark departure from his prewar persona as a mysterious divine force. It is important to keep in mind, moreover, that the putatively unsanctioned tours that worked to legitimate Hirohito's *humanity* through extrajuridical means took place concurrently with efforts to adjudicate his wartime *inhumanity* at the Tokyo War Crimes Tribunal. In giving tonal consistency and human shape to an emperor who was incompetent, whether in an endearing or infuriating sense, these rumors, I propose, contributed to exonerating Hirohito, as well as the Japanese nation, from crimes of war and aggression.

America's promulgation of Japan as a model democracy vis-à-vis Hirohito worked to *suppress* war memory. The 1980s, however, saw widespread American attempts to *revive* war memories in order to identify a precedent for Japan's putatively undemocratic trade policies and business practices. This latter period also accounted for a resurgence of "know your enemy" rhetoric, which included a demand for native informants who could provide intelligence on the specifically Japanese qualities of an "economic miracle." Such was the role for which Kazuo Ishiguro's early novels were slotted. My claims in this chapter will pertain to Ishiguro's writings as a whole, but I devote particular attention to *An Artist of the Floating World* (1986) in order to best contrast the pressures of racial self-representation during the 1970s and 1980s versus the 1940s and 1950s.[19] Like Hirohito, our narrator Masuji Ono embarks on itinerant "tours" of postwar Japan, targeting sites of economic reconstruction. The motif of the tour not only recalls Hirohito's efforts to remedy his public image through inspections. It also shows how Japan's economic rise made the lure of native guidance foundational to Ishiguro's early success. Lumped with other Japanophilic and Japanophobic texts, Ishiguro's "Japan Decade" novels, which also include *A Pale View of Hills* (1982) and *The Remains of the Day* (1989), allegedly helped readers "understand how Japanese people think."[20] Although Mark McGurl has shown how a surging information economy turned literary spokespeople into mid-level employees and how a robust "experiential economy" turned literary reading into "quasi-touristic imaginary experiences," Japan's specific influence on the work of character and the character who works has yet to be fully accounted for.[21] Why have Ishiguro's later novels been interpreted as commentaries on new routines of overwork, while his early novels have been interpreted as commentaries on antiquated regimes of excessive nationalism?

I address this impasse by showing how all of Ishiguro's characters, Japanese or otherwise, perform a kind of "knowledge work," to the extent that all of these characters circulate rumors about "identity." Rumors are an overriding theme for Ishiguro. This is because his status-conscious protagonists are perennially fixated on what others say about them. On a more formal level, rumors function as a structuring principle, mediating the relation between narration and dialogue. In every Ishiguro novel, characters are constantly talking about each other, and the narrator is constantly recounting these conversations. This intricate narrative infrastructure leads us to repeatedly encounter the same choice words and turns of phrase. Ironically, the phrases that spread most abundantly in Ishiguro's novels concern likeness ("the likes of") and distinction ("rise above"). Yet the more that Ishiguro's narrators rehearse the language of their myriad interlocutors—and the more that characters discuss forms of distinguishing, marking, typologizing, and locating identity—the more difficult it becomes to keep track of who said what, when, and where. In presenting recurring conversations between superficially differentiated characters who ventriloquize nearly identical lines, Ishiguro's works demonstrate how the whirr and murmur of rumors attenuate not only the meaning of a repeated message but also the integrity of the characters through which this message passes.

In *Artist*, rumors issue from and pass through what appears to be a classically unreliable narrator. Masuji Ono's recollections revolve around conversations that serve to validate his unparalleled influence as a wartime propaganda artist. Reproducing these conversations, however, creates a formal tension between character narration and peripheral prattle, as well as between culturally specific information and anonymous chatter. As in the case of Hirohito's tours, the rumors that accompany Ono's listless journey produce a certain tonal effect. I argue that this busy and buzzy tone, which accounts for the peculiar "quietness" of Ishiguro's novels, allows us to perceive the continuity between Japanese identities and post-Fordist identities. Rather than isolate Ishiguro's Japan novels as a passing phase, therefore, I read them in conjunction with Ishiguro's other works in order to reconceive how racial intelligence is transmitted. The leveling of narratological speech acts into a general hum—a flat and neutral tone—reframes racial representation as a kind of informational interfacing. In recruiting a host of indistinct and immaterial laborers to relentlessly talk about distinction, even Ishiguro's most racially allegorical novels produce a monotonous tone rather than an intelligible identity. We might say, then, that the rumor circulating within and across Ishiguro's novels is that there is something "Asian" in the air—even if there isn't a racially marked character in sight.

If contradictory rumors gave shape to a free Asian ally in the case of Hirohito, we have the opposite effect in Ishiguro's novels. Here, tediously redundant rumors not only disaggregate race from character but also transform "character" into a site of dialogic intensity and information overload.

I bring together these two geopolitically charged sites of identity production with the aim of theorizing rumors as a life form of racial information that saturates and undercuts—even as it is constantly shadowed by—the singular, authoritative figure of the autoethnographic informant. Fleeting, anonymous, and overwhelming, rumors alert us to the tremors of identities-in-formation, not through what they posit but through how they spread. Using the rumor circulation index as a tonal index allows us to apprehend "Asian" as an anxiety *about* racial intelligibility rather than as a statement on race as such. With respect to Ishiguro in particular, the mobilization of rumors as a formal principle circulates the myth of distinct identities—of likeness and distinction. A compulsive, repetitive tendency that severs the genetic line to original sources and cultural origins, Asian-as-rumor, we will find, yields the precise opposite of historical facts and racial truths.

THE LAST DAYS OF WAR, THE FIRST DAYS OF PEACE

In *Artist*, it is a character named Matsuda who, during Japan's military campaign, turns our narrator, the young Ono, toward politically engaged art. Matsuda is a stiff royalist: "Our Emperor is our rightful leader, and yet what in reality has become of things? Power has been grasped from him by these businessmen and their politicians." Although in Asia "Japan stands like a giant amidst cripples and dwarfs," Matsuda yearns "for us to forge an empire as powerful and wealthy as those of the British and the French." Such an empire requires a military that is "answerable only to his Imperial Majesty" (173). Matsuda's miscalculations are easy to recognize. In the postwar present of *Artist*, the United States has seized the reins from Britain and France, the empires that Matsuda holds up as paragons for Japan. Matsuda's take on the emperor likewise marks a departed era. His militaristic bromides have been overtaken in the novel by routine homages to democracy. Finally, instead of becoming a powerful imperial presence, postwar Japan has been reborn as a child. Says one character, "we Japanese have been shown to be like children. We've yet to learn how to handle the responsibility of democracy" (120).[22]

The narrative structure of flashbacks in *Artist* allows Ishiguro to compare and contrast wartime Japan and postwar Japan. Yet, despite the obvious discrepancies between a past coded as militaristic and a present coded as democratic, what stands out in Matsuda's speech is the striking similarity between the United States' tutelary model and Matsuda's imperialistic model when it comes to the status of the emperor. That is, Matsuda's indignation about the emperor's victimization by his military advisers is not an anachronism of the defeated Japanese empire but a foundational tenet of Washington's transitional policy in free Asia. For much of the war, the American public, the State Department, and the Allied leaders had called for Hirohito's arrest.[23] But near the war's end, U.S. national interests outpaced the Allies' military considerations, and the postwar fate of the Japanese emperor and of the imperial institution became a cold war problem.[24] Given the threat of Soviet encroachment in Asia, Washington increasingly saw preserving the emperor as a tactical necessity. Although former ambassador Joseph Grew is typically credited with pushing to retain the emperor in March 1943, more than two years before the war ended, a lenient emperor policy was floated in conversation as early as July 1942, just months after U.S. involvement in the war began.[25]

Regardless of the policy's origins, the nomination of Hirohito as a pillar for Japan's democratization became axiomatic thanks to MacArthur's military secretary and head of psychological warfare, Bonner Fellers. In a widely circulated memorandum, Fellers paints the emperor as a tragic hero whose efforts to make peace with the United States were stymied by both his own military advisers and Soviet warmongers. The shifting terms of the emperor's involvement are palpable not only in the broader historical narrative of the war but also in Fellers's drafts. Here, Fellers crosses out the phrase "ordinarily indecisive monarch" and substitutes the word "rebuke." When recounting the final retreat of Japanese troops, he strikes through and then reinserts the phrase "at Hirohito's command." At some moments, the emperor is "worn" and "harassed." Mostly, though, he appears bold and intrepid, his actions no less than "revolutionary," as he defied the strictures of the ancient emperor system to "face down his own fanatic militarists, usurp their power, and compel them by sheer strength of will."[26]

Fellers's editing at the level of character rather than outcome affords an early glimpse of how plastic Hirohito's image could be. Washington's increasing conviction regarding Hirohito's plasticity coexisted with its belief that the emperor exercised an unaccountable control over his subjects. During the war, military strategists had considered "painting the emperor's picture on the sides of Allied ships to deter kamikaze suicide attacks."[27] In the months leading up to Japan's surrender, the Joint Chiefs of Staff briefly contemplated whether the emperor's surrender would lead to "national suicide" and "virtual extinction."[28] Preventing mass chaos thus provided a popular line of reasoning for protecting the emperor from prosecution. In his memoirs, MacArthur, one of the emperor's chief defenders, speculates that Hirohito's "unjust" indictment would produce "tragic consequences" and require "one million reinforcements" for damage control in Japan and the Pacific theater. Yet more dramatically, MacArthur proclaims that his erstwhile foe "had a more thorough grasp of the democratic concept than almost any Japanese."[29]

Hirohito's radio broadcast of surrender paved the way for his democratic "humanization." And if the announcement of Japan's defeat wasn't shocking enough, this broadcast was the first time that the emperor's own subjects had heard his voice. The experience was utterly baffling. According to Marilyn Ivy, the "reedy," "disembodied" prerecorded speech, proceeding in "impossibly archaic language," made both the speaker and his message unrecognizable.[30] A journalist writing in 1948 recalls, "It almost sounded as if he were not human." Some listeners even "misinterpret[ed] the message . . . as a call for greater resistance."[31] Following Japan's surrender, the U.S. occupying forces would expedite and formalize the demystification and humanization of Hirohito. This effort included publicizing the Imperial Household's assets, submitting textbooks and literatures to U.S. censors, updating imperial portraits in public spaces, and reworking the Japanese constitution so that a refurbished emperor system could serve a functionally democratic state. The most memorable and most official move toward humanizing Hirohito was his public address on January 1, 1946. Drafted by the State Department and the Occupation regime, the "Humanity Declaration" decreed that the relationship between the emperor and his subjects was to be one of "mutual trust and affection" and not based on "mere legends and myths."[32] U.S. officers were quick to denounce Japan's "legends and myths," both during and after the war. Yet the United States' own transwar emperor policy also included what John Dower describes as the "remythologizing of Hirohito."[33] Retaining but reoutfitting the throne at the level of governance required transforming the emperor into a merely symbolic figurehead—Hirohito was to remain head of state, but to be voided of actual political power. Remaking Hirohito into a "human emperor" at the level of myth, however, required a more public and embodied approach—something that would bring him into direct contact with his subjects. The emperor's tours were a core component of this "remythologizing" project. These tours indeed democratized and humanized Hirohito, but not because he gave express articulation to any individual or representative identity. Rather, Hirohito became what Nancy Ruttenburg calls a "democratic personality," insofar as he dynamically yet unconsciously performed the role of a "vocal current": he helped circulate a "translatable and transferable form of subjectivity" among his subjects, a process that in time also produced a cold war political sensibility.[34]

The cold war project of crafting Japan's national self-conception through Hirohito's humanization provides one avenue for grappling with the peculiar memory effects of Ishiguro's early writings on Japan. In these writings, we often encounter two kinds of characters: those who, in a rapid about-face toward an American tomorrow, have forgotten Japan's imperial past, and those who continue to cling to prewar ideals, but more due to habitual conformity than genuine belief. *Artist* is remarkable for charting the course from a character's overattachment to imperial Japan to his forgetting of imperial Japan. Our narrator's most unreliable moments are when he ostentatiously repents for his wartime involvement. As other characters dismiss this propaganda artist's attempt to claim responsibility and express culpability, we, too, become inclined to view him as an ordinary man who misguidedly thinks that his role in the war was more important than it actually had been. This subtle exoneration of the narrator, by the embodied contemporary reader as well as by the novel's postwar Japanese society, introduces a number of questions: Why are the novel's ordinary Japanese subjects so forgetful about the past? What made this forgetting both possible and necessary? How exactly did it come about? As we will see, Hirohito's inspection tours across Japan offer one site for understanding how the nation came to be absolved of its war crimes. More subtly than laws or proclamations but arguably more effectively, the emotional norming effected by these tours created an assumption of national innocence that bound the emperor with the people and that limited responsibility for the war to a select clique of militarists.

THE EMPEROR ON TOUR

Hirohito's first public outing was in November 1945, a handful of weeks before the Humanity Declaration. Donning a "railwayman's uniform" clearly designed for the public eye, the emperor visited a shrine in the Mie Prefecture.[35] The tours conducted expressly for "inspection" commenced the following year on February 19, 1946, when he visited a factory and black market.[36] These inspection visits were billed as occasions for the emperor to express condolence for war losses and to boost morale for reconstruction. However, they were as much for Hirohito to be inspected as they were for him to do the inspecting. How did the emperor find his way into this public persona of sympathetic cheer? How does one perform a part that has never existed? The shedding of a worker's uniform for a Western-style business suit shows that the Occupation regime and the emperor's advisers were improvising along the way. The degree of control they exerted can perhaps be gleaned from the emperor's typical itinerary, which was programmed down to the minute. "Inspection" brought the "human emperor" to farms, hospitals, shipyards, mills, mines, and a variety schools and factories. In the morning, Hirohito was to encourage fishermen unloading their catch and farmers hauling rice; in the afternoon, he "rubbed elbows with coal miners." One day found him waving at baseball games and another planting trees for Arbor Day. Wherever the emperor went, onlookers, officials, and journalists glorified his austere lifestyle. The emperor rejects "special facilities, furniture, or beddings . . . for his comfort," it was reported. He would be "satisfied with simplest meals."[37] Other commentators pursued the opposite spectrum of divine mystification, exoticizing his "use of weeds for food" and his insistence on wearing his cravat "until it is threadbare."[38] Such accounts show that the inspection tours were accompanied by a "pilgrimage on paper," a "deluge of so-called 'Emperor Articles.'"[39] Some of these articles were akin to contemporary tabloid coverage, featuring the royal family posed in quotidian settings. The paper trail that I'll be following documents the responses that the inspection tours elicited, for it was Hirohito's interactions with his subjects that presented the most mystery and therefore generated the most speculation. Simply put, there was no precedent for what to do once "the thick curtain of tradition and Government policy that separated the Emperor from his people [was] lifted."[40] Occupation staffer Guy Swope attempted to survey the range of possibilities:

Some individuals were apathetic, some moved to tears and uncontrollable emotion, some only curious, some frightened, some confused as though not knowing what the entire affair was about. One man fell to his knees and thrust his face into the mud when the Emperor spoke to him. Others stared without emotion; some were embarrassed. Numerous incidents might be related, but it is believed fallacious to ascribe too much importance to individual actions, and folly to attempt conclusive deductions from them. . . . Some people love him and some hate him; some are amused, and some are afraid. He is all things to all men, and his very presence is, to some, not quite real.[41]

Swope is right to refrain from overemphasizing the significance of "individual actions," and I agree that it is difficult to arrive at "conclusive deductions." Yet these myriad reactions to the emperor also do not cancel each other out. If we look more closely at what people were saying about the emperor, we find that they often arrived at dramatically divergent conclusions by following nearly identical signposts. In particular, two symbolic conceits recur: a worn felt hat and an earnest yet unhappy "ah so." Z. Tomiya, for instance, expresses a "friendly feeling" in seeing Hirohito interact with his subjects and sadness over the sight of him "waving his hat . . . on the roof in the rain and snow." Others fete Hirohito's heroism: "When we think of the Emperor . . . , sailing across the channel in the cold wind and even saying smilingly, 'Ah so! Ah so!' waving his hat, without showing any trace of fatigue, our hearts ache."[42] Far less charitable observations, however, picked up on the same tropes. A journalist writing in October 1948 was one of many who demanded Hirohito's abdication: "you, Emperor Hirohito, signer of the war declaration, remain unconcerned and neither acknowledge your error nor beg forgiveness. With an air of nonchalance, you go on tours with your bland reply, 'Ah so.' "[43] American observers also differed on how the emperor was faring. Some commented on his stiffness and nervousness. Others praised him for "sweating it out manfully." For many, the imperial tours became known as the " 'ah so' tours."[44] While sympathetic images of "the smiling, hat-doffing emperor" obviously worked to encode Hirohito as the democratic "emperor of love and peace," one could say that the more derogatory characterizations had a similar effect.[45] The new symbolic regime of a battered hat and a banal "ah so" cast Hirohito as alternately innocent, incompetent, pitiful, and reprehensible. But whatever affective interpretation the slightly awkward majesty solicited, it's clear that a "human emperor" was above all a powerless one.

This new emperor, with his faux-worn hat and cryptic "ah so," generated sentiments and statements that were logically conflicting yet tonally

FIGURE 2.1. Slightly awkward majesty: Emperor Hirohito in 1946

coherent. Sara Ahmed's theory of "affective economies" is useful for understanding this paradox. According to Ahmed, "emotions create the very surfaces and boundaries that allow all kinds of objects to be delineated. The objects of emotion take shape as effects of circulation." Although Ahmed focuses on "shared feelings," in the case of Hirohito, a human shape is the effect of the *varied* emotional responses to his embodied presence. Even if these responses cannot be resolved into a consistent message, they nonetheless produce "a thickness in the air, or an atmosphere."[46] Ahmed's invocation of Silvan Tomkins's "emotional contagion" is noteworthy here, given how commonly the viral metaphor is used to convey the active, uncontrollable nature of a rumor that mysteriously takes on a "life of its own."[47] For Hirohito, rumors were able to give the persona of the "human emperor" a "life of its own," in part because the emperor himself lacked the savoir-faire to step into this new role. Hirohito became a "human emperor," in other words, not because he animated the positive traits of humanness but because his lack of a clear message and lack of a legible affect had the effect of inviting conjecture. Further, it seems in the above examples that Hirohito's voicelessness and lifelessness provoked a kind of overcompensation, whereby viewers reacted all the more strongly, with great emotional force and even hysterics, precisely because the emperor himself was so affectively vacant. This emotional dyad of no expression and overexpression, likely reinforced by American documentation, converges with the tenor of U.S. WWII propaganda, which depicted the Japanese as emotionally repressed until "an opportunity for the first time in his life to express himself" leads him to "go completely berserk."[48]

In feeding the life of rumors, the emperor tours show how an overriding public tone—rather than a "humanity declaration"—could transform a mystically divine monarch into a human-shaped vessel, a suit and a hat without a warm body. Paul Kent, a U.S. official assigned to follow the imperial tours in 1947, offers a compelling and succinct account of Hirohito's humanity effect:

The impression he makes upon one is less than inspiring. He is nervous to the point of looking physically handicapped; his gestures and movements are jerky and uncoordinated. He hesitates before speaking or acting. If not thoroughly self-conscious, he is certainly ill-at-ease. His influence can spring only from his position and the ancient tradition attaching to the sovereign. His force as a man is negligible. On almost all occasions his face was devoid of any expression. He did smile a few times, when speaking to children, and when the *Banzai's* assumed great proportions. He is even poorly dressed. The head of a state might be expected to wear black shoes, on occasion, when clad in a black suit. The Emperor wears only brown.

The report goes on to conclude that the tours were ineffective in both demystifying the emperor and de-indoctrinating the citizenry: "humanization has assuredly in no wise reduced, if, indeed, it has not actually increased, the power and influence of the Imperial tradition." In the same report, Kent also reiterates many complaints, among both Japanese and Americans, that the tours were "completely unjustified in a nation standing upon the verge of financial collapse."[49] I don't disagree that Hirohito's performance was uninspiring and uncommanding, but my interpretation of this performance veers in the opposite direction: I believe that Hirohito's excessive nervousness, lack of coordination, painful self-consciousness, inexpressive face, and poor dress turned out to be unexpectedly advantageous for securing his democratic identity. To redirect Kent's assessment, Hirohito's "force as a man" was valuable *because* it was "negligible." Specifically, the emperor's lack of affective and linguistic expression allowed him to provide a model of democratic leadership based on a pliant and passive personality. Taken together, Hirohito's indecipherable sigh ("ah so"), bodily discomfiture ("jerky and uncoordinated"), and ill-fitting getup (worn hat and brown suit) made him puppet-like, doll-like, and child-like—but neither man-like nor leader-like. Dower evocatively describes Hirohito as "a figure of 'hollow' charisma." Naoko Shibusawa quotes SCAP officials who dubbed him a "dummy-on-the-knee," a "doll-like zombie," and "the little man who [wasn't] there."[50] Despite Kent's frustrations, the fact that such a persona is "less than inspiring" is more of a solution than a problem, for it was this sense of an embodied but vacant presence that made Hirohito so easily exploitable for the political agendas of others. By speaking as himself, the emperor offered his embodied speech for ideological conscription by interested parties.

Hirohito's inspection tours served various ends and had different scalar effects. In a local sense, the emperor became nicknamed "the Broom" because "every place he was scheduled to visit got cleaned up." Dower writes how in the city of Uwajima, an inn rebuilt expressly for the emperor's visit attempted to sell his bath water to local dignitaries. In Kyoto, meanwhile, the emperor's reception was more mixed. In 1951, university students fiercely protested the imperial tours amidst debates about Japan's role in the American cold war.[51] At the global level, it is hugely consequential that Hirohito's tours were contemporaneous with the Tokyo War Crime Trials. One can't say that Hirohito's exemption from standing trial in 1949 was a byproduct of his tours. But the affective cultivation of Hirohito's humanity vis-à-vis his fallibility contributed to creating the impression that Hirohito was basically innocuous, if not outright innocent. That is, Hirohito was a "human emperor," to the extent that he was as incompetent in his social interactions as he was impotent in Japan's military affairs. Locally and globally, the imperial tours illustrate the ideological importance of Asian self-representation to the legitimation of American empire. In later chapters, we'll see how performances of vocality became crucial to authenticating racial presence and ideological truth. On the one hand, Hirohito's affective blankness represents a departure from the archetype of the overly animated free Asian. Unlike the ebulliently progressive orator, the emotionally overwrought POW, and the perennially cheerful brother (all personas we'll meet in the coming pages), Hirohito's achievement of a free Asian subjectivity did not result from anything that he himself did or said—even though his advisers maintain that the tours were his own idea.[52] On the other hand, Hirohito, precisely because he was an empty shell of a man, provides an allegorical exemplification and an ideal case of the free Asian's availability for ideological manipulation. On this score, it is worth noting that Hirohito's status as clumsy, careworn, inarticulate, and "human" has helped his legacy fare better than that of Chiang Kai-shek, Syngman Rhee, Ngo Dinh Diem, Ferdinand Marcos, and other forceful, passionate, outspoken, and narcissistic personalities who pushed a strong nationalist or personal agenda that conflicted with the United States cold war priorities.[53]

Regardless of whether the free Asian appears excessive or impoverished in expressivity, what I will continue to stress in this book is not this figure's regrettable and abject puppetry but, to the contrary, its contribution to creating a new normal at a moment of heightened geopolitical instability. It is in this light that we can view Hirohito's formulaic messages and default "ah so" as garnering token support for the positions of American cold warriors and Japanese conservative royalists, who, despite their differences, plotted a common postwar future for Japan and honed a culturalist rhetoric of Japanese exceptionalism.[54] As it happened, even spontaneous protests against the emperor, venomous calls to overthrow him, and multiple threats to his life would only reinforce his democratic symbolism. These expressions of anger and distress, no matter their source or content, were often summarily attributed to communist agitators. MacArthur once declared that "only the Communists have objected strongly to the emperor's activities."[55] The emperor's efficacy was measured by military strength ("the Emperor alone is worth 20 divisions"), and his popularity became an indirect safeguard against communism ("the Japanese people do not pay homage to the Emperor as a protection against Communism, but in doing so, they naturally check its progress"). According to one press report, the "spirit of loyalty to the Emperor is the strongest bulwark against Communism."[56]

If in postwar Japan the circulation of rumors and emotions seems especially volatile—if the question of what binds a nation seems especially confusing—it is because times of national defeat and economic reconstruction are crucibles for the ideological work of emotional norming. In Anna

Parkinson's investigation of postwar Germany, this norming process reveals "the role of empathic identification that fuses a group together in an affective structure."[57] In the case of postwar Japan, the affects that fuse a defeated empire into a common identity necessarily possess a cultural and racial dimension. In contemplating what kind of "emotional regime" attended changes in a geopolitical regime, we must thus consider how transwar efforts to exonerate rather than indict the wartime emperor impacted Japanese national identity as well as free Asian racial formation. The emperor tours installed Hirohito as a serviceable figurehead for race and nation by cultivating a set bandwidth of emotional relations between the emperor, the everyday Japanese citizenry, the wartime military advisers, and the American occupiers. In contrast to postwar Germany where democratization required rendering guilt normative, the oddity of occupied Japan is that a confluence of U.S. interests produced the need to foster empathy toward Hirohito, ire toward his military advisers, and apathy toward Japan's imperialist project. In short, during a transwar moment, the emotions that had the power to bind together a rehabilitated Japanese nation as well as an anticommunist free Asian alliance were effectively enabled by Hirohito's flaccidity and harmlessness.[58] Regardless of whether an *individual's* relation to the emperor was positive or negative, therefore, the rumors sparked by the imperial tours produced a tonal situation that aligned the political figurehead with the everyday populace, based not on empathy or loyalty but on mutual innocence. These tours helped frame "military leaders, government elites, and perhaps some soldiers [as] responsible for the disasters," while establishing that "ordinary citizens were only victims of the war and the nation's colonial policies."[59] In refashioning a powerfully divine ruler as a fallible human, U.S. cold war policy steered Japan towards what Carol Gluck terms a "negative model for the postwar reforms," an apparent "inversion of the prewar" that made "an anti-past" the "original moment of memory, the first postwar redaction of the history of imperialism and war."[60]

In the domestic context of Japan, the new reforms introduced during the U.S. Occupation stripped the emperor of political power and codified his humanity into positive law. In the mid-century cultural imaginary, the notion of the symbolic emperor came to underpin emergent schools of thought among both Japanese and Euro-American thinkers, most famously with Roland Barthes's characterization of the Japanese emperor as "the sacred 'nothing'" and "an empty subject."[61] In the international realm of human rights, Hirohito's withdrawal from the Tokyo Trials deflected the question of his war responsibility and that of his legal humanity. That key legal proceedings concerning Hirohito's role in Japanese militarism and imperialism were never permitted to run their course has had serious and ongoing repercussions for Asia and the Pacific, the regions where the former Japanese empire and the ascendant American empire overlapped considerably. Cold war efforts to suppress the history of Japanese militarism offer a revealing contrast to the moral condemnation of Nazism. In *After Evil*, Robert Meister writes that the Holocaust has inspired a moral lament of "too late" and continues to justify military interventions in the name of preventing future evil.[62] U.S. transwar policy in Japan bears out the reverse temporal rationale, insofar as it operated on the principle of "never too soon": the domestic internment of Japanese American citizens, the nuclear bombing of Hiroshima and Nagasaki, and the anticipatory planning for postwar occupation all constituted an effort toward "winning the peace." This military strategy of preemption and moral rhetoric of peace would come to guide U.S. cold war operations in Asia more broadly. For example, in the weeks before Japan's surrender, "Koreans changed to quasi-enemies, and Japanese to friends" since a victor's justice in Asia required that the newly liberated "Korea [get] the occupation designed for Japan," the former enemy state.[63] Pursued in the name of freedom and containment, U.S. cold war policy not only interrupted decolonization in the region but also postponed redress for Japanese crimes. Unlike the moral certainty of the Holocaust, then, the question of "evil" among Japan's former territories seems elusive and unredressable: there is no "after evil." In creating an environment inhospitable to postwar justice or decolonization, the intermingling of Japanese and American empire turned the fruits of military occupation into "gifts for the liberated" and created an affective economy of indebtedness and gratitude.[64]

For our purposes, one of the most significant aspects of Washington's cold war policy is that Hirohito's new "human" identity facilitated a kind of organized forgetting as it helped make way for the dominant narrative of Japan's national identity. The problem of how war is remembered, especially among a nation's ordinary subjects, was a point of obsession for the young Ishiguro. In his first three novels, *A Pale View of Hills*, *An Artist of the Floating World*, and *The Remains of the Day*, national politics are in the background, but the politics of national forgetting are in the foreground. *Artist* and *Remains* in particular feature protagonists who seem immoral and anachronistic due to their attachment to prewar ideologies (militarism, fascism, colonialism) in the dawn of a new era animated by the political views, moral values, and cultural iconography of the United States. It is not only Ishiguro's characters but also Ishiguro himself who seems caught in the throes of history's unpredictable manifestations and ambivalent returns: he is the first to admit that he has essentially written the same book three times.[65] For someone who in his younger years claimed to be ignorant about Japan and impatient whenever the topic of Japan came up—for someone whose first stories were about a suicide pact, street fights in Scotland, and a teenager who poisons his cat—it seems incredible that Ishiguro's first published works would be a handful of short stories and two novels about wartime Japan. Even Ishiguro himself verges on citing some kind of mysterious force: "Then one night, during my third or fourth week in that little room, I found myself writing, with a new and urgent intensity, about Japan—about Nagasaki, the city of my birth, during the last days of the Second World War." Even the mature Ishiguro, in his 2017 Nobel Prize lecture, seems bewildered by this topical turn and return to Japan: "What was going on with me? What was all this peculiar energy?"[66]

In my assessment of this peculiar energy, the young Ishiguro's persistent revisiting of postwar Japan, which seems as compulsive as it was unexpected and even unwelcome, gets at the curious memory effects of a transwar period—a period when a world premised on the emperor's divinity was being remade in the image of the emperor's humanity.[67] The fate of the emperor bears out the broader trends and sentiments of transwar regime change, which entailed a wholesale reworking of the relation between individual memory and national history as well as between national amnesty and national amnesia.[68] In this section, we have seen how national forgetting was inculcated by an extraordinary national figure who attempts to transform himself into an ordinary human. In the following sections, we will meet an excruciatingly ordinary citizen, the titular character of *Artist*, who attempts to demonstrate that he is a renowned personage. At stake in my comparison of a literary character who is formalized as forgettable and a political personality who is absolved by selective forgetting is not so much what each figure has to say for himself—significantly, in both cases, it is difficult to ascertain if this figure *is* speaking for himself—but rather what, and how much, others have to say about him.

JAPAN: KNOW YOUR ENEMY (AGAIN)

U.S. cold war policy in essence renewed Japan's license to empire in Asia. It retained Japan's prewar domestic infrastructures, including the emperor as "the center of [its] new democracy" and the *zaibatsu* as the basis of its new economy.[69] Under the leadership of prime minister Yoshida Shigeru, Japan's pursuit of economic recovery became the "peaceful" alternative to military expansion. The topic of war-related reparations, meanwhile, was viewed "only as an economic burden for the recovery" and not "as an issue of moral or responsibility."[70] In the 1950s, such thinking became the basis for strengthening economic and geopolitical ties with the United States. In *The Inability to Mourn* (1967), Alexander and Margarete Mitscherlich posited a conflict between psychic recovery and economic recovery in postwar Germany. The equation of "democracy with little more than the postwar (capitalist) economic system," Parkinson writes, was seen as thwarting "the moral emotions befitting democracy, such as empathy, guilt, and ... mourning."[71] Whereas the Mitscherlichs saw economic development in Germany as a moral breach, in transwar Japan, national memory and the national economy functioned as related inflection points of postwar rehabilitation. The postponement of moral repentance and the embrace of capitalist vigor converged in the blank affect of the "human emperor," a soft and diminutive fellow awkwardly clad in his democratic business suit.

The business suit is an apt symbol for capturing the extent of U.S. influence on Japan's economic recovery and the threat that Japan's economic clout would come to pose. If during the Occupation Hirohito's business suit could be seen as signifying Japan's renewed vitality under U.S. stewardship, then by the 1970s and 1980s, the geopolitical terrain had shifted enough for Ezra Vogel to view the suited Japanese executive as a threat. In a 1989 reissuing of Ruth Benedict's *The Chrysanthemum and the Sword*, Vogel exhorted, "understanding the Japanese is perhaps just as critical now, when Japanese progress is made by troops of suited businessmen, as it was when troops of khaki-clad soldiers were advancing."[72] In 1966, Douglas Mendel used the term "pacifism" to describe Japan's remarkable "economic progress," which was "matched by an equally striking reversal of foreign and military policy."⁷³ By the 1970s, Japanese economic practices came to be discussed with the opposite term: "adversarial." Coined by Peter Drucker, "adversarial" includes an ethnocentric accusation. Japan's "adversarial" methods were seen as distinct from "competitive trade" in the Western industrial nations, for they sought "to create major *economic* damage."⁷⁴ Following a similar line of reasoning, Karel van Wolferen claims that one of the "central fictions" of postwar Western thought is that Japan belongs in the group of " 'capitalist, free-market' economies." Van Wolferen enjoins the West to solve the "riddle" of Japan: "Under such circumstances, a better understanding of the nature and uses of power in Japan is no luxury."⁷⁵

Western curiosity about Japanese workplace management dates at least to 1955. That year saw the nation return to prewar performance levels, and it was also then that U.S. businessman James Abegglen, funded by the Ford Foundation, returned to Japan to study its industrial practices. Abegglen's early stab at formulating a culturally specific model of the Japanese firm in 1958 was followed by a two-part series in the *Economist*, entitled "Consider Japan," published in September 1962. These accounts, among a number of others in the 1960s and 1970s, provided the lead-up to a flurry of Japan-related publications in the 1980s, beginning with Ezra Vogel's *Japan as Number One* (1979). As a counterpoint to this trend, James Fallows came out with *More Like Us: Making America Great Again* (1989), as well as a number of publications on how Japan and other Asian economic miracles might be contained rather than emulated. Efforts to explain Japan's extraordinary economic growth through its cultural distinctiveness also fertilized the popular imagination. Filmic and literary blockbusters such as Ridley Scott's *Blade Runner* (1982), William Gibson's *Neuromancer* (1984), Neal Stephenson's *Snow Crash* (1992), and Alexander Besher's *RIM* (1994) used Japan to imagine the dystopian possibilities of advanced capitalism. In a reprise of the anti-Chinese "yellow peril" discourse of the nineteenth century, California became ground zero for Asiatic invasion. Whether fictional or scholarly, wishful or hostile, such works were to help the Western industrial nations master the present economic situation by demystifying a new competitor.⁷⁶

This was the environment in which 24-year-old Kazuo Ishiguro embarked on a career in fiction. We might think of travel writer Pico Iyer's review essay as a representative "Japan Decade" reading of *The Remains of the Day*. Iyer opens with the following pronouncement: "of all the books tumbling off the foreign presses purporting to explain Japan to the West, the most revealing one so far is not, in fact, set in Japan, has nothing to do with Japan and, as it happens, is a novel about six unexceptional days in the cloistered life of an English butler in 1956." For Iyer, Ishiguro was "perfectly positioned to see... how the staff of an English country house, with its stiff-backed sense of 'self-training,' its precisely stratified hierarchy, its uniforms and rites and stress on self-negation, might almost belong to Sony or Toshiba."[77] Iyer's reading of *Remains* shows how deeply the geopolitical tensions of the time impacted Ishiguro's initial success and his readers' intuitive interpretations. An indignant Ishiguro recalls how a British television network "rang me up during rumors of a U.S.-Japanese trade war and asked me if I would go on a program to discuss things from the Japanese side."[78]

Perhaps it is because of such requests that Ishiguro would leave behind the bad politics of postwar Japan and Britain for more "universal" topics. Certainly, he is hardly the first writer to attempt a transition from the "ethnic" to the "universal," the particular to the unmarked. What distinguishes Ishiguro, the recipient of the 2017 Nobel Prize in literature, is that he has been wildly successful. The most surprising part of all this, though, is not the level of Ishiguro's success. It is that even as his novels have come to feature a diverse range of characters and settings, their defining tenor has remained remarkably consistent and recognizably Ishiguroan. In 1982, Malcolm Bradbury pegged the "Japaneseness" in *Pale View* to an "economy of emotion."[79] Seven years later, Ishiguro's move away from Japanese content reinforced a similar racial thesis: "His restrained personal style matches his literary tone. 'Quiet' has been perhaps the most common epithet applied by reviewers to *The Remains of the Day*."[80] However, Ishiguro's fourth novel, *The Unconsoled* (1995), set in an unidentified European city, prompted complaints about the absence of "discernible cultural, social or historical determinants." *When We Were Orphans* (2000), a novel that unfolds in wartime Shanghai, was deemed "so lacking in local colour as to be entirely inappropriate to the task in hand."[81] While Ishiguro has always preferred to ironize rather than to represent localizable "determinants" and "colour," it is true that his later novels exude a familiar quietness shorn of ready sociocultural explanations. Rebecca Walkowitz's astute readings of early Ishiguro (in her first book) and late Ishiguro (in her second) show how "quiet" came to be disarticulated from Ishiguro's racial particularity and adduced to explain his globality. As a Japanese British writer who came of age during the 1980s, "Ishiguro un[did] national allegory by allegorizing the invention of national identities." In ensuing years, as a cosmopolitan author devoid of a hyphenated identity, Ishiguro shifted his emphasis from critiquing origins as the final word on cultural authenticity to critiquing originality or uniqueness "as the defining quality of art, culture, and human life."[82] In particular, Ishiguro came to reject unique words—language that is too context-specific. Avoiding "cultural reference points" that "don't transfer geographically," he says, is what allows "words to survive translation."[83] This desire for maximal legibility in the global market transforms *quietness* from a racial trait signifying the Japanese native informant's exquisite self-control into a professional asset signifying a cosmopolitan novelist's translational efficiency.

Despite what appears to be an evolutionary shift from the culturally particular to the globally universal, my belief is that Ishiguro's quietness charges us to view his early and late works as giving expression to a shared historical ethos, a distinctive period style. This is to say that Masuji Ono, the Japanese wartime artist that *Artist* depicts as an antecedent to the "Japan Decade" employee, bears a historical continuity with the post-Fordist laborers that critics have located in novels such as *The Remains of the Day*, *The Unconsoled*, and *Never Let Me Go*.[84] A quiet style, in playing up the ambiguity between a racial trait (such as decorousness) and a professional trait (such as work ethic), clues us into the overlapping tonal registers of "Japan" and "global" at a time when Japanese management practices symbolized a change from Fordist specialization to post-Fordist flexibility. Readers of Ishiguro have readily attributed quietness (and, relatedly, apathy or complicity) to specific characters, maybe even to all characters. What I'm suggesting, however, is that "quiet" is less a trait than a tone. This tone arises from a narrative situation wherein words, phrases, and entire sentences travel among indistinguishable characters but are not "voiced" in any kind of self-willed way. In this regard, all of Ishiguro's characters can be understood as "stock characters," whose presence in the text is determined by "their connection with a stock of words that are transcribed and imprinted over and over again." Deidre Lynch is referring here to the literary servant in eighteenth-century literature—a minor character that embodies the "typicality of characterlessness."[85] I would posit that the twentieth-century equivalent of such a characterless character is the racial type. In *Artist*, this tension between stock characters and stock phrases gets worked out through a narrator who summons conversations from his past to substantiate his own distinctiveness. Yet the more that Ono talks about others talking about himself, the more that he—and the very notion of character—disintegrates into a circuit of rumors. Whereas Walkowitz might describe this narrative tendency as a translational style that indexes global circulation, I interpret it as a transferrable rumor that indexes racial tone.

In registering the intensity with which rumors circulate, the quiet tone of Ishiguro's novels simultaneously conveys the importance and the impenetrability of Asian identity in a post–cold war period when Japanese economic advancement invited analogies to an earlier era of Japanese military expansion. During this post–cold war period, U.S. efforts to soften Japan's image as an imperial aggressor gave way to an outpouring of demands for apologies from the Japanese government. Most of these redress movements have "involved the U.S. courts, American legislatures, and community politics."[86] The kinds of political justice and historical recovery pursued under such auspices warrant our suspicion and caution. One would be hard pressed to say that Ishiguro reproduces a victor's history or "writes back" with a redemptive counterhistory. But his eccentric approach to characterization shows that race cannot be easily assigned a trait—such as quietness or decorum—any more than historical memory can be reduced to guilt or innocence.

MASUJI ONO'S CRIME

Redolent with optimistic rhetoric about the future, *Artist* is superficially about progress. This, though, is not a *bildungsroman*. Our narrator Masuji Ono sways easily with the political winds of the time. Over the course of the novel, he swings from nostalgia for imperial Japan in 1948 to admiration for imperial America in 1950. At the novel's end, Ono arrives at a momentous realization. But, as will be familiar to Ishiguro's readers, the irony is that our peripatetic protagonist's physical and spiritual journey has actually been one of maximal motion and minimal mobility. Accordingly, from a formal standpoint, Ono, like many of Ishiguro's characters, does not develop; he is—pardon my glibness—all talk.

Rumors are a prominent theme in *Artist*, for they underpin Ono's faith in his own "prestige" and "high regard" (9, 25). Ono's memories are oriented around not events but conversations. As he leads the reader through pleasure districts, local parks, factory yards, and suburban villas, his memories of who said what float to the surface, assuming homologous forms with shifting content. These redundant dialogic encounters feature characters who utter nearly identical lines. For example, Ono attributes the phrase "height of impertinence" to Shintaro and "height of bad manners" to Mrs. Kawakami (20, 22). His daughters, Setsuko and Noriko, are both given to sounding deferential objections by noting how this or that is "very kind of Father." When considering the origin of the phrase "the greatest cowardice of all," Ono confuses Miyake, his prospective son-in-law, with Suichi, his current son-in-law, even as he asserts his sensitivity to the particularities of their character (52). As these examples demonstrate, not only is *Artist* crowded with talkers, but these talkers are basically interchangeable and literally forgettable.

Ono's most frequently recurring memory concerns the burning or confiscation of paintings. Convinced of art's power to bestow individual distinction, Ono in each vignette depicts the painter as a non-conforming hero whose tragic flaw is the audacity to defy society. The earliest references to confiscation are when Ono notes that his own paintings have been "tidied away" after the war (32, 79). These euphemistic references to Ono's disgraced status provide a textbook case of unreliable narration, whereby implied author and implied reader have occasion to share a wink over the narrator's head.[87] The reputation of the bygone propaganda artist, we are guided to think, has not fared well in the changeover from Japanese fascism to American democracy. Ono himself, however, seems unaware of this new political climate or his place in it. Evidence of Ono's political culpability and narrative unreliability gradually accumulates over the course of the novel. His starkest memories regarding confiscation are when his reprehensibility as a wartime collaborator seems the most transparent. These memories are also the source of the novel's most obviously recurring lines:

Ono recalls a conversation with his father, who burns an "untidy pile" of his paintings: "Masuji, are you sure all your work is here? Aren't there *one or two paintings you haven't brought me?* ... And *no doubt*, Masuji, the missing paintings are *the very ones you're most proud of*." (43, emphasis mine)

THE TONE OF RUMORS

Ono later recalls his teacher Mori-san destroying his paintings: "Incidentally, Ono . . . I was told there were *one or two other paintings* you've completed recently that were not with those I have now. . . . And *no doubt* these are *the very paintings you are most fond of.*" (178, emphasis mine)

Ono is in the middle of recalling his conversation with Mori-san, which appears in the second block quotation, when he suddenly alerts us that this memory has merged with another. This new recollection involves Ono's prize student Kuroda: "Of course, [Mori-san] may well not have used that precise phrase, 'exploring curious avenues.' For . . . it may well be that I am remembering my own words to Kuroda" (177).

The art-burning memory's recurrence builds toward an original shame: Ono's service to the Committee of Unpatriotic Activities led to the destruction of Kuroda's paintings and to this student's brutal imprisonment. The progression of increasingly clearer recollections thus appears to affirm our preliminary indictment of Ono when he had first intimated that his paintings had been "tidied away." But a few pages later, Ono's daughter Setsuko makes a surprising revelation that forces us to reassess the nature of Ono's guilt:

Taro-san was somewhat concerned Father should be so interested in [the wartime composer] Mr Naguchi's death. Indeed, it would seem Father was drawing a comparison between Mr Naguchi's career and his own. . . . Mr Naguchi's songs came to have enormous prevalence at every level of the war effort. There would thus appear to have been some substance to his wish that he should share responsibility along with the politicians and generals. But Father is wrong to even begin thinking in such terms about himself. Father was, after all, a painter. (192)

At this point in the novel, the reader who had initially wished for a more conscious exhibition of remorse from Ono may be backpedaling, for Ono's involvement in the war seems to have been not so significant after all. Furthermore, this revelation follows a scene in which Ono had eagerly and theatrically owned up to his wartime responsibility. This self-aggrandizing "declaration" is framed as "coming to terms with the mistakes one has made in the course of one's life." Yet acknowledging the "negative influence" of his career, as it happens, brings Ono neither contrition nor humility but "a satisfaction and dignity" (123–24). This turn of events calls for us to rethink the significance of Ono's recurring memory. At stake in this recurrence is not that Ono's character becomes more comprehensible as we learn more about his wartime activities but that the repetitious speech of the multiple characters he invokes makes these characters essentially indistinguishable from himself: he sounds like his father who sounds like Mori-san. Ono's true crime, it turns out, is not that he has wielded his influence as a steadfastly patriotic artist, but that he, like many of Ishiguro's narrators, has thought himself to be more distinguished—more distinct—than he actually is.

How does this situation compare to that of Hirohito? If there is a difference between the prewar and postwar emperor, it is not a matter of divine absence versus human presence but a matter of how different forms of absence provide historically specific kinds of leverage. We might interpret the uncertain nature of Ono's crime—whether he was responsible or negligible, distinguished contributor or forgettable nobody—as a commentary on the emperor's deflationary tactics, which served to render him indistinct from the Japanese people at large. In Ishiguro's novel, assertions of distinction bear a rough correlation with the scope of wartime complicity. This correlation is most apparent in conversations that feature the phrase "the likes of." Ostensibly, such a phrase distinguishes the individual in question. In *Artist*, however, "the likes of" is used to describe Kuroda, Kenji, Shintaro, Mrs. Kawakami, Mrs. Saito, Sasaki, Matsuda, and Ono himself. In isolated usage, the term implies that the character to which it refers is a distinct, recognizable type. Assessed collectively, it homogenizes a flock of characters who are distinguished on the exact same terms. Aside from Ono himself, the phrase is a favorite of Matsuda, the staunch militarist we met earlier. In most cases, Ono and Matsuda employ the phrase to champion the repute of wartime nationalists. To quote Matsuda: "Before long, a few more years, and the likes of us will be able to hold our heads high about what we tried to do" (94). Here, "the likes of" underlines the exceptionality of those at the forefront of Japan's imperial charge. At the end of *Artist*, this phrase shifts from signaling prestige to deflecting guilt. Again, Matsuda:

Army officers, politicians, businessmen.... They've all been blamed for what happened to this country. But as for *the likes of us*, Ono, our contribution was always marginal. No one cares now what *the likes of you and me* once did. *They look at us and see* only two old men with their sticks.... We're the only ones who care now. *The likes of you and me*, Ono, when *we look back over our lives and see* they were flawed, we're the only ones who care now. (201, emphasis mine)

Matsuda delivers the same message as Ono's daughter: Ono, the painter, played a "marginal" role in Japan's imperial war, and he need not atone for his "contribution." This passage, though, shows how modulating the degree of wartime complicity is concomitant with modulating the distinctiveness of character. In contrast to earlier moments when "the likes of" worked to elevate the Japanese nationalists, here the phrase performs a generalizing function by restricting responsibility for the war to a small clique and, consequently, absolving Matsuda, Ono, and the nation as a whole of their wartime involvement. This move is analogous to Hirohito's efforts to instantiate his own likeness to everyday Japanese citizens for the purpose of legitimating their shared innocence. Similar to how Matsuda proclaims that the nation sees the former militarists as "only two old men with their sticks," the Japanese people came to see the accused war criminal Hirohito as only a "human emperor." Reading these cases together makes it possible to detect the danger of relying on "the likes of" to designate the innocence of the general and the guilt of the exceptional. Moreover, "the likes of" functions like a hinge phrase that enables a fallacious mirroring: the smooth slide from "they look at us and see" to "we look back over our lives and see" demonstrates the ease with which a false likeness can be established, not only between self and other, emperor and subject, but also between looking and seeing, perception and conception, empirical evidence and historical interpretation.

From the American perspective of the 1940s and 1950s, Hirohito had to be innocent—inept, hapless, merely human—in order to secure Japan as an anticommunist friend. The particularities of this political environment steer Matsuda and Ono to view "the likes of us" as "old men with their sticks." They are no more responsible than any other minor character, including the modestly attired and stoop shouldered emperor. However, from the American perspective of the 1980s, Ono and Matsuda are imperial apologists. Careful readers might note the resemblance between the "old men with sticks" in the passage above and Ono's depiction of samurais with sticks in his confiscated paintings (168). Considered from this post–cold war standpoint, *Artist* contributes to the belated explosion of demands for Japan's atonement of its war crimes. The historical context for judging Ono and Matsuda, then, is both cold war Japan, the U.S. ally that anchored free Asia, and trade war Japan, the U.S. competitor that deployed unscrupulous economic practices.[88] In the former context, the reader finds Ono innocent; in the latter, Ono is guilty. To my mind, the extraordinary achievement of Ishiguro's novel is that it allows us to view these two historical moments together and to come up against their seemingly conflicting moral frameworks for postwar adjudication. The question of Ono's distinctiveness, though, concerns not only his level of complicity in Japan's imperial war but also his efficacy as an informant on Japan's economic miracle. What might it mean to treat Ono not merely as an anachronistic patriot but also as one of the flexible, professional, affective laborers for which Ishiguro has become so well known?

CHARACTERS WHO WORK, WORKERS WHO TALK

Scholarship on Ishiguro shows that his reputation as a global writer may have less to do with his predilection for switching up the geographic locales of his novels than with his demonstrated interest in the changing routines of work. Global Ishiguro, it seems, is a post-Fordist writer. Critical discussions on Ishiguro's post-Fordism invariably focus on Ishiguro's non-Japanese texts. Ryan Trimm, for example, views *The Remains of the Day* as a commentary on "a professionalism associated with increasing globalization." Bruce Robbins frames Ishiguro's depiction of post-Fordist "harriedness" as signaling a "blockage of caring," a "professional affectivity" that has no place for love or patriotism. In Robbins's view, even the "carers" of *Never Let Me Go* do not "care" in ethically responsible ways and are stricken by "an excessive devotion to one's work." Lisa Fluet draws on "Ishiguro's novels as a whole" to explore "the twentieth-century hegemony of knowledge-work." A footnoted addendum, however, notifies us that she has limited her study to "the later novels and their focus on the ramifications of displaced professionals emerging in the twentieth-century British context. The role of the nation, and of empire, as a supporter of the services that artists and intellectuals provide, is quite different in the Japanese context."[89]

No doubt context matters, and patriotism indeed plays a more obvious role in Ishiguro's "Japan Decade" novels. But I am reluctant to view globalization as separate from Japanese postwar reconstruction, knowledge work as separate from ethnic services, and racialized detachment (Oriental reticence) as separate from professionalized detachment (expertise). It is worth pointing out the extent to which the characteristics of post-Fordism that these critics invoke were attributed to Japan in the long 1980s. If "every period of organizational transformation has its archetypical expression," and if "Ford Motor Company" was the archetypal expression "of standardized production and mass consumption,"[90] then it is no accident that canonical reflections on the changing terms of empire have used the term "Toyotism" to denominate "the inversion of the Fordist structure" and the "fulcrum for rejecting Fordism."[91] As Stephen Wood puts it, "characterizations of Japan and of the new post-Fordist world are becoming increasingly one and the same." Martin Kenney and Richard Florida, writing in 1989, go a step further in framing the Fordism/post-Fordism split as a U.S./Japan rivalry: "In Japan, work teams, job rotation, learning-by-doing, and flexibility have been used to replace the functional specialization, task fragmentation and rigid assembly-line production of U.S. Fordism."[92] There has certainly been a good deal of back-and-forth regarding whether "Toyotism" is in fact distinct from Fordism, whether "just-in-time" actually originated as an American mass production method, whether management theory travels from the west outwards or from the east outwards, whether firms have really displaced factories, and so forth. But even the attempt to designate modes of production as an "American system" or a "Japanese system" clarifies the major economic players during this period.[93] And the ambiguity about origins and distinctions speaks to the broader global impact of changing employment practices while also reminding us of the mutual entanglement of American and Japanese imperial interests throughout the second half of the twentieth century.

How has the overlap between Japanese miracle discourse and post-Fordist discourse affected the meaning, the value, the content, and the *tone* of racial self-representation? Sianne Ngai has posed a related question that pertains to character representation more generally: "Under a late capitalist mode of production privileging ever more elastic relations to work and personality, is there something increasingly funny about character as an aesthetic form?" Ngai's examples are the eponymous protagonists of *I Love Lucy* and *The Cable Guy*, who possess a prodigious capacity to take on a startling variety of odd jobs. These examples show that for the service worker willing to perform any role, "character" is predicated on a principle of perpetual extension, an assumption that nothing is ever "out of character."[94] Viet Thanh Nguyen has called the racial version of this flexible laborer "the all-purpose literary fixer."[95] Nguyen's term names a middle ground between, on the one hand, the racially overdetermined native informant whose one-track purpose is to supply racially useful information and, on the other, the universalist literary character whose role in a text elides the instrumentalist function of serving a purpose or providing a fix. This middle ground is where we find Ishiguro's "quiet" characters. These characters challenge the reductive functionality of the stereotype, yet they are not without a racial purpose. Their usefulness as a racial guide lies not so much in the information they give (they are, after all, flagrantly unreliable) but in the inscrutable quietness of their overall effect. Like the affective laborer's smile that personalizes the service, quietness sells the "Japan Decade" novel by racializing it.

In their landmark study of a new imperial order, Michael Hardt and Antonio Negri have claimed that affect and information constitute the two "faces" of immaterial labor. The affective "face" centralizes "human contact and interaction;" "its products are ... a feeling of ease, well-being, satisfaction, excitement, or passion." The informational "face" follows the model of the computer: "Today we increasingly think like computers, while communication technologies and their model of interaction are becoming more and more central to laboring activities."[96] Laborers who gratify by delivering the racial goods show that these two "faces," affect and information, cannot be easily isolated. Alan Liu's conceptualization of *cool* as "the *cultural* face ... of knowledge work" exemplifies a racialized case of informational and affective convergence. Cool, Liu writes, marks the point "where ethnicity and the new corporatism are indistinguishable." Even more intriguing, cool seems to most readily locate ethnicity in specifically *Oriental* corporations—what Liu calls "tribes." In his assessment, it is the "*keiretsu, chaebol*, and other Japanese or Korean terms for business networks and conglomerates" that best illustrate the nebulous "line between 'tribe' and 'corporation,'" "ethnic diaspora and enterprise networking."[97] Liu's cool knowledge worker is a paradoxical "personality" that conflates ethnic selfhood with impersonal information: "The historyless specter now haunting the United States and much of the world besides is one that may seem to have the lumpen-ethnic traits of Japanese, Chinese, Koreans, Indians, and so on, but in reality washes out both ethnicity and class to focus on technological/technical structures and processes." Liu's vision of corporate selfhood is "Oriental" to the extent that it is evacuated of distinguishing features: "Global competition thus always resolves into the challenge to workers to be as minimalist in identity—that is, to be as self-sacrificing, to work as hard, to save as much—as zero-people, or so they seem, in the Far East or elsewhere." If cool initially appears to be the affect of information in Liu's study, then it eventually comes to signal the more specific (yet peculiarly generic) affect of the Oriental-as-information. Neither entirely warm-blooded nor entirely bloodless, cool casts the Oriental as the paradigmatic knowledge worker, someone whose "truest face" is the "interface."[98]

Although the nineteenth-century term *coolie* has been retired by more politic regimes of racial governance, it's clear that the referential field of "Asian" remains overdetermined by economic and technological tropes. Indeed, the *coolie*'s mechanical indifference to pain seems anticipatory of (though not etymologically) the *cool* knowledge worker's imperturbable work ethic.[99] This tension between the racially derogatory coolie and the racially non-specific cool is palpable in all of Ishiguro's novels. Put another way, what links the likes of Masuji Ono to the likes of Kathy H. is their status as cool knowledge workers—they provide a racial "fix," not by narrating the experience of racial difference, but by being impersonal, flexible, and detached. Here, though, is where I want to stop reading for race as an attribute of character. In Ishiguro's novels, the zero-self is less about a self-sacrificing work ethic/working ethnic. Rather, the apparent absence of distinct personalities has to do with the proliferation of racial information by way of rumors—a mode of transmission that renders "identity" ubiquitous but dislocated. We ought to first note that even though Ishiguro's characters heroically perform an array of tasks, they are largely *in*flexible, plagued by an overweening inability to adapt quickly enough to the shifting terms of work. Stevens in *Remains* struggles and fails to add bantering to his repertoire of skills. Kathy H., the carer clone in *Never Let Me Go*, is unable to summon the appropriate empathy when Tommy prepares for his fourth donation. In the case of *Artist*, Ono pursues a string of artistic enterprises over the course of his career: a stint at a "firm" churning out "paintings at very short notice" for foreign consumption (66); tutelage under a master who integrates "European influences" into "the Utamaro tradition" (140–41); and, finally, his professional apex as a wartime propaganda painter. Each of these endeavors ends up exposing the lag between the newest professional scene and Ono's late arrival. Professional inefficiency at the level of plot has a formal correlate in the failure of characters to properly *be* characters. Across Ishiguro's novels, we find characters whose pervasive inability to be maximally flexible takes the specific form of expending incredible energy toward being maximally redundant. Instead of having a single character take on multiple roles or multiple characters take on different roles, these novels mobilize a revolving crew of characters who perform the same roles in the specific sense that they tell the same stories, pass on the same rumors, and utter the same lines. To put this narrative calculus more concisely, Ishiguro's redundant characters labor toward producing distinctiveness, only to end up generating a surplus of frenetic, repetitive chatter. The Oriental-as-information—a post-Fordist revision of the enemy-as-rumor—renders race not the content but the tone of transmission, something that emerges through the pulsing energy of rapid, meaningless, and superabundant interfacing.

Ishiguro's character-workers show that the task of representing Asianness has been distributed across multiple platforms of racial intelligence—the allegory of a racial type, the first-hand account of a racial tour guide, and the anonymous talk of indistinct characters. It is this third category, I believe, that assumes primacy. For, despite the fact that Ishiguro's novels proceed entirely in a first-person voice, their overwhelming effect is to confuse the boundaries between the psychological truth of character-narration and the suppositional chatter of seemingly parasitic talk. This conflict between the singularity of narration and the superfluity of talk is structurally similar to Eve Kosofsky Sedgwick's contrast between the "strangely specific" speech acts of gay affirmation (associated with the declarative mode of "coming out") and the heterogeneous gossip bubbling under the cover of "closetedness." Sedgwick takes gossip—"immemorially associated in European thought with servants, with effeminate and gay men, with all women"—as a tool for "making, testing, and using unrationalized and provisional hypotheses about what *kinds of people* there are to be found in one's world."[100] What Sedgwick teaches us is that the provisional nature of gossip can chip away at affirmative assertions of identity. What Ishiguro's novels show, though, is that this vitiation is especially potent when gossip concerns not the panoply of possible social identities but the monolithic figure of "identity" itself. So whereas Sedgwick makes the case that gossip enables a "nonce taxonomy" of pre-legitimated identities and therefore a finer grain of sociality, in Ishiguro's novels, "tribes" or "teams" of characters empty out identity by glorifying it.[101] These self-absorbed stock characters declare their "stock" ad nauseum, to the point where the very idea of "character" comes to be associated not with distinguishing or differentiated traits but with a diffuse and incessant noise .

Let me return to *Artist* to provide a few examples. As we saw earlier, conversations that cycle redundantly among characters have the effect of dissolving the distinctions between one character and another: Ono becomes his father who becomes Mori-san who becomes Kuroda. Using the same "rumor" regarding art-burning, I want to shift our focus now from a rumor's participants to its circulation density and, correspondingly, its tonal register. This means shifting as well from "identity" as a property of characters to "identity" as a recurring topic of conversation.

"Masuji, are you sure all your work is here? Aren't there *one or two paintings* you haven't brought me? . . . And *no doubt*, Masuji, the missing paintings are *the very ones you're most proud of.*" (43, emphasis mine)

"Incidentally, Ono . . . I was told there were *one or two other paintings* you've completed recently that were not with those I have now. . . . And *no doubt* these are *the very paintings you are most fond of.*" (178, emphasis mine)

Notice here the repeated attempt to squirrel away "one or two" paintings from an "untidy pile." This ambiguity that always accompanies distinction permeates the entire fabric of Ono's narration: "One or two important respects," "one or two such moments," "one or two things to attend to," "one or two small points," and "one or two things in common with people like Mr Naguchi." And, as if testing the seams of numerical containment, the phrase "one or two" occasionally branches out into "two or three" and, at times, "three or four:" "two or three weeks later," "two or three splendid carp," "two or three songs," "three or four of the crayons," "three or four of my paintings," and so on. Such phrases are uttered with a distinguishing intent yet betray a fugitive inclination towards indistinction. Their ubiquity in *Artist*, as well as in Ishiguro's other novels, renders negligible the difference between "one or two" while at the same time insisting on the social value of distinctiveness. This discursive patchwork of casual differentiation also shows how the prevalence of distinction as a topic of discussion bears an inverse relationship to the discernibility of distinct discussants. A distinct identity is the most important to our narrator Ono and the *most frequently* discussed by him, yet this frequent discussion paradoxically means that Ono possesses the *least distinct* identity. In the course of reproducing a compendium of seemingly distinct conversations throughout his tour, Ono is constantly arriving at and returning to the one or two occasions when he had putatively "risen above" someone, something, somewhere:

"wished to rise above such a life" (47)
"to rise above the sway of things" (73)
"rise above the undesirable and decadent influences" (73)
"must all endeavor to rise above the sway of things" (73)
"aspires to rise above the mediocre" (134)
"deepest sense of triumph and satisfaction began to rise within me" (204)
"to risk everything to rise above the mediocre" (204)

In some of these instances, Ono is describing himself as someone who is distinctively capable. In others, he is recalling someone else describing him as distinctively capable. The net effect, however, is to convey a disproportionate worry about distinctiveness rather than to confer distinctiveness on Ono as such. Notably, this presents a very different scenario than Fredric Jameson's reading of Benito Pérez Galdós's novels. Jameson deems Galdós's characters "talkers par excellence," in that their speech "transforms every moment into an event." These characters demonstrate the "heightened value attached to the personal intonation as such, to the unique sound which is henceforth, in the realm of affect, the sound of the individual body."[102] In Ishiguro's novels, every character is likewise a talker. But these characters' attempts to pass on what someone else has said, over and over again, have an utterly distortive effect. The more they talk, the more the carefully crafted and subtly stilted language so specific to Ishiguro's characters—as a Japanese artist, a British butler, a senior citizen, or a carer clone—becomes wiped of its distinguishing traces. Every qualifying remark or conditional statement—an "indeed," a "no doubt," an "after all"—ends up belonging to no one in particular. Ishiguro's redundant characters employ the same turns of phrase (usually as a gesture of false modesty) and spout the same sound bites (usually about influence, dignity, pride, and distinction). It is this combination of importance and indeterminacy—this sense that characters who, in their ostentatious attempts to "rise above," are perpetually disintegrating into an anonymous circuit of noise—that gives Ishiguro's novels a racial tinge. Rumor has it that an Asian character is here—in the butler, in the clone, in the air, in the very ambiguity between one character and two.[103]

TALK OF DEEP TRIUMPH

The one, two, many disordered conversations that structure Ono's tour of postwar Japan, in the end, reveal very little about his wartime culpability or his ethnic identity. In contrast to more culturally and historically authoritative works, which seem to yield concrete facts and truths, the rumors that circulate in *Artist* operate more impressionistically by introducing a vague sense of import. In this regard, Ono is not a racial representative whose first-person story offers an accurate and authentic self-portrait; instead, Ono is simply the most concentrated point of overlap between one character and two, a dialogic node through which the novel amasses a tonal density. Ono in fact takes pride in characterizing himself as a privileged site of interfacing: "I could be having a conversation with someone, the rest of them talking amongst themselves, and as soon as an interesting question had been asked of me, they would all break off their own conversations, and I would have a circle of faces awaiting my reply" (73). Although Ono makes the familiar move of flaunting his prestige here, he also provides a fitting description of *Artist*'s novelistic structure: his role as a narrator is not to "speak" his own story but to function as a kind of information hub or call center through which all conversations must be routed.

Thus far, I have largely limited my analysis to *Artist*. I want to conclude by considering the ways in which all of Ishiguro's novels are tonally preoccupied with identity. At the level of description, Ishiguro meticulously avoids thick characterizations. He does not locate race in either phenotype or interiority, in racism as an objectifying mechanism or racial consciousness as an empowering mode of subject formation. His only attribution of "color" to characters draws on the play of light and shadow: "The pale light from outside fell on one side of her face, but her hands and sleeves were caught in the glow from the lantern" (*Pale View*, 175). Or: "I noticed all the more the effect of the pale light coming into the room and the way it lit up the edges of my father's craggy, lined, still awesome features" (*Remains*, 64). Even in *The Buried Giant* (2015), published three decades after *Pale View*, we can still find the same "feeble light" through which "they could even make out each other's outlines."[104] With this "pale view" approach to rendering color, Ishiguro makes not just race but also character a perceptual illusion. If there is a connection among Ishiguro's novels, it is this indefatigable rumor of an "identity" that no character actually possesses. Witness, for instance, how the painter Ono, the butler Stevens, the detective Banks, and the pianist Stephan all share a "deep . . . triumph" of distinction in character as well as a surface level indistinction in speech:

> But then as I continued to stand there, . . . *a deep feeling of triumph started to well up within me.* . . . I had, after all, just come through an extremely trying evening, throughout which I had managed to preserve a "dignity in keeping with my position." (*Remains*, 227, emphasis mine)

> And it was as I sat there, looking down at the villa, . . . *that deep sense of triumph and satisfaction began to rise within me.* . . . It was a profound sense of happiness deriving from the conviction that . . . one has achieved something of real value and distinction. (*Artist*, 204, emphasis mine)

> when this case has become a *triumphant* memory—she will be truly glad *I rose to the challenge* of my responsibilities. (*Orphans*, 149, emphasis mine)

> The hotel manager . . . turning to his son had given another wink, this time with *an air of triumph*. At that moment the young man had felt something *very powerful rising in his breast*. (*The Unconsoled*, 67, emphasis mine)

This comparison shows how the same kind of talk about the same kind of character produces the same general tone in Ishiguro's works. The hum of repeating words and phrases traveling up and down Ishiguro's oeuvre is allegorized in *Remains* as "all sorts of rumours buzzing through the servants' halls up and down the country" (30). In this novel, the butler Stevens's peripheral relation to the central political conversations of the day offers an analogue for our own status as a reader listening in on the rumors buzzing through Ishiguro's novels. Like Stevens in Darlington Hall, we shuffle "in and out of the various rooms." And as we listen in on voices "deep in discussion," we cannot "avoid gaining a certain impression of the general mood" (80). Our eavesdropping, like his, is structured by passing moments of clarity that yield a decontextualized yet presumably significant phrase: "in contrast to their quiet mood at dinner, [the gentlemen] had begun to exchange words with some urgency.... I did not stop to listen, but I could not avoid hearing his lordship shouting: 'But that's not your business, my boy! That's not your business!'" (217). As with Darlington Hall's rumor mill, an atmospheric buzz allows us to take the temperature of a particular "room" (that is, a particular novel), even if this buzz cannot be disaggregated into the specific statements of distinct speakers. Similar scenes of casual eavesdropping and distracted listening are rife in Ishiguro's works. At Hailsham, where "everyone [was] always listening in," a number of Kathy H.'s conversations take place under the eaves (150). In *Pale View*, we frequently find Etsuko putting a surreptitious ear to the door before entering a room. In *When We Were Orphans*, British detective Christopher Banks is constantly recalling conversations that he overhears and mixes up. Take, for example, an exchange between his parents, in which Banks occasionally manages to catch "whole phrases": "I heard her repeat: 'A disgrace!' a number of times, and she referred often to what she called 'the sinful trade.'" And, as the conversation proceeds: "'It's not so simple. It's not nearly so simple" and "'It's too bad.... It's too bad, it's just too bad!'" (70). The "whole phrases" that Banks is able to decipher are also repeating phrases. They are laughably wooden and rather parrot-like. Banks uses such conversations to formulate hypotheses about his parents' lives, but what he actually hears is a crescendo of the same banal line, persisting as an urgent yet eerily disembodied drone.

By employing rumors as a representational technique and characterological principle, Ishiguro's novels disable our reliance on anthropomorphic coherence as the baseline for locating the presence of race. In this respect, all of Ishiguro's works invite us to read for an aestheticized racial tone. Or, we could as well say, reading race tonally requires us to account for all of

Ishiguro's novels, for the rumor of identity can hardly be limited to the confines of one text. *Artist* is especially useful for my study, however, because it stages the circulation of rumors about an inflated national identity in relation to cold war structures of forgetting. At this novel's end, we find Ono sitting on a park bench where the city's pleasure district used to be: "But to see how our city has been rebuilt, how things have recovered so rapidly over these years, fills me with genuine gladness. Our nation, it seems, whatever mistakes it may have made in the past, has now another chance to make a better go of things. One can only wish these young people well" (206). Although all of Ishiguro's characters are forgetful, and although this quality always contributes to the novelistic dissemination of hearsay, *Artist* allows us to perceive the specifically imperial underpinnings of mundane forgetfulness and everyday conjecture. Ono's casually forgetful attitude toward the past is bound up with a budding optimism about Japan's future generation.[105] This attitude is similar to what we will find in the memoirs of Induk Pahk, the focus of the next chapter. For free Asians whose nations were "liberated" by the U.S. occupying forces, forgetfulness is what enables a forward-looking orientation, a peering ahead toward an American future. The fact that forgetfulness also makes Ono appear so ordinary—so fallible and so human—does not universalize this trait. Rather, *Artist*'s evocation of forgetting through the dispersal of mundane conversations and repetitive rumors dramatizes the geopolitical work of affective norming. Forgetting appears ordinary not because it is human but because it is an effect of a purposefully engineered order of global governance.

In both my case studies, rumors disclose an uncertainty about identity, as everyday people try to work out and catch up to a historically unprecedented situation. In the case of Hirohito's tours, a blank affect and an ambiguous tone enhance his appeal as a subject of curiosity and speculation. By appearing as an uncoordinated puppet, an awkward salesman, a poorly dressed doll, and a bespectacled putty—by appearing as a passive vessel through which rumors could pass—Hirohito gives credence to U.S. efforts to deflect accusations of wartime responsibility. Specially suited to be a suit, this friendly free Asian seems incapable of war crimes to the extent that he seems incapable of individual agency at all. In Ishiguro's novels, characters are even more like inert vessels and rumors even more like an indomitable force. If the American cold war required the service of racially representative free Asians, a service that Hirohito provided through his hollowness, then Ishiguro's *Artist* stages a "Japan Decade" version of self-negation through what Alan Liu characterizes as impersonal knowledge work. In my reading, Ishiguro's novels do not offer racial information through what particular characters say or do. It is not reticence, work ethic, guilt, or narrative unreliability that produces a sense of Asian-ness but rather the intensity of rumors that circulate about distinction and likeness, personality and typology. In neutralizing the presence of characters, the tone of Ishiguro's novels prevents us from looking for racial meaning in an exotic name, a marked trait, a bloodline, an official document, or any kind of verifiable source. At the same time, this disquietingly quiet tone also shows how the unavailability of a legible identity and a coherent politics, particularly at times of historical transition and geopolitical turmoil, can contribute to the racialization of Asians as unknowable.

At both of the historical junctures that I've examined, rumor circulation evidences the desire for and the impossibility of stabilizing a distinct or typical racial subject. Whether through a thicket of anonymous paperwork or a jumble of indistinct character dialogue, the quantity of rumors, which also translates into the liveliness of rumors, presents a telling contrast to the unidentifiable human vessels that facilitate their transmission. Neither literary novel nor governmental archive offers a usable record of who was where and who said what. Both, however, bear out a tangible suspicion and an unresolvable tension about the meanings and manifestations of race at a moment when tomorrow's wars loom and yesterday's wars linger.

Chapter Three

THE TONE OF THE TIMES

Historical Temperament in the Works of Induk Pahk and Theresa Hak Kyung Cha

> she tells me it's always the woman operator
> she tells me it is sixteen hours
> sixteen hours from here
>
> —THERESA HAK KYUNG CHA, *TEMPS MORTS* (1980)

It has become something of a ritual for Western-educated South Korean scholars of a certain generation to reflect on their homeland after years abroad.[1] For example, Choong Soon Kim left to study anthropology in the United States in 1965. In *The Culture of Korean Industry*, Kim recalls his first return visit in 1981: "Experiencing so suddenly the results of economic development and industrialization, I felt a case of 'future shock.' The entire country seemed to vibrate with economic progress."[2] Sociologist John Lie was born in Korea but grew up in Japan. He describes "Seoul in the early 1960s" as "my childhood conception of backwardness." Two decades later, Lie returned from the United States to teach at Yonsei University in the midst of Seoul's preparations for the 1988 Olympics: "In Apkujong-dong, I encountered upper-middle-class housewives sporting *haute couture* and affluent youths leading lives of invidious distinction and dissolution. Clean and well-lit coffee shops had replaced the dark and dingy cafes."[3] For U.S.-trained anthropologist Seung-kyung Kim, the story of industrialization takes place in the Masan Free Export Zone among female factory workers, who were at the forefront of labor organizing in the 1980s. Although Kim notes the divergence between her own life path and that of the women in her research, she emphasizes how "the political climate of the universities" provides a point of continuity between anthropologist and subject, diasporan and citizen.[4]

The return narrative that most intrigues me comes from economist Ha-Joon Chang. In recounting Korea's economic history through his intellectual biography, Chang accentuates the disorienting gap between the life he's lived and the changes he's witnessed by employing the language and tropes of science fiction, a rhetorical move that Christopher T. Fan has theorized in relation to U.S.–Asian economic relations.[5] At the time of Chang's birth in October 7, 1963, "the sorry country" of South Korea was "one of the poorest places in the world." As Chang grew up, magical transformations abounded. Cigarettes, gum, chocolates, and cookies changed from being illicit luxury goods introduced by the U.S. Army to everyday household items. Samsung shifted from the fish and vegetable industry to the semiconductor and electronics industry. A school playground became a campsite for soldiers following Park Chung-hee's imposition of martial law. By the time Chang was finishing his graduate studies in England in the late 1980s, Korea was by all counts a wealthy nation: "A country whose main exports included tungsten ore, fish and wigs made with human hair has become a high-tech powerhouse, exporting stylish mobile phones and flat-screen TVs." Chang is liberal with references to time travel in his recollections. He writes: "The material progress I have seen in my 40-odd years is as though I had started life as a British pensioner born when George III was on the throne or as an American grandfather born while Abraham Lincoln was president." Cell phones, a "science-fiction product" at the time of Chang's birth, had become one of Korea's leading exports at the time of his writing. The "miracle on the Han," Chang leads us to believe, was miraculous for scholars in particular: "I felt like an historian of mediaeval England who has actually witnessed the Battle of Hastings or an astronomer who has voyaged back in time to the Big Bang."[6]

In returning to Korea, these social scientists travel not only spatially but also temporally. Korea, with its new rhythm and sheen, is hardly recognizable. All four scholars, moreover, show that it is impossible to chronicle Korean economic modernity without referencing the intensification of state authoritarianism. A futuristic Korea, they imply, includes a dystopian element. With respect to both politics and economics, all marvel at the ability to *see* change—to witness history in motion. This awe arises from the fact that the visible signs of social, political, and economic transformation do not seem to properly link up with the measurements of historical time provided by calendric units. How is it that one can experience an epoch in the abbreviated span of a decade? Or, to quote Reinhart Koselleck, is there a "method for determining the time from which the history of one's own time was sensed to be emphatically new?" Koselleck defines "new time" (*neue Zeit*) as the moment when history appears to occur *through* time rather than *in* time: "Time is no longer simply the medium in which all histories take place; it gains a historical quality." As a force rather than a void, history appears "in and for itself in the absence of an associated subject or object."[7] The above cohort of Korean social scientists illustrates how history has become so powerfully transformative that it appears to have abandoned its subjects in a different time-space. These Korean returnees can only look on agape, unable to connect the dots from then to now.

Diasporic return narratives demonstrate how the qualitative experience of time can deviate from the quantitative measure of time. We might go a step further and posit that a key function of such narratives is to make this deviation palpable and poignant. As a documentation of profound spatiotemporal dissonance, return narratives show how a sense of one's place in history is coextensive with a temporal consciousness, a sense of one's being in time. This chapter is concerned with two Korean American writers who, in relaying their life stories of shuttling between Korea and the United States during periods of geopolitical transition, depict a kind of mundane time travel. That is, both Theresa Hak Kyung Cha and Induk Pahk allow us to glimpse "the expected otherness of the future and, associated with it, the alteration in the rhythm of temporal experience."[8] Like Choong Soon Kim and John Lie, Cha left South Korea for the United States in the 1960s and returned in the 1980s. Accompanied by her brother James, a cinematographer, Cha visited Seoul in May 1980 to shoot *White Dust from Mongolia*, a project intended as her magnus opus.[9] Did the Chas, too, confront what Kim calls "future shock?" Theresa Cha was raped and murdered in 1982, and her impressions of Korea are not well documented.[10] But though *White Dust* never came to fruition, Cha's footage from the trip presents a very different Korea than the one the social scientists describe. Whereas these scholars relay a sense of unexpected acceleration, an ever quickening "progress" or "advancement" that gets congealed into the decadent forms of phones, TVs, haute couture, and coffee shops, *White Dust* conveys a sense of slowness and stillness. If for Chang living through two decades of Korean history is akin to witnessing the Big Bang, then for Cha the difference between a moment and an eternity seems hazy, the present stretching like a line of abandoned railway tracks.

Cha had been working on *White Dust* at the same time as *Dictee*, the 1982 experimental memoir for which she is best remembered. Both these works employ a melancholic aesthetic, insofar as both squarely locate "Korea" in a traumatic past. This circumscribed historical vision in *White Dust* bewilders critic Ed Park. Hadn't Cha arrived in Korea during its most famous pro-democracy movement, the Kwangju rebellion? Weren't she and her brother "harassed as they tried to work on their film, possibly suspected of being North Korea spies?" Given that Cha's "abstract, dream-state conception of history ran up against, was broken by, *real* history," Park writes, "perhaps this should have become the topic of her film." But, he laments, "it doesn't appear that she made any concessions to the reality of what she had witnessed in Korea."[11]

One can imagine Park filing similar accusations of ahistoricity against Induk Pahk. Pahk also spent much of her adult life in the United States, and she also returned to Korea during massive anti-government protests. Pahk's return journey in 1961 coincided with the military coup that brought Park Chung-hee to power; this was exactly nineteen years before the Kwangju uprising, which coalesced in the aftermath of Park's assassination. When referencing these events in her 1976 memoir *The Cock Still Crows*, Pahk, like Cha, does not even mention Park's regime or the populist outrage it provoked: "News of a revolution's starting in Korea came twelve hours before my departure from Washington, D.C. All my friends... advised me not to proceed, but I knew what I was doing. God was in this plan."[12] In Pahk's telling, an unanticipated "revolution" is dwarfed by a divinely foreordained "plan." Pahk is so devoted to executing this plan—specifically, establishing a vocational boys' school—that she is not swayed by political tumult, be it democracy protests or military coups. And yet, Park's presidency turns out to be a great boon for Pahk. First, his administration grants her permission to remove more than two hundred graves for her new school: "By this arrangement, I inherited seventy-six magnificent granite tombstones and tables," she writes. "Others were used for stone flooring in the entrance to the main building" (92). Three years later, President Park would again assist Pahk when a cement company lobbied to displace her school: "We won this case by the intervention of God through Madame Park" (97). Pahk's repeated deference to God as the sole driver of her personal fortunes and her surprising disregard for the graves of the dead disclose the tensions in her experience of historical time. On the one hand, Pahk seems old fashioned and pre-modern in her submission to a transhistorical omnipotent power. On the other hand, Pahk embodies a fanatical form of modernity in her single-minded, even ruthless, commitment to futurity. By turning old tombstones into new stone flooring—by treating "a dead body as if it were ordinary organic matter"—Pahk reveals the "extreme violence" that enables extreme modernization. In her uncompromising surge ahead, Pahk appears to banish history and deny humanity.[13] The dead are not to be remembered but surpassed.

In chapter 2 of *Tonal Intelligence*, I proposed that Japan's transwar evolution from the United States' enemy to its ally entailed an affective norming among everyday subjects that indefinitely deferred discussions of the nation's guilt and accountability. In this chapter, I remain concerned with subjects who are incapable of processing the magnitude of historical transition. Pahk's progressive and providential outlook makes her seem untouched by Korea's serial wars, occupations, and regime changes. Her memoirs have the effect of hurtling her forward toward a divinely guaranteed future. By contrast, Cha's aestheticization of "Korea" both monumentalizes and abstracts history. Where Pahk's self-representations leave no room for contingency during a time of seismic disruptions, Cha's self-representations are all about contingency and offer no possibility of historical change. Both these approaches end up seeming ahistorical. But rather than dismiss Cha and Pahk for their inattention to *historical events*, this chapter will show how their self-representations document their experience of *historical time*. With the term historical time, I am referring to "how, in a given present, the temporal dimensions of past and future [are] related."[14] Because what concerns me is less a chronology of events than a historically situated experience of time, I find Cha and Pahk insightful not for their explicit depictions of Korean colonial history but for their indirect interpretations of temporality in the midst of dramatic geopolitical realignments. Instead of grounding us in specific historical moments through thick descriptions or overt representations, Pahk's and Cha's works allow us to discern, at the level of tone, a measure of historical movement, of history proceeding either too quickly or too slowly at a particular juncture in U.S.–Japan–Korean relations.

As my opening example shows, Pahk and Cha are generationally proximate, yet epochs apart. Pahk's career as a transpacific Christian speaker was coming to a close just before Korea's rapid industrialization. Meanwhile, Cha's career as a Bay Area mixed media artist was taking off just as the economic and political paradoxes of rapid industrialization were coming to a head. Pahk's cold war Christian memoirs and Cha's post–cold war mixed media productions are historically specific and stylistically distinct. Yet they also explore identical themes within modern Korean history: Euro-American Christianity, bodily amputation, national division, technological progress, and, most significantly, women's literacy and speech. For Pahk, speaking was a professional vocation, patriotic duty, and moral calling. Between 1926 and 1977, Pahk traversed the Pacific Ocean twenty-one times and the United States seventy-two times as an "unofficial goodwill Ambassador" on behalf of numerous American organizations, from Christian missions to governmental organs.[15] She revisits these speaking adventures in three English-language memoirs: *September Monkey* (1954), *The Hour of the Tiger* (1965), and *The Cock Still Crows* (1977).[16] That Pahk published essentially the same Christian memoir three times speaks to the popularity of this middlebrow genre in cold war America. For example, Louise Yim's *My Forty Year Fight for Korea* (1951) and Helen Kim's *Grace Sufficient* (1964) cover ground remarkably similar to Pahk's memoirs.[17] They, too, document the writer's conversion to Protestantism at a young age, pursuit of graduate studies in the United States, return to Korea to establish educational institutions, and assumption of governmental posts within the Republic of Korea (ROK). Though Pahk was hardly the only participant in "Cold War imperial feminism" or "Cold War cosmopolitan feminism," I focus on her here because her political compass is especially prone to fluctuation.[18] Across her writings, Pahk presents herself as anti-Japanese in one phase of life, pro-Japanese in another, and pro-American in yet another. These strategic adjustments never appear as fickle. Instead, Pahk's memoirs are portraits of a progressive Korean woman on the move. In her obsession with showing how up-to-date she is, Pahk leaves little room for either reflection or growth. In fact, her pet rhetorical devices, the statistic and the aphorism, dramatically diminish individual and historical agency. These numerical facts and moral truths convey the feeling of acceleration and propulsion, of moving the speaker ever forward, but not of her own volition. A tone of haste and hurry sweeps up the speaker, casting historical time as accumulative, irreversible, and transcendent. I interpret the vertiginous breathlessness of Pahk's memoirs as specific to a transwar moment when pro-American anticommunism became impossible to reconcile with anti-Japanese anticolonialism. Pahk's surge toward a glorious future arises from a desire to overcome the messy politics of colonial wars. Her seemingly frictionless forward movement creates the impression that anticolonial nationalism (the dominant sentiment of the Pacific War) naturally precedes, rather than messily coexists with, anticommunist nationalism (the dominant sentiment of the cold war). This view of historical time as smoothly sequential implicitly casts all manifestations of anti-Japaneseness—be it demands for reparations or charges against collaborators—as antiquated, something that must be rapidly overcome in the name of anticommunist modernity.

Like Pahk, Cha explores a female speaking subject through tropes of Christianity, militarism, colonialism, and nationalism. These themes come together most succinctly in *Dictee*.[19] The disproportionate critical focus on *Dictee*, however, obscures the fact that Cha's interest in her Korean heritage developed in the later years of her life. Although it's impossible to speculate on Cha's exact motivations, I'm struck that Korea's growing visibility in her work coincides with the nation's growing visibility on the global scene. It seems meaningful that Cha was reexamining Korean colonial history at the same time that a broader international community was seeing this history anew thanks to increasing Korean calls for reparations and apologies from Japan. Because of this timely convergence, it is not uncommon to find Cha's *Dictee* cited in criticism on Korean redress movements. Indeed, the scholars who are best known for bringing *Dictee* into the fore—in particular Elaine Kim and Laura Hyun-Yi Kang—were at the same time writing about the ongoing history of militarized sexual exploitation in South Korea.[20] Grace M. Cho's 2008 study *Haunting the Korean Diaspora* repeatedly cites *Dictee* to evoke the spectrality of the *yanggongju*, a transimperial figure whose sexual services to military forces include both Japanese comfort stations and American camptowns.[21]

While Cha has become a ready example for late twentieth-century redress culture, she has rarely been considered in relation to the other aspect of Korea's global visibility—its "miraculous" economic growth.[22] Korea's dual presence within the domain of human rights redress and that of capitalist development exemplifies Pheng Cheah's claim that "the moral universalism of human rights discourse can, paradoxically, be used to justify economic globalization as a form of postcolonial civilizing mission."[23] Implied here is that contemporary manifestations of a "postcolonial civilizing mission" may elude recognition as a form of colonialism. David Scott has cautioned that "picturing colonialism in one way—as a system of totalizing degradation—enables (indeed obliges) the critical response to it to take the form of the longing for anticolonial overcoming or revolution."[24] Scott's insight reminds us that during the time of Cha's writing—the 1970s and 1980s—"colonialism" and "cold war" in Korea looked dramatically different than it had in the 1950s. Although the "miracle on the Han" has often solicited the language of ethno-nationalism, it is actually premised on two enduring colonial relationships, one with Japan and the other with the United States. In the human rights realm, Lisa Yoneyama has shown how Japan's centrality to redress movements reveals an "inability to fully challenge U.S. predominance in the region" and thus reinforces "the production of the Cold War historical epistemology."[25] Within the economic realm, Korea's rapid industrialization in the 1960s was only possible through the Park administration's contributions to the American war in Vietnam and its normalization of Korea–Japan relations. It is this economic genealogy that most interests me. For although Cha has become expedient for upholding a particular imagining of Korea's colonial history (one that is characterized by loss, violation, suppression, fragmentation, and exceptional violence), I find that her informational aesthetic in fact evidences an alternate version of this colonial history (one that is more commonly known as late capitalism, post-Fordism, the New Economy, and Toyotism). In my view, Cha's depictions of diagrams, anagrams, lists, letters, envelopes, and speech parts are no less a commentary on colonial wars than her depictions of Korean heroes, public beheadings, Japanese history textbooks, and American immigration documents: late capitalism is late colonialism by another name. Reading Cha's well-known preoccupation with female speech in the context of her broader interest in post-Fordist communication systems will thus deter us from interpreting Korea's economic miracles of the 1970s and 1980s as a historical break, a clean passage from war to peace or from colonialism to sovereignty. Rather, Cha's post–cold war aesthetic, I will show, animates the paradoxes of postcolonial capitalist modernity and the transformation of cold war imaginaries.[26]

If, for Pahk, time feels rushed and frenzied, then for Cha it is slow and aimless. And where Pahk beatifically portrays her headlong rush toward modernity, Cha's aestheticization of lists, conjugations, permutations, anagrams, mnemonics, and other taxonomic systems has the effect of stretching time and flattening tone. Cha's representation of her contemporary world dramatizes not the scale or pace of change but a disconcerting sense of suspension. In portraying an activity that yields no advancement and an informational aesthetic that bears no message, Cha's mixed media productions induce an immersion in an ongoing present—a present where cause-and-effect relations are supplanted by an incessant, directionless vacillation and where clear indices of racial difference give way to the exhaustive systematicity of sheer variation. For me, then, the most crucial violence documented in Cha's post–cold war works is a violence of perception, of being unable to discern the markers of "war" and "race." This reading not only complicates Cha's status as a haunted subject, who is fractured by a spectacular trauma and consequently produces a melancholic history. It is also intended as a corrective to scholars of the "contemporary" and "postmodern," who unreflectively use phrases such as "after World War II," "post-1945," and "postwar," as if "war" could be a neutral marker of time.[27]

WARTIME: FLOW AND AMPUTATION

As recounted in *September Monkey*, Pahk delivered her first oration at age 12. The occasion was her graduation from an American mission school, and the topic was suffering: "They that sow in tears shall reap in Joy" (40–41). Pahk's educational and spiritual journey then led her to Ewha Girls' High School.[28] Here, Pahk participated even more intensively in public speaking and debate. These activities were "new to Oriental womanhood in my country" and "gave us training in expressing ourselves." One topic of debate was "Is It Necessary for Women to Have Higher Education?" Another queried, "Which is More Important, Physical Power or Spiritual Power?" (49). Pahk's biography shows how female educational achievement came to function as a measure of Korean spiritual modernity for both American missionaries and Korean nationalists. This transnational itinerary of American Christian internationalism eventually brought Pahk to Wesleyan College in Macon, Georgia, in 1926. It was here, on one day in Sunday school, that Pahk delivered "an extemporaneous speech in English" (112).

This speech was so well received that Pahk became a Sunday regular. From there, public speaking turned into a vocation. The pivotal moment was January 1, 1928. On this day, the 31-year-old Pahk delivered her first public English-language speech at the Quadrennial Convention of the Student Volunteer Movement for Foreign Missions (SVM), an evangelical organization that peaked in the 1920s. Donning a traditional Korean dress, Pahk lowered the microphone toward her and declared: "of all the discoveries made in the latter part of the nineteenth century, the discovery of womanhood in Korea, as representative of all Asia, was the greatest of all" (119).

Pahk would deliver some version of these charismatic lines again and again, at church luncheons, in school classrooms, and with strangers on the Greyhound bus. From her stint as the traveling secretary for the SVM to her employment by the U.S. government to her alliances with nongovernmental organizations such as the East–West Foundation and the Red Cross, Pahk's lectures brought her to forty-five American states and nine Canadian provinces as well as to Europe and Asia. The bulk of Pahk's ambassadorial service for the U.S. government took place during the years of regime change. Following the American "liberation" of the Korean peninsula from Japanese rule in 1945, the United States Army Military Government in Korea (USAMGIK) asked Pahk to visit women's organizations, U.S. military bases, Army hospitals, and Red Cross clubs. During this time, Pahk also served as a radio lecturer for USAMGIK's Department of Public Information on "Democracy and Women of Korea." Then, in December 1947, U.S. military governor John Hodge invited Pahk to return to the United States on a Korean Cultural Mission: "He offered me his fullest cooperation if I could be financially responsible for the trip. He wanted me to present the situation of Korea to American audiences, to paint a true picture for them. We agreed that I was not to go as a government representative but rather as a free agent" (244). Despite Pahk's official status as a "free agent," it was common for news outlets to note her sponsorship by USAMGIK.[29] Just days before Pahk was to leave the United States, the infamous North Korean shot was fired across the 38th parallel. Instead of returning to South Korea, Pahk stayed behind, "waging a long-range war against the Communists from the U.S." through Voice of America radio broadcasts.[30] Every week for eighteen months, Pahk delivered "a thirteen-minute message of encouragement, cheer and inspiration" to Korean listeners (262).

Pahk discusses her services to the U.S. government only in her first and most popular memoir, *September Monkey*. This memoir is also explicit in allegorically linking Pahk's personal life to Korea's colonial history. I quote from this memoir at length to show how a seemingly familiar allegory of woman as nation also includes an allegory of historical time. In the passage below, the year is 1931, and Pahk is returning to Korea after a five-year stay in the United States followed by a worldwide sightseeing and speaking tour:

I was in the same land with my children! I would soon see my mother and mother-in-law. Korean women getting on the train with their familiar garb and hairdress and with babies on their backs caused a great wave of happiness to flow over me, followed by a great burden of regret because my fellow countrywomen were not free. Suddenly I felt again that I was hemmed in by circumstances. Five years and two months had passed since I left my homeland. I had seen much of the world, I had experienced freedom, moving freely among free peoples. Now I was coming back to my own people who were oppressed by the Japanese and also I must face my own personal problems which must be solved. I knew the action I was about to take in regard to my marital status would create a lot of criticism and I might have to pay for it all of my life. But unless ills were cured they would go on hurting. I would rather have an arm amputated and live than to die because it was diseased. I was confident that I would find a way to work out by [sic] own problem with God's help, but what of Korea's problems and the world's problems? I was certainly a part of the whole. Could I be used of God [sic] to help meet the larger problems also? Probably I was the first Korean woman in history to have a chance to know intellectual America as widely and intimately as had been my opportunity. (161–62)

Known for being one of the first Korean divorcees, Pahk contemplates here "the action I was about to take in regard to my marital status."[31] In describing marriage, Pahk employs a figurative phraseology: "hemmed in by circumstances," "unless ills were cured they would go on hurting," and "have an arm amputated." Marriage is the painful constriction of the body over time. Gender oppression, moreover, gains poignancy through its rhetorical connection to national oppression: "I was coming back to my own people who were oppressed by the Japanese and also I must face my own personal problems." This alignment between Japanese colonialism and patriarchal marriage leads Pahk to project her "personal problems" onto all Korean mothers: "Korean women getting on the train ... with babies on their backs caused a great wave of happiness to flow over me, followed by a great burden of regret because my fellow countrywomen were not free." In this line, maternal yearning (to see her children) and wifely dread (of returning to her restrictive marriage and her colonized nation) have a temporal dimension. Marriage and motherhood are not just allegories for an unfree nation, but they also figure historical time as "flow," "wave," and "burden." Pahk's wave of maternal joy, which overcomes the weight of both colonial bondage and marital obligation, positions her to speak of her impending divorce with something like proud anticipation: "I would rather have an arm amputated and live than to die because it was diseased." In this instance, amputation refers to an action necessitated by the colonial era of anti-Japanese nationalism. Later in *Monkey*, Pahk redeploys similar metaphors of amputation to describe actions necessitated by the cold war era of pro-American nationalism, for example by personifying national division as a South Korea that has "legs but no head" and a North Korea that has "a head but no legs" (250). In narrating Japanese colonialism from a cold war standpoint, Pahk suggests that multiple imperialisms have begotten multiple emergency amputations. Only through "amputation"—through the unburdening of imperial histories, grievances, and sentiments—can Korean nationalist time freely flow toward a transcendent future.

The flow of anticipation and the burden of dread allegorize two familiar paradigms of temporality. One, embodied by the returning mother, is a harmonious circadian movement toward maternal (and national) reunion. The other, embodied by the embattled divorcee, is a surgical "amputation," an emergency operation that saves the self (and the nation) by eliminating harmful burdens. Reinhart Koselleck attempts to steer us away from this schematization of "time in a bipolar manner." He writes disapprovingly of how "time is either portrayed as linear, as an arrow of time that heads in a teleological direction, or toward an open future, or conceived of as recurrent and cyclical."[32] In Pahk's case, teleological progress and cyclical return give credence to an ideal of modern womanhood that can countenance divorce and an ideal of modern nationhood that is conditioned by division. A tonal rather than allegorical reading of Pahk's memoirs, however, allows us to comprehend historical time through differentiated speeds and movements rather than geometric shapes. Employing a geological metaphor, Koselleck imagines history as sediments of time that "set themselves apart from each other at differing speeds over the course of the so-called history of the earth."[33] If "differentiating conditions must enter so that concrete historical motion might be rendered visible," then in Pahk's memoir we register this motion through a superfluous haste, an excessive expedience. That is, the temper of historical change becomes perceptible through the misalignment between Pahk's buoyant hubris on the one hand and her rather pedestrian excursions through churches, clubs, schools, and auditoriums on the other. So even as Pahk attempts to integrate cyclical natural time and linear modern time into a chronology of national progress, the unusually urgent and euphoric tone of her memoirs attunes us to history's "differing speeds" and "differentiating conditions." In the passage alluding to divorce, readers might notice that Pahk lends her account a heroic touch by couching her return to Korea within the memory of "moving freely among free peoples" in the United States. Superficial expressions of self-doubt ("Could I be used of God to meet the larger problems also?") are immediately subsumed by the triumphal language of being "the first woman in history to have a chance to know intellectual America." In describing "a burden of regret," Pahk does not actually seem regretful.

Breathless, rapturous, and aggressively future-oriented, Pahk's memoirs give tonal expression to the historical temperament in which they were written. This hurried and harried tone connotes sheer advancement rather than rounded development. It suggests a dramatic overshooting of the expected pace of individual growth and national modernization. Although distortive, this sense of disproportion in Pahk's memoirs is precisely what allows us to "conceptually deduce progress, decadence, acceleration, or delay, the 'not yet' and the 'no longer,' the 'earlier' or 'later than,' the 'too early' and the 'too late,' situation and duration."[34] Pahk may never slow down long enough to provide anything in the way of context or explanation, yet her perfunctory and propulsive account of progress—a progress that cannot afford to pause—nonetheless marks out the "situation and duration" of a transitional moment. Specifically, in her unremitting press forward, Pahk indirectly signals a disjuncture between the temporality of anticolonial nationalism (coded as anti-Japanese) and the temporality of anticommunist nationalism (coded as pro-American).

THE TONE OF THE TIMES

MODERN FACTS AND MORAL TRUTHS

As discussed in chapter 2, Lisa Yoneyama's term "transwar" is useful for understanding how U.S. cold war policy in Asia exploited and extended Japanese colonial power. Many of the free Koreans in this chapter, like the free Filipinos we will meet in chapter 5, were pro-Japanese "collaborators" who sought to clear their names by casting their lot with their American "liberators." To consolidate a democratic and capitalist free Asia, the United States called on the colonized to forget the crimes of their former colonizer, Japan. Christianity became a resource for authorizing this forgetting in the name of nationalist advancement. Expatriate intellectuals who returned to Korea after its "liberation" from Japan in 1945 were predominantly Christian-educated—even those on the left, and even including Kim Il-sung. But the U.S. occupation and its support for Syngman Rhee definitively "changed the political atmosphere in the church." Lacking a political base after returning to Korea, Rhee seized upon Christian support. As a result, Korean Protestants received disproportionate representation within both the U.S. military government and the ROK's rightist regime.[35] Furthermore, persecuted Christians escaping from the north were heavily recruited by the U.S. Information Agency to preach "the evils of communism and the benevolence of the UN."[36] During the Rhee era, the church would "enhanc[e] the cause of anticommunism to the point of equating it with the Christian mission."[37] A Christian genealogy of Korean nationalism drew on the legacies of American moral internationalism. By narrating the kinship between American Protestantism and Korean nationalism from the nineteenth century onwards, cold war Christians, both Korean and American, were able to present the U.S.-backed and Rhee-led ROK "as the only legitimate descendant of this nationalist movement."[38]

This rescripting of Korean nationalism as requiring anticommunist allegiance and national division was no small feat given that that the Korean independence movement had long understood sovereignty and liberation through an anti-Japanese program. Cold war Korean Christian memoirs published by American presses were part of this broader effort to refashion Korean nationalism so that it harmonized with American geopolitical interests. These memoirs plot a common educational, professional, and political trajectory for free Koreans. Particularly noteworthy are the writings of Induk Pahk, Louise Yim, and Helen Kim, three women who all undertook journeys across the Pacific Ocean to American universities and then returned to South Korea to build schools and serve the Rhee regime. By detailing a female writer's achievement of modernity through American missionary education and English-language publication, Pahk, Yim, and Kim helped frame American Christian internationalism of the early twentieth century as a natural precursor to the state-backed American geopolitical internationalism of the cold war present.[39] The biographical parallels between these women's narratives would have us believe that since the beginning of time—since the arrival of U.S. missions on Korean shores—the United States has *continuously* supported Korean independence, whether it's against the threat of colonialism (exemplified by the Japanese empire) or that of communism (exemplified by the North Korean state). Yet these similarities between Pahk, Yim, and Kim also make the incommensurable strains within their memoirs more glaring. Although all three women viewed themselves as patriots, their writings do not in the end avail a unified understanding of "Korean nationalism." The crucial issue around which nationalism splinters is pro-Japanese "collaboration." Yim, writing at the outbreak of the Korean War, when the ROK and Japan were technically allies, feels the need to justify her *anti-Japanese* sentiments: "In becoming aware of what the Japanese were doing to Korea, I developed prejudices that have remained with me to this day—a feeling that the Japanese are a bad people."[40] Kim, on the other hand, faces the opposite challenge of justifying her *pro-Japanese* activities, despite the fact that the Pacific War has technically concluded. Writing in 1964, Kim implies that "collaborating" with the Japanese was merely consistent with her lifelong objective of putting the cause of women's education above self or nation. To fulfill her "humble service to the womanhood of my country" by keeping Ewha College afloat, Kim had to sacrifice her own integrity and succumb to Japanese demands.[41] Yim's explanation of why her anti-Japanese prejudice has lingered into the present and Kim's explanation of why her anti-Japanese patriotism was not potent enough bear out a confusion about what constitutes properly nationalist feelings during a transwar period of geopolitical upheaval. Read together, Yim's and Kim's memoirs show how emotional regimes take longer to recalibrate than the political regimes instituted by governing bodies.

Unlike her contemporaries Yim and Kim, Pahk avoids taking strong political positions. In *Tiger*, when a British student probes Pahk about the

Japanese occupation, she responds: "Politics absolutely fascinates me. But I am no politician" (48). Pahk's professed political disinterest empowers her to be resolutely forward looking, such that she never bothers to defend or deny her record of "collaboration." By imagining the temporality of Korean modernity as flow and amputation, she is able to cut her losses and move unflaggingly toward the future. This forward movement relies on two rhetorical devices—numbers and aphorisms—and calls forth a specific narrative tone—that of transcendent progress.

Numbers serve to quantify Pahk's achievements. Across three memoirs, Pahk attempts to put a number on the miles she's traveled, the speeches she's given, the minutes she's spoken, and the amount of applause she's received. For example: "In my gypsy life I traveled about forty-five thousand miles a year and each year made about two hundred and fifty speeches" (*Tiger*, 59). Other estimates are more precise. In 1965, Pahk calculates she has made a total of 5,387 speeches. By 1977, that number has increased to 6,808. In addition to counting speeches and miles, Pahk often offers statistical analyses. To highlight her productivity, she may provide a granular account of a specific pit stop: "I stayed with this friend one week, speaking three times a day, twice in the morning and once in the afternoon, in different schools" (*Cock*, 29). Or, she may try to impress the reader with her efficiency and impact. At the First International Assembly of Women in October 1946, Pahk was not on the scheduled program of speakers, yet she "felt a definite responsibility to let this great group of women know that Korea was represented." Compounding this sense of responsibility are the 8,000 miles that Pahk has traveled and the $1,000 she has spent to attend the conference. While the already scheduled speakers were allocated fifteen minutes, Pahk requests only one minute. When she is told that "even a minute is impossible," she proudly does more with still less: "I reached [the speaker's platform] almost instantly," and "I said what I had wanted to say in less than thirty seconds" (*Monkey*, 231–32).

In these examples, we cannot fully grasp just how many speeches Pahk has made or just how many miles she has traveled, but we know that there have been quite a lot of both and that each increases steadily. This feeling of numerical magnitude overpowers the narrative arc of Pahk's memoir. It doesn't matter that we cannot remember each individual number or its purpose, for the mere presence of numbers holds more power than their content or context. This representational strategy illustrates Pahk's faith in what

Mary Poovey calls the modern fact. Poovey writes, "numbers have come to epitomize the modern fact, because they have come to seem preinterpretive or even somehow noninterpretive at the same time that they have become the bedrock of systematic knowledge."[42] Numbers communicate transparency; it is less that they *are* facts than that they have the *quality* of fact. This is what makes them seem irrefutable, what allows them to buttress "systematic knowledge." Unlike Poovey's case studies, Pahk does not use numbers as an argumentative tool, something to certify a scientific or economic theory. Indeed, it seems unusual to find *so many* numbers in an autobiography, a genre presumably better suited for nourishing interpersonal empathy. Why is statistical evidence recruited to do so much work in a personal narrative? If, as Poovey claims, facts are abstractions that have material effects, then to what end do Pahk's transparent numbers substantiate credibility and inspire conviction? By substituting a narrative account with a numerical count, Pahk's self-representations appear to link individual progress to the unidirectional passage of time. Numbers provide a degree of biographical elucidation, but they are more significant for advancing a vision of history as flow. By referencing objective counts of miles and speeches, Pahk documents not only her own travels but also modernity's irreversible movement forward.

As a statistical representation of spatial, temporal, individual, and civilizational "progress," Pahk's memoirs seek to convince us with concrete factual truths. Yet despite the preponderance of numerical evidence, the tone of Pahk's memoirs isn't exactly cool, hard, dispassionate, or objective. Tallying speeches, miles, and minutes elicits not so much painstaking exactitude but vertiginous quantity. The sublimity of numerical magnitude, moreover, seems incongruous with the forgettability of mundane content—of counting the steps from one small town to another. Yoon Sun Lee has written about this paradox in the context of Asian American literary realism: "We commonly tend to invest numerousness with importance.... But the everyday upends this way of linking quantitative measure and qualitative significance. In this domain, the more iterations, or the more instances there are, the more negligible something seems." Numerousness affords not only a "minimal narrativity" but also a "minimal sociality": "the weakening of emplotment more often results in the emergence of a schematic thingness, of small emptied shapes placed side by side in a way that suggests functional equivalence over time but not meaningful interconnectedness."⁴³ Pahk has a clear stake in numerousness—a term that encompasses both the quantity and the quality of numbers. Numerousness establishes social progress and temporal flow as analogous structures proceeding apace toward the future. But despite their self-evident facticity, these statistical representations also make Pahk's cold war speaking career seem uneventful and ahistorical. The act of counting implies "progress," yet it reads as a straightforward and anti-climactic sequence, proceeding almost automatically in a detailless vacuum.

If Pahk's numbers constitute modern facts, then her witticisms function as eternal truths. In *Cock*, Pahk explains that her "love [for] acronyms, phrases, idioms, and jokes" has to do with her "being a foreigner learning to speak English" (43). This love of aphoristic wit culminates in a 1970 collection of "Asian proverbs" called *The Wisdom of the Dragon*. In the context of Pahk's memoirs, rhyming slogans and witty sayings combine individual savvy with God-given insight. They evidence both individual ingenuity and divine sanction. Only in *Monkey*, Pahk's first memoir, do we find proverbial wisdom serving a geopolitical purpose. Take, for example, Pahk's first joke in English: "In America when men get together they call it a stag party.... Now I can see why Korea has been a backward nation. It has had nothing but stag parties and a country which has only stag parties soon approaches stagnation" (124–25). This joke about stagnation showcases Pahk's contribution to modernizing her nation, both by making a smart joke in English and by diversifying Korea's "stag party." It also preempts further interrogation: the joke provides an explanation to the very problem it poses (Korea stagnates because it is run by stags), and it allows Pahk to present herself as an antidote to this problem. In another recurring joke reproduced in *Monkey*, Pahk outlines three types of communists and similarly serves up a tidy political resolution in the punch line: "There are the 'red apple,' the 'tomato,' and the 'watermelon' Communists." When asked "what we can do about them," Pahk replies, "we make applesauce from the apples, tomato juice from the tomatoes, and pickles from the watermelon—and eat all of them up" (251).

Monkey's descriptions of postwar modernization often use proverbs that indirectly engage flow and amputation:

Through all of these new developments we were constantly bombarded with propaganda by the Communists.... They condemned any Koreans who had ever found it necessary to deal with the Japanese for any reason, calling them traitors and creating suspicion among Koreans. The only way to meet Communist propaganda was to outdo it with democratic propaganda, including the doctrine that "bygones should be bygones" and that from the time of Liberation everyone's conduct would be judged from that day on. (218–19)

Pahk's reference to "new developments" renders communism temporally prior to democracy. This move conflates present-day communism with an antiquated anti-colonialism. Pahk reasons that the Korean communists who dwell in anti-Japanese feelings are stuck in a previous war and a previous iteration of nationalism. In denouncing pro-Japanese "collaborators" as traitors, these Koreans have let "bygones" intrude upon a new future. With the "democratic" doctrine of "bygones should be bygones" Pahk stipulates that in order for history to progress—or flow—toward modernity, one must relinquish—even amputate—the premodern past.

Unlike those who hold up the flow of progress, Pahk has swiftly adapted to "new developments." In the 1910s, Pahk sacrificed herself to the Korean independence movement. *Monkey* provides lengthy descriptions of Pahk's time in a Japanese jail following the March 1, 1919 pro-independence protests:[44] "Upon entering the detention station I faced a group of horrible-looking men seated before a square of cages, into one of which I was thrust" (59). In the 1930s, "new developments" have considerably softened Pahk's attitude toward Japanese colonial rule: "My girls were reading magazines written in Japanese, so I too would read them. We have a saying, 'If one wants to catch a tiger one must get to the place where the tigers are'" (195). Like the "bygones" doctrine, this saying about catching tigers turns a sensitive political issue into a fundamental moral axiom. But since Pahk's receptivity to Japanese rule has more to do with keeping up with the times than adhering to a moral code, the reference point for "new developments" changes from Japan to the United States in the 1950s. In explaining her "cultural mission" to the United States, Pahk writes, "I was sure that Americans would be deeply interested in Korea when they understood the facts, for I know that 'when they are interested, people care; when they care, they share'" (247). Here, Pahk's narration of her achievements maintains a calculated myopia toward the relic of Japanese colonialism, while framing American interest, care, and generosity as an asset for Korean nationalism. Because the strategy of amputation allows Pahk to cut away past burdens, she doesn't see any contradiction in participating in anti-Japanese protests in one phase of life and adapting to Japanese norms in another. These are merely the progressive stages of Korean modernity rather than the contradictory forces underpinning it.

Pahk's statistics and aphorisms are rhetorical structures that, in coordination, document a propulsive movement forward and sound a tone of intrepid progress. If Pahk's speeches, miles, and minutes are devices for tracking and quantifying her passage through time, then her "transhistorical and transcultural" aphorisms are also, in an analogous sense, "vessels that travel everywhere, laden with freight yet buoyant." As Andrew Hui has noted, the etymology of aphorism can be interpreted as a journey toward a receding horizon.[45] A compact bundle of infinite, aphorisms promise a spiritual transport that parallels Pahk's nautical, locomotive, and automotive adventures. The statistic and the aphorism, both rhetorical vehicles of transport, distinguish Pahk from those who feel defensive or remorseful about former political allegiances. In her later memoirs, Pahk becomes increasingly uninterested in individual and national development. The result is that numbers and aphorisms all but entirely displace the allegory of woman as nation. These modern facts and moral precepts provide little historical clarity, but they do create a historically specific tonal effect. In supplanting narrative details with a tone of delirious exhilaration, Pahk's writings frame Korea's colonial past as something that, in the name of modern progress and divine good, requires amputating rather than redressing, overcoming rather than describing. To the extent that Pahk's numerical tabulations provide empirical proof that time *can* only move forward, her piquant maxims provides moral justification for such a view, suggesting that time *should* only move forward. Pahk's steady accrual of miles and speeches and her canny droppings of analectic truths map modern progress onto temporal progression. Thanks to the laws of science and the laws of God, the national forgetting of Japanese colonialism as well as the national forgiveness of pro-Japanese collaborators appear as progressive and principled stances. At a time when a smooth acceleration away from the colonial past was geopolitically necessary, Pahk's euphoric pursuit of futurity normalizes an ideal of cosmopolitan modernity based on Japan as a free Asian ally and the United States as a free world leader.

And yet, a war narrative that seems so happily unencumbered—that insists on the natural and normal flow of time—also captures the *strangeness* of regime change. A temporality that proceeds uninterruptedly toward the future both marks and masks a crisis in historicity. We can detect this crisis in Pahk's tone of surpassing hurry. As a transwar mode of writing, Pahk's compression of historical time into a sequence of numbers thoroughly abstracts Korea's experiences of colonialism and militarism. It refuses to acknowledge the distinctions between past, present, and future, even as it inadvertently reveals that U.S.–Japan inter-imperial relations have compelled revisions of the recent past and stymied visions of the near future. Pahk's numerical facts and moral truisms bespeak a dutiful avoidance of historical details. At the same time, this avoidance also connotes a historically motivated alteration in temporal experience. A transwar moment suppresses the past and forestalls historical justice by concealing the violence of transition—by quickening the journey forward without hitch or burden.

EVEN MORE HURRY

The Hour of the Tiger and *The Cock Still Crows* are in essence rewritings of *September Monkey*. These later memoirs recount the same turning points in Pahk's life: acquiring her first pencil, attending a boys' school in disguise, traveling with the Student Volunteer Movement, answering the call of General Hodge, and so on. In contrast to *Monkey*, however, *Tiger* and *Cock* present Pahk's speaking engagements as separate from any nationalist or internationalist cause. All her life's work, we are told, go toward fulfilling God's plan. This plan is to create a vocational boys' school in Korea modeled after Berea University in Kentucky. In rewriting her life story so that "Berea in Korea" appears as her divine purpose, Pahk sidelines war, colonialism, and geopolitics to the point of irrelevance. For example, in *Cock*, Pahk again recalls her five months "in solitary confinement in Westgate Prison, Seoul, during the Korean Independence Movement." But unlike in *Monkey*, Pahk's involvement in this movement has little to do with patriotism. Instead, Pahk explains that "waiting endlessly with what patience I could muster" in a Japanese prison was a way of "preparing myself to wait for buses" as she traveled the United States (75). A newspaper interview with Pahk more explicitly establishes her imprisonment as the origin of a divinely wrought plan: "An idea born 35 years ago in a Japanese jail will within the next three years be spreading education among the free Asian youth who need it most—the underprivileged of Korea. That was the hope expressed yesterday by Mrs. Induk Pahk, a lady of Korea who has traveled 776,420 miles in her efforts to found Berea College of Korea."[46] Recasting Korean nationalism as a divine project dedicated to mothering Korea's future generations reshapes the temporality of Pahk's biography. If *Monkey* tracks Pahk's adaptability to "new developments" emerging from regime change, then *Tiger* tracks Pahk's commitment to an "extraordinary plan" that subordinates personal, national, and historical *developments* to preordained *patterns* (23): "the pattern of my life . . . appeared to be shaped in the direction of a single purpose" (12).

A pattern-oriented narrative requires both momentous events and mundane routines to always already be serving the divine cause of boys' education. Such a narrative is even more liberal with numbers and maxims. Yet even when Pahk is not providing numerical and moral evidence, her narrative still retains the same "progressive" tone of fervent activity and exalted haste. This tonal quality severely undercuts both historical causality and individual agency. Stripped of personhood, Pahk's narrative presence in her later memoirs becomes a channel for divine and technological forces. In *Cock*, Pahk recalls how, before one speech, "I flashed my wire to God: 'Please speak through me'" (24). On several occasions, she uses the figure of the "telephone operator" to describe her ability to connect "the needy children in Korea and those friends here in America" (*Cock*, 55–56; *Tiger*, 252). This vehicular notion of the speaking self produces a narrative that is not merely progressive but altogether transportive:

While reading the above verses in the Bible, I could hear the crash of the hammer, the buzz of the saw, and the noise of the chisel on the stone, breaking the silence into an active life. Korea has been too quiet for too long a time; but through modern education in technology, we can see the old Korean mind being awakened by the rhythmic noise of working with hands and heads. The mission of our school in this transition is to put the spirit of God into it—to make a pleasing rhythm of noise instead of *just noise*" (*Cock*, 103, emphasis in original).

In this passage, the construction of Pahk's school appears technologically modern and spiritually transcendent. First, Pahk onomatopoetically describes the "crash" and "buzz" of industry, jubilant noises "breaking the silence" of Bible verses. Then, she proposes that this "rhythmic noise of working with hands and heads" requires a conduit to "put the spirit of God into it." The conduit for transforming "*just noise*" into "a pleasing rhythm" is none other than Pahk herself. The sounds of a schoolhouse speedily going up under God's watch are tonally reproduced in narrative. A "rhythmic noise" and "pleasing rhythm" thus bring not only Pahk's school but also her memoir "into an active life." Even though Pahk is speaking about her role in Korea's postwar transition, the tone of this passage seems to be addressing a subject loftier than individual or nation. Shorn of biographical, historical, and geopolitical coordinates, progress is recast in the transportive language of spiritual and technological miracles.

In *Monkey*, "new developments" in Korean modernity were dictated by successive geopolitical regimes. In *Tiger* and *Cock*, by contrast, Korea appears technologically and spiritually advanced but politically agnostic. To explain this shift from the geopolitical to the divine, the opening of *Tiger* stages a "rebirth" (93). In a dreamlike scene set in a Massachusetts church, a clock striking midnight triggers a memory of a train arriving in Kyoto while Pahk is en route to the United States:

I was traveling across Japan by train, before World War II, bound for Yokohama where I was to board a ship for America.... En route to Yokohama, I was half-dozing in the railway carriage when I heard the conductor call out, "Kyoto! Kyoto!" Kyoto! It had always been a magic name to me.... The Japanese are so punctual in the running of their trains that when the conductor spoke the word "Kyoto," it was as if a clock had struck the hour.... Kyoto! Midnight! The dividing point. The darkness of deep night had ended; the new day had just been born. And so it was with my life. The past with its suffering was behind me. My new day had begun. Here, in this little chapel in western Massachusetts, once more I had the same feeling.... An impulse came over me to speak to that clock as to a faithful friend. I paused on the landing, smiled, and said in my mind, "Thank you, Mr. Big Chime Clock. I am a changed person." (10–11)

Occurring at the beginning of the memoir, the clock striking midnight occasions a narrative reconstruction: a "new day" offers an autobiographical "rebirth." This ebullient newness serves to normalize an allegory of colonial modernity. In Pahk's telling, "Korea" is banished to "the darkness of night" and "the past with its suffering." "Japan," meanwhile, symbolizes the punctual arrival of modernity, an event foreordained by God. In creating a clock that is synchronized to God's plan, Pahk rewrites the experience of

Japanese colonialism as a spatial, temporal, and spiritual passage. Colonialism appears here as a "dividing point" of place (Kyoto) and time (midnight) that enables her eventual arrival in modern America. Kyoto is invoked not as a signifier of colonial power but as an attempt to evacuate such signifiers of meaning and force. What replaces the colonial, national, and historical particulars of this narrative is an incantatory tone. As Pahk's cries of "Kyoto!" and "Midnight!" echo the train conductor's, we encounter a journey toward modernity that is mystical and scientific, and that, for this reason, lacks any historical grounding.

The synchronization of space and time through clock and train has received considerable attention. In nineteenth-century American and European nation-building, trains precipitated the standardizing of clock time and generated an "energetic atmosphere" of "haste."[47] Gerhard Dohrn-van Rossum suggests that the "experiential change" ushered in by trains engendered a new awareness of history. In mediating one's experience of time, trains spurred "the identification of the historical change with the progressive 'Zeitgeist.'"[48] The Japanese railway system, which developed in response to Euro-American influence, imparted a similar time consciousness. Naofumi Nakamura analyzes a shift from being "completely nonchalant about being ten or twenty minutes late" to "strict time control with a tolerance of only a few minutes."[49] Railroads have also symbolized Japanese *imperial* modernity.[50] In Ishiguro's *An Artist of the Floating World*, Masuji Ono's "tour" proceeds by way of tram lines, which he repeatedly describes with pride and nostalgia: "I believe it was 1931 when the present lines began to operate," he enthuses. "Whole districts seemed to change character overnight" (61–62).

We can surmise that 1931—when Japan solidified its "railway imperialism" by taking control of a 400-mile railway line in Northeast China[51]—is around the time of Pahk's journey through Kyoto. Though Pahk avoids dates, her experience of time "before World War II" is nevertheless historically conditioned. Put another way, Pahk's overt rendering of train time and clock time offers an indirect commentary on wartime. To appreciate this point, we must briefly revisit Leo Marx's 1964 study *The Machine in the Garden*. Here, Marx observes that nineteenth-century American literature proceeds in "an unruffled, contemplative, Augustan tone," signaling "a timeless, recurrent pattern of human affairs." This pastoral scene is then intruded upon by industrialization, figured as a roaring locomotive, a symbol of "history as an unpredictable, irreversible sequence of unique events." Although this allegorical train appears to be interrupting the pastoral calm, Marx shows how "the machine in the garden" actually reconciles two seemingly disparate notions of time. On the one hand, train technology normalized the "idea that history is a record of more or less continuous progress." On the other, this superhuman miracle, in annihilating time and space, also imagined "history as an upward spiral, a movement that dispels all doubt, carrying mankind back, full circle." In bringing line and circle together, the railroad thereby became "the chosen vehicle for bringing America into its own pastoral utopia."[52] In this analysis, it is not merely that trains go through gardens (as in a plotted chronology); rather, their temporalities coexist. Perhaps, then, the "unruffled" garden and the "roaring" train are not so tonally dissonant after all. As Koselleck has shown, historical time is plural because it is structured by different durational schemes that "sediment" at different speeds—the *longue durée* of an economic cycle settles differently than a political event such as March 1, 1919. In Pahk's case, a tone of haste indicates that historical time is synced not just to clock and train but also to war. If for Marx the time of the machine coincides with, rather than succeeds, the time of the garden, then for Pahk an unruffled and roaring tone shows that wartime has become indistinguishable from peacetime. In Pahk's recollection of her rebirth, the phrase "before World War II" is practically negligible, no different than if Pahk had written "after World War II" or "during World War II." But while God, clock, and train all seem powerfully determinative compared to this negligible war, I'd make a case for the reverse: it is in fact the irresolvable burden of "wartime" (a combination of persisting Japanese colonial influence, escalating American imperial ambition, and ongoing Korean reunification and independence struggles) that compels Pahk's recourse to spiritual and technological transport. At this transwar scene, the United States, as the new hegemon in Asia, attempts to circumvent the difficulties of geopolitical transition—to extinguish both residues of anti-Japanese sentiments and desires for Korean reunification—by cultivating obeisance to technological progress and divine will. Taken together, the miracles of modern transportation and the miracles of spiritual transport establish not only historical time but also an American-led free world as irreversible and inevitable.

MATERNAL AND MEDIAL SELF-REPRESENTATIONS

For Pahk, the present marks a point of no return. This ahistorical present is fundamentally superior to an obsolete past and already eclipsed by a transcendent future. As a result, the difference between past and present can only be quantified rather than qualitatively described, while the convertibility of present into future depends on the ratifying powers of God. Theresa Hak Kyung Cha's representations of a post–cold war present also seem ahistorical. But if Pahk's present vanishes instantly, Cha's present extends indefinitely. To draw out this difference, let us compare Pahk's and Cha's respective portrayals of Yu Guan Soon, the famed heroine of March 1, 1919.[53] On this day, Yu, a sixteen-year-old student of Ewha Girls' High School, slipped out to join the masses in the streets and rallied her village toward independence. When imprisoned by the Japanese, Yu instigated protests, which led to harsher treatment. Denied a fair trial, she died from brutal torture. In the years after 1919, Yu was sustained in "the underground of Korean memory" and also held up by American sympathizers who deemed the March 1 movement "Christian as well as patriotic."[54] After 1945, Yu became the "the epitome of patriotism." Her legacy lives on through a museum built in her name, a statue in Seoul, and songs celebrating her sacrifice.[55]

Pahk and Cha take very different approaches to engaging with Yu's lore. One practical explanation is that Pahk is of the same generation as Yu, whereas Cha is not. At the time of the March 1 demonstrations, Pahk had been a teacher at Ewha and was also arrested. In *Monkey*, Pahk recalls encountering Yu in prison, seeing her awaiting trial, and hearing her crying.[56] Pahk's account of her flash encounter with Yu may seem reminiscent of Georg Lukacs's theory of the historical novel, insofar as this incident allows us to access history from the perspective of a character who is on the periphery of the action. Lukacs, though, emphasizes the middling status of this peripheral character, someone who can be generalized as an average type.[57] Pahk, by contrast, invokes Yu in order to elevate her own importance. This narrative maneuver establishes Yu as an unreal heroine, whose life is necessarily contained within the time-space of March 1, 1919. Pahk's personal story, consequently, can cross with Yu's mythic history *only* on this day. Pahk describes their diverging timelines this way: "My heart was moved to do something for this young girl, but I was quite helpless" (68). Where Yu is heroic, Pahk is helpless. In being more mother than comrade to the "young girl," Pahk is able to live on and progress forward while Yu dies and becomes fossilized as myth. We see then that even though Pahk and Yu are contemporaries, their biographies are structured by different temporal paradigms. Pahk's progressiveness depends on her uninhibited advancement. Yu's endurance as myth, by contrast, depends on the circumscription of her life story by the events of March 1.

This mythic, circumscribed form is how Yu appears in Cha's *Dictee*.[58] Born 32 years after Yu's death, Cha has no personal recollection of Yu. But Yu's mythification has less to do with a generational difference than with Cha's artistic vision. On the whole, *Dictee* is far less personal than archaeological. Its nine sections are named after muses and bear no clear relation to each other or to Cha's life. Yu appears alongside Joan of Arc, Cha's mother, and a host of anonymous and historical personas. If Yu's heroism allows Pahk to place herself near the heart of the action, this same heroic quality allows Cha to communicate estrangement and effacement. In *Dictee*, we encounter Yu in a section entitled "Clio / History" (figures 3.1 and 3.2).

These images invite us to coordinate two lines of criticism on *Dictee*. The first concerns Cha's relation to the official historical record. Anne Cheng, for example, reads *Dictee* as "a critique of the desire for documentation."[59] Most of the photos in *Dictee* withhold captions and footnotes. The photo *does* have a caption (not included in the image below). Yet the reference to birth and death dates, as well as to birth by "one mother and one father," anonymizes rather than distinguishes the subject. The caption conveys Yu's biological lifespan but not her historical identity. The other body of criticism focuses on Cha's interest in media or, to borrow the language of film theory, "apparatuses." Looking below, we see that the medium of the photograph suppresses rather than restores the subject. As Thy Phu writes with respect to another image in *Dictee*, "the decomposed quality of this composition and the withholding of its context further suggest that the task of historical writing is incomplete, that historical picturing cannot illustrate the whole story."[60] We cannot extract any historical lesson from the images of Yu. Instead, what stands out most immediately is their graininess—their speckles and scratches, the traces of the photographic medium. Cha's critique of historical documentation and her treatment of

FIGURE 3.1. Yu Guan Soon in *Dictee*

documentary media are related points of emphases. That is, Cha expresses her antipathy towards archival recovery by paying over-close attention to the materiality of specific media.

To recap, we might say that Pahk's relation to the Korean patriot Yu is maternal, while Cha's is medial. As a maternal figure, Pahk appeals to the moral language of sympathy but is "helpless" when it comes to Yu's sacrificial cause. In expressing a sense of constraint and powerlessness, Pahk appears able to only move on. Cha, on the other hand, encounters not Yu herself but her photograph. Her efforts to intensify the materiality of the artifactual image enhance the viewer's experience of duration and dwelling. So while the maternal allows Pahk to shape historical time into an eternal myth and an unyielding line, the medial allows Cha to suspend time altogether.

FIGURE 3.2. A girls' school (Yu Guan Soon on far left)

A photograph is in some sense the definition of a suspended present. Kia Lindroos writes, "If the reproducibility is thought of as changing the temporal and spatial ways of perception, the most influential technique . . . is photography."[61] Cha heightens this distorted and suspended perception of time by presenting the same photograph of Yu twice: careful readers will notice that the first image of Yu, cropped and enlarged as a portrait, is taken from the second image, the group shot of young girls. In the 1982 Tanam Press edition, the first image appears in the body of the text and the second on the book's back cover.[62] How does this photographic cropping compare to Pahk's narrative depiction of Yu? If narratives have been seen as providing privileged access to the rhythms and structures of historical time, a photograph is "undevelopable" and bespeaks "an intense *immobility*." For Roland Barthes, undevelopable and immobile are not the same as ahistorical. In fact, in Barthes's view, the photograph that condenses time and affect into a *punctum* works to *restore* temporality to history. Defined as a "prick" or "wound" that is "at once brief and active," the *punctum* provides "the lacerating emphasis of the *noeme* ('*that-has-been*')."[63] At issue here is not overt eventfulness or detailed particulars. Barthes would be less inclined to locate a *punctum* in the photo of the girls, whose traditional dress, conservative hair, and formal pose are evocative of a turn-of-the-century girls' school. Informative but detached in its historicity, this photo perhaps compels us "to glance quickly and desultorily, to linger, then to hurry on."[64] By contrast, the cropped photo of Yu arrests narrativization and intensifies attention. Where the group shot offers visual context as a descriptive caption might, the cropped portrait "buries" the subject (to play on Barthes's metaphor of the corpse) by building up temporal layers.

This temporal multiplicity has to do with the fact that we are viewing not Yu's corpse, but the photograph's. In experiencing the *punctum* of Yu's photograph, therefore, we cannot ascertain *who* or *what* has been and can only grasp who or what *has been*. This distortion of time contrasts with Pahk's teleological understanding of progress. The suspended present of the photograph suggests that "time does not flow like a river but, rather, stands still like a work of plastic art such as a statue, mosaic, or temple."[65] The paradoxical stillness and plasticity of Cha's photograph call to mind Barthes's dictum that "every photograph is a certificate of presence." In certifying that "the past is as certain as the present," the photograph's "testimony bears not on the object but on time."[66] A certificate of presence refers to the evidence of time rather than the essence of a person. Barthes's searching for the truth of his mother via photographs thus yields not her *essence* but her *presence*—not her eternal self but her being in time. Likewise, Cha's aesthetic manipulations of Yu's photograph deflect questions of periodicity (what we find in the group shot) and identity (what we expect to find in a caption). Not only do these strategies of de/composition inhibit the intelligibility of essence, whether of a person or event, but they also augment the experience of duration.

Like the photograph of Yu, *Dictee*'s narrative of Yu shifts our attention from subjectivity to temporality. "Clio / History" opens with the lines "She makes complete her duration." Is this a complicated way of saying that Yu has lived her full life? No, Cha quickly indicates that "duration" refers to how Yu has been "rendered incessant, obsessive myth" (28). Again, Cha's concern is not the duration of a biographical life but that of an incessant present. "Clio / History" concludes with a meditation on the different temporal rhythms that make up this present:

Eternal time. No age. Time fixes for some. Their image, the memory of them is not given to deterioration, unlike the captured image that extracts from the soul precisely by reproducing, multiplying itself. Their countenance evokes not the hallowed beauty, beauty from seasonal decay, evokes not the inevitable, not death, but the dy-ing.

. . .

The decapitated forms. Worn. Marred, recording a past, of previous forms. The present form face to face reveals the missing, the absent. Would-be-said remnant, memory. But the remnant is the whole.

The memory is the entire. The longing in the face of the lost. Maintains the missing. Fixed between the wax and wane indefinite not a sign of progress. All else age, in time. (37–38)

In this passage, an organically whole "memory" seems to be the ideal against which we are to measure the deterioration of a "captured image." This deterioration is how we perceive the passage of time. Memory, meanwhile, is not associated with life but with timelessness—with being outside of time ("The memory is entire . . . All else age, in time"). In never referencing Yu's lived life, Cha gives these lines a melancholic feel: we have only a fixed, timeless memory and a decaying, captured image. But if the profile of Yu is a profile of presence rather than essence, then it makes sense that we are pushed to grasp time not through a lived life but a recorded one. The "decapitated forms" are not the result of a violent Japanese execution (the image shown on *Dictee*'s adjacent page). Instead, decapitation refers to the wearing away of recorded media, the marring of "previous forms."

What Cha calls a "captured image" indexes not only decapitation and deterioration but also mechanical reproduction. The coexistence of these conflicting modes of temporality within a captured image—natural decomposition and artificial regeneration—perhaps explains Cha's account of beauty: "the hallowed beauty, beauty from seasonal decay, evokes not the inevitable, not death, but the dy-ing." A beauty that is both hallowed and mortal, deified and decaying, describes not Yu herself, but her recorded and reproduced image. This mediated and manipulated portrait of a Korean heroine, Cha writes, is "fixed between the wax and wane indefinite not a sign of progress." By aligning the nationalist heroine Yu with indirection rather than progress, Cha imagines time as slowing rather than flowing. Barthes has said something similar about photograph enlargement: "I enlarge, and, so to speak, I *retard*, in order to have time to know at last."[67] Visual enlargement appears to move us closer to the subject, but in *Dictee*, this technique ends up replacing the truth of an individual life with a multiplicity of temporal orderings. As different temporalities collide, the captured image of Yu conveys neither progress nor stasis but suspension. As with Pahk's breathless harriedness, a suspensive slowness is borne out at the level of tone. A dilatory tone, in transforming the direction and temporality of modernity into a question, registers a critique of cold war modernization theory, which licensed American intervention in putatively backward nations such as Korea.[68] More than a critique, though, the directionless feeling of immersion in Cha's work also evidences an understanding of time that, as we will see, is specific to her post–cold war and post-colonial moment.

THE IMMERSIVE PRESENT

Yu Guan Soon is not the only nationalist trope that Pahk and Cha share. Both also use the metaphors of "operator" and "messenger" to describe a Korean female speaker. In fact, I'd contend that all of Cha's mixed media productions are preoccupied with this metaphor, for they literally and prolifically reproduce the mediums and mechanisms of communication. Related to communication technologies is the shared theme of amputation. For Pahk, amputation illustrates a belief that national modernization requires cutting one's losses: in the 1930s, this meant eliminating a colonial presence; in the 1950s, it meant policing a communist threat. In *Dictee*, we find a similar allegory: anatomical textbook images of "amputated" speech organs are immediately followed by a textbook map of a divided Korea. In Cha's case, however, these amputations invite a post–cold war reading. Where Pahk saw her speeches as channeling God for a cold war cause, Cha's speech parts—including both disembodied vocal organs and grammatical parts of speech—must be considered in relation to a post–cold war imaginary of information technologies.

Despite Cha's melancholic representation of Korean colonial history, her strategies for aestheticizing circuits of information in fact give symptomatic expression to a revised set of Korean, Japanese, and American relations. The South Korean state has often described its extraordinary capitalist gains in the language of economic nationalism and supplemented this economic discourse with appeals to Korean foundational myths. Yet it is neither economic strategy nor ethnic stock but two crucial geopolitical developments that account for Korea's economic takeoff in the 1970s. The first is the normalization of diplomatic relations with Japan in 1965, a surreptitious process that stoked public outcry. The strengthening of Korean–Japan security and economic cooperation was contemporaneous with demands for reparations, redress, and apologies as well as disputes over the sovereignty of the Liancourt Rocks.[69] In other words, Korea's relation with its former colonizer was characterized by economic intimacy on the one hand and political abrasiveness on the other. The second economic stimulus of the 1960s was the United States' colonial war in Vietnam.[70] Unlike the normalization treaty, Korea's contributions toward this effort stirred little controversy. And while the treaty with Japan included reparation payments, the dispatching of troops to South Vietnam was framed as repaying the United States for aiding South Korea's war against the communist north.[71] The Vietnam War not only paved the way for Park Chung-hee's militarized bureaucracy, but it also catalyzed industry, absorbing 94 percent of Korea's steel exports and 52 percent of its export of transportation equipment. Bruce Cumings writes that this economic boost "was a welcome irony, since Japan had gotten its economy off the mark through allied procurements in the Korean War."[72] These new arrangements with Japan and the United States, rooted in but departing from prior colonial relationships, were vital sparkplugs for Korea's so-called miracle economy. Through the treaty with Japan, Korea received $600 million in grants and loans. Through the Vietnam War, it received $920 million in U.S. military and economic aid.[73] More than aid, both these colonial relations also imparted long-standing cultural regimes. Chung-in Moon and Byung-joon Jun show how Park's "administrative democracy"—also known as "Koreanizing democracy"—"mixed the Japanese ethos of top-down mobilization and the U.S. ideas of technocracy with Korean nationalism in most un-Japanese and un-American ways to clear the way for economic growth."[74] Park's admiration for Meiji Japan has been well documented. John Lie adds, "much of South Korea's military-cultural revolution can be traced to the management ideas and practices of the U.S. military."[75] In short, the post–cold war triangulation of U.S.–Korean–Japanese relations begot an evolving set of ideas and practices. Through these, President Park instilled the belief that national vigor depends on an ethnocentric and patriarchal culture of militaristic discipline and industrial efficiency.

These revised neocolonial relations receive no direct representation in Cha's work. Yet her diasporic, "off-center" view of Korea can nonetheless "restore asymmetry in our perception," allowing new insights to emerge.[76] As we have seen with Pahk, historical transition means not only changes that one can mark out through discrete events and dates but also changes in how one inhabits, understands, and represents time. The increasingly transcendent tone of Pahk's cold war narratives shores up an ideal of civilizational progress and historical progression that obscures the competing temporalities and irreconcilable agendas of anticolonialism and anticommunism. Like Pahk, Cha is writing during a transitional phase in U.S.–Korean–Japanese relations. The tone of Cha's mixed media productions, however, is dilatory and directionless. If Pahk's accelerated thrust appears to smooth over the discrepant demands, logics, and timelines of Korea's colonial wars, then Cha's techniques of deceleration immerse us in an expansive present that we cannot see beyond. Even when Cha directly engages Korea's history of war and colonialism, for instance with the photograph of Yu, her suspensive strategies abolish clear cause-and-effect relations and impede our comprehension of beginnings, middles, and ends.

Such strategies communicate little through narrative or visual content, but they tonally evoke the experience of ongoingness. As the reproduced photo of Yu shows, ongoingness has both a monumental and mechanical quality. This tonal and temporal effect, moreover, often involves manipulating the viewer's frame of reference, for instance through cropping. To reinvoke Barthes, cropping is a technique of enlarging and retarding that allows one to "have time to know at last."[77] An even more exaggerated cropping of the sacrificial Korean heroine appears in the 1975 video *Mouth to Mouth*.[78] This eight-minute video opens with a brief pan of the eight Korean vowels. The majority of the video consists of a disembodied female mouth "speaking" these vowels against pixelated static. Instead of language, the audio track presents white noise intermingled with occasional birdsong and trickling water. *Mouth to Mouth* riffs on the colonial-era "articulatory organ" myth, which posits an organic continuity between the shapes of the

Korean script and those of the Korean mouth. The video also alludes to the association between Korean women and Korean vernacular culture.[79] But even without this knowledge, one can still locate an allegory of gendered nationalism. The physical duress displayed by the feminized and Orientalized mouth, a symbol of the vernacular and the organic, indicts a technological modernity that is coded as imperial, Western, and masculine. If interpreted allegorically, *Mouth to Mouth* would have us conceive of "mouth to mouth" as a mode of narrative and genealogical connection. It steers us forward through the successive appearances of one mouth and another or one vowel and another. A national language appears, then, as a source of genealogical descent that persists despite the encroaching forces of colonial modernity.

Yet despite its title, Cha's video actually hinders our ability to devise a narrative chronology or a national genealogy based on the relation of *mouth to mouth*. Instead, Cha insistently plays up the relation of *mouth to video*. Through the mouth's mechanical jerking motion, Cha "refigur[es] voice as a physical rather than subjective operation."[80] This biomechanical voice suggests that mouth and video are contemporaneous and competing technologies of representation; the operations of one trouble the integrity of the other (figures 3.3 and 3.4).

Mouth to Mouth displays a mutual dispersion of mouth into static and static into mouth: "Image and sound move in slow-paced dissolves," as the video's "restless 'snow' motion" generates a spatiotemporal slow motion.[81] Subverting our perception of direction and depth, the video closes off any assessment of closer or farther, inner or outer, convex or concave, forward or backward, foreground or background. As with Yu's photograph, we have no orientation or momentum for "advancement." The video's dissolution of ontological boundaries and enhancement of textured fissuring thus change our temporal framework from narrative progression and genealogical transmission (mouth to mouth) to directionless forms of ongoingness (mouth to video).

Mouth to Mouth "engulfs," "submerges," "suffuses," and "immerses" the viewer. These quoted words recur throughout Fredric Jameson's study *Postmodernism, Or, The Cultural Logic of Late Capitalism* (1991). For Jameson, the immersiveness of postmodern art testifies to the attenuation of historicity during capitalism's "late" or "multinational" phase. "Historicity," Jameson maintains, "can first and foremost be defined as a perception

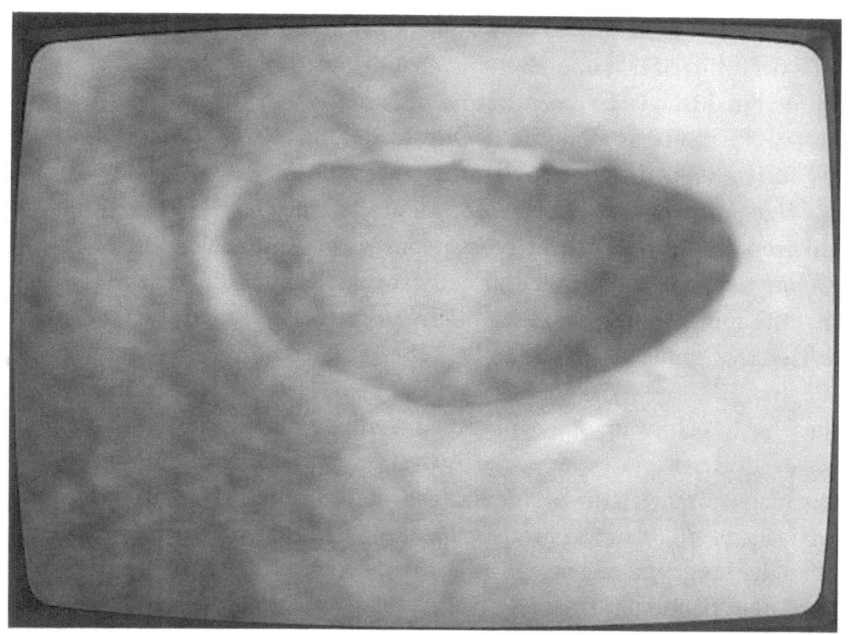
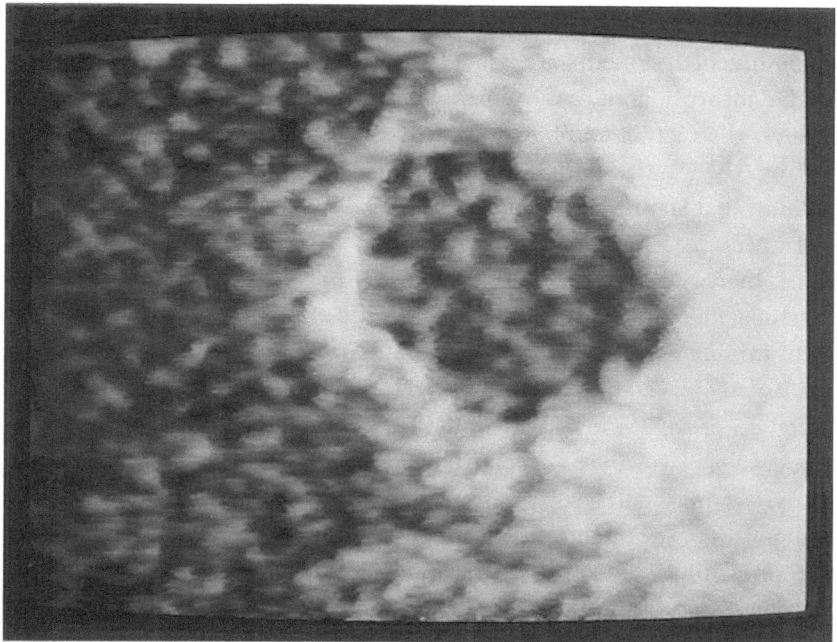

FIGURE 3.3., 3.4. *Mouth to Mouth*

of the present as history; that is, a relationship to the present which somehow defamiliarizes it and allows us that distance from immediacy." What blunts our historical perception is "our immersion in the here and now (not yet identified as a 'present')." Only by pulling out of this immersion can we initiate some distance so that the present becomes "not merely a 'present' but a present that can be dated and called the eighties or the fifties."[82] Jameson would likely identify two sources of "immersion" in *Mouth to Mouth*: the body and the medium. Regarding the body, he writes, "I believe that the contemporary or postmodern 'perpetual present' is better characterized as a 'reduction to the body.'" The "isolated body," he goes on to say, "begins to know more global waves of generalized sensations, and it is these which, for want of a better word, I will here call affect."[83] The "global waves" of sensations experienced by the body are akin to the "never-ending stream" characteristic of media, especially video art.[84] In Jameson's analysis, *medium*, or its plural *media*, is "a word that has tended to displace the older language of genres and forms." Genres "offer the richest symptom" of a "particular time and place." Media, on the other hand, produce extreme forms of depersonalization, to the extent that that "the auteurs themselves are dissolved along with the spectator."[85] In sum, for Jameson, embodiment and media are related forms of ahistoricity. Instead of a collective absorption into a movement of historical agents, passive immersion induces distraction and boredom. It is an aesthetic experience that shifts us from the Kantian notion of the sublime to the "anti-auratic, anti-cynical tedium" that Sianne Ngai calls "stuplimity."[86]

In *Mouth to Mouth*, immersion produces an expansive ongoingness rather than a clearly delineated "regime of the past-present-future" in which "personal identities and destinies" receive full elaboration.[87] Although Cha's eight-minute video is much shorter than Jameson's own example of video art, its "stream" is similarly unmoored from chronology.[88] Jameson's interpretation of *Mouth to Mouth* would perhaps mirror his analysis in *Postmodernism* of a "Language poem" by Bob Perelman called "China." In this analysis, Jameson first surmises that Perelman's poem does "capture something of the excitement of the immense, unfinished social experiment of the New China—unparalleled in world history." But Jameson then lambasts Perelman for erasing the historical and political content of "China" with stylistic techniques of "schizophrenic disjunction or *écriture*."[89] The "China" poem is one of many instances in *Postmodernism* when Jameson uses Asian references, namely China and Vietnam, as shorthand for a bygone socialism. In other words, "Asia" signifies a historical period of failed political revolution that precedes the ahistorical period of multinational capitalism. This sequential ordering of Western capitalism and Asian socialism makes it impossible for Jameson's theory of postmodernism to accommodate the changing profile of "Asia" at a post–cold war and late capitalist moment. Of course, Jameson would never mistake South Korea for a lost socialist utopia. Nonetheless, works such as *Dictee* and *Mouth to Mouth* raise kindred questions about how a rapidly morphing historical present influences aesthetic interpretations of the near past and the encroaching future. Cha's "Korea," like Jameson's "Asia," is also overdetermined by a specific conception of colonialism (culturally oppressive, physically violent, sexually exploitative) that is fixed in an irretrievable past. Just as Jameson's nostalgia for Asian socialism raises questions about contemporary formations of Asian capitalism, Cha's work compels us to ponder why all things "Korean" seem aligned with a prior colonial trauma at a time when Korea was becoming known as "the miracle on the Han."

Cha's mixed media productions emerged in the context of Korea's high-profile economic push and redress demands. Put another way, Cha inhabits the same historical present as the Korean military-state and wide-ranging populist movements, both of which attempted to exploit the binding powers of *han* (melancholy) toward national unity.[90] Though a diasporan, Cha is not immune to "a cultural regime of governmentality which aims to shape Koreans with signs of 'origin' and 'progress.'" This post–cold war cultural regime, according to Hong Kal, explains the continuity between Korean American Nam June Paik's video text *The More The Better* (1988) and a patriotic memorial hall in South Korea called *The Spirit of March First* (1987). Despite differences in style and content, these works both frame Korean modernity "as evolving from the 'local' ancestral origin to the utopian aesthetic (or anesthetic) space of perfect harmony and fulfillment with the 'global' world."[91] We can discern a similar dynamic in Cha's "postmodern" depictions of Korean suffering. Because Cha so emphatically centers the melancholic subject of colonial violence, her aesthetic strategies of fragmentation and indeterminacy have often been interpreted as disrupting totalizing narratives of History. Viewing Cha's period style as *post–cold war* rather than *postmodern*, however, can help us better recognize the changing nature of "war" and "colonialism" during a time of Korea's socioeconomic transformations.

We can best glimpse Cha's post–cold war interpretation of historical time in her prolific representations of communication systems and structures. I'm thinking here of the telegraphic codes in *Repetitive Pattern* (1975), the serial envelopes in *Faire-Part* (1976), the sentence diagrams in *It Is Almost That* (1977), the empty movie theater in *Commentaire* (1980), and the blank pages, undelivered letters, and anonymous phone calls across Cha's oeuvre. Considered alongside such works, *Mouth to Mouth*'s procession of vowels and *Dictee*'s reproduction of grammar lessons may be more in line with a post–cold war commentary on communication technologies than with the colonial disciplining of language and speech. Like many conceptual artists of the 1960s and 1970s, Cha has a penchant for aestheticizing lists, diagrams, copies, permutations, numbers, types, and inventories. These serve not to communicate a *specific* message but to foreground the *general* structures, components, and circuits that make up a communicative act. Lucy Lippard describes this aesthetic as replacing "traditional formal concerns of composition, color, technique, and physical presence" with "the process/product relationship of art, information and systems." Lippard interprets conceptual art's focus on "communication (but not community) and distribution (but not accessibility)" in relation to new regimes of knowledge work.[92] Even if these knowledge regimes were not exemplary of South Korea, which in the 1970s and 1980s grew its economy through export manufacturing, they nevertheless bear out a new hegemonic norm of labor within capitalist production, one that "creates immaterial products, such as knowledge, information, communication, a relationship, or an emotional response."[93] During the late twentieth century, the United States and Japan were more emblematic of the "new spirit of capitalism" and the new knowledge worker, whereas Korea was more often seen as an offshore site of assembly and manufacturing.[94] But the neocolonial intimacy between the American, Japanese, and Korean political economies also reminds us that immaterial labor and industrial labor grew up together during this period, even though the former is commonly viewed as superseding the latter. Although Cha never says in so many words that Korean rapid industrialization, Japanese Toyotism, and American post-Fordism are co-constitutive forces within global modernity, her aesthetic techniques help us see how post–cold war geopolitical rearrangements inculcate historically specific temporal experiences.

Cha's most "Korean" works are also the ones that most intensely dramatize an aesthetic of ruination. Take, for example, *Dictee*'s fossilized handprints, crumbling edifices, indecipherable etches, and fading photos. These artifacts serve to capture not lives but lapses. In contrast to artifactual ruins, which exaggerate a perspective of categorical temporal remove, Cha's troping of "immaterial products" (knowledge, information, communication) presents a more conflicted temporality. I'm especially drawn to *Exilée* and *Temps Morts*.[95] These two works are variations on a theme, inasmuch as "the condition of exile *is* dead time (*temps morts*)."[96] In these works, Cha frames her distance from Korea—her "exile"—as temporal rather than geographical. And even though Cha doesn't name specific geographical locales, she is recounting a return journey of some kind: "it dawns on me just the other day that / i have been back for months" (*Temps Morts*, 61). Unlike Cha's overtly "Korean" works, *Exilée* and *Temps Morts* do not locate "war" in a traumatic past. Instead, they depict the "dead time" of exile not as a time apart but as a temporal disorientation that is co-produced by ongoing, residual, and emerging regimes of colonialism.

Exilée and *Temps Morts* were published together in 1980 by Tanam Press. They were then reissued in a single volume by the University of California Press in 2009. Ed Park recalls that the first editions of *Exilée* and *Temps Morts* were boxed before the ink had dried; pulling apart each copy inevitably damaged the cover. Even if unintentionally, this 1980 edition made the sticky residue of ink an unavoidable part of the textual encounter, enhancing these works' emphasis on the medium of language. The glossy 2009 edition of *Exilée* and *Temps Morts*, on the other hand, has a commemorative feel. Its cover features Cha's photograph and "give[s] off the refulgent glow of relics."[97] The event of Cha's death endows *Exilée* and *Temps Morts* with new meaning. The remnant-words in these texts appear as refulgent relics because they are all that remain of Cha. The medial quality of the textual apparatus and the auratic quality of the deceased artist combine to give *Exilée* and *Temps Morts* a "somber tone." As a work of conceptual art and a crypt of authorial remains, the 2009 collection—not unlike the heavily edited image of Yu Guan Soon—has the feel of both a "multimedia display" and a "tomb."[98] This paradox is captured on the very first page of *Exilée*:

EXIL
EXILE
  ILE
  É
  É E (33).

One of *Dictee*'s most quoted lines concerns exile: "Our destination is fixed on the perpetual motion of search. Fixed in its perpetual exile" (81). Unlike this poetic description of spatial searching, the visualization of the word "exilée" invites a temporal interpretation, one that introduces heterogeneity into the inert absolutism of "perpetual exile." This visual arrangement is less a single word than a collection of alphabetical letters, each discrete and distant from the other. The atomization of communication into parts—sounds and letters—recalls the opening of *Dictee*, which also reproduces broken speech—groans, gulps, gasps, and swallows. As we might expect from Cha, the addition and subtraction of letters do not point us in any temporal direction. What may at first glance appear as a work of *de*composition—letters wearing away over time—could as well be a work of composition—letters that contribute to the formation of a multivalent linguistic expression. Cha's presentation of "exilée" as something in process, rather than a fixed state, compels us to wonder not who is exiled from where but toward which direction the present is unfolding. The text is caught between the competing directions of composition and decomposition, creation and destruction, wax and wane.

This oscillation is similar to what we find in *Dictee* and *Mouth to Mouth* insofar as it indexes the off-center location of a diasporic subject viewing "Korea." In *Exilée* and *Temps Morts*, however, the temporal distance between the diasporan and her homeland is figured not as ruination (crumbling remnants from an archaic past) but as jetlag (a condition of late capitalism and late colonialism). In both *Exilée* and *Temps Morts*, Cha names neither the United States nor Korea; we get no clear sense of where she is returning to or where she is exiled from. Instead, Cha represents exile as the experience of a sixteen-hour time difference. In *Exilée*, Cha attempts to evoke the "now" that lies "in between the one actual / to the another actual present."

This "simultaneous" and "alternate" present is calculated as "sixteen hours ahead of this time" (37). These lines portray Korea and the United States as parallel universes; the lived present of one place is the alternate reality of the other. Cha's avant-garde account of a return journey interestingly dovetails with the science fictional account of "future shock" discussed at the beginning of this chapter. For the social scientists, the experience of shock arises from an inability to reconcile the late capitalist Korea that they are returning to with the war-ravaged Korea that they had left. For Cha, the experience of lag is described as "exile," a term that indicates her similar reliance on "wartime" as a way to make sense of "dead time." In different ways, then, these diasporic returnees allow us to grasp the temporality of war as disorienting in its ongoingness—as troubling our expectations of exceptional violence, economic stagnation, and physical ruin. For all their thematic, stylistic, and generic divergences, these diasporans share a preoccupation with the feeling of history moving on when one is not present, of being left behind or exiled in a "Korea" of one's memory. Whether cast as future shock or jet lag, historical change feels like time travel.

To convey the lag and shock of being abandoned by history, *Temps Morts* conjures the figure of a telephone operator:

she tells me it's always the woman operator
she tells me it is sixteen hours
sixteen hours from here a head. (69)

In Pahk's case, you will recall, the female telephone operator underlines her ability to connect people across different cultures. Cha uses the same persona to describe the task of connecting people across different time zones. If, for Pahk, the operator renders the female speaker vehicular so that she can channel God, then for Cha this figure symbolizes the diasporan's inhabitation of a disjointed present. Instead of delineating an actual speaker, Cha documents the hesitations, shuffles, and half-steps of a subject whose perception of history is profoundly constrained—who is an exile because she can perceive but not process the velocity of historical transformation. This diasporic subject is

advancing memory collecting memory just to
just to look back in advance for souvenirs
happened or not happened at all (*Temps Morts*, 72).

The above passage on collecting memory/collective memory may seem to present us with Cha's melancholic subject, an exiled subject fixed in a perpetual search. But Cha actually guides us to view these repetitive yet intransitive actions—of looking back and advancing, happening and not happening—as the activity of a protracted "wartime." Representing this protraction, it seems, requires the late capitalist grammar of post–cold war globalization. By this I mean that the dead time of exile is a disjunctive, disconcerting temporality which, as Cha's grammatical tics imply, can only be described through conjugations of intransitive verbs: it is an experience of not knowing where one is located in relation to what has already happened, what has been happening, what is happening now, and what will happen.

Those familiar with Cha's work will know that verb conjugations appear across her corpus, most memorably in *Dictee*'s schoolbook lessons:

TRADUIRE EN FRANCAIS:

1. I want you to speak.
2. I wanted him to speak.
3. I shall want you to speak.
4. Are you afraid he will speak?
5. Were you afraid they would speak?
6. It will be better for him to speak to us. (8)

If *Dictee* casts translations and conjugations as language exercises for the colonial subject, then *Exilée* and *Temps Morts* reframe language as a privileged medium of late capitalist modernity. Cha's most illuminating account of exile as dead time thus appears in *Temps Morts* as a formal letter about corporate decision making, which then seamlessly transitions into a series of incomplete verbal phrases:

Dear Colleague,
It's amusing. But serious. You make decisions everyday; large and small. Decisions that could and often do affect your profession, your life-style, where you live and even with whom you live. They are important and necessary decisions that could have a <u>far-reaching impact on your life</u> not just today but in your future as well.

Far too often in today's quick-changing, fast-paced world, <u>new events and trends come along</u> that can catch us off-guard and <u>lead us into the dim world of "future shock</u>," the disorientation that occurs when the world changes faster than we can rearrange our thinking patterns, attitudes, and values.

It doesn't have to be that way. Not if you take are taking took have taken have been taking have had been taking had taken will take will have been taking will have taken will have had taken know are knowing have known have been knowing have had been knowing had known will know will have known will have had known say are saying said have said have been saying have had been saying had said will say will have said will have had said decide are deciding decided have decided have been deciding have had been deciding had decided will decide will have decided. (72–73, emphasis in original)

This letter departs noticeably from Cha's typical poetic idiom. Yet Cha also suggests that the letter's corporate speak forms the very stuff of her poetics. Phrases such as "far-reaching impact," "news events and trends," and "future shock" initially seem to convey something momentous, but they actually have an anesthetic effect. When the third paragraph declares "It doesn't have to be that way," one wonders if an alternative is indeed in order. The rhetorical shift that follows both is and is not a departure from the corporate jargon. The procedural enumeration of grammatical action hyperbolizes the repetition of cognate words such as "impact," "events," and "shock." In the long wake of intransitive verbs, subjects and objects fall away. What remain are permutations of the same action in different tenses. These verbal exercises dramatically elongate the action that they describe. In a sense, they provide the linguistic version of Barthes's observation that to enlarge is to retard. Neither simultaneous nor sequential, the subject-less and object-less verbs stage an energetic deceleration, or perhaps a perpetual vacillation. They falter rather than flow, producing a non-progressive movement, a layering of different times and tenses rather than a frenzied rush forward or a tripartite division between past, present, and future. Instead of purposeful historical change, clear-eyed individual decision, or divinely ordained patterns, we have an inventory of sheer variation. Compared to the euphoria of Pahk's physical and spiritual *transport*, Cha's aesthetic of systematicity offers but a vague feeling of *transience*. The shifts and stutters produced by this aesthetic bring to bear a tone of irresolvable uncertainty that lacks a subjective referent or an explanatory cause.

Exilée and *Temps Morts* provide conjugations of *to speak* and *to know* rather than *speech* or *knowledge* as such. This economy of verbs is reminiscent of Ishiguro's economy of rumors. But while Ishiguro's rumor aesthetic involves literally reproducing the same lines, Cha's permutations suggest a preoccupation with exhaustive variation and endless seriality. In Ishiguro's novels, a post–cold war tone is located in the rumor of race, which disables the autoethnographic truth of first-person narration. The tone of Cha's works, an effect of her procedural reproduction of communication structures, even more forcefully conveys motion without movement. Their enumerative intensity, moreover, shows that post–cold war regimes of perception—including the perception of historical change and the perception of racial difference—are conditioned by *variation* rather than *difference*.[99] Sianne Ngai has offered a helpfully historicist account of conceptual art's propensity for variation. Not only do serial displays of types and systems paradoxically beget a "lack of distinguishing characteristics," but this seriality produces a "*historically distinctive* characterlessness."[100] Ngai's diagnosis seems especially pressing for Cha, who uses informational systems to comment on race, ethnicity, gender, war, and colonialism—topics that rely on *difference* for their very conceptualization. The terms war and colonialism, for instance, imply *differentiated periods*. Hence, "post–Cold War" most often refers to 1989 and "post-colonialism" tends to designate the 1950s and 1960s. Meanwhile, race, ethnicity, and gender imply *differentiated subjects*. This is why our conversations about these identity categories tend to concentrate on those who are explicitly marked. In Cha's works, historical distinctiveness and racial difference are frequently supplanted by a taxonomic aesthetic. Instead of historical events and racial subjects, therefore, we encounter an enchantment with variation—with characterlessness *through* variation. *Variation* takes *difference* to an indiscriminating extreme. It is the tenuous threshold where difference shifts from a perceptual certainty to a perceptual challenge. What Cha's work obliges us to consider, then, is how the attenuation of perceivable difference in a "quick-changing, fast-paced world" (to quote from her "Dear Colleague" letter) undercuts our understanding of "race" as empiricized evidence and "history" as eventful change.

The many critics who have studied Cha's "aesthetic of infidelity" have endowed her work with extraordinary critical power.[101] By contrast, Ngai's concept-word for the post-Fordist evocation of serial variation is *interesting*—a descriptor that is notoriously held up as an example of critical vacuity. Cha's work, I think, demands our attention to both a resistant politics of strategic difference *and* a weak aesthetic of indifferent variation. Whereas an aesthetic of infidelity honors Cha's critique of cold war militarism, colonialism, and imperialism—exercises of power allegorized as the disciplining of female bodies and female speech—an aesthetic of the merely interesting situates Cha's work in relation to the geopolitical regimes of her own historical moment. By allowing for the presence of and tension between perceivable difference and exhaustive variation, a tonal reading helps us complicate not only politically redemptive readings of Cha's aesthetic but also critically dismissive readings of her alleged ahistoricity.[102] In this chapter, I've tried to avoid suggesting that Cha's work, by virtue of being more temporally advanced and aesthetically experimental, is more politically savvy than Pahk's "complicit" cold war autobiographies. At the same time, I've the rejected the claim that Cha's "postmodern" and "avant-garde" aesthetics are historically unrevealing, that they do not have anything worthwhile to say about the period from which they emerged. Rather than celebrate Cha's aesthetics of infidelity or denounce this aesthetic as historically benighted, I've shown how Cha's interest in the temporal dimensions of exile make her work unexpectedly insightful for understanding the vicissitudes of perception at a time of historical transition. A passing sense of variation may withhold any historically detailed representation, but it does communicate a post–cold war tonality and temporality. In using systems of variation to evoke a minimal nonactivity, Cha frames both racial difference and historical change as perceptual problems. Her time-based aesthetic neither redeems nor refuses a colonial past and instead documents the difficulty of perceiving and processing "difference" at a post–cold war moment.

THE HIGH PITCH OF HISTORICAL TRANSITION

At stake in a tonal reading is the ability to take stock of the strange and elusive temperament of geopolitical transitions. This historical temperament inheres not in a chronology of events but in "the tensions between competing historical directions" that erupt in "a particularly high pitch."[103] In this chapter, we first saw how Pahk's quick-witted, happy-go-lucky memoirs present a model of progress that valorizes steady and uninhibited forward movement. By thinking on her feet, Pahk disentangles herself from the quagmire of difficult politics that might bog her down. She deals lightly and swiftly with the past; to dwell is to stagnate. For her, self-representation is a kind of self-propulsion, a method of moving the individual ahead. As a narrative persona, Pahk does not so much develop as simply advance. In Cha's work, we encounter the inverse: self-representational strategies of delay, suspension, and hesitation dilate a singular essence into a stagnant presence. Dwelling in the long, hypnotic present of Cha's works, we have no resources for making meaningful distinctions between present, past, and future, and we have no firm basis for anticipation or recollection. An administrative and taxonomic aesthetic that "clocks the variations" dulls the prick of the *punctum*, turning it into the immersive expanse of tedium.[104] This recasting of Cha's work as more informatic than melancholic is not intended to deny her interest in colonialism and militarism. To the contrary, my contention has been that colonialism and militarism are just as central to the story of South Korea's miracle economy as they are to the stories of Yu Guan Soon, militarized sex work, and language education. In examining Pahk's and Cha's ostensibly ahistorical works, I've demonstrated how their self-representations can help elucidate the relation between global regimes of governance and the everyday people who inhabit these regimes but cannot yet recognize, analyze, or represent them. My aim has not been to condemn or celebrate Pahk and Cha for exposing or occluding the presence of "war" and "colonialism." Rather, both show us how settling an account of "war" and "colonialism" is never *against* colonialism or *after* war but profoundly implicated *within* them.

Chapter Four

THE TONE OF DOCUMENTATION

Combating the Brainwashee's Drone in Korean War "Testimonies" and "Confessions"

> There were many great historical events in China, yet there have not been outstanding historical novels.
>
> —HA JIN, "THE INDIVIDUAL'S STORY IN HISTORICAL EVENTS," LECTURE AT THE INSTITUTE OF EUROPEAN AND AMERICAN STUDIES, ACADEMIA SINICA, TAIWAN

The various immigration stories in C. Y. Lee's novel *The Flower Drum Song* (1957) may ultimately be less interesting than the author's own. Lee arrived in the United States in 1943 to study comparative literature at Columbia University. He ended up in Yale's playwriting program. After graduating in 1947, Lee moved west. In 1949, he was living above a Filipino nightclub in San Francisco's Chinatown, searching out "city scandals" for a newspaper column. By this point, Lee was sitting on an overstayed student visa. Each phone call he received brought fresh worries that U.S. immigration officials were onto him. One afternoon, Lee found himself on the line with a "gravelly voice" fielding probing questions. "Officer," Lee recalls saying, "I'm all packed. Deport me any time." The caller, it turns out, was from *Reader's Digest*. And the news was not deportation but publication: Lee had won a contest for his short story "Forbidden Dollar."[1] The combination of Lee's literary success and America's cold war liberalism would help him gain permanent residency. His novel *Flower Drum Song* would go on to inspire a popular Broadway play and film. Lee himself would be naturalized as an American citizen.

I start this chapter on Ha Jin with C. Y. Lee because their life stories offer parallel accounts of what it means to be an exilic author writing back to communist China. Like Lee, Jin views his literary career and his immigration history as inseparable. This link, moreover, was secured by

U.S.–China geopolitics. In Lee's case, the ability to come by legal residency and literary success shows how "World War II and the Cold War had dramatically improved the possibilities for Chinese students to resettle permanently and become Americans."[2] Like the Chinese Communist victory of 1949, the Tiananmen protests of 1989 "stranded" Chinese students in the United States.[3] Jin had been a graduate student in comparative literature at Brandeis University on June 4, 1989. He was among the 30,000 Chinese students whom President George H.W. Bush granted political asylum.[4] Post-1989 Chinese asylees and immigrants "substantially altered the demographics of Chinese America" in a way comparable to the post-1949 escapees from the Mainland.[5] In depicting newly arriving PRC immigrants, Jin and Lee both draw out the alienating experience of living in the United States and mingling among Chinatown Chinese. They also similarly tout the perspectival advantages of dislocation. Given the oppressive politics of the Chinese Communist state in 1949 as well as in 1989, both writers position the Chinese in America as singularly capable of presenting the most culturally authentic (Lee) and historically accurate (Jin) version of China.[6]

I'm hardly the first to place Jin within a cold war literary lineage. For Belinda Kong, Jin writes in the tradition of Chinese diasporic authors such as Lin Yutang, Han Suyin, and Eileen Chang, who all "produced novels in English about China."[7] Jing Tsu likewise cites Lin and Chang as Jin's analogues, although she focuses on their bilingualism.[8] To me, the key trait that Jin shares with these cold war writers is a critical stance against Chinese communism. What does it mean to use literature to take up an anticommunist stance in the 1990s and 2000s—that is, after the breakup of the Soviet Union and, more significantly, after China's economic liberalization? I view Jin, the recipient of numerous literary awards, as an especially representative figure among a cohort of writers and artists who together constitute one of the most socially legible versions of *post*–cold war anticommunism in Anglo-American culture. I'm thinking here of PRC writers whose works are banned in China and who self-consciously use literature—as opposed to journalism, scholarship, autobiography, or activism—to express dissent against the Chinese state. What links Jin to Mo Yan, Gao Xingjian, Bei Dao, Ma Jian, and Yu Hua is literary exile vis-à-vis state censorship. What distinguishes Jin from this prestigious cluster is his insistence on writing in English instead of Chinese.[9] But even though Jin has publicly committed himself to the English language and to an

American setting, his work has found a mixed reception in Asian American Studies.[10] Steven G. Yao, for example, accuses Jin of "critiqu[ing] a totalitarian communist regime primarily for consumption by an audience in the United States." Yao's aversion, though, is not just to Jin's pro-American content but also to his "plainly realist style."[11] This plain style does seem at odds with Jin's Asian American contemporaries, whose literary writings often ironize the task of racial and ethnic representation. By contrast, Jin is entirely earnest in his desire to represent Chineseness with the utmost accuracy. He intends his unadorned mode of writing as a distinctly literary choice, one that corresponds with his strong stake in both historical truths and humanist universals: "Unlike most academics, I do believe in universals and that there is truth that transcends borders and time."[12] Jin, in short, is a bit of a throwback. He is more anticommunist, ethnographic, and universalist than his contemporaries—and unabashedly so.

What can Jin's documentary style tell us about post–cold war anticommunism? How did enthusiastic declarations of anticommunist commitment during the cold war years give way to apparent political disinterest in a post–cold war era? This chapter tracks a shift in the relation between emotional expressivity and political credibility by reading Jin's fictionalized autobiography of a Korean War POW alongside the first-person accounts of actual Korean War POWs. Among the actual POWs, I devote particular attention to the U.S. Psychological Warfare Division publication *Wang Tsun-ming, Anti-Communist: An Autobiographical Account of Chinese Communist Thought Reform* (1954).[13] Wang's "autobiographical account" was obtained, transcribed, and translated by his captors. In other words, it is both a testimony and an interrogation report. I juxtapose Wang's account with Jin's *War Trash* (2005), also a generically ambiguous text.[14] Not only is *War Trash* a novel passing as a memoir, but it is also the product of in-depth research, complete with a bibliography of Chinese- and English-language primary and secondary sources. Fictional POW Yu Yuan and actual POW Wang Tsun-ming possess strikingly similar profiles. Both exploit their access to the Communists of the Mainland as well as to the Nationalists of the Republic of China.[15] In doing so, both strategically manage their ideological affiliations. Yet despite this apparent waffling, both in the end testify to the United States' moral supremacy. The most curious point of convergence between Yu and Wang is that both claim to be uniquely resistant to political indoctrination. This last point gets at one of the Korean War's defining features: it was largely fought at the negotiating table and in the POW compounds, both sites where "war" came to be construed as a primarily *psychological* kind of combat. Each side—the U.S.-led United Nations and the Chinese and North Korean Communists—sought to show the humaneness of their respective positions by turning captivity into an educational experience. The UN pejoratively referred to the Communists' version of this experience as "brainwashing," "menticide," "mind control," and "thought reform." Their own was called "reeducation," "reorientation," "reclamation," "rehabilitation," and "deindoctrination." Whatever its name, and whichever the side, the goal of prison education was to make a moral impression on "students" so as to effect a political conversion. Without a military victory in sight, the Korean War was to be won through armistice negotiations based on a tally of prisoners' hearts and minds.

Yu and Wang both tout their ability to survive "brainwashing" and, it would seem, to transcend their historical circumstance. Their dramatically different approaches to evidencing their psychological fortitude, however, illustrate the historical specificity of cold war versus post–cold war understandings of narrative and political reliability. Wang's first-person account, as the title indicates, is supposed to be an intelligence report on "Chinese Communist thought reform." For this task, one finds it exceedingly wanting. But what Wang lacks in factual coherence, he makes up for in ideological verve. His autobiography, like many first-person POW statements produced in captivity, parades his voluntary and unequivocal loyalty to free world democracy. The difficulty of reporting on communist indoctrination while demonstrating anticommunist allegiance results in a strange tonal quality. To make sense of Wang's excessively emotional and uncompromisingly ideological tone, we must take a closer look at the American overreaction to "brainwashing," allegedly a new mode of warfare innovated by the Chinese Communists that turned democratic individuals into unthinking automatons. Portrayed as a process of rewiring and rewriting, "brainwashing" shows how mid-century American concerns about psychological warfare and mass media found a common idiom. In other words, "brainwashing" was seen not only as a method of indoctrination but also as a technology of inscription, a way of impressing communist messages onto "washed" minds. This operation was most often likened to the workings of a phonograph, and the voice it produced was described as proceeding in a detached and even disembodied monotone. It is against this image of the brainwashee as an eerie phonographic voice that Wang uses a passionately embodied mode of speech to substantiate his psychological integrity. Wang's anticommunist vocality is also played up through the comments of his U.S. interrogators. In privileging fervor over fact, these interrogators reveal that in the context of a Korean War stalemate, a POW's autobiographical performance of American "reeducation" is more valuable than his intelligence report on Chinese "brainwashing." As a double agent serving a double function, however, Wang's interrogation-turned-autobiography ultimately exhibits an ambivalent tone and an uncertain agency. Has Wang been successfully "reeducated," or is he in fact still "brainwashed?" Are we encountering a thinking individual or a preprogrammed machine? By pursuing a tonal reading of Wang's report, we will find that the voice of a "reeducated" POW is just as strange, equivocal, and unhinged as that of a "brainwashed" POW.

War Trash's extensive focus on the volatility of inscriptional technologies inclines me to view ideological indoctrination—"brainwashing" and "reeducation"—as its unspecified but overwhelming topic. In Jin's novel, signatures are lifted and repurposed, military citations are verbally conferred but never documented, promissory notes are liberally distributed, and tattoos are repeatedly altered. Most significantly, the narrator copiously depicts forms of spoken propaganda, emphasizing the chasm between a party line and individual bodies. *Ideology*, as the novel defines it, is a disjunction between inscriptions and media. In this novelistic world, Jin's narrator is anti-ideological in more than the conventional sense. On the one hand, Yu Yuan's self-described "documentary manner" extends Jin's attempt to provide an objective account of the Korean War. In this regard, Yu's professed political disinterest is concomitant with his conscientious narrative detachment.[16] On the other hand, Yu's documentary style may have less to do with political belief than he'd like us to think. For if we understand ideology in the POW compounds as the alarming separability of inscriptions from physical matter, then we can also view Yu's documentary function as an effort to resecure this relationship. As I see it, then, Yu's "documentary manner" signals not an ability to maintain political objectivity but an ability to control inscriptional technologies—including even the tattoo on his body. Where Wang backs his anticommunist commitment with embodied passion, Yu shows how post–cold war anticommunism, directed against

Chinese state censors, takes the form of historiographic legitimacy. In *War Trash*, this legitimacy requires Yu to limit his speakerly presence and to compartmentalize *ideology* into a stable piece of historical evidence.

For Jin, the humanist, a documentary manner makes historical preservation a function of aesthetic autonomy (I will say more about this in the next section). For his detractors, such as Steven Yao, a documentary manner preserves not history but ethnographic exotica. For me, a documentary manner is an invitation to take "the cultural impulse to preserve... down to the unit level of records and documents."[17] A unit-level investigation allows us to contemplate what counts as historical truth by tracking how inscriptions find their media and by asking who mobilizes inscriptional media. This unit-level perspective also reveals that a documentary manner's capacity to preserve depends on a paradoxical literalness. Literalness here refers to both Yu's reproduction of the "notes and files" that he brings with him and Jin's consultation of the "notes and files" that he lists in *War Trash*'s bibliography (3). A documentary manner with a literal orientation is how Jin's work achieves its truth-effects. So powerful are these truth-effects that a number of reputed scholars, including Korean War historian Bruce Cumings, have cited *War Trash* with high praise.[18] However, the literalness of Jin's novel has also spawned numerous historical, ethical, and aesthetic quandaries. For example, in 2005, a Chinese journalist accused Jin of plagiarizing Zhang Zeshi's Chinese-language collection of first-person Korean War POW accounts. These charges turn the common accusation against Jin (that he is appropriating Chinese voices) into a matter of intellectual property. In the United States, *War Trash* has been subject to another kind of intellectual property dilemma, one that centers on its alleged creativity deficit. Criticisms of this book's stylistic and linguistic shortcomings fall in line with Jin's American reception history more broadly. A stripped and simple prose, it seems, makes Jin's work both stylistically distinct and distinctly styleless. Are we reading "a highly refined aesthetic of anti-excitability?" Or do we have an unrefined anti-aesthetic "conveyor belt" of "simple sentences, familiar sentiments, and uneventful three- to five-page chapters?"[19] These conflicting interpretations of Jin's documentary manner lead me to believe that post–cold war anticommunism exceeds the powerful historical determinant of the Tiananmen event. Certainly, a documentary manner, in signaling a strict adherence to historical truth, overtly corrects for the heavy hand of Chinese state censors. But the "conveyor belt" effect of a documentary manner also covertly clues us into the geopolitics of intellectual property rights insofar as a literal reproduction of the historical record discloses the inconsistent relation between political freedom and creative freedom.

If the cold war anticommunism of Wang Tsun-ming inaugurates a recognizably "free Asian" voice, then the post–cold war anticommunism of Ha Jin locates democratic freedom in authorship and creativity. Given the hypervisibility of the PRC artist in discussions of political expression,[20] it stands to reason that creativity discourse has not only given moral urgency to the Chinese government's suppression of free speech but has also consolidated a whole range of political issues under this catchall grievance. Because of its capaciousness, the slogan of free speech has been taken up by different factions and for diverse causes. The question that Jin's work raises is how to critique the authoritarianism of the Chinese state without automatic recourse to a triumphal American discourse of freedom.[21] Recognizing the importance of this balancing act, this chapter narrows the interpretive scope of free speech, which, in Jin's case, specifically concerns censorship—an issue of his publications being banned in China. As I will show, this specific issue articulates freedom to intellectual property, so as to align freedom of speech with freedom to publish. A commitment to literary publication, rather than to an openly political program such as "free Asia," is what gives the anticommunism of PRC diaspora writers a post–cold war cast. Jin is a particularly interesting case, for while his *authorial profile* has relied on equating political freedom with aesthetic creativity, his *authorial style* worries the relation between the two. Among American readers, Jin's documentary manner has been lauded for its uninhibited political expression, yet this same compositional style has also been denigrated for its lack of artistry and individuality. The lauders are gratified that Jin has produced a work that reads like an actual historical tract. The denigrators, meanwhile, deem his writing a plagiarized copy or a sloppy translation. A documentary manner, then, in the guise of both Yu's suitcase of archival documents and Jin's bibliography of consulted works, at times indicates reliable evidence and at other times suggests uncertain property status. A fidelity to the historical record may accord political freedom to the exilic subject within the geopolitical framework of Chinese authoritarianism, but this same technique shortchanges the credibility of the authorial subject within the geopolitical framework of Chinese piracy. These contradictions underpinning *War Trash*'s documentary manner make for a tonal effect that is differently estranging than the hyperbolically ideological accounts produced by actual Korean War POWs. In compelling readers to affectively confront the materiality of a document, the tone of Jin's novel conveys an instability between literalness and literariness, copying and creating. This documentary tone, I propose, lies at the core of Jin's *post–cold war anticommunism*.

THE ARTIST AS HISTORICAL VISIONARY

Like many generations of Chinese sojourners before him, Jin had planned to return to China. His goal had been to become a professor of American literature in a Chinese university. "I thought I would remain a Chinese writer and make book after book about China—in short, to translate history into literature," Jin says.[22] But after the events of 1989, Jin decided to stay in the United States. He also took up the pen for authorial instead of scholarly ends. And when he did so, he translated literature into history.

Jin's first English-language publication was a 1990 collection of poetry, *Between Silences: A Voice from China*. In the preface, Jin writes, "As a fortunate one I speak for those unfortunate people . . . who created the history and at the same time were fooled or ruined by it."[23] Two decades later, Jin would abandon the post of political spokesperson and refashion himself as a literary artist. In a 2009 essay collection, he expounds on the artistic condition of "rootlessness," which, for him, signifies not only a writer's lack of a homeland but also literature's immunity to political influence. Jin's artistic values are on the fullest display in "The Spokesman and the Tribe." This essay's humanist account of literature is hardly novel. The primary difference is that Jin specifies *historical preservation* as literature's "key function":

What was needed was one artist who could stay above immediate social needs and create a genuine piece of literature that preserved the oppressed in memory. Yes, to preserve is the key function of literature, which, to combat historical amnesia, must be predicated on the autonomy and integrity of literary works inviolable by time.[24]

In this passage, and in the collection as a whole, Jin does not name China. Nevertheless, judging from Jin's writings, lectures, interviews, and essays, it's clear that literature's "integrity" has been violated not by time but by the Chinese government. King-Kok Cheung characterizes Jin's position as such: "What is left unsaid in [Jin's] exaltation of literature is that its historiographical function can hardly be implemented in a country that polices and regulates publications." Cheung directly links Jin's "refrain about the primacy of literature" to his "political plea for artistic freedom in China."[25] Such a link indicates that, for Jin, delivering a historical truth requires transgressing the state-policed boundaries of individual expression and monitoring the moral boundaries of aesthetic autonomy. To contest the state by way of art is to fall back on the power of abstention. In the passage above, Jin renders both modest and heroic the "one artist who could stay above immediate social needs." He professes, "today literature is ineffective at social change. All the writer can strive for is a personal voice."[26] This diminishment of both literature and writer suggests that social inefficacy and political divestment are the prerequisites for being historically visionary. For Jin, "a personal voice" is one that projects an effete minimalism, a plain style for a plain person. The herculean tasks of preserving history and combatting amnesia, in other words, require both a minor subject and a minor method.

To be sure, this minor aesthetic of radical retreat privileges a masculine and anti-social position for critiquing the state. Jin's protagonists, conceived in his own image, are nearly all Chinese men whose victimization at the hands of the Chinese state is exacerbated by various forms of emasculation within their personal lives. These men tend to be some combination of scholar, poet, translator, and journalist. As artists and characters, they are both ordinary and exceptional. Their singular access to historical truth depends on their insignificance and fallibility—this is what distinguishes them from the communist flock. For example, in *War Trash*, Yu Yuan's *inability* to join his comrades in "laying down their lives for an idea" contributes to his *ability* to think beyond the polarizing ideological choices given him (250). The narrator of *The Boat Rocker* (2016) confides, "I knew I was relinquishing any chance of rising through China's officialdom to become a big man.... To be a free man also means to come to terms with my commonality."[27] At the compositional level, Jin's minor method emphasizes unobtrusiveness. Te-hsing Shan recalls a lecture in which Jin noted the difficulty of "finding a narrator who could be both close enough to observe the details of particular events, and yet free to move about so as to offer a broader perspective."²⁸ The narrator who possesses this profile is an observer-*non*participant, someone whose historical reliability is enabled by his impotence. While some of Jin's more recent characters are outspoken dissidents, Yu Yuan in *War Trash* is not. Yu's political, social, and sexual disengagement is a corollary of his narrative effacement. Rather than socialize with his fellow prisoners, Yu documents them. This self-effacing documentary approach allows a writer to serve historical justice on behalf of the "unfortunate people" without being their "spokesman." For both the narrator Yu and the author Jin, literary autonomy and literary integrity require presenting ideology from a distance—through the documentation of others rather than an individualized voice.

THE IDEOLOGICAL INSCRIPTION: THE PARABLE OF THE TATTOO

A closer look at Yu's self-introduction will clarify how my view of Jin's documentary method differs from his own. *War Trash* opens with a frame story. Here, we meet our narrator, a 73-year-old Chinese man who is visiting his son in Atlanta. We learn that during his time in the United States, Yu intends to compose a memoir about his experiences as a Korean War POW. The frame story explains this memoir's conditions of composition:

In eight or nine months I will go back to China, the land that has raised and nourished me and will retain my bones. Already seventy-three years old, with my wife and daughter and another grandson back home, I won't be coming to the States again. Before I go, I must complete this memoir I have planned to write for more than half of my life. *I'm going to do it in English,* a language I started learning at the age of fourteen, and *I'm going to tell my story in a documentary manner so as to preserve historical accuracy.* I hope that someday Candie and Bobby and their parents *will read these pages so that they can feel the full weight of the tattoo on my belly.* I regard this memoir as the only gift a poor man like me can bequeath his American grandchildren. (5, emphasis mine)

This frame story is a parable about authorship. The parable most obviously concerns writing in English and completing the manuscript in the United States, both tactics intended to ensure "historical accuracy." In this regard, Jin's protagonist in essence reiterates his own belief that "to preserve is the key function of literature." As we saw earlier, Jin, a humanist and an aesthete to the core, believes that literature, in its political disinterestedness, can transcend time and preserve history. The narrator Yu, however, introduces a more materialist and medial notion of historical preservation by likening his memoir to his tattoo. As a parable about authorship, *War Trash*'s frame story is also a parable about a "documentary manner," one that co-implicates the authorial body, the tattoo, and the memoir. *To preserve* is to inscribe marks onto a medium, whether it's words on a page or tattoos on a belly.

To make sense of this parable about documentation as inscription, we must backtrack to the novel's first lines: "Below my navel stretches a long tattoo that says 'FUCK ... U ... S ...' The skin above those dots has shriveled as though scarred by burns. Like a talisman, the tattoo has protected me in China for almost five decades" (3). Yu's tattoo is indeed talismanic. He receives it while imprisoned on Koje Island. When he wakes up to see the words "FUCK COMMUNISM" inscribed on his stomach, he reports: "As if stabbed in the heart, I blacked out again..., frightened by the thought that I might never be able to erase the words from my skin" (98). Despite Yu's initial alarm, his tattoo turns out to be an exceptionally malleable inscription. Upon relocating to a Communist camp, he has this tattoo modified to read "FUCK ... U ... S ..." so as to facilitate his repatriation processing. In the frame story, we learn that Yu, while in Atlanta, has arranged to have the tattoo surgically removed.

By opening his narration with the tattoo, Yu presents the body as subject *to* inscription rather than a subject *of* it. While compulsory tattooing during the Korean War indeed represents a staggering exercise of biopower, the subjection of Yu's body to inscription is less oppressive than has been supposed.[29] Yu's tattoo is no doubt involuntary, but its instability as an inscription repeatedly manifests as an asset—as a talisman even. Yu modulates his tattoo according to need. Meanwhile, his premonition of the tattoo's impossible erasure and his metaphor of being stabbed in the heart are fates lived out by other prisoners. In *War Trash*, memorable foils to Yu's advantageous tattoo are the grisly cases of Communist prisoners who have the skin bearing their tattoo physically slashed off, charred, or eaten. Yu even describes a Nationalist officer who cuts out and skewers a man's heart, thus turning the battle for "hearts and minds" into a literal mandate to "see the true color of [the] heart" (106).[30] Forcible tattoos offer us a version of "corpographies," a term that Andrea Bachner defines as allegories of citizenship in which "writing as a force ... takes hold of bodies and subjects them to meaning and power."[31] Yu's tattoo, however, is unexpectedly empowering. As a narrative device, it allows him to showcase his tactical management of the relation between inscription and body. Although Yu will turn out to be an exceptionally literary fellow, this early representation of "writing" is more physical than cognitive; it has to do with controlling the relation between inscriptions and the body. According to Carolyn Marvin, "bodies are displayed or concealed at different levels in literate practice to accomplish social work, namely, to locate their owners in a social and moral order." She writes, "the suppression of the body constitutes the condition and prerequisite for literate achievement."[32] As we will see, suppressing the body in order to achieve inscriptional authority is central to *War Trash*'s documentary manner. Yu's ability to regulate how inscriptions signify and how they transmogrify—beginning with his tattoo—appears in his memoir as an "ability to control the flow of information in Compound 602" (135).

Jin's frame story hints at the relation between bodily suppression and documentary authority by repeatedly showing how the fate of Yu's tattoo is tied to that of his memoir. Let us remember that Yu's tattoo provides the occasion for narration. The tattoo "FUCK ... U ... S ..." has protected Yu during his adult life in China, his opening lines tell us. Now that he is in the United States, however, "it has become a constant concern" (3). Yu takes pains to keep his tattoo hidden, not just from passersby on the street but also from his granddaughter and daughter-in-law. Fear of the U.S. authorities or of social stigma is one thing. But with regard to his family, Yu offers a very different rationale for keeping the tattoo a secret. When preparing a bath, he tells us: "I carefully lock the bathroom, for fear that Karie, my Cambodian-born daughter-in-law, might by chance catch a glimpse of the words on my belly. She knows I fought in Korea and want to write a memoir of that war while I am here. Yet at this stage I don't want to reveal any of its contents to others or I might lose my wind when I take up the pen" (4). Strangely, Yu presumes that exposing "the words on my belly" will divulge the contents of his memoir. Why should his daughter-in-law seeing his tattoo deter him from composing his memoir? The tattoo-memoir link appears once more in the closing paragraph of the frame story, which I quoted earlier. Here, Yu bequeaths his memoir to his Asian American grandchildren. He hopes they "will read these pages so that they can feel the full weight of the tattoo on my belly" (5).[33] Why doesn't Yu want his family to *see* his tattoo but to *feel* its weight by reading his memoir? How does Yu's composition of a memoir relate to the removal of his tattoo?

If the first two stages of the tattoo's evolution (from Nationalist slogan to Communist slogan) show that the legibility of a Korean War prisoner depends on ideological affiliation, then the removal of this tattoo seems to enact Yu's liberation from ideological inscription and to function as an analogue to his politically disinterested memoir. One key question begged by Jin's novel is whether being unmarked by ideology equates to being free from ideology. Since the answer is clearly no, the question then becomes why Jin's post–cold war anticommunist ideology requires not just the rhetoric of political disengagement but also the gesture of bodily suppression. Yu's commitment to shielding his family from his tattoo implies that their apprehension of ideology in its viscerally embodied form would invalidate his forthcoming documentation of ideology in a historically accurate form. Reading a documentary account about a tattoo allows one to access a history of ideological interpellation by experiencing the weight of this history without viewing "ideology" directly. Or, put differently, Yu's readers can encounter history through its "feel"—through the heft of its inscriptions instead of the distortions of its content. Interestingly, a U.S. intelligence study published in 1958 adopts a similar perspective: "one of the basic objectives of the casebook is to supply the reader with a 'feel' for the realities of a psychological warfare operation, and thus through such means to enrich his experience directly without exposing him to the events themselves."[34] This language of "exposure" betrays an underlying worry about the reader's susceptibility to an especially insidious brand of ideological indoctrination. In such a scenario, providing a "feel" of history can protect readers from "the events themselves." In *War Trash*, indoctrination is not only a matter of ideological initiation, for it carries the additional danger of assimilating the wrong version of history. If, as I argued in chapter 2, the tone of rumors can have an affective pull independent of their content, then we might make a similar case for Yu's memoir, which conveys the feel of history through the tone rather than the content of documentation. Yu would have us believe that a documentary tone, the byproduct of a hefty inscriptional apparatus, can feel more historically accurate than an immediate encounter with the false evidence of a shape-shifting sign. For Yu, this shape-shifting sign is his easily manipulable tattoo, which he must shield from his family's direct gaze. For Jin himself, the physical manifestation of indoctrination is his source material—the ideologically tainted "true stories" provided by Korean War POWs, which he has taken upon himself to transcribe and translate through a documentary style.

Yu's administration of the relationship between body and tattoo—medium and inscription—secures his documentary authority. Whereas other prisoners succumb to ideological indoctrination (and, literally, ideological inscription), Yu is distinguished as a *character* by his literary rather than political interests, and he is distinguished as a *narrator* by his management of, rather than submission to, inscriptional technologies. In *War Trash*, the horrifyingly compromised relations between words and papers, slogans and bodies, intensify the sense of crisis and confusion in the POW compounds. Not only does the "double character" of inscriptional forms seem especially exploitable during times of war, but an incongruity between the "material and semiotic" may constitute the very terms of ideological warfare.[35] For Yu, we might then say, "ideology" lies not in the content of a message, "fuck communism" or "fuck US," but in the unstable relationship between inscriptions and media that makes the two slogans so easily interchangeable. Yu's documentary manner corrects for the unreliable media that circulate throughout *War Trash*. He has at his disposal a raft of documents, which he transcribes to authenticate the historical reliability of his story. In a sense, Yu's ability to stabilize inscriptions and to render them accountable exemplifies what constitutes a document as such. Matthew Hull writes, "documents [are] instruments for materializing reference and predication in order to establish and communicate a stable relation between discourse and individuals, actions, objects, and environments."[36] By this account, the stable document and its materialization of reference can create an impression of reliability that is entirely separate from any literary virtue that one might associate with a narrator who reads a lot.

War Trash's portrayal of ideological indoctrination as a process of material inscription is integral to my understanding of the Korean War. That is to say, it reinforces my belief that "brainwashing"—the management of inscriptional technologies in relation to the impressionable mind—was the key terrain on which "war" was waged. The rhetoric of brainwashing that the Korean War popularized reflects the more general characterization of communist warfare as a psychological assault, a process of turning individual voices into automatic recordings. To understand the significance of brainwashing discourse during this time, we must acquaint ourselves with why the Korean War was seen as exceeding the boundaries of "conventional" warfare.

"BRAINWASHING" AND THE PRISONER REPATRIATION CONTROVERSY

The notion of conventional war is related to conventions of periodization. Bruce Cumings has observed that it is because "most American wars have begun when 'the other guy' fired the first shot" that the bombings of Hiroshima and Nagasaki have been remembered as the means to end the Second World War instead of as the rush to "start the cold war."[37] By a similar logic, we tend to view June 25, 1950, when a North Korean soldier opened fire, as the *start* of the Korean War instead of the *continuation* of an ongoing war "by other means."[38] Based on this periodization of the Korean War—to be sure, a conventional periodization of a conventional war—President Truman mobilized U.S. forces to assist South Korea as a defensive response to North Korean aggression. Fifteen other nations also contributed troops to the United Nations Command (UNC).[39] Five months later, the Chinese People's Volunteer Army (CPVA) entered the war to back the Korean People's Army (KPA). Defining and dating the Korean War based on the firing of shots, however, grossly mischaracterizes this war. Equally misleading are terms such as "police action" and "proxy war," which contribute to diminishing the Korean War into an altogether forgettable war. The Korean War caused no shortage of alarm—but it had little to do with the conventional fronts of combat.

One of the many skirmishes that rivaled the war being fought on the battlefield took place at the negotiating table. The Korean War truce talks began on July 10, 1951, in Kaesong, before moving to Panmunjom. Journalists placing bets on how long negotiations would last put the "pessimistic estimate" at six weeks.[40] These negotiations would end up requiring 575 meetings over the course of more than two years[41]—perhaps a premonition of the still protracted negotiations between North Korea and South Korea, which continue to be brokered by the United States. Inarguably, the most contentious issue in Panmunjom, the one that held up negotiations for fifteen months, was prisoner repatriation. Rosemary Foot writes, it is "astonishing to consider that the U.S. administration would contemplate unleashing nuclear war against a supposedly secondary enemy [the Chinese and North Koreans], ostensibly in response to the failure to agree on this one outstanding point."[42] In the face of a military stalemate, prisoner *non*-repatriation became the basis for claiming a moral victory or, as Foot puts it, a "substitute victory." Each side wanted POWs to realize the moral rightness of their captors and to voluntarily refuse repatriation to their homeland. Article 118 of the 1949 Geneva Conventions thus became subject to intense scrutiny. This article had been devised in response to the Soviet retention of German and Japanese prisoners after WWII. It provided that POWs "be released and repatriated without delay after the cession of hostilities." The Chinese and North Korean negotiators pushed to enforce the article, phrasing the issue as "the withholding of prisoners versus their automatic return." The UNC, however, contested the article by asserting a distinction between "voluntary repatriation" and "forcible repatriation." The consequences of forcible repatriation were dire indeed: "To return [a prisoner] into slavery would amount to enslaving a free person, and neither the United States nor any officer under their authority can enslave any human being."[43] In essence, a CPVA or KPA soldier's experience of captivity in the "democratic" UNC compounds was seen as the attainment of freedom, the transcendence of the Communists' "slavery." To force this newly freed prisoner to repatriate to North Korea or China after their release was thereby tantamount to enslavement.

The repatriation dispute begot a number of racially motivated suppositions. For example, the UNC accused the Communists of violating Article 17, which required prisoners to identify themselves to their captors. U.S. officials lamented that Oriental POWs could only be identified by fingerprints, for it was impossible to put name to person: some names could not be Anglicized, some prisoners provided false names, other prisoners exchanged names, and still others—in keeping with assumptions of the Oriental's psychological infirmity—"actually forgot their original names and gave another name." Thwarting identification was one way that a "new type of prisoner," the "Oriental Communist prisoner of war," took the fight from the conventional battlefield into the prison compounds. One study alleges that prior to May 1952, the U.S. "had no conception of either the Oriental mind or the Communist ideology. The combination of the two created a major puzzle for camp authorities."[44] The figure of the new prisoner was closely tied to that of the new negotiator. Communist delegates at Panmunjom were even accused of masterminding prisoner mutinies on Koje Island and Cheju Island.[45]

The most sensationalist version of Korean War Orientalism was the elevation of propaganda or indoctrination into the mystical domain of "brainwashing." A range of authorities, from government officials to journalists to scientists, stipulated that the Chinese had "persisted in violating the provisions of the Geneva Conventions by . . . subjecting the POW's [sic] to a peculiar, and heretofore unknown, mental indoctrination." Putatively honed by Oriental cunning, the "techniques used by the [Chinese] Communists" were believed to be "so advanced" that they resembled "a psychoanalytic or almost hypnotic process."[46] The American public's fears of UN prisoners' mass susceptibility to communist ideology escalated following Edward Hunter's 1950 story in the *Miami Sunday News*. Hunter estimated that one-third of UN POWs had been "turned" in captivity.[47] The nation's increasing concern about the democratic virility of young American men not only stoked fears of enemy infiltrators but also fanned the fires of homophobia. One *Newsweek* article speculated that of the Americans who were reported to be brainwashed, "about half . . . were bound together more by homosexualism than Communism." In a similar vein, Michael Rogin discusses how "momism" gained explanatory power for the POWs'—as well as the United States'—lack of manly fortitude. Race, religion, criminality, and education also factored into these public conjectures. Adam Zweiback reports, "Discussion of the black nonrepatriates in the white press highlights public perceptions of Communism and civil rights in the mid-1950s."[48] In 1953, "brainwashing" mania reached a fever pitch. This was when Americans discovered that of the 12,773 UN prisoners held in Communist custody, 21 U.S. prisoners (along with one British and 347 Chinese and Korean prisoners) had snubbed the chance to return to their homes in the free world. These non-repatriates were derided as "brainwashed" turncoats. Ironically, though, of the 75,801 total Communist prisoners, the 21,820 Chinese and Koreans who refused to return to the PRC and North Korea were seen as affirming the superiority of democracy.[49] The implication here is that only Americans can be brainwashed. The same strategies, when applied by Orientals to Orientals or by Americans to Orientals, fall into another realm. The Communists were embarrassed about how their numbers panned out, but the U.S. public was no less than alarmed. In the showdown of "mind to mind, culture to culture," the Americans "not only did not hold our own, but we failed signally."[50]

The entry of the CPVA into the war was seen as shifting the battlefield from the body to the mind through a "lenient policy." While the North Koreans were known for their brutal treatment of prisoners, the "Chinese to our great bewilderment would greet each captive with a smile, a cigarette, and a handshake," Colonel Willis A. Perry recalls.[51] What followed such civilities was perhaps the distribution of writing utensils. This is because the "confession" was a premier instrument of brainwashing. To quote one study: "Seldom did the brief autobiography prove sufficient. The prisoner was usually compelled to write more, and in greater detail." Then, someday, he "might discover that he had written a confession of some kind."[52] These confessions logged in private and used in interrogations could extend up to 500 pages.[53] The most notorious confessions, however, were of the public variety. UN "progressives" confessed to an array of crimes across multiple media platforms. An especially worrying case was the apparent brainwashing of high-ranking U.S. airmen Frank Schwable, Floyd O'Neal, and John Quinn, who in radio broadcasts confessed to bacteriological warfare. Prisoners also mailed their families communist publications with lurid titles ("Out of their Own Mouths") and made dramatic confessions ("torture, rape, arson, looting, and cold-blooded murder").[54] To riff on the famous characterization of the Korean War as a proxy war, we might view "brainwashing" as feeding broader cold war fears of agents speaking in a proxy voice: out of his own mouth, the POW "speaks 'his master's voice.'"[55]

Monica Kim has shown how the story of the Korean War interrogation rooms, as a paradoxical site of liberal warfare, cannot be reduced to brainwashing. Yet her suggestive characterization of the POW's body as an archive—as "a kind of text to be read, assessed, and evaluated"—offers a useful starting point for my interest in how brainwashing provides the scaffolding for broader cold war preconceptions about forgetting and remembering, falsity and truth.[56] The term "brainwashing" designates a specific relationship between body and inscription. According to the *Oxford English Dictionary*, to *forget* is to "lose one's hold"; it is to be dispossessed in a bodily sense—to forfeit a "getting." In the U.S. cold war imaginary, brainwashing was a forgetting in that it produced a grotesque disjuncture between a free world speaker and a communistic message. Its iconic image was of a prisoner speaking in a trance-like state, as if programmed to produce "a whole train of thought, from beginning to end" and "to go on as if manipulated by instincts alone."[57] A year after the Korean War armistice, President Eisenhower would adopt similar language to describe the war against communism: "They preach a material dogma that is abhorrent to us, a dogma coated with false promises. They speak it with a single and a tireless voice, while the free world speaks with diverse tongues a message that demands from each responsibility, perseverance and sacrifice."[58] By drawing a contrast between "a single and a tireless voice" and "diverse tongues," Eisenhower frames a battle over political "dogmas" as a matter of whether the voice that speaks is connected to the mind that thinks. Brainwashing tropes also proliferate in David McLean's documentation of the "cranks, nuts, and screwballs" who sent the CIA tips: "A fairly common complaint of the walk-ins is getting messages from the Communists by thought-transference or through the fillings in their teeth. One disturbed gentleman from Buffalo claimed the Communists had kidnapped him, cut open his head, removed his brains, and substituted a radio."[59] Of course, the most famous cultural elaboration of brainwashing is the 1962 film *The Manchurian Candidate*. Here, the scene of brainwashing is introduced through an acousmatic voice, an off-screen speaker chirping about air drainage. To signal the American brainwashee's liberation at the movie's end, we are told that "the wires have been pulled."[60] These wide-ranging examples show how a media-inflected discourse of brainwashing came to be absorbed into cold war vernacular culture, even if its specific incarnation as a mystical weapon of psychological warfare had been more or less disproved on scientific grounds.[61] And because American culture so consistently imagined brainwashing as enacting the unnatural and immoral detachment of voice from body, it in turn promoted an ideal of the democratic subject as someone who could speak their mind with embodied zeal. This is the subject we appear to find in Wang Tsun-ming's documentation of his "reeducation."

"BRAINWASHING" AND "REEDUCATION"

Cast against the dreary drone of the "brainwashed" subject's confession, the free Asian's passionate testimony was to provide confirmation of a speaker's genuine presence and democracy's moral supremacy. In the actual testimonies of "brainwashed" and "reeducated" captives, however, we are confronted with a deep-seated ambivalence at the level of tone. This is the case even for Wang Tsun-ming, a POW whose testimony was so compelling that his American captors turned it into a standalone document.[62] This document, also known as the Wang Report, was contracted by the U.S. Army and conducted by William C. Bradbury, with the aid of Lloyd E. Ohlin and Richard P. Harris (for simplicity, I'll reference only Bradbury from here onwards). One possible explanation for the added attention Wang received is his comportment: "Wang Tsun-ming is clearly a vigorous man of action. He is also unusually lucid and articulate. He is tall, with an impressive military bearing" (vii). By introducing Wang through his exceptional vigor, unusual lucidity, and impressive bearing, and by linking Wang's physicality to his articulateness, this intelligence report already seems more concerned about Wang's style of delivery than his actual statement. Indeed, Wang's recollections of the events between March 1950 (when he was taken into Communist custody) and May 1951 (when he surrendered to the UNC) will turn out to be more valuable for the tonal effect they produce than the intelligence they provide.

In order to comprehend Wang's tonal performance of "reeducation," we must first unpack the logic of "brainwashing" that he outlines. In Wang's telling, Chinese brainwashing appears as a finely tuned mechanism that inscribes ideological scripts onto blank brains. This inscriptional mechanism operationalizes a symbiotic relation between speech and writing, one that structures the POWs' daily "lessons." These lessons include:

1. a lecture requiring "voluminous notes";
2. a "small class" in which students "read their notes from the Big Class";
3. a discussion of "aspects of the current topic that are still not understood";
4. a public "report to each instructor"; and
5. group "criticism of daily behavior." (28)

This interplay of note-taking and discussion, of oral and written confessions, casts indoctrination as reflex training. Rewiring is a process of rewriting: to inscribe an ideological message onto the brain, one must repeatedly inscribe it onto paper. If successful, this rewired and rewritten message will then flow automatically from the mouth. The confessional *I* produced by this Pavlovian mechanism appears as a dystopian counterpart to the liberal conception of the autobiographical self. If autobiographies enable personal truths, then confessions yield inevitable lies, for the compulsive telling and retelling of one's story through "formal instruction, group discussion, confession, and self and mutual criticism" creates occasions for self-contradiction (v–vi). To speak without end about oneself and about one's compatriots facilitates a kind of self-delusion, which in time leads to the "physical and mental liquidation of one's self by one's self" (33). Contrary to the *bildung* apparatus that transforms a self-referential speaker into a self-determining subject, we thus have a case of discursive self-annihilation. Wang explains: "Our senses were practically destroyed. We could think of nothing else. We could think of nothing. Our movements were mechanical. We became like tools" (46). Brainwashing may have been useful in helping the Americans explain how the "communists had come to accept their own 'enslavement,'" Timothy Melley writes, but this idea that autobiographical self-reflection could turn the individual into a tool "posed a serious problem for dominant western thinking about subjectivity."[63]

Edward Hunter uses a provocative metaphor to describe the conversion of a self-possessive individual into an unfree automaton: "The same topic is gone over again and again and again, until the mind of the student rings like a phonograph record that has stuck at a point where it soporifically sings." Elsewhere, Hunter writes that the eeriest element of a "confession" is not what the brainwashed subject said but "the unnatural way in which he said it." Specifically, Hunter writes, "His speech seemed impressed on a disc that had to be played from start to finish, without modification or halt."[64] While Hunter's first quotation conveys the gridlock of the mind's thoughts, his second suggests the unchecked flow of speech. When read together, these accounts of brainwashing delineate the mind's transformation from an agent into a medium, a self-willed speaker into a phonograph record, and a truthful testimony into an inhuman tone. The phonograph appears as well in Joost Meerloo's account of "automatic confessions": "The brainwashee lives in a trance, repeating the record grooved into him by somebody else." As "false admissions are reread, repeated, hammered into his brain," the confessor "is forced to reproduce in his memory again and again the fantasized offenses." Meerloo's study is distinctive in that it offers one of the most explicitly Orientalist explanations of brainwashing *and* one of the most painstaking accounts of brainwashing's link to mass media.[65] In the Korean War POW compounds, "the Communist propaganda lectures were directed toward retraining the prisoners' minds."[66] In

American society, we can find the same "slow hypnosis in the wake of mechanical mass communication."[67] In explaining the democratic world's gradual regress, Meerloo hypothesizes that as modern life brings "the entire world daily into each man's home ... there is scarcely any hiding place from the constant visual and verbal assault on the mind." Inspired by Pierre Teilhard de Chardin, Marshall McLuhan makes a similar point about the porous barrier between the inner self and the outer world: "This externalization of our senses creates what de Chardin calls the 'noosphere' or a technological brain for the world. Instead of tending towards a vast Alexandrian library the world has become a computer, an electric brain, exactly as an infantile piece of science fiction. And as our senses have gone outside us, Big Brother goes inside."[68]

McLuhan demonstrates how brainwashing rhetoric became a filter for more general concerns about the deleterious effects of mass media. For Susan Carruthers, this generalization of brainwashing marks a shift from "excoriating the 'communist threat' from without" to "probing the enfeebled American psyche" within.[69] The causes of the enfeebled psyche were legion. Throughout the cold war years, communist mass psychology was discussed alongside an assortment of cultural preoccupations, from homosexuality to hypnosis, experimental drugs to CIA conspiracies.[70] Despite their different connotations, these forms of psychological vulnerability all denote an uptick in national anxiety regarding democratic individualism. Moreover, the articulation of these fears as an encroachment on liberal subjectivity enforces the idea that brainwashing can only be meaningful for a highly specific Western individual. We might recall here McLuhan's well-known fascination with the infiltration of "ear-culture" into Western techno-society. As he would have it, only in advanced societies can television and radio produce trancelike states whereby "literate individuals are suddenly gripped by an electromagnetic field."[71] Being brainwashed is in a sense analogous to being what McLuhan calls "retribalized"; this degenerative process can happen only to the civilized and not to those who are *already* tribalized. It is interesting to note that while in the 1950s American behavioralists began calling for an explicitly anti-ideological and implicitly culturalist approach to the cold war, an approach that would espouse "conventional behavioral paradigms rather than a battle of ideas,"[72] Chinese American researchers of the same era were fiercely ideological in their denunciation of communism but deeply resistant to the notion that the

Chinese are somehow culturally predisposed to indoctrination: "exposure of the [Chinese] masses to the Communist propaganda does not necessarily mean their acceptance of the propaganda."[73] Despite these efforts to counter the suspicion that Chinese brains are naturally "washed" and American ones naturally intact, even the most matter-of-fact accounts of the Korean War indirectly endorse such a perception. Again, only the 22 American and British non-repatriates who opted to stay in the PRC were deemed "brainwashed." The Asian non-repatriate prisoners who chose the PRC and North Korea were not. The Asian non-repatriates who chose Taiwan or South Korea were likewise not seen as subject to ideological duress. To the contrary, these "reeducated" or "deindoctrinated" prisoners were commended for their voluntary decisions.

Wang Tsun-ming's autobiography allows us to perceive how the propagandistic portrayal of "voluntary repatriation"—a portrayal necessary for an American moral victory—operated in tension with the unstated assumption that Orientals are in some sense always already brainwashed. So even though the Wang Report is technically supposed to provide intelligence on communist indoctrination, we can actually view it as a study on whether Orientals can be successfully reeducated into free citizens. In this report, not only does Wang demonstratively flaunt his loyalty to anticommunism, but his privileging of ideological consistency over logical consistency also makes him a rather poor informant. For example, at one point, Wang scoffs at the Communists' lack of originality, for it is "possible for anyone to escape [their] deception" (51). Later, though, he reports, "A lot of the men just go crazy" (53). One suspects that the most fundamental aim of the Wang Report is not to gather an accurate picture of Chinese brainwashing but to render present a free Asian who can speak his own mind. This is why Bradbury largely ignores Wang's contradictory remarks and comes out in strong support of him, even as uncertainty clouds the report. On the one hand, Bradbury praises Wang's "unusually strong" sense of "distrust and dislike" toward the Communists and deems these sentiments the source of his success in resisting indoctrination. Yet in the very same line, Bradbury proposes that Wang's "conformity was not a mere surface yielding" (vi). This equivocation suggests that as much as Bradbury wants to acknowledge the alarming efficacy of brainwashing, he finds it more urgent to show that Wang has been successfully reeducated.

The double aim of the Wang Report—to net intelligence on Chinese brainwashing and to validate the presence of a free Asian—results in a generic conflict between a prisoner interrogation and a non-repatriate testimony. In the report's preface, Bradbury frames the forthcoming account as a "nearly verbatim record of Wang's replies," presumably to an interrogation (vii). Yet the body of the report flips the script so that Bradbury appears as an interpreting listener who is evaluating Wang's self-representation. In this body text, Wang's first-person narration is double-spaced throughout, whereas Bradbury's third-person commentaries appear single-spaced and with extra-capacious margins. The uncertain relation between Wang and Bradbury contributes to the report's ambivalent tone. Although someone who has "simultaneously served the purposes of the Communists and developed a bitter-end will for revenge" likely invites suspicion, Bradbury tries to subtly mitigate this suspicion rather than openly confront it. But even as Bradbury invites Wang to testify to his psychological integrity, he also can't seem to shake the possibility that this integrity may already be compromised. Bradbury's third-person commentaries are intended to summarize: they present "additional information acquired several weeks later." Yet this seemingly objective presentation of "additional information" often also shuffles in additional *emotion*. In some instances, the fact that Wang "launched into a long, impassioned description" serves to underscore his anticommunist commitment and psychological infallibility (21). At other times, there is a touch of skepticism in Bradbury's observation that Wang "seemed to place a great deal of stress on his own participation in organizing these breakouts, particularly as evidence of his resistance to Communism" (21).

Particularly noteworthy is Bradbury's reliance on asterisked footnotes to introduce emotion, vigor, and "presence" into Wang's account. This unusual use of footnotes appeared during a time when the footnote was being phased out of intelligence. John A. Alexander remarks, "the suppression of footnotes was part of one's overall conversion from scholarship to intelligence: the paramount need of intelligence was a timely answer to a current problem." Because reliable intelligence depends on timeliness, "the higher the level of intelligence product, the less complete is its visible documentation."[74] Although Alexander goes on to defend the footnote, others worry that footnotes detract from the authority of the intelligence officer by literally outsourcing it.[75] The dilemma presented by the Wang Report is that Bradbury's authority is linked not to external sources but to Wang's psychological status. As Bradbury's informant, Wang is only credible if he has been successfully reeducated. Bradbury's desire to certify the presence of a politically reliable and psychologically infallible speaker thus leads him to repurpose footnotes to reference Wang's inner resolve and embodied vitality. On one occasion, Bradbury's footnote makes mention of Wang's "considerable humor and laughter" (37). On another, it indicates Wang's "severe emotional stress" (40). The combination of Bradbury's excessively emotive observations and Wang's relatively measured testimony make for a disembodied tonal quality not unlike that of a brainwashed subject's confession. This disorienting tonality is especially apparent in Wang's recollection of being forced by the Communists to compose a false letter. This letter leads Wang to betray his Nationalist compatriots. He explains:

I knew that all the men felt guilty in violating the old moral code between officers and men, and I knew that they would not hold me strictly responsible for the letter I had written, because they too had realized that I had been forced to do what I did. (32)

Bradbury then offers the following asterisked interpretation:

As he told this story, Wang gave evidence of being highly emotional and upset. This seems to have been an extremely *distressing* experience and it was surely a *distressing* confession to make to strangers. Moreover, he manifested great bitterness toward the communist pressure and trickery which had forced this kind of behavior. (32, emphasis mine)

Notice the difference in Wang's account and Bradbury's description of it. Yes, Wang expresses guilt in being forced to betray the anticommunist cause. But it is only in Bradbury's account that we encounter *distress*. Curiously, the *experience* of Communist captivity and the *recollection* of this experience are said to be equally "distressing" for Wang. By using the same adjective, Bradbury underlines Wang's capacity to remember and experience afresh, drawing an implied contrast between the robotic automaticity of a brainwashed subject and Wang's emotional responsiveness in the moment and in the flesh. If "communist pressure" on the impressionable mind typically produces a sensory retraining, Bradbury implies that this pressure merely reinforces Wang's "bitterness." The net effect is that Wang's emotional capacity is doubled. While in Communist custody, Wang's emotional reserve ensures his resistance to brainwashing: "their consequent effort to remold and control him reinforced his hatred," Bradbury writes (vi). Then, while in American custody, Wang re-experiences the same emotions.

This emotional doubling suggests a parallel between the Communist-coerced confession that Wang is describing and the U.S.-endorsed testimony that he is currently making. Indeed, there are several parallels between these ostensibly antithetical experiences. The report tells us that Wang received "intensive political indoctrination for three months" under the Communists' watch in March 1950 and again completed a "three month rehabilitation program" after being repatriated to Taiwan in 1954 (x, xi). In addition to the parallel three-month experiences of "indoctrination" and "rehabilitation," he also underwent three "interviews" with U.S. personnel that mirror the "interrogations" to which he was subjected by the Communists. The autobiographies that the Communists used "to check our activities in the past" seem little different from the autobiographies that Bradbury collects, which "are mutually consistent at the many points of overlap" but with "one significant exception" (viii, 26). This significant exception appears in a section on "New Evidence of Unreliability." Here, Bradbury questions Wang's account of two incidents that had supposedly caused the Communists to mistrust him. Though it's unclear what exactly makes Wang untrustworthy, the "evidence" notably raised suspicion for both his Chinese captors *and* his Americans ones.

The Wang Report, in short, reveals "brainwashing" and "reeducation" to be related technologies of memory. If Chinese brainwashing was seen as exploiting the chasm between an embodied speaker and a preprogrammed message, then something called American reeducation might be glossed as an endeavor to re-secure the moral relation between body and voice. In strategically using documentary devices to corroborate Wang's successful reeducation, Bradbury seems to believe that the appropriate expression of emotion could distinguish the free Asian from the brainwashed Oriental. Through such documentary devices, we might say that the Wang Report brings into view the prosthetics of anticommunist feeling. The footnotes, asterisks, spacing, and indentations that this report mobilizes discreetly add and certify sincerity while also conveying a qualifying tone.

THE TONE OF DOCUMENTATION

FIGURE 4.1. U.S. leaflet depicting "brainwashing" (Credit: New York Public Library)

The footnote, as a designated instrument for notating evidence, warrants special consideration. Bradbury's use of the footnote to authorize the fact of anticommunist emotion constitutes an effort to align race with ideology. Put differently, footnotes allow Bradbury to provide evidence of the inner feelings—the true stirrings of anticommunism—that the POW, due to his already compromised "Oriental mind," may not have been capable of exhibiting.

TRUTH!

Once attuned to this tonal uncertainty of an interrogation/testimony, we must question all hyperbolic expressions of anticommunist commitment. Indeed, when we glance at other first-person accounts produced by

FIGURE 4.2. U.S. leaflet depicting "reeducation" (Credit: New York Public Library)

reeducated prisoners, we find that commitment cannot be but excessively demonstrative and prodigiously evidenced. U.S. propaganda leaflets dropped among CPVA and DPRK combatants often include words of endorsement from current POWs (figures 4.1 and 4.2). These are generously sprinkled with exclamation points, as if interrogations conducted (or testimonies solicited) in captivity elicited rousing shouts of joy and excitement instead of silence or fear. The tone of propaganda, whether an effect of "brainwashing" or "reeducation," always possesses an out-of-body quality, something asterisked and tacked on, a strategic punctuation that transforms a statement into an exclamation. This tonal effect is supposed to verify organic emotion, but it betrays an inhuman animatedness, an excessiveness veering on ventriloquism.[76] Rather than lending credence to the speaker's true beliefs, this propagandistic tone suggests that a POW's "reeducation" or "deindoctrination" was emerging from a highly pressurized situation of uncertainty and distress.

The tonal resonance between the brainwashed POW and the reeducated POW is unsurprising given the remarkable similarity between Chinese Communist "study" sessions and the American Civil Information and Education Program (CIE).[77] CIE was an "orientation program, planned to be the most effective means for the UNC to inculcate a more favorable attitude among POW's [sic] toward western and democratic ways and to instill distrust of communist ideology." In October 1950, the United States launched a pilot version of the program among Korean prisoners. Instruction began in earnest on a small scale in June 1951. These early instructors were "chosen from among qualified POW's [sic]." Later, 104 instructors were recruited from Taiwan and Hong Kong.[78] Although conversion to Christianity was an early indicator of the program's efficacy, the intensification of armistice talks around repatriation made "prisoner petitions and other forms of refusals of repatriation" the "ultimate test of success."[79] These letters and petitions detail the phenomenal results of CIE programming, framing U.S. imprisonment as the start of a new life free from communist slavery. One prisoner says: "[The Communist] method of teaching was to cram, push and repeat the subject.... The CIE program let the men think for themselves." Trying in every way to substantiate their ideological position, the prisoners curse "the Iron Curtain" and pledge to "fight the communists to my death."[80]

Although displays of maudlin sentimentality and hawkish patriotism ran rampant among non-repatriates, not all prisoner testimonies sat well with the UNC. One man, who lamented having to fight his "own people," was labeled "unreliable" for "his short military service and dislike of military life," which led to "disinterest ... in the information offered."[81] Another untrustworthy figure was Han Hak Kyo, a high school teacher. Han, "short and slender" and "not too neat" in appearance, was, according to his interviewer, "reluctant" and "very unfriendly." Han's report proceeds as follows:

It is good to be given the opportunity to write down a part of my lifetime as a poor man of Korea, a country which has had a 4,000 year history of struggle under adverse circumstances and enjoying none of the cultural advantages of other countries. I am very discouraged about my future, the merits of our ancestors and the happiness of our posterity. To be truthful, a happy sightseeing voyage on the smooth sea is a desirable thing, but we must have a firmer determination to overcome our future difficulties. We must be prepared for the rest of our lives to struggle for existance [sic]. I will try to become a well-educated man who is able to search for truth in the world.[82]

Han's sole reference to his captors comes indirectly, when he calls the interview an "opportunity" to recount his past. From there, Han becomes increasingly resigned. He doesn't pledge life and loyalty to the free world, nor does he glorify his captors' cause. His account of North Korea lacks personal particulars and political signposts. Rather melancholically, he hints at Korea's long "history of struggle" under successive colonial regimes. Instead of declaring his hopes of fighting the Reds to a valiant death, Han submits to being "very discouraged" about his future and Korea's. His take on this future is meandering and vague, alternating between hope and despair. Calling "the rest of our lives" a "struggle for existance," he implies that the "democratic" conditions of the UN compounds, far from infusing him with the promise of freedom, offer a foreboding indicator of postwar life. His concluding desire to be "well-educated" and "able to search for truth in the world" lets on that education and truth are lacking in his current environs.

Han's dream of "a happy sightseeing voyage on the smooth sea" is uncannily reproduced in *War Trash*. Here, we encounter Yu Yuan staring out at the water and dreaming of another life. Watching the boats at sea "for hours on end," he "imagined myself making a living as a fisherman on the ocean" and "longed for an untrammeled life" (101). For Yu, an untrammeled life means repatriating to another country, "a third choice" that would free him "from the fracas between the Communists and the Nationalists" (313). In an interview with Jin, Jerry Varsava writes that this "Third Way" is "the human way."[83] Similarly, Ian Buruma claims that Yu's ability to "think for himself" makes *War Trash* "a fine novel on the human condition."[84] But while Yu's desire to skirt political allegiances endears him to select readers, Han's expression of similar sentiments is interpreted by his interrogator as "very evasive" and "untrue."[85] This assessment is accurate in that Han *does* evade ideological specifics, and he *does* presume the existence of a "truth in the world" that is incongruous with Truth in the Free World. But that this desire for a truth shorn of politics is viewed as *un*reliable establishes Han's difference from Yu. As we will see, Yu's efforts to document a truth free from ideology reflect a disdain towards the effusive anticommunism fostered by Bradbury and the CIE. Whereas U.S. intelligence officers privileged embodied vocalizations of feeling, Yu associates the spuriousness of ideological commitment with the fickleness of spoken evidence. The affective relationship that *War Trash* seeks from the reader is not identification with an emotionally expressive narrator but belief in a documentary narrator's historiographic authority.

THE WEIGHT OF HISTORY

As discussed earlier, Jin, in framing his oeuvre as a response to Chinese state censorship, advances an ideal of literary aesthetics that takes *history* rather than *beauty* as an operative term. Nowhere is Jin's literary devotion to historical truth clearer than in *War Trash*.[86] Which is to say, insofar as this novel is generally regarded as Jin's most historical work, it stands to reason that it is also his most literary one. *War Trash*'s historical and literary aspirations culminate in its documentary manner. Jin, one might note, often uses a clipped, matter-of-fact prose to represent historical trauma—a style of writing that some have deemed inappropriate to the subject matter.[87] *War Trash*, however, is documentary in the narrower sense that our narrator has brought with him the "notes and files" to document his POW experiences. Yu's opening reference to "all the material I had collected for this memoir" perhaps corresponds with the bibliography of works that Jin had consulted in writing his novel (3). Both narrator and author use documents to render commonsensical the relation between media and inscriptions. Through this documentary method, Yu distinguishes himself from his fellow prisoners, and Jin distinguishes *War Trash* from the first-person accounts on which it was based.

If Jin's other "historical" novels seem jarring due to the contrast between their detached style and gruesome content, then in *War Trash* the more dramatic disjuncture is between the narrator Yu's sterile documentary manner and all the other characters' ardent speech. This tonal disjuncture pits Yu's human limitation against his compatriots' patriotic heroism. Yu's political effeteness is what gives him historiographic legitimacy. That is, his documentary manner allows him to speak truth through powerlessness:

The truth was that our field armies had advanced so fast and so deep that our supply lines had crumbled. (emphasis mine, 19)

In truth, although I was calm in appearance, I was apprehensive at heart. (emphasis mine, 38)

[*T*]*o be honest*, I'm not a Communist. The reason I cannot sign up for Taiwan is that I have an old mother at home. (emphasis mine, 76)

We see here that even at the most colloquial and nondescript level, Yu's modest admissions of incapacity merge with his intrepid assertions of truth. The above sentences show that unlike Wang, Yu's immunity to ideological indoctrination has little to do with the strength of political belief. Rather, Yu is able to document ideology without succumbing to it because he hardly *has* a presence, because he withdraws himself so thoroughly. This approach to truth-telling is the lesson imparted by the novel's most quotable line: "Who can bear the weight of a war? To witness is to make the truth known, but we must remember that most victims have no voice of their own, and that in bearing witness to their stories we must not appropriate them" (299). Yu's treatise against appropriating voices is ironic since this is the very accusation that has been leveled at Jin, most literally with the plagiarism scandal. Before addressing this aspect of *War Trash*, I want to more carefully scrutinize Yu's claim about witnessing truth but not appropriating voices. As I see it, the answer to the question "who can bear the weight of a war" is no one—or no *person*. Yu's recurring metaphor of weight—the weight of a war and the weight of a tattoo—always points us to the memoir as a historical tract. To convey the weight of a dehumanizing war and a humiliating tattoo, *War Trash* attempts to approximate the weight of inscriptions—of a tattoo that mutates into a memoir, of the "notes and files" that Yu transports, of the bibliography that Jin compiles. Despite championing historical accuracy, what the novel ultimately offers is less the *facts* of history than the *feel* of history—or, as Yu might put it, the weight of history.

Yu's bookishness, we are led to believe, is responsible for his psychological resilience and his historical reliability. But, Faith Watson writes, *War Trash* "is as much about the *uses* of text, language and identity as it is about the narrator's POW experiences."[88] Watson's observation helps shift the focus away from Yu's cognitive faculties and literary disposition and toward his relation to documentary technologies. Ideology, for Yu, consistently manifests as a disconnect between evidentiary forms and the party line. Yu's anti-ideological stance thus comes down to a disenchantment with how ideology warps documentary evidence. For example, Yu is "dubious" about the issuing of citations: "I had been awarded three already, but never had I seen a medal" (242). He is outraged when his higher-ups order him to impersonate another prisoner by taking his ID tag. After Yu receives a letter of recommendation from an American lieutenant, a Communist superior rips it apart.

Yu's most heroic achievements, meanwhile, involve righting these evidentiary lapses. In fact, when a fellow prisoner speaks up on his behalf to communist officials, every example spotlights Yu's dexterity at remedying the pitfalls of unreliable media:

"Look, Comrade Yu Yuan did make a mistake in mixing with Priest Woodworth. But he *got stationery from him* and passed it on to me. Unlike most graduates from the Huangpu Military Academy who paid only lip service to our Communist cause, Yu Yuan helped us and participated in our struggle constantly. He saved Commissar Pei by *speaking to the American commander* Smart before our comrades boarded the ships bound for Cheju Island. Nobody among us could do that, could we?" A few men shook their chins. Ming went on, "When he was jailed in the troublemakers' cell, he led two comrades in *creating the Pei Code*, without which communication between Commissar Pei and the camp would have been impossible. Later he helped his battalion chief *get a falsely signed document back* so that the enemy officer couldn't use it to clear himself of his crime." (343, emphasis mine)

Yu procures paper, retrieves a stolen signature, creates a semaphore system, and serves as an interpreter. With the exception of interpreting for Commissar Pei, all these examples present a decidedly *physical* approach to communication. More specifically, they provide thematic instances of Yu's centrality to the material movement of information and the material regulation of truth in the POW compounds. This materiality is also foregrounded in Yu's account of conducting literacy lessons for the prisoners. These lessons are far more about the finding, making, and using of tools than about the content or techniques of reading and writing. Yu inscribes transliterated Chinese characters on the ground to teach prisoners English. Tooth powder serves as chalk and rain cloths as the chalkboard. Stars made of iron sheet and red paint are distributed as rewards. Prisoners make pen nibs out of tinplate and use tobacco tar for ink. Lacking paper, they spread sand on the bottom of cardboard boxes. The novel's most impressive communication contrivance is the Pei Code, cited above as one of Yu's contributions. Part semaphore and part Morse code, the Pei Code, also called "the Walking Telegraphic Method," is used to transmit messages through body movements and walking. The method is ingeniously documented in a "booklet" made of toilet paper and a shoelace (224, 225). As these examples show, if there is anything about his fellow prisoners that Yu admires, it is their innovative approach to pursuing literacy under extenuating circumstances. Analogously, we might deduce that Jin admires the POWs' craftwork more than the actual words in their memoirs. From tin stars to recycled leaflets, *War Trash* provides an evocative picture of the myriad handicrafts undertaken by actual prisoners (figures 4.3, 4.4, and 4.5).

In depicting literacy as manual practices rather than mental ones, *War Trash* is less about a personal *voice* than a personal *touch*, a sense of writing as artisanal. To vernacularize writing is not to give it the inflections of speech but to describe the everyday tools and craftsmanship that go toward *making* it. But a handmade booklet, as one might suspect, is not among the "notes and files" that Yu brings with him. And if it is, it certainly doesn't appear in his cache of documents. Instead, Yu's documents include transcriptions of loudspeaker announcements; radio broadcasts; communist constitutions; excerpts of the Geneva Conventions; and various signs, agreements, receipts, and book passages. When we encounter Yu's transcriptions of these documents amidst various accounts of the prisoners' materialist compositional practices, we cannot but compare them.

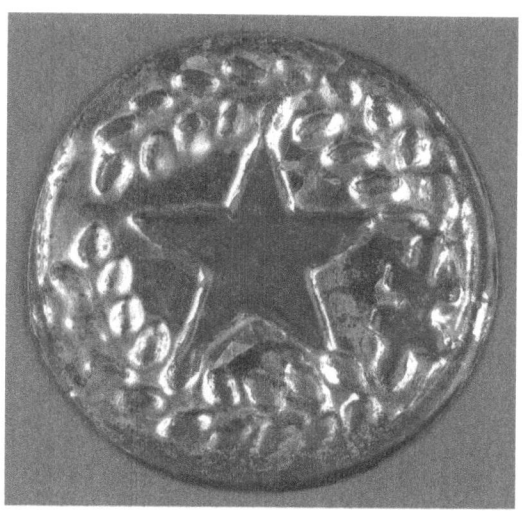

FIGURE 4.3. A star made of a Coca Cola bottle cap, created by Communist POWs on Koje Island and taken to the United States by Lt. Richard A. Weiss, U.S. Navy (Credit: New York Public Library)

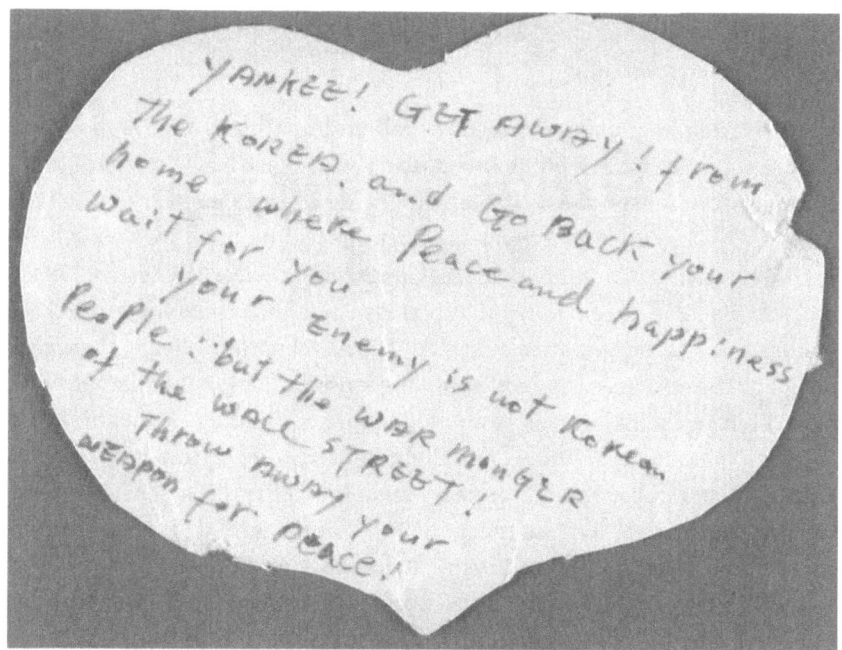

FIGURE 4.4. Heart cut out of scrap paper, created by Communist POWs on Koje Island (Credit: New York Public Library)

THE TONE OF DOCUMENTATION

FIGURE 4.5. Handmade booklet, created by Communist POWs on Koje Island (Credit: New York Public Library)

Yu's documentary manner possesses a literal quality in that he provides verbatim transcriptions of his "notes and files." These transcriptions, however, lack the "sensuous specificity" of writing as a species of "the mechanical arts."[89] They are not *actual* reproductions like the kind we find in Theresa Hak Kyung Cha's archival autobiography *Dictee*. What *War Trash* seeks to evoke is not a history that is fragmented or pieced together, but a history that is freighted with evidence. The novel's truth-effects, therefore, lie not in the document as an ethnographic object (texturally specific toilet paper) but in the document as an evidentiary instrument (a "frame" that certifies its content).[90] This is why Yu's documentary manner, in the service of "historical accuracy," appears less physical and less sensuous than the unconventional writing methods he observes and describes. To distinguish between the feel of historical accuracy and the feel of a physical document, we might note an anthropological precedent. While ethnographers have long documented the exotic writing practices of "primitives," it is only in the past three decades that they have begun to "look at" instead of "look through" their own documents.[91] Yu's description of how a young prisoner uses a pencil contrived of tinplate and a pipe is reminiscent of Claude Lévi-Strauss's observations of the Nambikwara people's unorthodox use of pencils and papers.[92] Inscriptional practices become more "material" when they are deployed by an "other." And given how many studies on paperwork have focused on colonial governance, and given how often a caged African antelope is cited as an example of a document's relation to evidence, we could also say that the provincializing gesture of scrutinizing "our" documentary methods is likewise easier when these practices are being applied toward an "other."[93]

The documentary tone of Yu's narrative—what I have been describing as the feel or the weight of history—serves as a foil to both the suspicious media in the compounds (propaganda) and the artisanal writing practices of his fellow prisoners (homemade pencils). To underscore the evidentiary function of his own "notes and files," Yu trains these documentary devices on the politically unreliable "others" in his midst. When we come across Yu's documents in transcribed form, the stability of inscriptions on paper is never in question. Instead, the document stabilized as evidence is the manifestation of Yu's implicitly thematized ability to fashion "truth" out of unreliable media. If rigorous documentation is *especially valuable* in the context of a war that has turned all media into a kind of propaganda, then Yu's documentary manner is *especially noticeable* when it reproduces propaganda as artifactual evidence. Just as Yu implies that his tattoo cannot be seen directly but must be "framed" or "documented," he seems keen to dramatize the act of documentation when dealing with other ideologically saturated inscriptions.

Nearly all the documents that Yu transcribes and thereby neutralizes are instances of propaganda. Some of these belong to the Americans and the Nationalists, but most are products of the Chinese Communists. An especially revealing example appears in the scene that Jin is accused of plagiarizing. This scene details the Chinese prisoners' capture of American General Matthew Bell. The document that's pivotal to the incident's resolution is an agreement drafted by the prisoners that outlines the conditions of Bell's release: "I promise to immediately stop our barbarous behavior, our insult and torture of Korean and Chinese prisoners, such as forcing them to write reactionary letters in blood, threats of solitary confinement, mass murdering, rifle and machine-gun shooting, using poison gas, germ weapons, experiments with the prisoners for the A-bomb"

(182). Yu expresses alarm over this "wild piece of writing," which essentially accuses the UNC of "brainwashing." His alarm is echoed by Bell himself, who refuses to sign the document and deems its language "inappropriate" (183). While the events that take place in the chapter on Bell are based on the actual capture of Francis T. Dodd, the chapter's documentary effects, such as the above agreement, are fictionalized. Unlike the elaborately quaint descriptions of how the prisoners produce and use inscriptional media, this document—like all of the documents that Yu reproduces—is a bureaucratic instrument in and of itself. Such documents do not exaggerate their sensuous materiality, and they are not particularly significant for their content (I wonder how many of Jin's readers have read the entirety of the United Communist Association's constitution). However, for these reasons, Yu's documents are all the more effective at evoking the feel of history: they are reproduced rather than made, and they emphasize the framing rather than the content of evidence. The tone of documentation *connotes* historical accuracy to the extent that it *denotes* reproducible documents.

As the case of "wild" writing suggests, Yu's exhibits of documentation serve to underscore the outlandishness of communist propaganda. This show of documentary remove is especially crucial when propaganda comes in the specific form of overemotional speech. In fact, Yu is so keen to distance himself from spoken propaganda that he hardly speaks at all. As a character, Yu possesses a retiring asociality that makes him a keen observer and a passing participant: "I was quiet and preferred to be solitary whenever it was possible" (246). Rather than socialize, he enjoys "reading English-language newspapers" and often "craved a good book" (271). When arguments take place among leaders, we can find Yu "on an upturned crate listening without expressing my view" (253). Yu's social isolation exempts him from dialogic participation. Speech, when attributed to Yu's fellow Chinese prisoners, is shot through with ideological jargon, be it the communist enjoinder "Comrades, we must live or die together!" or the equally ardent anticommunist declaration "Fight the Red bandits to death!" (29, 328). If Chinese speech is coded as propagandistic, then American English is vernacularized as racist:

Someone said in English, "Damn, we let some of the gooks get away."
A breezy voice answered, "Relax, man. We got eight of them, not bad."

THE TONE OF DOCUMENTATION

"Are they Koreans or Chinese?"
"Must be Chinks."
"How can you tell?"
"They don't wear no uniform." (40)

An especially hot-blooded strain of speech, one that Yu frequently transcribes, is the spirited scene of a rallying assembly: "Applause broke out. A man shouted, 'Fight the Red bandits to death!' We all raised our fists and repeated the slogan" (77). Another kind of gathering is the songfest, which, Yu tells, us is the "most popular form of entertainment." The prisoners compose songs for every occasion. One such occasion is a prison battle for a flag. Yu reports that he disliked this "fighting anthem." Yet despite the fact that he supposedly "never learned to sing it," Yu nonetheless provides a verbatim reproduction of the anthem's lyrics. Such a move is no doubt aberrant within the world of the novel. Indeed, Yu's entire documentary apparatus, his capacity to "recall these events with almost photographic accuracy," defies logical explanation.[94] But when we consider the novel's historical stake in a documentary aesthetic, the uncensored transcription of all nineteen lines of the prisoners' "fighting anthem" seems entirely in keeping with Yu's task of providing historical weight. Through this transcription, Yu gives us a feel for the difference between experiencing ideology up close (seeing an actual tattoo, hearing an actual song, reading an actual memoir) and experiencing its depersonalized documentation from a distance (269–70).

"Brainwashing" and "reeducation," let us recall, relied on literacy lessons to smuggle in political doctrines. In Wang's autobiography, brainwashing was depicted as a kind of reflex training enabled by the feedback loop between oral self-criticism and autobiographical writing. This notion of indoctrination as an inscriptional mechanism, as well as the associations of indoctrination with mind-numbing mass media, created a scenario in which emotional pronouncements of ideological allegiance could verify a speaker's presence of mind. In *War Trash*, by contrast, almost all dialogue is propagandistic and emptied of individuality. Yu's substitution of a personal voice with a documentary hand is integral to his ethics of witnessing history without appropriating voices. In prioritizing the feel of historical weight over the facticity of historical content, this documentary manner makes "historical accuracy" a function of *literalness* as a special kind of *literariness*. This ambiguity between literalness and literariness is what I understand as the tone of Jin's *post*–cold war anticommunism.

"CAN TRANSLATIONS PLAGIARIZE?"

Dissident, exile, and spokesman—such labels have placed Jin's work, regardless of topic, in the context of the 1989 Tiananmen event. Jin may decline such labels, but he actively pursues the context, often naming Tiananmen as his literary *raison d'être*. Alternately, some might say that Tiananmen is the *only* context in which Jin has validity as an author. Julia Lovell locates Jin's key value in his "insider's knowledge of China" and his "political freedom to write about it." Her otherwise scathing review of *War Trash* lambasts Jin's "stylistic infelicities" and lack of "linguistic fluency." At his best, Jin produces "a sober prose that does nothing to call attention to itself." At his worst, this prose is intruded upon by "small solecisms." Michael Upchurch describes a "split reaction" to Jin's short story collection *The Bridegroom*: "The first is gratitude for the vivid picture the book gives of Chinese society in the era just after the Cultural Revolution. . . . The second is a feeling that Jin, National Book Award or no, is in sore need of a copy editor." *The Bridegroom* has "a kind of documentary value," but at times it reads like "a Chinese-language original that hasn't had the best of treatments from its translator."[95]

In Jin's reception history, the geopolitics of post-Tiananmen censorship has far overshadowed the geopolitics of infelicities and solecisms. But Jin's documentary manner evinces both. Jin's nondescript style has led to observations about his misuse of American colloquialisms, awkward importations of Chinese idioms, poorly executed translations, and appropriative acts of plagiarism. In the case of a deeply researched work such as *War Trash*, a documentary manner also creates the effect of an actual historical record. In other words, even though Jin views the English language and a documentary aesthetic as central to literature's historical vocation, these are also the precise points that have driven readers to wonder if he *has* an aesthetic—if he is author or translator, creator or transcriber, originator or forger. In the context of the 1990s, such uncertainties about Jin's claim to authorship say at least as much about China's changing relationship to intellectual property as they do about its relationship to human rights. For Jin, the attainment of political freedom is best exemplified by the attainment of a copyright; freedom of speech is the right not only to *express* but also to *own* one's ideas. This notion of freedom results in a tonal conundrum: Jin's documentary manner seems the most historically reliable from a human rights standpoint when he is least authorially present from an intellectual property standpoint.

A global intellectual property rights (IPR) regime implicitly structures many familiar debates about Chinese literary production. For example, Laikwan Pang proposes that "censorship can also be seen as a protectionist policy, . . . protecting certain law-abiding local creative industries from international competition."[96] My aim here is not to defend PRC censorship. But seeing as there are many ways of contesting the Chinese government and many avenues for pursuing free speech, it is significant that Jin's reception history has so resoundingly singled out authorship and publication. Being barred from free expression in general is often equated with being banned from publication in particular. When a Chinese publisher pulled the translation of Jin's novel *Waiting* (1999) just after he had won the National Book Award, American journalists tried to connect the dots. John Pomfret suspects that the censorship of *Waiting* was a consequence of "the jealousy many in Chinese literary circles feel over Jin's book, which was written in English in a foreign country. Despite a glorious ancient literary tradition, no Chinese author has won a Nobel Prize for literature, which many here blame on government controls on writers."[97] Neither ancient traditions nor authoritarian rule is commensurable with a regime of creativity and innovation.[98] Furthermore, in contriving a causal link between the lack of free speech and the lack of creativity, Pomfret assumes that intellectual property rights naturally follow from political rights.

Jin himself likewise conflates political liberty with intellectual property. In the closing lines of *War Trash*, Yu's former comrade begs him: "Please write our story!" (349). But lest we interpret Yu's memoir as fulfilling this plea, his parting words instruct us to "not take this to be an 'our story.' In the depths of my being I have never been one of them. I have just written what I experienced" (350). This self-deprecating gesture is entirely in character. It comes from someone who calls his memoir "the only gift a poor man like me can bequeath his American grandchildren" (5). But if Yu just wanted to write what he experienced as a POW, and if he just wanted the memoir to be a gift within the family, it seems unlikely that Chinese authorities would stop him from writing it or bequeathing it. It is the prohibition of publication in particular, rather than the prohibition of expression in general, that conditions Jin's understanding of freedom and exile: "Imagine your books are banned—you can go back but your books are not allowed. I wouldn't feel comfortable accepting those terms."[99] Censorship also accounts for the blinders imposed by the state on readers in China: "I think that people in the diaspora like my books, though some Chinese have some misgivings about them partly because most of my books are not available there."[100]

In the 1980s and 1990s, China gained global visibility as an authoritarian state and a global pirate. Although some say that the Tiananmen protests were a factor in U.S. efforts to push for Chinese compliance on IPR, Andrew Mertha claims that the "USTR [Office of the United States Trade Representative] has been more successful when concentrating on issues substantively related to one another." For example, U.S. promises to support China's bid for the World Trade Organization (WTO) provided leverage for the 1992 Sino–U.S. Memorandum of Understanding on Intellectual Property Rights. While many believe that these IPR reforms have been achieved by "delink[ing] trade and human rights," the concurrent timing of events is also not without meaning.[101] Coincidentally, it was one week before the Tiananmen protests, on May 25, 1989, when the USTR released its inaugural Special 301 review, designed to "identify those foreign countries denying protection of intellectual property rights and market access to U.S. firms."[102] Such coincidences mean that unease about China's economic advancement by way of IPR infractions have tended to coexist with unease about its political regression by way of authoritarian rule.

The PRC's accession to the WTO in 2001 was the symbolic culmination of a process that began with Deng Xiaoping's economic reforms in the 1970s.[103] Between 1989 and 1996, the United States and the PRC signed four bilateral agreements on IPR. The narrative of China's integration into the global economy includes several conflicting threads. Some emphasize the Chinese state's introduction of IPR reform, while others stress its negligent enforcement. Paradoxically, China's accession to the WTO has strengthened its association with various forms of illegitimate production and black-market activity. The PRC's extreme stigma within the IPR regime is both the extension of long-existing discourses on civilizational inferiority and the sign of an imminent imperial changeover. Adrian Johns has perceptively proposed that piracy is "a phenomenon of geopolitical thresholds": it "always lies just beyond the sway of the civilizing process" and is "identified with the barbarians at the gates."[104] This mutinous dimension of piracy is perhaps why Chinese counterfeit production, cultural and otherwise, has been viewed as an anti-imperial, quasi-populist challenge—a "knock-off" of innovation, creativity, and branding.[105] Less utopian critics have considered the affinity rather than the antagonism between creating and copying. This affinity also arises from the codependency of informal and formal economies—counterfeit products enhance the value of brand-name products.[106] The IPR regime and its rhetoric of innovation have drawn trenchant critique, particularly from scholars sensitive to U.S. cultural hegemony. Joseph Slaughter has contended that IPR policies signal a shift "from industrial to information capitalism as a basis of national wealth." This shift reflects the "effort of the intellectual property-rich countries of the North to reorganize the global economy of the new world order to consolidate their own trade-related advantage by inventing and securing new streams of revenue in the international seas of stories."[107]

In Jin's reception history and in his own commentaries, the lack of political freedom amounts to the lack of creative freedom. Jin's choice of protagonists renders this link explicit: artists, scholars, journalists, and intellectuals all express their ideas by publishing them. Jin's style of writing, however, makes creative and authorial freedom more difficult to pin down. This is to say that Jin's use of a "documentary" English-language novel as a corrective to Korean War historiography has introduced ethical predicaments aside from freedom of speech. On July 24, 2005, journalist Chen Li reported that 10,000 characters from Zhang Zeshi's edited collection of Korean War POW memoirs appear unmodified in Jin's *War Trash*. The case was settled quickly and remained relatively hush within the United States, but it likely grew out of abiding unease about Jin's alleged appropriation of Chinese voices.[108] I bring up the plagiarism charge for two reasons. The first is Jin's response to the allegations. As Jing Tsu notes, "Much of Ha Jin's defense builds on interpreting Zhang's account as a piece of a historical document rather than an original creation; this interpretation allegedly does not involve questions of intellectual property."[109] The second reason is that regardless of whether the plagiarism allegation holds water, there is something disturbing about reading fiction that appears to, or purports to, carry the weight of history. Jin's American readers have picked up on this as well. Russell Banks characterizes *War Trash* as a "seamless, somewhat unsettling fusion of invention and reportage."

Banks writes: "Appearances to the contrary, then, though 'War Trash' is indeed a work of fiction, one has to keep reminding oneself of that fact."[110]

Tsu's question—"Can translations plagiarize?"—guides us to revisit Jin's documentary manner with both post-WTO China and post-Tiananmen China in mind.[111] This question shows that there are different kinds of accountability at stake. A translation is supposed to be accountable to the original. A documentary novel is supposed to be accountable to the historical record. *War Trash* is not a translation, but it relies on Chinese-language texts, and, in Banks's account, it reads "almost as if it had indeed been translated from Chinese." *War Trash* is not a historical record, although to John Freeman, it "winds up feeling less like a novel than a slice of actual history."[112] Jin has justified his use of Zhang's memoir by characterizing it as a Chinese-language historical reference. Yet the above reviews reveal a symmetry between how Jin treats Zhang's memoir and how American readers treat Jin's novel. Even though *War Trash* is a novel, it reads as "actual history." And even though this novel is technically an "original," the nagging feel of translation that so many readers experience effectively demotes the author into an invisible, "second-order" figure.[113] These readings of *War Trash* converge on the defining feature of Jin's documentary manner: the author as something other than a creative actor, whether this be a transcriber, translator, copier, or plagiarizer.

For the Chinese reader, *War Trash*'s documentary commitment to an existing record manifests as cultural appropriation. For the American reader, it manifests as creative lack. When an American reviewer notes that *War Trash* "seems to be merely importing information from the sources ... on which it draws," the point is not that Jin is guilty of illegitimate filching, of selling out the Chinese people for a book prize, but that he may not be worthy of such a prize.[114] In Jin's adopted country, an overattachment to transcribing the historical record reads as a negligence of style, plotting, and aesthetic matters. Perhaps in response to such criticism, Jin has made an increasing effort to demonstrate that a documentary manner is a politically, morally, and aesthetically informed choice. His later novels provide monuments not only to history and truth (as his past characters are wont to do) but also to clean writing. The narrator of *A Map of Betrayal* (2014) comes down on the "purple prose" of her Chinese students, who "mistook verbosity for eloquence and ambiguity for beauty."[115] *The Boat Rocker* contrasts the balanced prose of its journalistic narrator with his state-endorsed ex-wife, who "dropped pretentious expressions right and left, calling mung-bean noodles 'dragon's beard' and aniseeds 'octagonal stars'" (8). By thematizing the problem of overly colorful writing, Jin reminds readers that his own documentary prose is intended as both antithesis and antidote to the always already distortive Chinese language and the always overly ornate Chinese style.

Jin's most concerted attempt to turn a documentary manner into an aesthetic enterprise comes in *A Free Life* (2007), a 600-plus-page tome known for initiating Jin's entry into "Chinese America." This third-person novel employs a somewhat byzantine tripartite typography. When representing Chinese characters speaking English, Jin fashions an exaggerated pidgin, which may be more visual than aural: "No, sanks. I reelly cannot."[116] When representing the characters speaking Chinese to each other, Jin uses italics. Finally, the third-person narration takes place in conventional typescript; here, instead of documenting otherness, Jin hones an authorial voice that is capable of narrating in the American vernacular. Despite looking different on the page, *A Free Life*'s typographical scheme is similar in logic to *War Trash*'s documentary manner. In both novels, there is a showy quality to the copious depiction of Chinese speech as markedly propagandistic or markedly foreign. Jin's attempt to reproduce Chinese pidgin operates something like overly literal translations: "The more convincingly the translator observes the protocols of 'nearness,' the more exquisite the reader's sense of strangeness, of distance from the original text."[117] Tellingly, Jin's "natural" American vernacular has drawn more (negative) attention than his affected pidgin.[118] Pervasive derisions of Jin's attempt at literary narration and the near total disregard for his documentary typography reaffirm the documentary bias: Jin is the most useful and least offensive when presenting impersonal documentations of Chineseness. This explains why Michael Upchurch's prescription for Jin isn't to dress up his already simple prose but to strip it down even further: "Jin is on safe ground when he keeps his language utterly plain. But his ventures into the vernacular go off track."[119]

To return to the comparison with which this chapter opened, Jin is not wholly unaware of the Chinese exilic writers who preceded him. However, in "The Spokesman and the Tribe," Jin finds Conrad, Nabokov, Rushdie, and Naipaul more laudable than Lin Yutang, his more obvious predecessor. In Jin's critique, Lin's "vision of himself as a cultural spokesman of China" exacted severe aesthetic compromises. With Lin's work as an example, we learn that "a creative writer should aspire to be not a broker but a creator of culture."[120] Jin has not directly discussed C. Y. Lee, whom I offered as his cold war counterpart. But when asked if he planned to publish in Chinese as Lee had done late in life, Jin responded, "No, I have to concentrate on my survival in English. Life is too short for me to change back and forth."[121] Why doesn't Jin embrace his political or ethnic kinship with Lin or Lee? Don't they possess a shared antipathy toward communism and a common commitment to providing a truer representation of the Chinese people? Jin's insistence on his linguistic and stylistic difference from these cold war writers can be chalked up to his creative ethos. His assertion of language and style as the principal axes of comparison shows how anticommunist ideology in a post–cold war era surfaces not as any openly political statement but as an apparent harmony between political freedom and creative freedom.

As a post-Tiananmen *and* post-WTO figure, Jin represents the prestige of anticommunist freedom when it is commuted as creativity. But, in the final analysis, a notes-and-files compositional method may actually make Jin closer to a "broker" rather than a "creator." In *War Trash*, a documentary manner recasts the author as a mere recorder who produces the feel of history. The fact that the feel of history is also a plagiaristic feel and a translational feel—the fact that Jin can call himself a creator but write like a broker—reflects the peculiarity of post–cold war anticommunism. Does the tone of documentation convey the weight of history or the lightness of the copy? Does the literalness and literariness of a document yield a higher truth, or does it provoke suspicion and estrangement? For Wang Tsun-ming, embodied vocality was crucial to validating his "autobiography." Jin's documentary approach, by contrast, seeks historical validation in the total suppression of a speaking presence. The figure of the exilic and uncensored PRC author gives credence to the American mantra of free speech by exhibiting the right to copyright. But, ironically, freedom of speech mandates that the PRC author not take any liberties with an already existing record. Exercising the political freedom to set the record straight thus requires curbing the creative freedom that might distort this record. In order to recreate the feel of history, Jin must convey the literalness of reproduction. He must, in short, sabotage his own bid for literary authorship.

Chapter Five

THE TONE OF INTIMACY
Imperial Brotherhood and Trinh T. Minh-ha's
Cinematic Interviews

> It is not the clandestine triumphs that justify the billions spent on intelligence.... It is the steadiness and pervasiveness of a kind of close contact which will unmistakably reveal an opponent's real capacities and approximate intentions. Intelligence services touch, watch, and listen to each other at a thousand points. The intimate knowledge revealed by the wrestler's embrace freed both sides from the ignorance, rumor, and outbreaks of panicky fear that spark big wars no one wants.
>
> —THOMAS POWERS, "THE TRUTH ABOUT THE CIA" (1993)

On June 1, 1954, as delegates in Geneva contemplated how to partition Vietnam, a sprightly Edward Lansdale boarded a plane at Clark Air Force Base in the Philippines. About five hours later, he touched down in Saigon. Armed with just a used typewriter and a box of files and clothes, Lansdale set up shop in a small bungalow. This was to be his office. It was also his home.

Such humble and spartan beginnings belie the mission at hand. The first of a dozen or so U.S. counterinsurgency specialists to arrive in Vietnam, Lansdale was tasked with two related objectives: creating a government in the south that could stand up to the immensely popular Ho Chi Minh and organizing a paramilitary team in the north to infiltrate the Viet Minh. The fact that the Geneva Accords would expressly prohibit both these tasks only increased their allure for Lansdale. This, to be sure, was a man who, plying himself with a steady diet of frontier tales, relished orchestrating covert schemes in a lawless land. In keeping with such tales, Lansdale saw these schemes as entirely harmonious with his sympathetic support for "the little guy." Although a black operative, Lansdale was also, unironically, a folk hero. No surprise, then, that so many critics have deemed him a personification of American intelligence's dual identity.[1]

It may be more precise, though, to understand Lansdale as invested in normality rather than duality. For him, secrecy and openness were the same side of the same coin. The confidentiality of a grand conspiracy was always shading into the intimacy of everyday friendship. One of the best examples of this dynamic is "Operation Passage to Freedom." At once a covert mission and a public relations campaign, this operation sought to facilitate the flow of Vietnamese migrants across the newly established 17th parallel and into the U.S.-controlled southern region. Publicly, the United States government framed the "exodus" as refugees heroically fleeing from communism and "voting with their feet."[2] Covertly, the CIA gave Lansdale's team the green light to use whatever "dirty tricks" necessary to stimulate this flow—tricks such as spreading rumors that "the Blessed Virgin had gone South," reporting that Chinese communist troops were raping northern village girls, dropping leaflets warning of an American atomic bomb in the north, hiring Vietnamese soothsayers "to write predictions about coming disasters to certain Vietminh leaders," and offering "five acres and a water buffalo to every relocated refugee."[3]

In a classified report eventually published with the Pentagon Papers, Lansdale recalls one such trick with something like amusement, if not pride:

Major [Lucien] Conein was given responsibility for developing a paramilitary organization in the north, to be in position when the Vietminh took over.... Among cover duties, this team supervised the refugee flow for the Hanoi airlift organized by the French. One day, as a CAT C-46 finished loading, they saw a small child standing on the ground below the loading door. They shouted for the pilot to wait, picked the child up and shoved him into the aircraft, which then promptly taxied out for its takeoff in the constant air shuttle. A Vietnamese man and woman ran up to the team, asking what they had done with their small boy, whom they'd brought out to say goodbye to relatives. The chagrined team explained, finally talked the parents into going south to Free Vietnam, put them in the next aircraft to catch up with their son in Saigon.[4]

Although this report proceeds in third person, it is customarily attributed to Lansdale, perhaps due to its spirited style. And, although Lansdale relays this anecdote from a distance, his storied résumé of pranks makes it probable that he was the key driver behind this Vietnamese family's seemingly serendipitous journey to freedom in South Vietnam. In Lansdale's telling, the indiscriminate snatching of a child becomes a humanitarian rescue mission. The blunder makes for a good story, in part because all the signs of

American intervention are multiply displaced. The "refugee flow," we are told, is being organized through a French airlift and executed by the Taiwanese commercial airline Civil Air Transport (CAT). In this setup, the American supervisory presence seems as incidental as the kidnapping itself. The moral of the story is that the kidnapping was, in the end, fortuitous. An unexpected turn of events—events beyond anyone's intention or control—enabled a boy and his parents to escape from communism.

And so we have one family's path from anonymous bystander to militarized subject—from inscrutable Oriental to political refugee. One wonders what exactly Lansdale's "chagrined team" had said when they "finally talked the parents into going south to Free Vietnam." Did they use the idiom of "freedom"? Did "voting with your feet" come up? Did the parents chastise or thank the "chagrined team"? This family of three was among the nearly 600,000 to one million Vietnamese who, often with the assistance of the CIA, journeyed across the 17th parallel between August 1954 and May 1955. This mid-1950s Vietnamese refugee migration offers an early instantiation of the "militarized refugee," a term that Yến Lê Espiritu uses to mark "the hidden violence behind the humanitarian term 'refuge.'"[5] Although Espiritu is referring to the post-1975 generation of "boat people," the CIA's administration of political-psychological warfare through refugee resettlement shows that the "militarized refugee" came to be the public face of U.S. covert operations more than a decade before the arrival of combat forces in Vietnam.

The comingling of force and benevolence, what Chandan Reddy calls "freedom with violence," is often taken to be a signature feature of "liberal war" and "liberal modernity."[6] From some angles, the story of counterinsurgency—the story of the CIA's underhanded role in the refugee exodus of the 1950s—reinforces this characterization of American empire. Laleh Khalili writes, "If enemy-centric counterinsurgency depends on coercive or punitive measures to deter the civilian population from supporting the unconventional forces, then population-centric counterinsurgency is meant to win over that population by 'securing' and 'protecting' them, as well as by providing services that would win over the population." Khalili's study of post-9/11 counterinsurgency identifies U.S. operations in Southeast Asia as a crucial precedent for making "the military into the kind of modernizing instrument of social engineering that could build schools and clinics as easily as fighting."[7] Yet what's interesting about this

Southeast Asian genealogy of counterinsurgency, which seeks to unite the people with the soldier, is that it originates not in Western liberalism but in Chinese Maoism. Lansdale was ever eager to cite the communists as innovators of a brand of political warfare that could pass as populism. The free Asian subject, he believed, must be modeled on "the Vietminh soldier." This friendly soldier "conscientiously made friends with civilians as a helpful comrade, to fulfill the Chinese Communist dictum that 'the people are the water and the soldier is the fish.'"[8]

In this chapter, I show how this ideological heterodoxy informed U.S. psychological-political operations that predicated Third World self-sufficiency on militarized assistance. Specifically, I'm interested in how this interplay of warfare and welfare informs two Vietnamese refugee "exoduses": the movement of refugees from North Vietnam to South Vietnam in the 1950s and the movement of refugees from communist Vietnam to "the free world" (but really various permanent way stations)[9] in the 1970s and 1980s. I study the different vehicles of intimacy that cold war and post–cold war refugees brought into play through discourses of help and self-help. One such vehicle, which I explore through counterinsurgency specialist Edward Lansdale, is the *brother*. Another vehicle of intimacy, which I explore through experimental filmmaker Trinh T. Minh Ha, is the *interview*. Both Lansdale's counterinsurgency strategy of the brother and Trinh's cinematic strategy of the interview are ideologically impure. Lansdale modifies the communist concept of the brother to promote a cold war spirit of volunteerism that runs counter to decolonial Third Worldism. Trinh, meanwhile, adapts the liberalist tool of the interview to open up a quasi-utopian post–cold war space unencumbered by the paternalism of American humanitarianism and the patriarchy of Vietnamese socialism.

Both Lansdale's brother and Trinh's interview promise intimacy. Yet these vehicles facilitate different kinds and different tones of intimacy. We will find that, in Lansdale's counterinsurgency exploits, brotherly intimacy is produced by the free Asian's voluntary labors. As a volunteer, the brother was a figure who both gave help and needed help, who was able to model free Asian citizenship for Vietnamese refugees thanks to the informal guidance of American intelligence. Lansdale's most successful effort to operationalize the brother in South Vietnam was a Philippine medical humanitarian group called Operation Brotherhood (OB). Among the CIA's many "civic action" programs, medical aid was seen as particularly effective. That OB was allegedly "conceived in Asia by Asians" further elevated its propagandistic value.[10] In fact, U.S. officials saw OB's humanitarian cover as secondary to its political work. As a result, records of the organization's accomplishments devote far more attention to the volunteers' entertainment skills—their casual, affective, off-duty labors—than to their medical expertise. The records of OB produced by Lansdale are especially interesting at the level of tone. This is because Lansdale's notoriously freewheeling, laissez-faire approach to intelligence operations permeates his writing as well. An informal yet intimate tone is broadly characteristic of Lansdale's intelligence style, yet I show that this tone carries distinctively racial and sexual connotations when the subject of his representation is the Asian br/other—a figure whose voluntariness is paradoxically best exemplified by the OB Filipina.

Where Lansdale's informal model of intimacy is derived from the brother's voluntary labors, Trinh's formalist model of intimacy is derived from the interview's predetermined structure. Interviews are subject to defamiliarization in nearly all of Trinh's films and in many of her critical essays. I focus here on the 1989 experimental ethnodocumentary *Surname Viet, Given Name Nam*.[11] In *Surname*, Trinh stages a series of interviews with four women in post-1975 Vietnam. The film eventually reveals, however, that these interviews have actually been reenacted by recent Vietnamese refugees who are located in California. *Surname*'s interviews openly display the "cinematic tricks" that make a speaker's voice seem voluntary and her truth seem intimate.[12] I show how this adaptation of the interview reorganizes the relations of intimacy that interviews typically bring into play. Specifically, Trinh's technique of tracing the edges, borders, and surfaces of a framed subject serves to marginalize the speaker-viewer relationship and to centralize the speaker-filmmaker relationship. In this way, *Surname*'s interviews formalize a diasporic filmmaker's tonal expression of love toward her subjects.

As geopoliticized instruments for creating and manipulating intimacy, both the brother and the interview may seem compromised by their imbrication in American empire. This compromised status explains why the brotherly volunteer and the refugee interviewee have so often been viewed as puppet-like figures, made to regurgitate someone else's message. These political subjects have been at worst complicit sellouts and at best powerless victims. I push against such characterizations because they inhibit us from recognizing the subjects of empire as, finally, historical actors. When I explore Lansdale's efforts to operationalize the brother, therefore, I want to search out the instances in which the free Asian subject appears to us not as a self-Orientalizing ventriloquist but as the powerful motor enabling the illusion of American benevolence. And in analyzing Trinh's preoccupation with the interview's shape, structure, and outline, I aim to show how the formalist evocation of intimacy—a tonal intimacy—not only disables the empathic bonds between a refugee testifier and an American benefactor but also functions as an effort to carve out alternative ways of political co-belonging.

THE BROTHER: ASIANS HELPING ASIANS

"'Counterinsurgency' was another word for 'brotherly love,'" Lansdale liked to say.[13] In the context of Southeast Asia, counterinsurgency was intended to mobilize free Asian brothers to bring social services, friendly cheer, and, most significantly, political literacy to their untutored Oriental kin. But although Lansdale saw the brother as the friendly protagonist of American counterinsurgency, this figure was hardly native to the United States or to Asia:

The "brother" is the real newcomer to Asia. He has been seen in every country in Asia since 1920. He is the skilled and highly disciplined advance party for Communism in the initial phase of the struggle. . . . Usually, he is a person of deep sympathy and sincerity—an attractive personality. The paddy farmer first notes him as a newcomer to the local community who is helpful—helpful with farm and household chores, since he is insistent on earning the privilege of board and keep in the community. . . . From sympathy with the farmer for every real or imagined injustice, he turns easily and with conviction into an advisor who points out the one and only way to right these wrongs. This "brother" has brought great changes in Asia in our time; he is working now to change tomorrow.[14]

For Lansdale, the communist idea of the "brother" rhymed with the American coinage of "little brown brothers." The latter term had entered the United States' lexicon during its "benevolent" colonization of the Philippines.[15] Given Lansdale's personal connection to the Philippines, it makes sense that he saw the brother as a hinge figure that brought together the

THE TONE OF INTIMACY

United States' colonial history and its cold war present, a figure that was best personified by the Filipino. Because "only in the Philippines has Democracy been demonstrated in its full functioning," the newly independent nation was deemed "the down-to-earth, workaday exponent of Asiatic freedom."[16]

Lansdale's efforts to transform the Philippines into a "workshop of empire" inspired former intelligence officer Joseph B. Smith to declare, "The United States' fateful engagement in Vietnam began in Manila in the early 1950s, not in Saigon in the early sixties."[17] Smith is referring specifically to how, at Lansdale's behest, the CIA sponsored numerous Philippine organizations in Vietnam and across free Asia in the name of fraternity. Technical teams, military trainers, social workers, and medical staffers all aimed to make "Philippine democratic 'Know-How' available to the brother nations of Southeast Asia."[18] Of the various organizations in South Vietnam, Operation Brotherhood was the most successful, arguably because its core values of love and friendliness dovetailed with Lansdale's own "informal" and "personal" approach. According to a 1959 memo, "The Operation Brotherhood Program does so much for so little. Its value cannot be measured only in terms of medical service, though its medical services alone would fully justify its continuance. It must be considered as one of the maximum political impact activities in the country."[19] Political impact through informal care brings to bear the key brotherly traits that Lansdale outlines in the block quote above. The Filipino brother, like the communist brother, is skilled in ideological struggle, sympathetic towards the everyman, helpful with household chores, and assumes an advisory role toward younger family members. All this the brother does freely and openly—out of familial love and without hidden motivations.

To an extent, brotherhood was of a piece with U.S. propaganda's focus on the nuclear family and, more broadly, with the imperial domesticities that Laura Wexler calls "tender violence."[20] Not only did "images of gender and the family" become "valuable tools" for U.S. officials in "explaining the American way of life to foreign audiences," but the American public also "embraced domesticity and traditional gender roles as an antidote to anxieties unleashed by atomic weapons and political instability."[21] In both propaganda abroad and middlebrow culture at home, therefore, we can find "the problem of political obligation to Asia as a problem of family."[22] The link between the nuclear family and the paternal empire is palpable in Senator John F. Kennedy's characterization of the United States as "the parents of little Vietnam" and South Vietnam as an "offspring ... we cannot abandon."[23] Lansdale saw "brotherhood" as a departure from this top-down paternalism that structured the free world "family of man."[24] Where paternal relations reeked of colonialism, a horizontal model of fraternal relations among different Asian nations emphasized *volunteerism*. Brotherhood, in short, located individual and collective agency in helping others help themselves.

A pan-Asian brotherhood founded on volunteerism distanced itself not only from American paternalism but also from Third Worldism. According to a 1955 *New York Times* article on the Bandung Afro-Asian conference, "Asia for the Asians" is a disillusioned strategy "directed against the West" and "a tragedy for everyone except the Communists."[25] Speaking from a similar perspective, Oscar Arellano, the nominal founder of Operation Brotherhood, clarifies that the organization promoted an agenda "not of Asia *for* the Asians, but of Asians *helping* Asians."[26] To call OB a "citizen-to-citizen program" and a "self-help project" downplays self-determination and underlines a volunteerism rooted in civility.[27] In this respect, we can trace volunteerism to a long history of U.S. colonialism and neocolonialism in the Philippines. Since the early twentieth century, transnationally mobile Filipino professionals had been assisting the United States' management of local governance and its regional exercise of soft power.[28] This domestic capitalist class's activation of a "horizontal sphere of voluntarism and spontaneity" provided both the infrastructure and the ideology for Operation Brotherhood, which was run through the International Jaycees, an organization that, like the 4-H, Lions, and Rotary clubs, drew its membership from a class of elite men who promoted civic action in the form of economic propserity.[29]

Although "Asians helping Asians" was pitched in a humanitarian register, its appeal to racial kinship ultimately served the purposes of defense and security. The brotherly spirit of volunteerism thus informed not only service initiatives such as Operation Brotherhood but also regional anticommunist organizations such as the Southeast Asia Treaty Organization (SEATO) and the Association of Southeast Asian Nations (ASEAN). Whether through formal treaties or informal volunteerism, "brotherhood" showed how the language of racial affinity could lay the groundwork for collective security. In examining the U.S.-led formation of SEATO in 1954, Jim Glassman argues that the intertwined themes of mutual defense and cultural kinship in American propaganda essentially created "Southeast Asia" as an "area." That is, this area was to require collective security against communism to the extent that it was culturally distinct from Chineseness. Based on this geostrategic rather than Third Worldist instantiation of regional unity, "South Vietnam can then be portrayed as a more fundamentally Southeast Asian realm endangered by attack and threat of assimilation from the more Sinicized north."[30] The likes of Lansdale contributed to this remapping project. Lansdale used the language of brotherhood to reconceive of Southeast Asia as a region where "a Communist insurgency, like a civil war, can seem to be a most intimate, family matter."[31] To repair this "intimate, family matter" is not to reconcile the two sides of this "civil war." Brotherhood could not refer to the blood ties between communist Asia and free Asia—say, between North Vietnam and South Vietnam. Nor could brotherhood refer to an anticolonial fraternity that championed Third World liberation, anticolonial sovereignty, and national independence. A free world brotherhood of volunteerism, as Lansdale saw it, required *enforcing* national division and *prohibiting* self-determination.

How do Americans fit into this notion of brotherhood? Lansdale writes, "This 'family quarrel' aspect, of a Communist insurgency in a foreign country, poses the thorniest challenge ever faced by free Americans. We cannot look on, aloof, while a people are enslaved or murdered, and still have our own freedom bright and clear." The role of "free Americans" in the "family quarrel" of communist insurgency is not aloofness. But nor is it official intervention, in the way of an overbearing parent. The American presence that Lansdale advocates is friendly but informal. It is hospitable to the point of being domestic. Recalling his success in uniting soldiers and civilians against local communist threats in the Philippines, Lansdale writes: "We, as American advisers, only used our 'good offices' as interested friends to bring these men together in an informal atmosphere, provided plenty of coffee—and then let them alone to do a 're-think' on their campaign."[32] In South Vietnam, Lansdale availed his "good office" for a similar purpose of letting the Vietnamese alone to "re-think":

Under informal American auspices, (usually in my house, at my personal invitation), meetings were held in August 1954 between Vietnamese government officials and Vietnamese Army staff officers, to work out a modus vivendi for establishing the government throughout South Vietnam. The provision of neutral (American) "good offices" permitted bringing together officials who were deeply suspicious of each other including staff officers who were plotting a coup and government ministers who would be targets of the coup. An uneasy team of Vietnamese civil and military officials was formed. "Indians" who would carry the brunt of the work for the "chiefs" were selected and taken, under American guidance, to the Philippines for first-hand observance of Philippines Army-Government teamwork in stabilizing former Communist Huk areas.[33]

At first glance, Lansdale's rapturous incantation of American frontier mythology in this speech shows how Old West narratives, which gained renewed popularity in the 1950s, "found their echo" in policy.[34] In fact, Lansdale's frontier charisma set the tone for Eugene Burdick and William Lederer's *The Ugly American*, a 1958 novel that, Richard Slotkin writes, "treat[ed] 'Asians' as Hollywood . . . treated 'Indians.'"[35] If we look closely at the above speech, however, the Old West drama appears in adapted form. The language of suspicion, violence, and hierarchy is restricted to describing local relations—the "civil war" or "family quarrel." The Vietnamese personnel are ascribed with ulterior motives (plotting a coup), assigned an official task (establishing a government in South Vietnam), and delegated to a specific program (observing Army–Government collaboration in the Philippines). In this picture, the United States appears not as a conquering hero but as a congenial yet neutral presence, a "good office" or domestic respite within the Asian wilds. A good office is a makeshift contraption. Because CIA employees were not allocated workspace, Lansdale's team was frequently on the move.[36] Yet the lack of a clearly marked governmental structure actually fired up Lansdale's frontier imagination. Instead of forging officially recognizable relationships in a bureaucratic office, Lansdale excelled at contriving "unofficial gathering place[s] where Americans and Vietnamese could meet and get to know each other informally, minus the rigid protocol and pecking-order of the Establishment."[37]

The casual coffee chats convened in Lansdale's good offices are repeatedly cited as a counterinsurgency innovation that allowed Americans to unofficially intervene in the internecine problems of an Asian nation. In describing these casual, friendly gatherings, Lansdale employs a casual, friendly tone. That is, just as he brings the quarreling brothers together at his "personal invitation," he recounts the scene as if he were writing personal notes rather than an intelligence memo. This informal tone that accompanies the counterinsurgency strategy of informal guidance appears to be what makes "Asian self-help" possible. In Lansdale's memoir, for example, he nonchalantly admits to fudging a few details in order "to give Asians some sorely-needed heroes from among their own."[38] This condescending yet altruistic language of *giving*, which recurs throughout Lansdale's writings, thrusts the heroic Asians into the spotlight. It is a sleight of hand that many have rightly found troubling. Yet the "good offices" scenario suggests that at issue in "brotherhood" is not so much agency but intimacy. If heroic agency demands a spotlight, then the casual intimacy that enables "manifest domesticity" introduces a more complicated relation between openness and secrecy.[39]

INFORMAL TONES: THE X-FACTOR

Lansdale's official cover was the Air Force. He explains: "I served part of my career as a military man as a volunteer on CIA duties. The period when this happened was only in a short span."[40] Lansdale's flippancy in describing his volunteer duties is integral to the very concept of the volunteer. Volunteers, after all, are just as easily on duty as they are off duty, and we might even say that their flippant affect arises from this casual activity of flipping back and forth. There is a charm to the flippant volunteer that the steadfast officer lacks. The charm needed to maintain a cover and build a legend explains why Lansdale's volunteer CIA duties account for the entirety of his fame. These duties, most of which took place in the Philippines and South Vietnam in the 1950s, included the blackest kinds of clandestine operations, yet they also tended to carry the outward appearance of a practical joke or a frat boy gimmick. In the Philippines, Lansdale's team drew on local charms and vampire legends to defeat the Hukbalahap (Huk) movement, an anti-Japanese and pro-independence peasant force that the U.S. government viewed as a communist threat. Lansdale's Philippine adventures also included creating a "home-made substitute for napalm" by "fool[ing] around with coconut husks and gasoline."[41] In Vietnam, Lansdale planted explosives disguised as coal in rail yards and poured sugar into the tanks of Viet Minh trucks.[42] Years later in Cuba, Lansdale devised a plan called "Illumination by Submarine," which attempted to sabotage Fidel Castro's regime through a combination of fireworks, submarines, superstitions, and rumors.[43]

Lansdale troubled the distinction between diplomacy and counterinsurgency by bringing tricks, gimmicks, and folklore into the ambit of intelligence operations. Accordingly, he also distorted the tonal gradient of secrecy and openness by injecting color, style, and fancy into intelligence writing. Because he stood to benefit from maintaining his various covers, Lansdale, who was just as happy to play the naïf as he was to go native, tended to amplify rather than dispel the legends and myths circulating about him. Daniel Ellsberg, who happened to work under Lansdale before achieving Pentagon Papers fame, has commented on Lansdale's canny "willingness to appear simpleminded when he wanted to be opaque." Reporters would marvel at "how 'open' my boss was," Ellsberg recalls. They "had no idea, no clue, even the best of them, just how often and how egregiously they were lied to."[44] Jonathan Nashel's critical biography *Edward Lansdale's Cold War* offers the most illuminating account of how Lansdale built his legend through a certain stylistic panache. According to Nashel, Lansdale's expansive corpus of writing—"everything from official reports, memoranda, and lecture notes to diary jottings, letters, and memoirs"—is striking for "how little he varied his pitch or his tone."[45] This tonal factor is, I think, related to what Lansdale himself has called the "X factor." Lansdale had once pointed out to Secretary of Defense Robert McNamara that McNamara had "left out the most important factor of all" in a "long list of entries of a computer, including the body count type of stuff, enemy casualties." When pressed by McNamara to define this factor, Lansdale replied: "What the people out on the battlefield really feel; which side they want to see win and which side they're for at the moment."[46] It is fitting that Lansdale refers to this "human factor" as the "X factor." For what drove Lansdale was not just human sympathy but human psychology, both of which required exploiting "what the people on the battlefield really feel." The "X factor" names something not only central but also censored. It is this extra element—an element of pitch and tone combining sympathetic feeling with psychological manipulation—that makes it difficult to discern where Lansdale's friendliness ends and his cover begins.

An especially representative case of this ambiguity between Lansdale's open face and his "black mind" is his 1972 memoir.[47] *In the Midst of Wars* allegedly became required reading at three service academies and is frequently referenced in the *Foreign Relations of the United States*, the official record of U.S. foreign policy.[48] Yet Lansdale's "tales of high adventure" have also been viewed as "leaving far too much unsaid," especially regarding his volunteer CIA duties. Because Lansdale needed to conceal his role in covert affairs, he created not merely a cover story for himself but also a genre cover for his memoir. That this memoir doesn't offer "any major historical revelations" was interpreted as a shortcoming at the time of its publication.[49] But it is in fact a testament to this memoir's success that readers who took issue with the omissions in Lansdale's narrative could not help but comment on matters of style, tone, and genre in the same breath. For example, David Chandler wrote, "What aroused terror and respect for Lansdale was his expertise in guerrilla warfare, his operational *carte blanche* and his bureaucratic adroitness. The hero of Lansdale's book, however, resembles a character in *Our Town*, given to phrases like 'the battlecry of freedom' and 'A smile is a great passport. Use it!'"[50] While readers occasionally commended Lansdale for his idealism, most found it sobering to revisit U.S. interventions in Southeast Asia in the 1950s from the perspective of the 1970s. Sherwood Dickerman called Lansdale's memoir "a period piece," something that "reads like an adventure of Frank Merriwell in Asia, a daring lark for a good cause with no regard for consequences that are now dismally apparent."[51]

Chandler's comparison of *In the Midst of Wars* to Thornton Wilder's all-American play *Our Town* and Dickerman's invocation of Burt Standish's pulp hero Frank Merriwell imply that Lansdale's ham and pluck are poorly suited for a referendum on the Vietnam War, which by 1972 was unanimously viewed as an American tragedy. My guess, though, is that Lansdale, who was happiest when rollicking in the gray area between credibility and incredibility, may have actually been delighted that readers found the tone-deaf exuberance of his memoir reminiscent of pulpy genre fiction. As he told a friend, "I really wrote it for folks who otherwise would buy the usual run of adventure stories."[52] And it's not just Lansdale's memoir that does this genre-bending work. Even his classified writings—those intended for limited circulation within the intelligence community—mimic the style of heart-racing and/or heart-tugging middlebrow fiction. President Kennedy once found a classified report by Lansdale so absorbing that he deemed it "an excellent article for a magazine like *The*

Saturday Evening Post." The report entitled "The Village That Refuses to Die" then appeared in this very publication as "The Report the President Wanted Published." Richard Drinnon writes, "in outlook and tone the story was a perfect fit. It seemed inspiring proof that the republican values of middle America flourished in the swamps of Southeast Asia."[53] In this report, Lansdale describes a "Viet Cong attack" in 1959: "Lacking weapons, the settlers fought back with Boy Scout staves and knives. It seemed almost incredible." The story concludes with the villagers giving Lansdale "the three-fingered Boy Scout salute."[54] Lansdale's field experience and dramatic flair set him up to advise Vietnam War content for television shows such as *The Twilight Zone* and popular magazines such as *Reader's Digest* and *Life*.[55] Nashel conjectures that Lansdale's "style of personalized storytelling" is why the *New York Times* featured his report on the first day of the Pentagon Papers exposé.[56]

We see, then, that Lansdale knew how to "defy bureaucratic restraints" and operate within "shades of blackness" in his writing as well as in the field.[57] His tonal performance of openness creates the effect of someone who is hiding nothing and someone who is hiding in plain sight. As we will see, in Lansdale's documentations of Operation Brotherhood, an informal, lively, and accessible tone is more than a cover for himself; it also serves to enhance the voluntariness of little brown brothers. In displaying his blasé, hands-off approach to "nation-building" (the American parlance for "empire-building"), Lansdale is also executing a counterinsurgency operation to endorse OB's can-do spirit of self-help. In the previous chapter, I showed how Wang Tsun-ming's embodied performance of a consistent ideological line outweighs the factual inconsistencies in his intelligence report. Analogously, OB's consistent demonstration of voluntariness in promoting democratic capitalism was more valuable for U.S. interests than its provision of medical care. Lansdale readily concedes, "The village problems are not necessarily medical. The need is more economic."[58] OB's medical work was to provide a cover for the more critical task of winning deceived hearts and reeducating brainwashed minds. This cover also assisted the more specific aim of converting recent refugees and displaced locals into supporters of the U.S.-backed Catholic Ngo Dinh Diem for an upcoming presidential election. In pursuit of these psychological-political objectives, OB doctors and nurses modeled capitalist self-sufficiency to forestall "the workings of what is called 'belly communism.' "[59] Delinked from U.S.

governmental aid programs and funded by "men who believed in free enterprise," OB was not to be a clinic where healthcare is indiscriminately doled out. Instead, Lansdale's team orchestrated two-week "visits of mobile units," consisting not only of doctors and clinical nurses but also of public health nurses, home demonstrators, and socioeconomic workers.[60] While these OB units did offer their fair share of medical services, they also introduced "lessons in hygiene, first aid, nursing assistance, nutrition, practical home economics such as the canning of home-grown food, and even agricultural methods."[61]

Because OB's mission was more ideological than medical, Lansdale tends to provide more anecdotal than statistical evidence of its success.[62] The following is excerpted from the memorandum "'Pacification' In Vietnam":

The outstanding medical and public health work was carried out by Filipino volunteer doctors, nurses, dentists, and nutritionists of Operation Brotherhood. This organization had been founded shortly before by the International Junior Chamber of Commerce, with its leading spirit, organizer, and operational leader being Oscar Arellano, a young Filipino architect, who was then Vice-President for Asia of the International Jaycees. Operations Brotherhood was privately funded; many Americans contributed. Initially, the teams were all Filipino volunteers. Later, many nations contributed medical volunteers to the teams.

The esprit de corps of the Filipino volunteers of "OB" was a major factor in overcoming Communist political work. These were Free Asians, who cheerfully and energetically helped their fellow men—in strong contrast to the grimness of life during the long war. The Filipinos had defeated the Communist Huk guerrillas at home, and imparted hope for the future. The "OB" teams made up their own songs, held parties in off-duty hours, and were a real tonic to the dispirited; (many an American MAAG [Military Assistance Advisory Group] on duty in the provinces was later "adopted" by the "OB" Filipinos and will confirm this psychological impact). One side effect of the presence of pretty Filipino girl doctors, nurses, dentists, and nutritionists was that many a male Vietnamese started learning English so he could talk to them.[63]

As with the report that became published in the *Saturday Evening Post*, this "Pacification" memo was initially classified as "secret," but its tone suggests otherwise. And, in both cases, the transformation of a covert counterinsurgency project into a public relations campaign is enabled by the subject matter. Thanks to Lansdale's earnest telling, both the Vietnamese village that refuses to die and the Filipino brothers who model free Asian citizenship come across as enthusiastically committed to the anticommunist cause. In the above passage, Lansdale's tone of openness has the added effect of enhancing the voluntariness of the Filipinos he's describing. Although Lansdale compares the OB's "esprit de corps" to the communist notion of "political work," he largely characterizes this "spirit" as distinctly Filipino. OB volunteers spontaneously generate cheer and energy by making up songs and holding off-duty parties. Their figurative "tonic to the dispirited" seems far more restorative than any medicinal tonic they can offer. The Americans' role in this feel-good story of brotherly aid is framed as more corporate than militaristic. Lansdale makes a point to credit American private funders for supporting OB's operations.[64] By contrast, the American Military Assistance Advisory Group (MAAG) is relegated to a parenthetical side note. Lansdale's own role appears even more obliquely: "The Filipinos had defeated the Communist Huk guerrillas at home, and imparted hope for the future." In an account of brotherly bonds between Filipino volunteers and Vietnamese refugees, this line about the Huk guerrillas seems out of place. What connects the defeat of the Huks in the Philippines to the success of OB in South Vietnam is, of course, Lansdale himself.[65] This discreetly incongruous sentence illustrates the tonal work that Lansdale's writing performs. A casual reference to the anti-Huk campaign on which Lansdale had built his fame is his way of giving the Filipinos heroes. It positions Filipino brothers at the forefront of a global fight against communism by foregrounding their spirit of volunteerism. In being above all volunteers, these brothers can flip between being both here and there, on duty and off duty, soldiers and lovers; they are just as willing to fight the Huks as they are to help the Vietnamese.

CONFIDENTIAL INTIMACIES

It's easy to see why so many critics have credited Lansdale with "inventing" Operation Brotherhood—as well as with "inventing" Ramon Magsaysay, Ngo Dinh Diem, and South Vietnam. In such accounts, accepting Lansdale's inflated persona tends to produce the related move of reducing Operation Brotherhood, the Diem regime, and all free Asians to lurid puppetry or specious façade. For example, one critic refers to Diem as

Lansdale's diminutive "understudy." Another derides efforts to "use Filipinos as our alter egos to spread democracy through the SEATO security area." Yet another describes Filipinos as "brown Americans" who "spoke English with a slightly out-of-date American slang" and whose presence "announced that the CIA owned the place."[66] This theatrical idiom of puppets, actors, roles, and understudies condemns U.S. intelligence for its self-aggrandizing acts of deception while suggesting that the performance of democratic friendship fell short: "Operation Brotherhood made for great anticommunist theater, but it was not terribly successful."[67] As a theatrical production, the Vietnam War is an American melodrama.[68] In it, free Asians have no existence outside of a predetermined role. Recent scholars have done the important work of challenging the Lansdale-as-puppeteer and Asians-as-puppets scheme by exposing the ineptness of the former and returning agency to the latter. Nick Cullather, for instance, explores Philippine President Ramon Magsaysay's ability to manipulate Lansdale (rather than the other way around) and suggests that this ability has been refined through years of living under arrogant colonial advisers. Far from being happy dupes, Filipinos saw Lansdale as a bad director, someone who too brazenly claimed credit for Magsaysay's success.[69] Looking at the Vietnam side of Lansdale's operations, Simeon Man challenges the idea that the members of Operation Brotherhood unthinkingly carried out a scripted life. These volunteers "had transnational itineraries facilitated by Lansdale, but their trajectories far exceeded his doing," Man writes.[70] Most influential to my own thinking is Andrew Friedman's analysis of the imperial intimacies that sustained Lansdale's "good office." Friedman's survey of Lansdale's parties, klatches, chats, and "one-on-one experiences of extreme intimacy" shows how American counterinsurgency's experiments in brotherhood "came to target, regulate, and destroy Vietnamese domestic spaces in the very name of producing an idealistic, sustaining domesticity that stretched beyond politics."[71]

In designating voluntariness as the defining feature of "brothers," I want to ask what made counterinsurgency's intimacies seem like everyday domestic fare rather than a poorly staged production. To start, we might note that in the "Pacification" memo, Lansdale champions Oscar Arellano as the "leading spirit" and "operational leader" of Operation Brotherhood but singles out "pretty Filipino girl doctors, nurses, dentists, and nutritionists" for "inspiring Vietnamese men to learn English." These are related moves, insofar as they show how gender norms inflect the fakeness of the puppet and the genuineness of the volunteer. James Fisher writes that the idea of the "Junior Chamber of Commerce sponsoring Operation Brotherhood represented one of the more audacious fictions of the cold war, as American donors were encouraged to picture earnest young Asian businessmen meeting for luncheons."[72] This cover organization was an "audacious fiction," however, not merely because of its surreptitious relation to the CIA but also because of a gendered split in its dominant representations. Such a split is apparent in journalist Gloria Emerson's recollections of volunteering with the OB team in 1956. Published in 1975 after two decades of reporting in Vietnam, Emerson's memoir carries the veneer of antiwar cynicism. On the one hand, she recalls: "Vito, Magdalena, Buddy, Paul, Carola: They were cheerful, young, hard-working and nice. Most of them were women. They traveled in teams throughout the south, opened first-aid stations and taught some public health." On the other hand, Emerson expresses disgust about running into Arellano in the 1970s and listening "in astonishment [to] the same mush I heard so eagerly in 1956 about the wonderfulness of American intentions and the importance of O.B." Twenty years later, Arellano remained "a fine actor, pouring his life into that odd, unnatural role the Americans had elected him to play."[73] In these passages, Emerson associates OB with both a spirit of conviviality and a façade of puppetry, yet she arrives at these familiar conclusions by separating the naturally "cheerful, young, hard-working and nice" female volunteers from Arellano, the face of OB, who had been playing an "odd, unnatural role" all along.

As a counterinsurgency strategy, "brotherhood" propagated images of elite men chatting over lunch, yet this fiction of democratic vigor, patriotic service, and moral fortitude was enabled by the disproportionate presence and invisible labors of female volunteers. Heeding Cynthia Enloe's injunction to apply "gender-analytical investigatory skills" to international relations, we might ask: What "racialized ideas about femininities and masculinities are shaping the myriad relationships" that go toward sustaining a brotherhood?[74] How might reading the records of U.S. counterinsurgency for the figure of the Filipina volunteer help us comprehend brotherhood not only as a fraternal bond between men and nations but also as a patriarchal structure of desire?[75] In an astute analysis of statesman Carlos Romulo (who, not incidentally, was a vocal supporter of OB), Neferti Tadiar has shown that the "masculinist posturing" of Filipino politicians conceals not so much the puppet strings of American hegemony but rather "the inordinate burden that Filipino women have had to bear" in order to legitimate the "fraternal ideals" that subtend the Philippine–American alliance.[76] In shifting our focus away from evaluating whether OB was genuinely brotherly or merely puppetry, Tadiar's formulation sets us up to investigate how the dominant trope of the male ambassador—be he a brother or a puppet—came to naturalize and conceal the informal labors performed by teams of anonymous Filipinas. To be clear, both men and women contributed to Operation Brotherhood's day-to-day operations, and there is a well-plumbed history of Asian men being conscripted for feminized labors. What the annals of counterinsurgency reveal, however, is the specificity of the Filipina as a paradigm for the volunteer—that is, a figure whose most important contributions are not skilled or professional services but informal ministrations of love, care, and cheer.

The legacy of OB shows how a gendered division of labor can produce a problem of representation: the Filipina volunteer's *over*representation in OB's daily operations is symptomatic of her *under*representation in

FIGURE 5.1. Nurses of Operation Brotherhood treat a Vietnamese patient (Credit: National Archives)

archival and scholarly accounts of OB. Although we can find this paradox across representations of OB, I'll concentrate on Lansdale's writings in order to highlight the significance of his informal tone in imbuing the free Filipina's informal labors with a sense of voluntariness.[77] We have already seen the racializing and gendering of informal labors in Lansdale's "Pacification" memo, both when he commends the OB team for holding parties during "off-duty hours" and when, in the very same sentence, he notes that American officers "on duty in the provinces" have reaped the benefits of these off-duty labors. Lansdale then lauds the "pretty Filipina girl" for enticing male refugees to learn English, thus portraying her most valuable services as the off-duty variety.[78] Elsewhere in Lansdale's writing, the strategic emergence and immediate disappearance of the pretty Filipina girl also blur the distinction between technical aid and personal care as well as between on- and off-duty services. In his memoir, Lansdale recalls the time when the OB team was barred from entering Camau. Note how the flippancy of the volunteer appears sexualized here, a quality that Lansdale's flippant tone reinforces:

The refusers were male, and there were some mighty pretty girls among the Filipina nurses. I suggested that Operation Brotherhood take several of the prettiest nurses on a visit to Soc Trang, where I was meeting with Vietnamese Army leaders for a last-minute check of the Camau march-in. When our Soc Trang military meeting broke up for a bountiful luncheon, I managed to have the Operation Brotherhood group invited to join us. The senior Vietnamese officers vied with one another to have pretty Filipinas seated beside them at the luncheon. Lunch had hardly started before the Vietnamese had decided that Philippine medical teams simply must accompany them into Camau. Arrangements were made on the spot. There is an ancient Asian custom of using a pretty girl as a negotiator. I kicked myself for not thinking of it sooner.[79]

At an operational level, this anecdote illustrates Lansdale's willingness to "break the rules of personnel assignment" in the spirit of "warm friendships and affection": he is happy to recruit pretty Filipinas to provide an informal service that exceeds their formal training as nurses.[80] At a tonal level, the passage is casually coercive. Lansdale takes pride in his ability to extemporize—the nurses-turned-negotiators are not initially supposed to attend the luncheon among "officers" and "leaders," but they tag along because Lansdale has "managed to have the Operation Brotherhood group invited." The presence of the pretty Filipinas in this scene helps transmute the air of CIA coercion into the spirit of brotherly voluntariness. Although the women are *technically* nurses, they are *naturally* pretty. This natural trait of prettiness receives the lion's share of attention because it is something that the women can give freely—that they can volunteer. The women, in other words, do not have to perform any actual negotiation on behalf of Lansdale's team, for such overtures would surely come across as spuriously affected. Their mere presence—their self-evident prettiness—is enough to convince the Vietnamese officers to insist that OB teams "simply must accompany them into Camau." Even as the passage calls our attention to what Lansdale has "managed" to do, it also suggests that neither Lansdale nor the nurses has had to do anything or give anything in order for prettiness to lubricate the fraternal feelings between Vietnamese, Filipino, and American men.

Lansdale largely presents pretty women as the enablers of brotherhood and upper-class men such as Arellano as the ambassadors of brotherhood. On one occasion, however, he does lobby for Felisa Urbano to appear on television:

My friends tell me that [Miss Felisa Urbano] would be well qualified to give a talk on Operations Brotherhood work in Laos on TV while [in the United States]. Since the judgement of my friends in such matters as appearance, personality, and articulateness is above average, I feel sure that this girl, who is unknown to me, must be unusually attractive and worth letting the American TV audience have a look at. So we are making some informal arrangements for TV appearances.[81]

In this letter, Lansdale concedes that Urbano is "unknown to me," yet he deems her "well qualified to give a talk on Operation Brotherhood's work in Laos on TV." Urbano's qualifications for speaking have little to do with her oratory or professional skills (she is a nutritionist), just as the nurses mentioned above do not need any medical expertise in order to persuade the Vietnamese officers to admit the OB team into Camau. Lansdale's recommendation of Urbano, moreover, rests upon the opinions of his friends. That Urbano was the subject of a kind of locker-room talk allows Lansdale to deduce that she "must be unusually attractive." Similar to the nurses at lunch, Urbano does not have to overextend herself to be an effective negotiator but simply needs to volunteer her pretty looks. She is "worth letting the American TV audience have a look at" because she can give so much while doing and saying so little. As with the impromptu lunch invitation that Lansdale secures for the OB nurses, Urbano's TV appearances are said to be "informal arrangements." In both these accounts, Lansdale's flippant evaluation of a pretty volunteer's "worth" turns his colloquial style of writing into a force for the casualization of labor. His breezy tone not only diminishes the potential darkness of a secret counterinsurgency program by emphasizing circumstantial developments and spontaneous affections, but this tone also makes an overtly feminized trait such as prettiness appear both incidental and central—the X-factor, as he might put it.

OUT FROM THE DARKNESS AND INTO THE LIVING ROOM

An offhand remark that becomes the kernel of determinative action shows that an ethos of informality conditions not only what unfolds but also what gets documented. As the examples I've presented make clear, OB women appear in Lansdale's writings only when they are pretty. Prettiness, then, is less an inborn attribute than a template of femininity that shapes these women's encounter with power. I borrow this language from Michel Foucault, who proposes that "lives destined to pass beneath any discourse and disappear" come to "leave traces—brief, incisive, often enigmatic—only at the point of their instantaneous contact with power." Prettiness, Foucault would say, provides the evidence that the women were "snatched" from "the darkness in which they could, perhaps should, have remained." Although Lansdale's affection for pretty women signals his faith in the usefulness of sexual intimacy within intelligence operations, Foucault guides us to view prettiness as withholding an intimate knowledge—as, indeed, indexing the unknowability of a subject. That this subject's sudden appearance—and just as sudden disappearance—is enabled and marked by prettiness imbues this trait with a touch of tragedy and violence. Foucauldian interpretations of archival loss often underscore the exceptional brutality of the archive and, it follows, the compensatory possibilities of unintelligibility.[82] My own interest in how intelligence relates to intelligibility leads me to a hypothesis that is more specific to cold war geopolitics. What we've seen is how the archival intelligibility of Filipina volunteers depends on the intelligence value of their prettiness. The violence that illuminates the pretty Filipina is not the cool bureaucratic indifference often attributed to state machinery but the soft intimate violence of imperial brotherhood[83]—the shades of blackness that turn covert affairs into love affairs, the confidential tones that combine stealth with seduction. The Filipina volunteer appears not through the grid of bureaucratic documentation—the surgeries performed, medicines distributed, diseases treated, or courses taught—but through her off-duty, informal labors—the extra party, the extemporaneous luncheon, the ad hoc TV appearance.

Even though Lansdale steers us to applaud his ingenuity in facilitating Operation Brotherhood's festivities, the fugitive presence of the "pretty Filipinas" also implicitly frames Lansdale as someone whose extraordinary capacity for love and levity has depended on unacknowledged help. Recent scholars have revealed the centrality of Lansdale's romantic dalliances to his anticommunist projects in Southeast Asia. In *The Road Not Taken* (2018), Max Boot claims to expose "the hitherto unrevealed importance of his love affair with Pat Kelly." According to Boot, Patrocinio Yapcinco Kelly, Lansdale's longtime lover and eventual wife, is responsible for his "sympathetic understanding of the Filipino people." Since Lansdale himself had neither command of Tagalog nor connections in the Philippines, he relied on Kelly's "role as an invaluable intermediary and interpreter, not only of language but also of customs and mindsets."[84] Andrew Friedman's *Covert Capital* (2013), as the title suggests, offers a more critical and less nostalgic take on Lansdale's network of intimate relations. In Friedman's account, it was not just Kelly but a whole company of Filipino and Vietnamese "friends," "intimates," "brothers," and "volunteers" whose informal labors created the aura of merriment that seemed to follow Lansdale from one good office to another. Not unlike the Filipina nurses, these helpers lent their services even when they didn't realize it. "Family meals" with Ngo Dinh Diem, for example, allowed Lansdale to "secretly [cycle] these intimacies into marketable knowledge back in the Pentagon and the CIA, where he provided U.S. militarists with microscopic details of Diem's life that transcended traditional ideas of useful diplomatic data."[85]

Lansdale's brand of psychological warfare made covert affairs of love and espionage an open secret, an everyman strategy of hiding by mingling, learning by loving. Love was Lansdale's cover, what allowed him to be the "most open and public of spooks."[86] Pat Kelly, Felisa Urbano, and the scores of "volunteers" who contributed to crafting Lansdale's open-faced cover and maintaining his "good offices" have remained largely invisible, precisely because their labors were of the off-duty variety. Although there is a nearly endless list of Lansdale's helpers, they appear only in glimpses and snatches, bustling in and out, hovering in the wings. In September 1954, Lansdale was living at 260 Rue Legrand de la Liraye where he hired "a 'grandmotherly' cook named Ti Bah." Lansdale wrote to Kelly, "She's doing her best to fatten me up."[87] In 1955, Lansdale would move to a new home at 51 Duy Tan, which served "as home and office" and included "a smaller building for the servants' living quarters." His driver and guard Proculo Mojica was a skilled guitarist and often joined the harmonica-playing Lansdale in entertaining guests.[88] Lansdale's memoir presents a different set of domestic presences: "My houseboy, Pham van Ty, followed a Vietnamese custom and had two wives, both of whom lived with him and helped keep house for me. I was fascinated and awed by the conjugal duty chart the wives had posted on the door to their quarters."[89] Journalist Joseph Alsop, who visited Lansdale in April 1955, paints yet another scene: "Lansdale's main house was a low-lying, rundown structure, the interior of which was very unkempt and disorderly. The same Filipino lady was always present, advertised as Lansdale's cook but who did more, I think, than cooking."[90] These Vietnamese and Filipino domestic laborers are among the many who "fill the margins of texts devoted to their superiors," appearing in radically truncated form and only for the "momentary performance of useful functions." Yet these minor figures nonetheless hold tremendous sway, "producing effects incongruous with [their] social position."[91] The voluntary labors of U.S. counterinsurgency's domestic hands are what bring them into view. Like OB nurses who wield their prettiness over lunch, the helpers adumbrated above—a cook who did more than cooking, a security guard who performed duets, and housekeepers who kept a "conjugal duty chart"—are all figures marked by, and rendered intelligible by, an ability to juggle a second or third duty beyond their officially designated task.

In his memoir, Lansdale writes, "I was to go to Vietnam to help the Vietnamese much as I had helped the Filipinos."[92] Long Bui has shrewdly observed that the case of Vietnam "updates the old Western 'civilizing mission' of *helping others help themselves*, infusing this ever-problematic effort with a postcolonial maxim: *We can't help you if you can't help yourself.*"[93] The "volunteers" we've met invite yet another revision, showing that U.S. efforts to build brotherhood were as much about Asians helping Americans as they were about Americans helping Asians or Asians helping Asians. That these volunteers achieve intelligibility almost entirely through their informal off-duty labors calls our attention to the domestic setting of voluntariness. On the one hand, these brotherly volunteers have helped buff the profile of "a man who never thought in terms of systems or larger social forces," who "had faith in his own good motives," and who "believed that Communism in Asia would crumble before men of goodwill with some concern for 'the little guy.'"[94] The extensive biographies devoted to Lansdale, as well as the prolific cultural representations he's inspired, speak to the durability of his self-mythification. A crucial part of this automythography is Lansdale's supposed ability to exploit the naïve superstitions and primitive cultures of "the little guy." Far from viewing natives as equals, he often took them for simpleminded stooges who needed to be tricked into "self-help." On the other hand, the fleeting presence of the volunteer—the free Asian who labors freely out of love—repositions us to view Lansdale as the recipient of help. From this perspective, Lansdale's "invention" of Operation Brotherhood is neither a story of free Asian puppetry nor American humanitarianism. It is, rather, an exposé of how the American officers of empire may be more susceptible to myth and in need of help than their Third World conscripts.

THE INTERVIEW: A HUMANITARIAN SUCCESS STORY

In the public memory of the American war in Vietnam, refugees are more often associated with the 1970s and 1980s than the 1950s. What these two refugee migrations share is a myth of help. As scholars have shown, the sense of déjà vu in the still-unfolding story of refugee migrations is no hitch, exception, or edge case but a fundamental feature of American empire. Insofar as "the gift of freedom is not simply a ruse for liberal war but its core proposition," Mimi Thi Nguyen writes, the Vietnamese refugee was "subject to the gift twice over": first "as an object of intervention in the Cold War" and again "as an object of deliverance in the aftermath of military defeat."[95] Moreover, scholars such as Marguerite Nguyen and Vinh Nguyen have taught us that the language of singular eventfulness surrounding refugee crises obscures the history of the United States as a settler empire and compresses the complex temporalities of "refugeetude."[96] Far from being a one-off crisis, the refugee figure testifies to the power of American liberal mythology and the recursive violences and violations it has simultaneously licensed and occluded.

Lansdale, too, saw the 1950s refugee migration to South Vietnam and the 1970s refugee migration to the free world as indelibly linked, but for very different reasons. In 1975, Lansdale penned a gallant letter to the *New York Times*: "Twenty years ago, it took ten months to move nearly a million Vietnamese in orderly fashion. . . . Today's prospects are that at least twice as many Vietnamese are in desperate need of another exodus, over a greater distance." He urges American communities to welcome this "splendid citizenry who would make fine neighbors."[97] In 1983, corresponding with historian William C. Gibbons, Lansdale maintains a similar line but with a shade of defensiveness: "Your statement that the refugee flow enabled U.S. officials to 'claim' that a million Vietnamese voted with their feet bothers me. Did you mean 'claim' in a pejorative sense? . . . Vietnamese are still 'voting with their feet' even today, without any encouragement from others and under horrible conditions."[98] As Lansdale would have it, well-meaning Americans are saviors who magnanimously open a door into a living room. In the 1950s, this door led to raucous festivities in Lansdale's cozy bungalows. In the 1970s, Lansdale helped move the paperwork on the behalf of numerous Vietnamese formerly employed in his counterinsurgency programs, and he even welcomed these brothers-turned-refugees into his suburban Virginia home.[99] To Lansdale, refugees who vote with their feet are another kind of volunteer. When a door opens, these autonomous agents, as an expression of their confidence in American democracy, simply choose to walk through. The narrative that Lansdale pushes denies any American interest in the outcome of voting with your feet. This ideal of humanitarianism shorn of political intent perpetuates an image of the United States as giving help rather than needing help and as "a refugee-providing rather than a refugee-producing nation."[100]

As an extension of American militarism, the myth of humanitarian assistance has had the effect of transforming the United States' oft-noted "Vietnam syndrome" into its "We-Win-Even-When-We-Lose" syndrome.[101] A vital driving force behind this transformation of national anxiety into national hubris is the Vietnam War's enormous memory apparatus. The most obvious culprit is the Hollywood blockbuster: the strategic conversion of "Vietnam" into a film has elicited biting critique from wide-ranging scholars and inspired extravagant satires from Vietnamese American and

THE TONE OF INTIMACY

Philippine American writers and artists.[102] Trinh T. Minh-ha, too, has come out strong against the war/film. The voice-over in her documentary *Surname Viet, Given Name Nam* tells us, "Nothing separates the Vietnam War and the superfilms that were made and continue to be made about it. It is said that if the Americans lost the other, they have certainly won this one." Trinh's critique of the war/film, particularly in *Surname*, is closely related to her critique of another hubristic genre: the refugee interview. In fact, although Trinh has expressed antipathy towards mainstream aesthetic practices that deny the individuality of the Vietnamese people, her far greater preoccupation has been the left-liberal aesthetic practices that purport to confer agency to a minoritized subject by letting her speak in her own words. Trinh's interrogation of the Vietnam War's memory industry thus unfolds around a problematic that she calls "giving voice."

"Giving voice" is coextensive with giving refuge. One definition of a refugee, after all, is the fact of sponsorship: "In comparison with all the immigrants from Europe and from Asia, the Vietnamese people were 'sponsored.'"[103] The sponsorship of voice, like the sponsorship of a new life, upholds a system of paternalism and compels a response of gratitude. Refugee testimonies, like refugees themselves, are expected to provide a moral solution to a tragic war.[104] Because the gift of voice arises from this geopoliticized and militarized context, it involves much more than handing a refugee a microphone. According to Trinh, the gesture of giving voice consists of not only providing an opportunity for "others" to "speak for themselves" but also incorporating representational techniques that render this speech accessible. In order for a "given voice" to be heard, it needs a more authoritative "Voice" to "objectively describe/interpret" it.[105] Presented this way, the authenticity guaranteed by a "given voice" appears analogous to the intimacy guaranteed by brotherly love: both are the products of "dirty tricks," whether in the realm of cinema or counterinsurgency. As can be expected, the agency of the Vietnamese refugee in testimonial accounts has been greeted with as much wariness as the agency of the Filipino brother in "self-help" initiatives. Both the brother's voluntary help and the refugee's voluntary voice appear to depend on a paternalistic source and to reinforce an imperialistic relationship.

The structure of Voice/voice that Trinh identifies can be found in nearly all English-language Southeast Asian refugee narratives published between the 1970s and the 1990s. Among memoirs, this structure manifests as co-authorship. Of these, the most popular are Le Ly Hayslip's *When Heaven and Earth Changed Places* (1989) and *Child of War, Woman of Peace* (1993).[106] Whereas autobiographies often conceal the contributions of "collaborators," collections of multiple "testimonies" or "oral histories" tend to explain and justify the superintending presence of an editor. Such anthologies include the Rand Corporation's *The Fall of South Vietnam: Statements by Vietnamese Military and Civilian Leaders* (1978); François Sully's *We, The Vietnamese: Voices from Vietnam* (1971); Darrel Montero's *Vietnamese Americans: Patterns of Resettlement and Socioeconomic Adaptation in the United States* (1979); Al Santoli's *To Bear Any Burden: The Vietnam War and its Aftermath in the Words of Americans and Southeast Asians* (1985); James Higgins's *Southeast Asians: A New Beginning in Lowell* (1986); Lucy Hong Nhiem Nguyen and Joel M. Halpern's *The Far East Comes Near: Autobiographical Accounts of Southeast Asian Students in America* (1989); Joanna C. Scott's *Indochina's Refugees: Oral Histories from Laos, Cambodia, and Vietnam* (1989); James Freeman's *Hearts of Sorrow: Vietnamese-American Lives* (1989); John Tenhula's *Voices from Southeast Asia: The Refugee Experience* (1990); and Robert Proudfoot's *Even the Birds Don't Sound the Same Here* (1990). All the editors listed here are white Euro-Americans, with the exception of Proudfoot, who is Native American. Many recruited the services of Southeast Asian translators and mediators, though only Hong Nhiem Nguyen is credited with authorship. While these collections often include prefatory remarks that address the ethical contingencies of collaboration, they ultimately frame the "voices" to follow as legitimate, representative, illuminating, and important. One editor tells us that "the person's voice came through more clearly on paper than through the microphone" and that editorial assistance resulted in a "more coherent, concise" text.[107] Another reassures us that each story "has been carefully checked with the story-teller" and that "as far as is humanly possible, they are accurate as told to me."[108] These editors are akin to Ha Jin's "documentary" narrator, who, as we saw in chapter 4, corroborates his political neutrality and narrative reliability by using inscriptional devices to frame, mark, and distance himself from the overwrought speech of others. In *Hearts of Sorrow*, James Freeman writes: "In collecting and editing these life stories, my aim was not to advocate a particular political position but to give people the opportunity to express their views, which are emphatically not neutral."[109] The likes of Freeman offer the objectivity of *framing* as a remedy for the distortions of *saying*: editors provide an objective frame, and respondents fill in this frame with feeling, tragedy, culture, and politics.

The late 1980s and early 1990s were responsible for the most prolific outpouring of refugee oral history projects. We ought to remember that this same period also gave rise to a decisive shift in Vietnam's relation to the United States and to its Southeast Asian neighbors. In the preceding decades, from the 1950s to the mid-1980s, security agreements involving Southeast Asia served to defend against communist infiltration. The United States' disengagement from the region after 1975 allowed Sino–Soviet and Sino–Vietnamese rivalries to flourish. This period also saw Vietnam invade Cambodia. Southeast Asian regional stability thus became increasingly defined against the ramifications of distinct yet related communist threats. By 1986, changes were underway. This was the year that Vietnam officially initiated its *doi moi* (renovation) policies, leading to what has been called socialist marketization. The nation's withdrawal of troops from Cambodia in 1988–1989 marks another key moment in the region's transformation. During this time, Vietnam was under consideration for entry into ASEAN, a cold war organization that had achieved visibility as a defense pact against Vietnamese military aggression.[110] In 1992, deliberations on Vietnam's membership were pursued in the broader context of "repositioning ASEAN to take account of the new economic and strategic realities of the post–Cold War era."[111] By 1995, the year of Vietnam's official accession into ASEAN, an economic rationale had wholly displaced a security rationale for regional cooperation among a cluster of Newly Industrialized Countries (NICs). It is noteworthy that in searching out an "NIC model," Vietnam looked not to the Philippines, the erstwhile show-window to democracy that now suffered from economic predation, but to ASEAN nations such as Singapore, Malaysia, and Thailand, which were benefiting from rapid industrialization and touting "Asian values."[112] Vietnam's outward-looking economic restructuring also resulted in significant social restructuring at home. *Doi moi* policies drew up new relationships between the state and the individual, propagated alternate conceptions of public and private, and established the family as both a site of anxiety about traditional values and a vehicle of social change.[113]

Vietnam's economic and social reforms, its withdrawal from Cambodia, and its admission into ASEAN rarely come up in mainstream discourse on the post–cold war. Nor are these developments mentioned in the refugee testimonies that began filling American bookshelves in the 1980s. While these testimonies drew emotional power from the traumas of war and the opportunities of resettlement, the geopolitical milieu that they were documenting—one that dramatized the split between "communism" and "freedom"—had already begun to change in marked ways. I'm drawn to Trinh's works from the late 1980s and early 1990s because they depict the relation between American liberal war and Vietnamese socialist and postsocialist governance as non-oppositional. Most explicitly, Trinh critiques the paternalism of American liberalism, which purports to "give voice" to the refugee. Yet works such as *Surname* also strive to expose the patriarchy of Vietnamese socialism, which exploits the labors and images of women. According to Trinh, the fact that liberal humanitarianism and revolutionary socialism are not mutually exclusive poles has confused viewers, who either are unable to reconcile "the feminist struggle" with "other struggles of liberation" or are "constantly casting the Vietnam reality back into the binary mold of communism and anti-communism."[114] *Surname*'s rejection of the cold war's polarized discourses on the basis of their shared patriarchal investments undercuts the structuring telos of the refugee testimony, a genre that moves from war to freedom, communism to capitalism, and Vietnam to America. By organizing *Surname* around two halves, Trinh points out these cold war binaries while also dismantling them. The film's first half is more "experimental"; it presents conspicuously staged interviews that appear to take place in Vietnam. The film's second half is a "realist" exposé; we learn here that the interviewees are in fact Vietnamese refugees living in the United States, and we are invited to peek into their everyday home and work lives. Through this setup, Trinh recasts the refugee's spatiotemporal passage from war to freedom as a formal shift from overtly reenacted interviews to apparently unscripted reality: "*Surname Viet* allows the practice of interviews to enter into the play of the true and the false, the real and the staged."[115] Perhaps *Surname*'s central drama comes not in either half but in the transition between them. Here, Trinh, speaking as a voice-over, calls out the interview as "an antiquated device of documentary." As she talks, the camera sweeps high and low over a series of framed photographs, pausing arbitrarily at images, spaces, and body parts.

Surname's reenactments are based on a collection of interviews conducted and translated by Mai Thu Vân in *Vietnam: Un peuple, des voix*

(1983).¹¹⁶ Trinh's self-awareness about representational politics is what distinguishes her from Mai, whose self-awareness more fundamentally concerns class politics. Put another way, where Mai focuses on socialist deception, Trinh's interest is filmic deception. As a formal parody of the ethnodocumentary, *Surname*'s interviews are interwoven with archival footage of traditional songs, dances, and rituals as well as of families, laborers, worshippers, and historical figures. The immobility of photographs and stills often calls attention to the dramatic framing movements of the camera. The mechanical eye roves across images to pause on specific faces, to visually dissect a body into its component parts, to abandon the foreground for the negative space, and to test out a range of apertures and angles. This visual framing always operates in tension with, and is sometimes undermined by, a multilayered audio track. Throughout *Surname*, subtitles do not correspond with what is spoken; Vietnamese-language songs and poetry intended to accompany the interviews end up overpowering them; stock footage of uncertain provenance or relevance are counterposed with a speaker's narrative; and English voice-overs intermingle with a speaker's interview. As these examples show, Trinh uses visual and audial framing devices that typically complement each other to relentlessly compete with each other. This formalist approach to the interview converts a truth-bearing instrument into a framing event. In *Surname*, the interview is less an interface for dialoguing or truth-telling than a platform for displaying the film's sutures and contingencies.

Surname's formal engagement of the interview initiates some degree of temporal and critical distance from the socialist context that preoccupies Mai. On the one hand, what remains constant across Trinh's documentary film and Mai's edited collection is the ideological and thematic content of the interviews themselves, which largely address the gap between a socialist regime that celebrates mothers and wives and the women whose labors have been exploited by this regime. On the other hand, Trinh's efforts to portray the interview as an ensemble of techniques and tricks estrange us from the ideologically laden content of these interviews. Her cinematic strategies have the effect of making the interviewee's diatribes against Vietnamese socialism seem as stagey as the interviews themselves. For example, before we see the face of the speaker, an excerpt from her interview is textually reproduced on screen. This quoted excerpt frames the interviewee we are about to meet by highlighting the travesties of the socialist state:

THE TONE OF INTIMACY

LY: "In principle, a foreigner is already a spy.... Even a socialist.... Or even you."

THU VAN: "A society that imposes on its people a single way of thinking, a single way of perceiving life, cannot be a human society."

CAT THIEN: "In the beginning, I tried to make things work [at the hospital], but slowly, we found ourselves in an atmosphere of distrust, then of suspicion!"

ANH: "If only men reread their history books, they would never dare send their people killing each other for ideologies. The Vietnamese people fought to [throw off] the yoke of domination. They didn't fight for some ideological principles."

In a way, these quotations prepare us to interpret the interviewees as victims of socialism. At the same time, it seems that Trinh has selected these quotations precisely for their didacticism—only Cat Thien's statement comes across as more personal than ideological. We should also remember that reading these excerpts on the page is a very different experience than reading them on the screen. In the latter case, the quotation often appears after the interviewee has already started speaking. Because the quoted text and the spoken word do not correspond, the viewer has difficulty processing either. What's more, the excerpted quote appears on screen alongside the interviewee's name, region, age, and profession. These, too, serve to frame the interviewee while also competing for our attention. By animating multiple, conflicting frames, Trinh produces a cinematic encounter where, instead of receiving straightforward information about the speaker, the viewer is thrown into a state of sensory overload.

Introducing yet interrupting the interviewee, the socialist sound bites excerpted above turn out to be exceedingly chaotic framing events. As such, these sound bites destabilize both the liberal (American) notion of voice and the socialist (Vietnamese) notion of revolution. Trinh's essays show how these twinned components of *Surname*'s interviews have been recurring points of contention among viewers. In the critical volume *When the Moon Waxes Red* (1991), Trinh stages in italics two interview-like exchanges between "a woman viewer" and "the woman filmmaker":

A WOMAN VIEWER: *By having the women re-enact the interviews, you have defeated your own purpose in the film!*

THE WOMAN FILMMAKER: *What is my purpose? What do you think is?*

THE VIEWER IRRITATED: *To show women's power, of course!*

THE TONE OF INTIMACY

A WOMAN VIEWER:—*In dealing with socialist Vietnam, why don't you show what has been acquired through the Revolution?*
THE WOMAN FILMMAKER:—*The women in the film wouldn't have spoken as they did without the Revolution.*
THE VIEWER:—*... True, but I mean real acquisitions, real attainments ... something tangible! Do you understand me?* (ellipses in original)[117]

These rebarbative reactions to *Surname* identify two sources of potential empowerment for Vietnamese women: the interview's giving of voice and the socialist state's liberation of society. The crux of the hypothetical viewer's complaint is that Trinh's reenacted interviews have turned these liberal and socialist ideals into set pieces and, in so doing, have derailed the Vietnamese woman's deliverance from patriarchy. Trinh's experimental touches, it is suggested, render her film's subaltern interviewees casualties of the Western director.

What Trinh's cinematic strategy of the interview shares with Lansdale's counterinsurgency strategy of the brother is the appearance of being contrived, staged, and artificial. The interview purports to affirm a speaker's voluntariness, yet it also evidences the manipulations of outside forces. The reader will recall that I wanted to sidestep metaphors of puppetry in discussing Operation Brotherhood, since these had the effect of highlighting the powerlessness and inauthenticity of the free Asian brother. My analysis of *Surname* likewise refrains from using theatrical metaphors to level accusations of cultural impurity and imperial complicity. In my reading, the interview is not, as Bill Nichols proposes, an instrument of ventriloquism.[118] Nor do I agree with Peter X. Feng's insinuation that the reenacted interviews in *Surname*'s first half "call attention to Trinh's intervention," while "Trinh has somewhat less control over her actors in the second half."[119] These critics remind us that acts of framing are always caught up in power relations. But while Trinh's interviews do serve to frame the speaker, they also announce to us the alternate encounters that a framing gesture can facilitate. This brings me to the key difference between the brother and the interview. In a sense, this difference is obvious: the brother is a person and the interview a device. To rephrase this in a more useful way: Lansdale's brother is purposefully informal, generating an intimacy that is casually volunteered rather than officially solicited; Trinh's interview, by contrast, is hyperbolically formal in a way that forecloses the intimacy between a speaker and a listener. In this regard, *Surname*'s abstracted socialist quotations are less about stimulating the audience's sympathy for victims of socialism than about reconceiving what an interview frame can do. The impression left by these quotations has little to do with their content and more to do with how they crowd up against other channels of information and how they slip away too soon. As an interruptive force, these framing quotations not only bar us from the speaker they presume to describe, but they also rework the relation between—and, more surprisingly, blur the distinction between—the speaker being framed and the frame itself.

All the ideological content in *Surname*—whether it's the characters' critiques of the Vietnamese socialist state or the actresses' tributes to American capitalist society—are presented through these disorienting and estranging formal techniques. Just as Lansdale's informal intimacy repurposes familial relations to assist the cause of free world alliance, Trinh's formalist intimacy reimagines affective and political relationships at a time when post–cold war developments were thoroughly transforming understandings of kinship. The framing event of the interview is central to this reimagining of intimacy. While the frame provides a convenient metaphor for the barriers imposed by the interview—a metaphor for the interview as a kind of impasse—it also demonstrates Trinh's interest in how an "impasse turns out to be a passage, and a creatively dangerous passageway."[120] Acts of framing usually serve to maintain the distance—to erect a wall—between an interviewer and a speaker, an editorial presence and an ethnographic object, a Voice and a voice. Trinh's techniques of framing, however, close this distance. Playing with the impasse thus not only creates a creative passage but also introduces new configurations of intimacy. This is what I see Trinh doing when she remakes the hegemonic interview into what she calls an "inter-view."

SUPERFICIAL INTIMACIES

The interview is a vehicle of authentication that, according to this term's etymology, allows its participants "to see each other." In this "meeting of persons face to face," the speaker-viewer relationship is typically understood as a direct address.[121] As a kind of reflexive seeing, the interview demands that interviewees "discipline their bodies to oblige the camera's requirements." To be interviewed is to be held "in the grip of the mise-en-scene."[122]

Trinh's attention to the filmmaker–speaker relationship, rather than the speaker–viewer relationship, explodes this idea of the interview as a meeting between one face and another along a horizontal axis. Her conception of the "inter-view" as "a cinematic frame" is based on interruption and suture. Understood as a repertoire of cinematic techniques, the inter-view "thereby refus[es] to reduce its role to that of a mere device to authenticate the message advanced."[123] Trinh's experimental documentaries and critical writings direct us to approach the interview as a resource for a more formalist and less intrusive mode of intimacy, one that is primarily tonal. Tone here is similar to what Eugenie Brinkema calls "a formal affectivity." In a remarkable close reading, Brinkema interprets the tear shed by a crying subject as a pure exteriority, an affect that, through form, "has fully shed the subject."[124] The disinterested yet intimate camerawork in *Surname*'s interviews invites a complementary reading. An intimate tone borne out by the *form* of the interview arises from the camera's repertoire of framing activity and has little to do with what the actresses themselves are saying. As P. Adams Sitney has written, "The structural film insists on its shape, and what content it has is minimal and subsidiary to the outline." Such a film does not reproduce an empirical real but creates "a conscious ontology of the viewing experience."[125] Catherine Russell applies this definition to ethnographic viewing in particular: "structural film conveys a means of representing 'the gaze' or the look at the Other"; it "is an exemplary incorporation of a theory of looking into ethnographic representation."[126] In *Surname*, we will find that this representation of an ethnographic gaze not only stimulates our consciousness of a viewing experience but also creates an alternate plain of relationality. More than a critique of "the gaze," the framing event of the inter-view transforms "representation" into a means of intimate cohabitation.

Trinh's preferred metaphor for the inter-view is not a horizontal line or a picture frame but a net. In contrast to anthropologists who "act as if they were fishermen," positioning themselves "as observers who throw a net, thinking that they can thereby catch what they look for," Trinh writes, "I would have to be the net myself, a net with no fisherman; for I'm caught in it as much as what I try to catch. And I am caught with everything that I try to bring out in my films."[127] This quote shows that unlike other self-reflexive documentarians who display themselves interacting with their subjects, Trinh prefers to use self-representation to destabilize subject/object relations and to controvert the autonomy of the self. For her, the inter-view is not a mutual face-to-face encounter but a distribution of the filmmaker across a film's formal apparatus: "You can recognize me or locate me everywhere in my film, in every framing, every cut, *every camera gesture*."[128] This association of the camera's movements with gesture rather than capture introduces tactility into film. It offers "the possibility of a break with the specular structure of hegemonic discourse and its scopic economy." The inter-view, then, might be thought of as "the interstice between the visual and the haptic." Or, as Trinh writes, "Sight, crossing over, is not merely sight, but speech freed from the limitations of speech."[129] In translating and restaging Mai's interviews, Trinh activates a disordering of the senses so as to reconfigure the interview's predetermined relations. "Catching" (but not capturing) the myriad participants in the net of representation renders them intertwined and inseparable. Caught together, filmmaker and subject are bound by a relation of inextricability that Trinh calls love: "However possessive it can be in its proffering, a love relationship does not allow one to speak about the subject filmed as if one can objectify it or separate oneself from it unproblematically."[130]

To explore the inter-view's enactment of this love relationship, I will focus on the interviewee Thu Van, who is played by the actress Khien Lai. Whereas *Surname*'s other three interviewees are shot in more obviously artificial mise-en-scènes with more distorted lighting while wearing ethnically or professionally coded clothing, Thu Van's three interviews present a discreetly staged minimalism. Throughout these interviews, the lighting is soft and even. Thu Van wears a white blouse, black pants, and black shoes. She appears against an unadorned white wall behind a set of wooden tables. Other than speaking, Thu Van's movements are minor. Mostly, she remains sitting, and on one occasion, she paces slowly. I'm drawn to Thu Van's interviews because they allegorize the *form* of the inter-view. The camera's movements adhere to a grid, rarely breaking from a vertical and horizontal axis. Thu Van is never "in" a visual frame. Instead, the inter-view functions as a kind of *mutual* framing: Thu Van's slowness and stillness answer to, and harmonize with, Trinh's "camera gestures." What these interviews unveil, in the end, is neither a framed subject nor, as Trinh might say, a "framer framed," but various kinds of frame-to-frame encounters—an assortment of angles, geometries, lattices, and nets.[131]

Thu Van is a 35-year-old member of a health technical cadre, who's being interviewed in Vietnam in 1982. Her three interviews take place in the same room. In the first, Thu Van directly faces the camera, which is locked in a very tight close-up. This camera appears to "scan" Thu Van, up and down, left and right. This scanning activity is broken up by systematic pauses—a beat or two on the mouth, the hands, and each quadrant of the face. Susan Lok describes this interview as the work of "an interested and indiscriminate eye." Even as it is "articulating its/my/your desiring gaze," this eye is also "refusing mastery."[132] The camera is indiscriminate insofar as its movements are predetermined; it tracks not Thu Van's body but the outlines of the representational field. In being indiscriminate, the camera aims not to capture Thu Van's subjectivity but to articulate the boundaries of the inter-view as a cinematic frame. Importantly, indiscriminateness is not synonymous with objectivity. Where the disinterest that enables objectivity confers authority, the disinterest that is bound to a grid connotes limitation. Instead of rounding out the subject, this almost passive practice of seeing models for us a different mode of attention, one that, in being indiscriminate, is incurious and uninquiring about the testimonial speaker. Indiscriminateness, in Thu Van's interview, is not opposed to interestedness. The camera signals its interest not through disclosure but through a surpassing closeness. The camera's roving activity is less probing than tactile: its "gestures" transform the industrial superfilm into a thin gossamer film, a penetrative technology into a gently refractive tone. Expressed tonally, intimacy involves not so much focusing on or looking at the subject but rather pausing on a block of the face or a slice of the hands (figures 5.2, 5.3, and 5.4). Hesitant, lingering, and idling, the camera's pause intensifies the sensuousness of details—the opening of the sleeve, the fines lines of the hand, the gloss of the nails, the weave of the blouse. But this tonal intimacy never seems salacious, for its expression is purely formal, entirely contained within a tightly controlled path.

The first interview "makes the framing itself an event," such that "people's faces are viewed like landscape."[133] The camera sweeps, circles, hovers, and loiters; its movements are far more conspicuous than the interviewee's. In the second interview, this relationship changes. We begin this interview with Thu Van sitting behind two tables, her hands resting in the

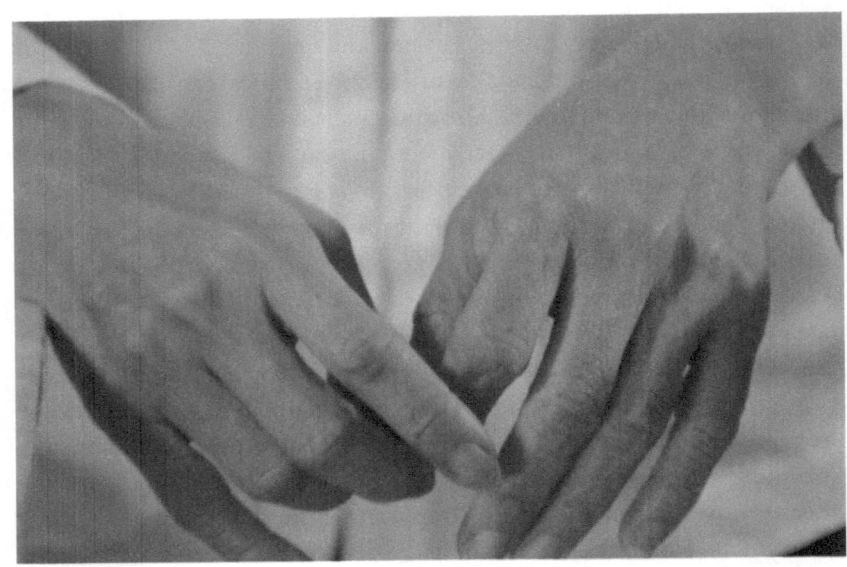

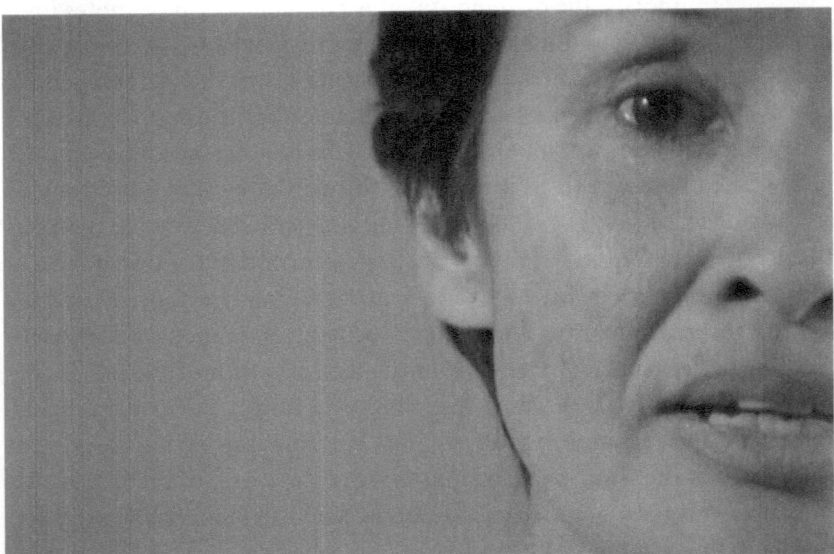

FIGURE 5.2., 5.3., 5.4. First interview with Thu Van in *Surname*

FIGURE 5.2., 5.3., 5.4. *(Continued)*

open space between them. The arrangement is peculiar. If the first interview compelled us to view the subject as always exceeding the frame, here Thu Vu appears not so much as a subject but as a part of the framing situation (figure 5.5). The center crease of her blouse is perfectly perpendicular to the center crease of the table. Together, these creases have the effect of quadrating our frame of reference. Thu Van's hands, meanwhile, are less expressive communicators than structuring vectors, creating an arrangement of symmetrical vertices, crevices, seams, and folds. Instead of the interviewee meeting the interviewer face-to-face, the two personas are radically emptied out, formalized as a frame "meeting" a frame.

If anything does enter this frame, it is "ideology." Compared to the other women, Thu Van's interviews bear a more potent political charge. Instead of relating her personal circumstances, she declares her preference to love a bicycle rather than a man and pontificates on the treatment of street sweepers. Because of Thu Van's penchant for political symbolism and political allegory, everything about this scene seems to "oscillate between function and metaphor."[134] Thu Van's black shirt and white pants, her placement between two tables, the red scarf in her hands, and the pair of scissors to

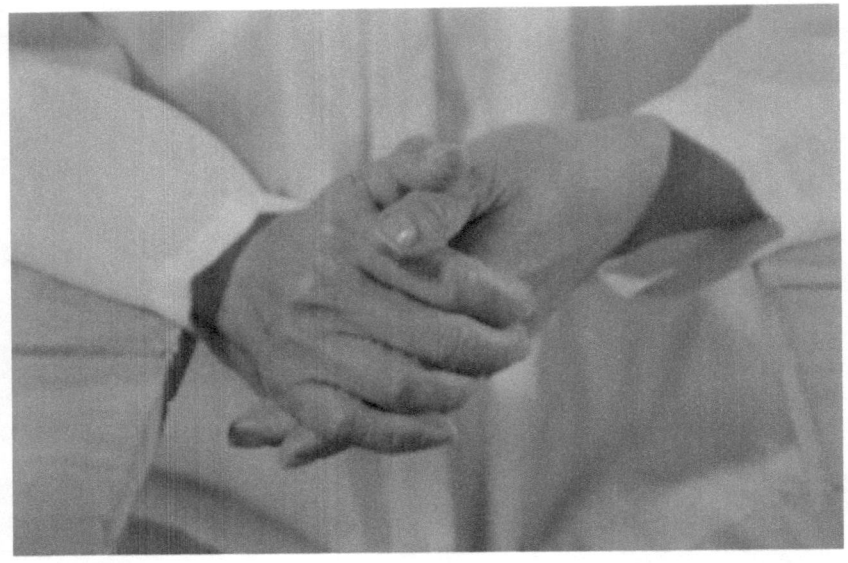

good mothers, good wives, heroic fighters. Ghost women with no humanity! They display us in shop-windows for foreign visitors who come to look at our lives, as if we were polite animals. The image of the woman is magnified like that of a saint!. We are only human beings. Why don't we want to admit that these women are tired of seeing

FIGURE 5.5., 5.6., 5.7. Second interview with Thu Van in *Surname*

THE TONE OF INTIMACY

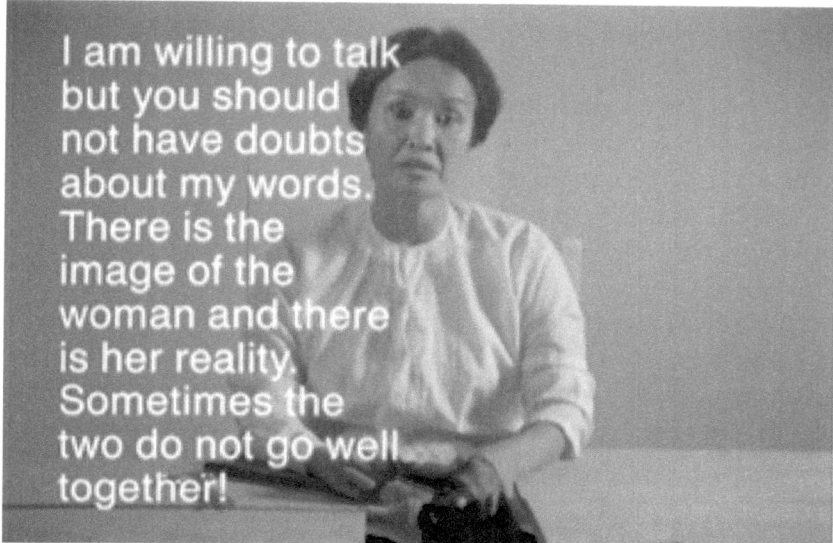

FIGURE 5.5., 5.6., 5.7. (*Continued*)

her left (figure 5.6 and 5.7)—these props and arrangements become weighted with significance as Thu Van tells us: "They display us in shop-windows for foreign visitors"; "The image of the woman is magnified like a saint"; "There is the image of the woman and there is her reality"; and "I am caught between two worlds: the socialism which I reject and the capitalism which I do not know." What deters us from interpreting this interview as a black-and-white allegory of cold war politics—a division of north and south, socialist and capitalist, "the image of the woman" and "her reality"—is the camerawork. Similar to the first interview, the camera movements in this second interview disinterestedly mark out a frame, tenderly pausing on the face, the hands, and the feet. Unlike the first interview, these pauses are accentuated with the flashing of quotations—a cross between subtitles and sound bites. Despite their loaded content, however, the subtitles/sound bites do not actually clarify or exemplify a political subject. In fact, the visualization of words across the screen makes Thu Van appear even more muted and flat. These interviews are ultimately less an allegory about cold war politics than an allegory about the politics of framing. The white letters superimposed on the white blouse and against the white wall appear as a screen, a contraption that both administers and obfuscates an inside and an outside, a subject and a frame. In this setup, even the political allegory of cold war Manichaeanism gets repurposed as a documentary device. The fraught binaries of socialism and capitalism that Thu Van discusses with such zeal are more about spectacle than content, appearing to us as a visual transposition, a bisected frame.

In the last reenacted interview, the camera seems to entirely cede authority and action to Thu Van. Whereas our initial understanding of the interview as a framing event came from the camera's dramatic sweeps and scans, the third interview presents a more mobile subject. If, before, the camera's movements overshadowed Thu Van's, here Thu Van appears to have more agency by walking in and out of the camera's frame (figure 5.8). Yet by this point in our viewing, the difference between a "frame" and a "subject" has become fully undone. The ambulatory subject's casual pacing is not so different from the sitting subject's minimalist mannerisms in that both these embodied gestures actively and reciprocally participate in the camera's framing gestures. The point isn't that Thu Van escapes the frame, just as the point of *Surname* isn't to reject representation *tout court*. What's

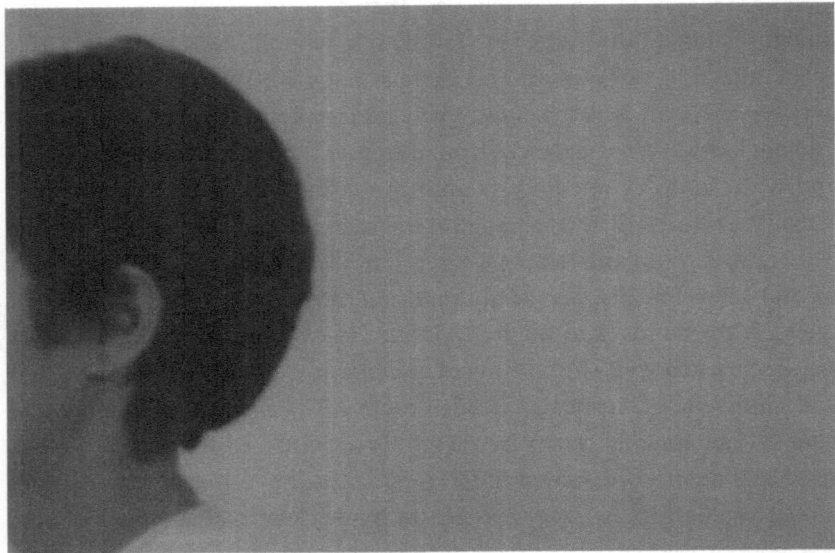

FIGURE 5.8. Third interview with Thu Van in *Surname*

significant in the third interview is that the camera's dilatory movements become inseparable and indistinguishable from Thu Van's own. Neither camera nor interviewee possesses mastery: the camera does not capture Thu Van, and Thu Van does not refuse the camera. As both move along a horizontal axis, it becomes unclear whether the camera is following Thu Van or vice versa. Or, it may be more accurate to say that neither wants to catch or catch up to the other, but they pace side by side, their strides intermingling.

THE OTHER HALF

Interpretations of racial self-representation still often swing between redemptive agency and traitorous complicity, cultural authenticity and false stereotype. When agential and authentic, individuals act on their own behalf; when complicit and false, they act on the behalf of and under the influence of someone else. Rather than use Lansdale's exploitation of the Asian brother and Trinh's exploitation of the refugee interview to condemn puppetry and valorize autonomy, I've recast "self-representation" as a collective project that implicates multiple historical actors and mobilizes heterogeneous affective relationships. In my analysis thus far, I have discussed self-representation through spatial metaphors: for both Lansdale and Trinh, self-representation involves a kind of cohabitation. In Lansdale's case, cohabitation is a domestic enterprise enabled by free Asians, who volunteer their informal labors to create an intimate living room. In Trinh's, cohabitation describes the formal entanglement of a filmmaker and her subjects, who are caught together in a fisherman's net. In this chapter's concluding remarks, I'd like to contemplate how racial self-representation, as a kind of collective cohabitation, is not a singular event but unfolds over time. As I've mentioned in passing, both Lansdale's brothers and Trinh's interviews have a second life: the brother, "created" by Lansdale in South Vietnam, is eventually transported to suburban Virginia, indeed to Lansdale's own home; the interview, conducted in a fictional Vietnam staged by Trinh, reappears in a realist documentation of domestic life in quotidian California, where Trinh herself resides. If refugee narratives tend to essentialize the differences between violent displacement from socialist Vietnam and peaceful resettlement in capitalist America, then these case studies of the cold war brother and the post–cold war interview command our attention to the spatiotemporal *continuity* between now and then, here and there.

In Lansdale's case, the continuity between superficially disparate timespaces is provided by the confidential "good office." In this domesticized space of intimate relations, the cold war safe house of brotherly counterinsurgency doubles as the post–cold war sanctuary of refugee resettlement. Filipino nurses who first earned their stripes in the living rooms of American counterinsurgency sometimes found themselves in the operating rooms of American hospitals. J. "Pete" Fuentecilla describes how with the American retreat in 1975, Operation Brotherhood volunteers in Laos became refugees themselves, escaping to Thailand and, eventually, to France, Canada, Australia, England, and the United States. Because "the OB program was somewhat patterned to the U.S. licensed practical nursing course," those who ended up in the United States "earned their RN licenses" and "continued nursing."[135] We can find a parallel story in the case of the brothers once employed in American counterinsurgency programs, who became refugees in Northern Virginia following the Fall of Saigon. The suburban resettlement narrative, like the counterinsurgency "good office" narrative, troubles the distinction between battlefield and home. Andrew Friedman describes how on June 7, 1975, Lansdale "hosted a gathering at his house 'where newly arrived refugees could organize some self-help programs.'" As in South Vietnam, these "self-help programs" doubled as a form of political warfare. Refugees sponsored by Lansdale were even involved in efforts by anticommunist "freedom fighters" (and U.S. intelligence veterans) to retake Vietnam in the 1980s.[136] In Lansdale's living room, the cold war crusade for collective security merged with the post–cold war program of humanitarian refuge. Moreover, for Lansdale, and many other American veterans, the open festivities of the living room were contiguous with the more confidential intimacies of the bedroom. Intimates who became informants also became immigrants. In 1973, after the death of Lansdale's wife, his lover Pat Kelly relocated to Virginia, where they were eventually married.[137]

At first glance, Trinh's *Surname* appears to dramatize the difference between wartime in Vietnam and peacetime in America through its stylistically distinct "halves." The reenacted interviews of *Surname*'s first half are so conspicuously choreographed that they might be mistaken for dramatic monologues. In *Surname*'s second half, the formal interviews have become informal conversations. These take place in the United States and in more natural and everyday settings, often outside. For example, when we meet Khien, the actress who plays Thu Van, she is engaged in an animated conversation over an outdoor meal with friends. Filmed in one continuous take, this scene shows Khien eating as she talks; her interlocutors occasionally laugh or ask a question; a person walks by with a tray. Instead of ventriloquizing someone else's words at someone else's direction, Khien appears to be speaking to her friends on her own accord. What ties together *Surname*'s two halves is the theme of women's labor. Although the character Thu Van vociferously spurns socialist Vietnam's valorization of "heroic workers, virtuous women," it so happens that heroism and virtue are central to the actress Khien's own self-understanding. In the conversation with friends, Khien speaks of three different jobs that she held after the war. Khien portrays these demeaning and dangerous jobs as sacrificial; she took them on to feed her children. If Khien's work life seems to draw from socialist ideals of heroism and virtue, then her American leisure life seems to reinforce ethnic and gendered ideals of beauty. The long take of Khien's conversation is interleaved with footage of her feeding fish with her son, sipping tea in a Japanese-style garden, and modeling the traditional Vietnamese dress in an American elementary school.

What do we make of these apparent inconsistencies? As I see it, *Surname*'s overriding message is not that only the actresses in the first half are playing a role, nor that women are always playing a role, but that the abstraction of the natural from the role gives femininity its value. Trinh's concern with the social productivity of femininity in *both* socialist and capitalist contexts, as well as in *both* theatrical and occupational roles, manifests in myriad scenes of singing, dancing, courting, and marrying that proliferate *across* the film's two halves. An overemphasis on the differences between these two halves therefore not only divides wartime from peacetime but also divides women's labor into waged and unwaged, formal and informal, public and private. Such divisions, when cast as a problem of representation, compel us to view the liberation of autonomous voice (in conversations) as a remedy to the violence of conscripted ventriloquism (in interviews).

In this chapter, I have positioned *the interview* as a post–cold war counterpoint to *the brother*. As social technologies for producing intimacy, the interview and the brother have both been weaponized within psychological warfare campaigns. A second refugee migration has required a second round of psychological warfare not only to continue buoying the United States' global reputation and self-conception but also to maintain a narrative predicated on the increasingly untenable polarities of American benevolence and Asian need, capitalist plenty and socialist privation, self-willed individuals and propagandistic mouthpieces. Through the brother, Lansdale contributed to these political-psychological campaigns by attempting to actualize anticommunist affiliation through cultural filiation. Trinh, however, equips us to conceive of the interview as generating forms of intimacy in excess of these cultural and political identities.

To offer one final encapsulation of Lansdale's and Trinh's distinct approaches to self-representation, we might compare how they differently take up the metaphor of the fish pond. Lansdale, as I noted in this chapter's opening pages, found inspiration in the Chinese communist axiom "the people are the water and the soldier is the fish." For, Trinh, meanwhile, the fisherman's net offered a way to describe the entangled relation—the love relation—between a filmmaker and her subjects. If Lansdale's metaphor of the brother as a fish sustains a fictive freedom of swimming together, Trinh's metaphor of the interview as a net emphasizes a mutual binding, a state of being caught together. For Lansdale, Operation Brotherhood's construction of fish ponds guaranteed both political and cultural legitimation: "Chinese 'volunteer' teams attempted social welfare work similar to that of 'OB,' suffering considerable loss of face when the Filipinos showed Vietnamese farmers how to build fish ponds just south of the 17th Parallel, which the Chinese failed to do."[138] In contrast to Lansdale, who promoted the fish pond as a powerful symbol of a pan-Asian friendship, Trinh uses the fish pond to draw out the unexpected conflicts in how two Vietnamese women understand self-representation. In recounting the production of *Surname*, Trinh notes how she had found it "disturbing" when Khien had insisted on being filmed by a fish pond for the film's "real-life" component, even though fish ponds had no actual bearing on her everyday life. Significantly, Trinh's opinion of the fish pond changes when she views the film footage: "having always been such a richly significative symbol in Asian cultures, the fish pond seems to point here to a dream space, a space of meditation where you can rest and retreat from the pressure of daily work."[139] The fish pond's transvaluation from a kitschy stereotype into a "dream space"—into something like film itself—suggests that the camera does not merely record an object but has the potential to actively transform subject-object relations. In using the formalist interview to enact entanglement rather than extraction, *Surname* shows that an interviewee speaks but only with the participation of myriad others, that a filmmaker conducting a documentary interview cannot but document herself too, and that a framing event is both a power relation and a co-production.

By reimagining self-representation as cohabitation, Trinh reworks the relation between intelligence and intimacy. In doing so, she also raises the question of how individual self-representation bears on collective solidarity. Is there a path between the two? Perhaps to tell the story of Asian self-representation through U.S. intelligence operations already primes us for political disappointment. It is not only difficult and uncomfortable but perhaps also problematic and parochial to consider a politics guided by the paradigm of Asian self-representation, which, in both cold war and post–cold war contexts, often accounts for the navel-gazing tendencies of mainstream Asian American activism. I find Trinh's reconceptualization of the impasse to be a helpful starting point for thinking through these challenging yet necessary questions. What if the impasse, the boundary, the barrier, or the divide were to "signal a departure and the possibility of a different presencing?"[140] Given the bugaboos of stereotype and essentialism—given these inexorable political and critical impasses—what kind of collective presencing can self-representation enable, especially in a way that allows one to move across and beyond proper identity categories? As the coda to this book will show, I find it much easier to ask than to answer these questions. But even without answers, my hope is that the question and impasse of Asian diasporic solidarity may still yet embolden our political critique and enlarge our political imagination.

CODA—THE TONE OF COMMONS

Solidarities Without a Solid

> Motion of the greater congregation
>
> Of being in and affecting
>
> —MYUNG MI KIM, *COMMONS* (2002)

Instead of using war to *measure time*—instead of assuming that *antebellum* America, *post45* literature, and *post–cold war* geopolitics have self-evident meaning—this book has contemplated how we *measure war*. To be sure, we already have many ways to measure war: casualties, territories, supplies, and public opinion are to gauge winning and losing; officially conferred medals and reparations can presumably calculate valor and injury. These metrics are in the end unsatisfying and misguided, I've argued, because they operate on a mischaracterization of war. In taking a *tonal* measure of the American cold war in Asia, *Tonal Intelligence* has contributed to a more fundamental project of rethinking what this war was. That is, my search for an alternate *measure* of the cold war has been entirely bound up with an effort to *discern* this war. In this regard, *Tonal Intelligence* extends the work of scholars who have characterized the cold war in Asia as a *perpetual* structure that became, and continues to be, a *perceptual* problem: this is a war that often passes as "governance" and that sometimes looks like "peace." My more focused interest in this book has been the role of U.S. intelligence in rendering war unconventional and total. Working through specific case studies, I've explored how the United States' desire for enemy intelligence coexisted with its worry about racial intelligibility. Tone has been useful for studying these matters of temperament. Whether through the pulse of viral rumors or the ecstatic excesses of POW testimonies, tone has allowed us to take an aesthetic and affective measure of a war preoccupied with the hidden meanings of race. Tone has also facilitated our attunement to the *periodic* aspect of a cold war *period*. Tobin Siebers writes: "We have seen the cold war come and go so many times that we must recognize that one defining feature of the cold war era is not knowing where we stand in relation to our enemies or friends."[1] Based on this formulation, the temperament of suspicion influences not only how one approaches an analytical object but also how one comprehends the chronology of war; the cold war continues to "come and go" at the same pace as the comings and goings of potential enemies. In a geopolitical order still permeated with cold war suspicion, tone has provided a device for tracking continuity and measuring change. It has helped us take the temperature of an evolving historical milieu by examining inscrutable figures side by side. Through this juxtapositional analysis, we have learned how the confusion of regime change can engender differential conceptions of modernity and differential experiences of historical time.

So—the previous chapters have used tone to measure "war," this way and that. In doing so, they have presented the temperament of the cold war as something like a historical climate, an atmospheric commotion that people are unknowingly steeped in or uncontrollably swept up by. The free Asian and Asian diasporic subjects we've met all experience the intimacy and immediacy of this climate of war—and for precisely this reason, these subjects are often stricken by a profound historical myopia. As an open-ended conclusion to *Tonal Intelligence*, I'd like to entertain a slightly different portrayal of historical temperament, one in which it is both a mobilizing force and a force that is mobilized. In this revised framing, modulations of atmosphere are what inject unlikely possibility into the status quo and enable a flare or flicker of a different future. The perception of a change in pressure—but not necessarily a change in substance—can make new ideas and feelings seem uniquely conceivable and new relations and aspirations seem potentially attainable. This flash of historical perceptiveness can initiate the minor estrangement that suddenly allows us to be other to ourselves—to encounter our own capacity for action of another scale, to recognize our commonality with a collective, and to initiate our absorption into a cause. In short, a temperament, climate, milieu, or mood is not simply something that one becomes passively caught up in. Moods can move us to move together.

Many critics have tried to put their finger on this galvanizing historical situation. Sara Ahmed writes, "'great movements' of feeling" link the personal to the historical, providing the glue that "holds or binds the social body together." Or, Jonathan Flatley: "if we want to form politically agential collectives, this is most directly a question of moods." Dora Zhang has offered an especially trenchant reflection on how a historical mood can become harnessed toward political ends: "What would it mean to bring about a climate in which a collective is moved to act in the service of social change?"[2] These critics describe what I think of as a movement-moment—an eruption of a *political movement* that helps crystallize a *historical moment*. In keeping with the distended temporalities that I've examined, this coda will be interested in a less monumental kind of moment and a less momentous kind of movement. This interest takes me to Myung Mi Kim, a poet whose extensive ruminations on "wartime" have also functioned as explorations of collectivity—specifically, the collective dynamic of both moving and being moved.

The two epigraphs I've chosen for this chapter come from Kim's 2002 poetry collection *Commons*. These poetic aphorisms offer us pedagogies for "standing in proximity"[3]—for being together in an affiliative structure that is uncodified and disunited. Kim's notion of a *commons* requires us to reframe a *collective movement* as "motion of the greater congregation," and it requires us to understand *individual agency* as "of being in and affecting."[4] Despite appearing to take the wind out of the political, this blueprint for coming into relation and proceeding as formation is more utopian than nihilistic. Kim's poetics situates us in an otherworldly time-space. Although devoid of social, cultural, racial, and historical notations, it is clearly a world racked by war, inequality, and violence. What's disorienting about *Commons*, however, is not its apocalyptic quality or its difference from "our" reality; it is the degree to which we are embedded *inside* the immediate present of an uncanny world. Because of this embedment, we can perceive no more and no less than an intimate surround. This pressing nearness is experienced as both a provocation and a proscription: through the sheer act of reading, we are tasked with imagining connection and fullness in a landscape of gaping lack. How might we move through, with, and toward a commons when confronted with scarcity and bound by limitation?

Commons explores race, diaspora, and culture mainly through depictions of plant and animal species. Its titular "commons" does not refer to any particular formation at any particular moment, but it does pose the question of how a form becomes a formation and when a movement produces a moment. Although *Commons* makes no explicit reference to "Asian America" or "Asian diaspora," it has made me realize that these also denominate dislocated time-spaces worlded by war and suffused with possibility. In the 1995 essay "Denationalization Reconsidered," Sau-ling Wong characterizes "Asian America" as more of a political desire than an empirically locatable place. This "quasi-geographical term," Wong writes, bespeaks "a yearning for the kind of containing boundaries and contained site enjoyed by the dominant society, a nation-state." To "denationalize" Asian America would be to both diffuse and defuse it: "the idea of an 'Asian diaspora' would be so inclusive as to be *politically ungrounded*." Wong thus recommends: "coalitions of Asian American and other racial/ethnic minorities within the U.S. should take precedence over those formed with Asian peoples in the diaspora."[5] Kim's phrase "of being in and affecting" is undeniably "politically ungrounded"—there is no individual or collective subject and no spatial or temporal orientation. *Commons* appeals to me, however, not as a political prescription but as a thought experiment in what an ungrounded politics might afford for an unbounded collective. As a leveling that produces relationality, a commons may seem like a gesture toward universality. I'd say, though, that Kim's agricultural motif is better characterized as diasporic rather than universal: her poems are patterned arrangements that mimic how a single diaspora spreads and how different diasporas interact. By taking differentiation—of society, history, language, and species—to the infinitesimal extreme, Kim's commons shows how individual incidents, idiosyncratic in their separateness, might nonetheless give rise to a relational formation—to co-incidence, so to speak. Overwhelming differentiation is what makes connection newly possible and unexpectedly meaningful.[6]

The "free Asians" and "Asian diasporans" in *Tonal Intelligence* fall on the outsides of the movement-moment called "Asian America," a political formation whose origin story is most often associated with the late 1960s. Free Asians such as Induk Pahk and Operation Brotherhood seem to precede the Asian American Movement, and Asian diasporans such as Theresa Hak Kyung Cha and Ha Jin seem to succeed it. This temporal remove from the heart of a revolutionary politics is exacerbated by a spatial interstitiality. Both free Asians and Asian diasporans are tricky to reconcile with a "domestic" notion of Asian America. Finally, even more difficult than placing such figures temporally and spatially is articulating them to a common political project. Sau-ling Wong, of course, is right. It is impossible to craft a consistent politics that can properly ground an Asian diasporic formation. With respect to a *cold war* Asian diaspora, we can at least identify a containment culture that influenced how far-flung artists, writers, critics, educators, prisoners, statespeople, and aid workers fashioned themselves as racial subjects—as "free Asians." This cold war geopoliticization of diaspora explains how someone like Jade Snow Wong could be better known by the label of "Overseas Chinese" before she was retroactively canonized as "Chinese American." A *post–cold war* Asian diaspora is a product of war. Such a diaspora is thus bound by commonality but not necessarily by cause. Indeed, in our contemporary moment, the geopolitical conditions that have been produced by an unresolved cold war have rarely resulted in a shared political vision among Asians and Asian Americans—and even more rarely among Asians, Asian Americans, and Oceanians. What I'm saying, then, is that the clunky locution I've been using, "post–cold war Asian diaspora," only *appears* to promise specificity—a ground to build on, an identity to organize around. In this locution, "post–cold war" and "diaspora" are essentially phantom descriptors. They give name to the process of living out a history that is not always recognizably one's own, of drifting through an otherworldly elsewhere that eclipses nations, oceans, and blocs. "Post–cold war" and "diaspora" have the paradoxical effect of emptying out the formation that they purport to describe, transforming it into a double elision, a displacement from both temporal and spatial coordinates. A placeless placeholder term, "post–cold war Asian diaspora" gives name not to a fully formed or already existing formation but to an ongoing process of accretion and dissolution.

Even if mutually unmoored subjects cannot become a politic, can they nonetheless become a commons? Even if diasporas are groundless, can there still be—to quote Nadia Ellis—a "coming together of people mutually claiming to have no relation to each other," a formation in which it is "separateness that constitutes the connection?"[7] Even if the shared moment that brings a diasporic commons together cannot in the end climax in the explosive force of a movement, might there still be an impactful motion of this greater congregation? In the previous chapters, we have already witnessed versions of a commons. In Ishiguro's novels, forgettable minor characters were linked together through groundless rumors—a tremor or tic that eventually outstrips any individual speaker and accords outsized power to a collective mood. Trinh offers another imagining of commons. In her films, an inter-view implicates its participants in a "net," such that the coincidence of being caught together becomes an intimate cohabitation. From one perspective, an amorphous, unintentional, and scattered social form seems incapable of congealing into an effective political formation. As Wong might put it, a diaspora cannot become a coalition. From another perspective, an ungrounded and unbounded formation gives rise to a fissiparous congregation in motion—a commons. In the remainder of this conclusion, I want to look at three contemporary writers whose representations of a commons indirectly comment on a "post–cold war Asian diaspora." Ed Park, Eugene Lim, and Pamela Lu have all explored the coincidental and unintentional bonds that form among characters who may or may not be Asian and, in fact, who may or may not be characters. Where Kim conceives of a post-apocalyptic commons as a product of militarism, Park, Lim, and Lu portray commons as a late capitalist condition of individual disintegration. These commons are, to be sure, the same. As we have seen time and again, a post–cold war Asian diaspora is both a militaristic formation and an economic one.

DENATIONALIZED AND DESOLIDIFIED

Ed Park's *Personal Days* (2008) is an office novel in which cost-cutting initiatives, corporate catchphrases, generically similar names, and mundane elevator talk combine to make its unmemorable minor characters indistinguishable from each other.[8] These characters are formally voiced as a narrative persona called "we." Park's deindividualizing approach to depicting "we" shows how contemporary office work have made it impossible to "establish an actual distinction between a stable 'inside' and an uncertain and telluric 'outside.'" In other words, the irony of "personal days" is the obsolescence of both the individual unit of the "personal" and the temporal unit of the "day." There are no personal days in a workaday life, which now bears "a direct and continuous relation with the world as such, with the imprecise context of our existence."[9] Park formalizes the imprecise context of a mid-level employee's existence by locating his characters at the vacillating boundary between "I" and "we" as well as between background and foreground: all the characters in *Personal Days* are so minor that their sole function is to stage their own retreat.[10] So while Min Hyoung Song is correct to observe that Park's novel contains "only trace references to race," we must note that it also contains only trace references *of* characters.[11] These two aspects of *Personal Days* are related. In Park's novelistic world, race is a simultaneously characterizing and characterless designation. It is the most stable, empirical, and embodied in the case of Jonah, a belatedly "self-identified 'half black' man," who is the sole survivor in a corporate apocalypse of downsizing. Through Jonah, Colleen Lye writes, Blackness becomes associated with "a narrative of individual emergence or distinction."[12] By contrast, the novel's "half-Asian British accented woman" (nicknamed HABAW) appears to us only in liminal flashes. Indeed, we encounter her almost exclusively in the context of elevator small talk. Although nominally distinguished by nationality, race, and accent, this token Asian character never materializes beyond silent, cipher-like acronymic "traces"—HABAW, .5ABW, AB, Tracy, Trace. Whether intentional or not, Park's coding of racial halfness, in one case enduring and in the other evanescent, shows that the "differential processes of Asian and black racialization constitute U.S. middle-class identity more divergently than ever before."[13] These divergent approaches to representing the waning and wavering markers of racial difference also point to divergent political paradigms. Whereas Black politics is conventionally figured as a charismatic male personality, Asian/American politics is conventionally figured as trace efforts and token causes.[14]

Although it is possible to read *Personal Days* from a "Black" lens or an "Asian" lens, the novel actively thwarts such efforts. It is not exactly a race novel (despite the Black hero), a diaspora novel (despite the British Asian character), or an American novel (despite the Manhattan setting). Rather, Park's interest in the slide between (racial) type and (print) typography makes *Personal Days* a cross between a stereotypical novel and a typographical novel. In studying the relation between commercial society and print culture, Deidre Lynch has shown how eighteenth-century English readers developed "a fascination with the puns that could link the person 'in' a text to the printed letters (alphabetic symbols, or 'characters' in another sense) that elaborated that text's surface."[15] Analogously, in the globalized twenty-first-century workplace that Park spoofs, the trace character—reduced to an alphabetic character—is also the race character—reduced to a graphic type.[16] Following Lye, we might read *Personal Days* as "critically responsive to and diagnostic of post-Fordist modes of racialization."[17] I would add that this novel also models for us post-Fordist modes of racial formation. That is, precisely because Park prefers to trace race instead of to represent race, *Personal Days* reads as a "commons" novel; it is a novel trying to imagine how depersonalized persons might come together through ways other than outright political legibility. Relatedly, I would submit that *Personal Days* is a tonal novel. This is because the reduction of all characters (even Jonah) into trace-effects makes an overriding *mood* rather than any individual or collective *personality* the site of political critique. Despite or because of her unimportance, it is Trace's "elevator talk" or "elevator pitch" that sets the tone for *Personal Days*. This overly generic tone is the product of various formal and thematic devices for disabling a "politics of recognition." One such device is the proliferation of forgettable J-names (Jack, Jack II, Jill, Jenny, Jason, Jules, and Jonah). Another more literal device is a voice recognition software called Glottis. Glottis is constantly malfunctioning at its specialized task of recognizing voices, for instance interpreting "Percival Davis" as "Personal Days." Or, just as likely, it could be that the novel's depersonalized trace characters—who all spew "office argot" (112)—do not in fact possess recognizable voices. Whatever the case, the stock phrases, trite colloquialisms, and cheap puns coursing through the novel bring into relief the inventive literary language—the "reams of Dada-ready sentences" (225)—produced by Glottis's malfunctioning. Where Glottis's voice is novel and distinctive, the standardized pitch of the novel provides the tone of the commons. Facilitated by characters who are always receding, this commons is a coincidental formation. As a "we," it accrues shape only through incidents of misrecognition: "We look like we've been squeezed out of a tube and haven't quite solidified" (5–6).

Eugene Lim's *Dear Cyborgs* (2017) and Pamela Lu's *Ambient Parking Lot* (2011) also feature not-quite-solidified solidarities.[18] I'll dwell a bit longer on these novels because their engagement of a disorganized mode of collective organizing more explicitly parodies the heroic politics of a movement-moment. Lu's and Lim's characters are also t/race effects.[19] As in *Personal Days*, these characters travel under the sign of pronouns, alphabetic letters, code names, and pseudonyms, and they flitter in and out of a "we" voice. Incapable of separating themselves both from each other and from their social environments, Lim's and Lu's characters inhabit a collective commons that is ubiquitous, expendable, expandable, and inconsequential. For Lim, the politics of this collective is called parasitic. For Lu, the keyword is ambient. These weak, improvisational, vacuous, and ambivalent politics cast "solidarity" as the liquid form of an amoeba-like blob and the vaporous form of invisible microbes. Because they are desolidified, Lu's and Lim's "solidarities" are hardly legible as such; they seep into and are borne out of the morass of work, life, and art. To borrow a line from Kathleen Stewart's peripatetic ethnography of late capitalism, ambience and parasitism are "[w]eirdly collective sensibilities" that "pulse in plain sight."[20]

PARASITISM: TALKING NEXT TO

Both Lu and Lim present landscapes of political declension—of parasitism and ambience—against mythic visions of a more potent politics and a sturdier solidarity. In Lim's *Dear Cyborgs*, the locus of such myths will be achingly familiar to academic readers:

The analysis of race and power that became institutionally codified in the Ethnic Studies departments in California, and which has since spread to institutions nationally and worldwide, has had, to understate it, a great impact. In many ways this ongoing analysis and study is the intellectual engine driving today's continuing battle for justice and civil rights. This is so much the case that one can not only excuse the late Fred Ho's defense of his friend but even believe to be true his statement, "If Aoki was an agent, so what? He surely was a piss-poor one because what he contributed to the movement is enormously greater than anything he could have detracted or derailed."

Still, the long-held lie is devastating. Especially, for better or worse, to those wanting heroes.

And Aoki's story is haunting and important—I want to say to Frank and Muriel and Dave—also, maybe chiefly, because it is such an American story in that it tells the tale of a particular kind of passing. (136)

Lim's narrator begins by noting that the lessons "institutionally codified in the Ethnic Studies departments" continue to be the "intellectual engine driving today's continuing battle for justice and civil rights." The academy's edifying relation to a larger political cause is then ironized through the case of Richard Aoki, a Japanese American Black Panther, who in 2012 was alleged to have been a CIA agent. By invoking renowned musician, activist, and intellectual Fred Ho, who insisted on preserving the narrative of "the movement" and Aoki's place within it, Lim raises the question of why Ethnic Studies is so committed to its own origin story, even in the face of incriminating evidence. The upshot of the anecdote, however, is not to indict the institution of Ethnic Studies, but to recognize the desire for Asian American political heroes. This desire belongs not just to Ethnic Studies scholars but also to the novel's protagonists, a cast of Asian American superheroes described as "depressed and anxious much of the time" (43). Let's be clear here. By superheroes, we are not talking about Clark Kent or Peter Parker, who passionately take on herowork as a side gig or a nighttime extracurricular. We are also not talking about Matt Murdock, Jessica Jones, or Luke Cage, heroes who turn their social marginality into justice-serving superpowers (enhanced senses for the blind man, physical strength for the white woman, and indestructible skin for the Black man). Departing from these genre conventions, the superheroes in Lim's novel—Frank, Muriel, Dave, and a flickering I—are the listless employees of Team Chaos who struggle in a very different way to maintain work/life balance. By the novel's end, political protest, artistic creation, and clocking the nonheroic superhero hours have all been reduced to their core features of routine and ritual. In other words, the novel's titular *cyborgs* have little to do with technology in the conventional sense. For Lim, the term *cyborg* simply refers to the fact that these exceedingly ordinary superheroes—these uninspired employees—have become preprogrammed in their most basic life choices, whether it's buying a book, taking a lunch break, doing drugs, ghostwriting a political autobiography, working as a stock broker, or engaging art and politics as "merely a way of living" (5).

Amidst these mundanely repetitive routines, parasitism emerges as a regenerative source of possibility and a recurring topic of conversation among Lim's pack of characters. Parasitism is first articulated parenthetically as "a sliver of protest still possible," a potentially "reactionary or collaborative tactic," and an "admittedly vaporous defiance." This last-ditch option, something just short of "utter acquiescence," is to "try without going into heroics to participate minimally, as a parasite does, getting one's needs and not much more" (8). Is this minimal participation selfish or selfless? Does it counteract individual heroism, or is it merely a form of shirking social responsibility? These questions are easier to consider through a concrete example. The following case involves the narrator's fellow superhero Muriel:

"I mean, since these temptations and shortcuts are unavoidable, impossible to outwit, maybe Muriel should use them to proceed with her own desires.... And she should pursue these desires using these corrupt means as would a freeloading parasite. Why not? Take your breaks and do your sketches and read poetry chapbooks at Wendy's or Burger King or McDonald's, especially—and this surely could be a measurement of your will, at least an exercise of it—especially if you can mostly avoid the food and only have a coffee. Or," I concluded, "a diet soda, even." (130)

Within the same conversation, Dave brings up a second example:

Then, after another minute, Dave said, "Some Koreans, elderly, a gaggle of grandmas and grandpas, did just what you're doing Muriel. They would use this McDonald's down the road from my apartment. At first it was three or four of them, but then slowly word started to spread and dozens of Korean senior citizens would habitually come and take the place over. They'd each buy just one cup of dollar coffee. Some would get there at five in the morning and stay past dark. You have to imagine coming in during the lunch rush and finding there a classroom of *halmeonis* and *harabeojis* talking the blues or gossiping or recounting what they saw on last night's soap opera installment; that is, raising a ruckus and having a grand old time. The franchise owner eventually got sick to death of this. He started calling the cops on the parasite geezers and kept having them thrown out. They'd just walk around the block and then come right back." (130–31)

In these two examples, the politics of self-interested parasitism is also one of apolitical occupation. The parasitic customer who orders a coffee from the dollar menu and parks herself in McDonald's for an entire workday is both a grubby freeloader and an unwitting activist. As a mode of politics, parasitism has two key features that I want to highlight. First, it exploits a tension between agency and proscription. Second, parasitism mandates an unusual relation between self and collective.

The central conundrum of a parasitic politics is its fraught relation to individual agency. Is parasitism an assertion of agency by those who "walk around the block and then come right back?" Or, is it a curbing of agency, if one must "avoid the food and only have a coffee?" The problem of agency leads to the question of whether parasitism can ever achieve the status of an intentional strategy. Does parasitism stop becoming parasitism once it is more widely and more consciously deployed? Such questions are on the characters' minds as well. Says Dave: "So the lesson here, Muriel, is that you have correctly found the locations to enact a strategy of parasitism; however, heed the warning, for if you become too noticeable a strain, too large or successful or seemingly independent, the host body will strike to destroy" (131–32). Dave's "lesson" is that parasitism can only remain effective on a certain scale—the scale of the imperceptible. On the one side, parasitism cannot become too large, for it draws its success from remaining unnoticed. On the other, parasitism is not a singular activity and thrives on multiplication—"three or four" senior citizens quickly swell into "dozens." Neither solidary nor solitary, parasitism makes for a strange sort of collectivity, for it is self-interest that provides the precondition for the parasite's pursuit of a social relation. "To parasite means to eat next to," Michel Serres writes. And "eating next to" is what makes the parasitic relation "intersubjective." Serres continues, "We parasite each other and live amidst parasites. Which is more or less a way of saying that they constitute our environment. We live in that black box called the collective; we live by it, on it, and in it."[21] In this account, the parasitic subject is a plural subject—a "we." Yet this "we" does not demonstrate a strong sense of shared purpose. In eating next to each other, parasites are joined by nothing more than a desire for subsistence. Serres appropriately associates the parasitic "we" with "milieu," a term that conflates a social formation with a social environment or a social climate.[22] The para-site refashions the collective as a peripheral site, an inhabitation of habit and habitat: "we live by it, on it, and in it." This quiet, invisible ubiquity of parasites explains how, in Lim's example, a single instance of freeloading can transform into a swarm of "parasite geezers" who "habitually come and take the place over." Parasitism, described another way, is how "the habit of protest becomes something else, something apart from, almost irrelevant to, one's initial desires. It becomes, to say it simply, a way of life" (5). This habituation of protest makes parasitism part of the everyday surround, dissolving collective passion into humdrum adjacency. We can thus find an artist who reads poetry chapbooks eating next to Korean senior citizens who gossip about soap operas, not due to their openly articulated motivations but due to their shared threshold of habituated tolerance for McDonald's coffee.

Perhaps the strangest aspect of the long passages on parasitism is their structure—or lack thereof. The narrator's recollection of Muriel's and Dave's anecdotes are presented through the framing device of a conversation, yet each actually turns out to be a long and searching soliloquy. Lim's novel consists almost entirely of such "conversations," which enact a narrative principle of parasitism. The superheroes of *Dear Cyborgs* are not goal-driven, action-oriented doers but listless, meandering talkers. What's more, they do not talk *to* each other so much as they talk *next to* each other. For example, one of Lim's common maneuvers for transitioning between conversations is Dave's line "Some Koreans, elderly, a gaggle of grandmas and grandpas, did just what you're doing Muriel." This superficial gesture of identifying a common experience conceals the lack of similarity between the things being discussed. A weak relation of "talking next to" allows characters to speak without end. This dialogic structure manifests in different ways. When Frank Exit confronts the supposed villain Ms. Mistleto in a Sri Lankan library, the two have an extended conversation through a projected hologram. Or rather, this conversation consists entirely of Ms. Mistleto recounting an Occupy Wall Street protest at Zuccotti Park led by Kim Jin-suk, a fictional character code-named Salt Flower who spends nine months in a metal box (19). A subsequent encounter atop a Himalayan peak triggers another long flashback, in which Ms. Mistelto narrates her engulfment within an "anonymous flow" of protestors in a public square (57). Like the memory of Salt Flower, whose protest through self-withdrawal sets other activists on a nine-month-long project to deliver her sustenance, this second flashback describes the leveling of a climatic protest into a habituated climate: "I passed hours and then days this way, the crowd not dispersing but growing larger, more permanent, with systems of rest and shelter and food emerging" (58). In addition to these encounters on the job, as it were, the superheroes of Team Chaos also talk during their free time, as they shuffle from Thai restaurants to Korean karaoke to art museums to bars to bookstores. This metafictional contrivance of embedding concentric layers of conversations, anecdotes, and hearsay within long, digressive monologues creates the narrative effect of individual speakers (including the narrating I) disappearing into a haze of cacophonous talk. On the one hand, the profusion of monologues seems incredibly self-absorbed. On the other hand, there is a paradoxically democratizing effect of fuzzily marked voices airing out their beliefs without regard to plot, action, or the integrity of one speaker versus another. One memorable instance of narratological parasitism is a conversation at a Shanghainese restaurant. Here, the speakers are identified only through impersonal pronouns and vague descriptions: "we," "one of you," "another," "you," "the one who'd asked the question," and "the one who had mostly been listening" (20–24). This anonymizing setup of rotating voices around a lunch table creates multiple levels of eating, talking, and standing in proximity. Despite being intensely solipsistic, this parasitic adjacency also seems potentially, if only tonally, collectivist.

It is during this lunchtime conversation that someone "who had mostly been quiet until now" enlarges upon the novel's prevailing concern: the artist as a metaphor for the parasitic activist, someone who participates in politics out of self-interest:

"So I think that a protest," she went on, "like a work of dance or a work of music, is something done, at least in part, by the protester for the protester." She saw I was about to interrupt so said, "One more minute. Let me explain. Of course one hopes and plans for impact, for audience, for change, for efficacy. But, like dance, like music, a protest can be a religious ritual too, one that needn't be derisively looked down upon as magical thinking, but a spiritual act where the act itself is the goal. And that act may on some other level be co-opted, but in the subjective world of the protester it is a way, in itself, to be. Even in solipsism, the subject can be moral. You can call it hokum if you wish, but for the protester, the protest makes a moral world in which she can abide." (24)

Like a conversation structured around unrelated monologues, the solipsism of the artist is a species of parasitism. What political protest and artistic practice share, the unidentified speaker speculates, is their status as "religious ritual." A protest is like a dance in that each is "a spiritual act where the act itself is the goal." This "act," moreover, isn't some dramatic grandstanding but akin to an everyday gesture, an indoctrinated habit—it is merely "something done." In keeping with these deliberations, the artworks referenced in *Dear Cyborgs* are more methodical than inspirational. Dave explains, "Every day after dinner I'd take out one of Ursula's pencils, and I'd start coloring in a section of paper. My goal was to color in the paper as completely as possible. I was trying to use up the pencil entirely, down to its last nub. I would work until I couldn't hold it properly anymore" (33–34). The content of Dave's drawings hardly matters. The goal of this art project is a systematic exhaustion, of both strength and supplies. The ritualistic procedure doesn't so much *produce* the art; it *is* the art. Given this overlap between art and routine, it makes sense that *Dear Cyborgs* takes Tehching Hsieh as a patron saint.[23] Hsieh, an artist named Sonny explains, "gave me a kind of realism about protest art. Tehching Hsieh says, *I don't think that art can change the world. But at least art can help us to unveil life*" (107, emphasis in original). The realism of protest art lies in its ritual character. What makes a ritualistic act "political" is unclear. In the long block quote above, the anonymous speaker conjectures that a ritualistic act "may on some other level be co-opted," even as it "exists within the subjective world of the protester." Which is to say, a self-interested act, something done "by the protestor for the protestor," can lend itself to a higher cause "on some other level." To "co-opt" a self-interested act so that it can become a mode of relation beyond the self—this is the dim promise of a parasitic politics and a parasitic narrative. To eat next to, talk next to, stand next to, or live next to does not contradict a parasite's self-interest, yet it opens up an "intersubjective" relation that enables resilience in numbers if not change through solidarity.

The core provocation of Lim's novel is that even the high-flying superhero—the intrepid social reformer, the distinguished artist, the successful careerist—is a parasite. The question of agency that haunts the parasitic activities of protest, art, and waged work is related to the question of race. In order to be effective, parasitic relations must be weak enough to fly under the radar of intelligibility. As Dave had warned Muriel, "a strategy of parasitism" risks becoming "too noticeable a strain," thus inviting the host body to destroy it. A parasitic politics of race is counterintuitive because racial intelligibility is often the prerequisite for—if not wholly conflated with—racial justice. Advocating for the presence of minorities on screen, on campus, and on syllabi has occupied much of our political thinking. Such efforts have existed in productive tension with desires for a nonessentialist politics of race. In *Dear Cyborgs*, race hovers, but its perceptual registers and origin stories are always in question. For example, the narrator guesses that the masked Ms. Mistleto was "around my age, in her fifties, Asian, perhaps Nepali or Korean" (52–53). Dave tells us that "Ursula was Bangladeshi and we happened to be the only nonwhite people at the party" but never reveals his exact racial identity (28). More interesting than character traits is the racial status of the invasive parasite. The "indissociably plural" vermin swarm is a familiar metaphor for the "minority which is not one."[24] In fact, U.S. counterinsurgency efforts in the Orient—from the Philippines to Vietnam to Afghanistan—are commonly known as "war against the flea."[25] In 1966, William Pfaff linked Chinese "wave" methods to the Viet Cong's guerrilla warfare by asserting, "The strategy of the weak is today a strategy of Asians."[26]

Whereas racial visibility has been the basis for a politics of embodied presence, Lim takes racial uncertainty as the basis for a politics of imperceptible parasites. This nonheroic model of political organizing calls to mind Rachel Lee's reappropriation of yellow peril discourse. Although Lee acknowledges that germophobic conceptions of "viral and bacterial contamination" target "certain human bodies—call them Asiatic," her primary aim is to critique human-centric notions of political justice. She asks, why is that when "proposing 'what is to be done,' advocates of social justice often implicitly turn to 'heroic' humans and their autonomous willful agency as also the presumed foremost agents of imagining and materializing a better world?" Lee encourages us to "view protoctists and bacteria" not as "germs or parasites" but as "endosymbionts as well as crucial partners in producing planetary atmospheres and conditions habitable simultaneously to all five kingdoms of life."[27]

Compared to Lee's posthuman take on Asian American biologies, the parasitic milieu of Lim's novel is more politically conflicted. In fact, *Dear Cyborgs* seems to conclude that parasitism can never provide a satisfying answer to the question of "what is to be done." Instead, parasitism stands for a nonstrategic mode of living that can yield at best an underwhelming, unsynthesized, and noncathartic politics. Parasitism offers a furtive and fugitive prepositional politics of adjacency (eating next to) when an actional or verbal politics of collectivity seems out of reach or perhaps even undesirable.[28]

AMBIENCE: GROUND AND BACKGROUND

Parasitism, a dwelling in common, is the source of a weak politics that cannot achieve the cohesiveness or prestige of a movement-moment. Protists cannot protest. This incapacity also pervades Pamela Lu's novels, *Pamela* (1998) and *Ambient Parking Lot* (2011). These novels bear out Lu's decade-long interest in the relationship between characters and cars. At this conjunction of individual and vehicle, heroism becomes subjected to relentless parodying. Of the two novels, *Pamela* addresses race more directly.[29] Styled after Samuel Richardson's novel by the same name, this work depicts the muddled roots-searching of identity-hungry students in the San Francisco Bay Area, who are identified only by an alphabetic character. We follow L, R, C, A, YJ, I, and other characterless characters to find Vietnamese noodle soup in Chinatown and observe their sampling of Taiwanese pop music. Searching for a common racial identity offers one explanation for why Lu's characters always appear to us as a congregation in motion. That this motion comes by way of cars crystallizes the novel's central characterological problem of agency: "I tricked myself out of desolation; I could not tell if I was moving or moved" (51). Oscillating between activity and passivity, Lu's identity-desiring and artist-aspiring characters are constantly "[finding] ourselves implicated in the same vehicle heading northeast toward a dinner party" or "[driving] ourselves deeper into the mystery that was our passing existence" (15, 49). These overly earnest naïfs cannot contain or restrain themselves—from communicating too much, from falling in love, from slipping out of character.

Ambient Parking Lot, published thirteen years later, is in many ways a sequel to *Pamela*. In a more intensely suburban and car-laden landscape, the wayward students of yore have graduated into itinerant musicians.[30] Where *Pamela* features a range of bending, evaporating, and thinning characters who are each indistinct from the other, *Ambient Parking Lot* takes the perspective of a single homogenized "we." The Ambient Parkers are both audiophiles and autophiles: their mission is to capture the mundane soundscape of parking lots. Such a mission makes depersonalization both more purposeful and more passive; the Ambient Parkers are always heroically disappearing into "the most unmusical of landscapes" (6). As explorers seeking to discover and document a never-ending expanse of parking lots, these musicians aggressively chase a lifestyle of blissful quiescence: "We surrendered to both forms of ambience and viewed them as distinctive movements of a composition that we listened to compulsively, like tonal junkies" (32). Or: "We surfaced from slumber, gurgling impressions of truck horns and carburetors, ham signals and telegraph buzz"

CODA—THE TONE OF COMMONS

(32). Part description and part declaration, these statements narrated by a lofty and even imperial "we" champion the harried pursuit of surrender and slumber.

In chronicling the mock-heroic performance of labors that are as tedious as they are meaningless, *Ambient Parking Lot* presents us with the opposite of what we find in *Dear Cyborgs*, where the so-called superheroes appear as a new kind of lumpenproletariat. The difference between parasitism and ambience is in part a matter of metropolitan setting. Lim's *Dear Cyborg*, which takes place in New York City, features a loosely formed pack of superhero amblers. Lu's *Ambient Parking Lot*, which takes place in a Los Angeles-esque suburb, features a homogenous band of musicians who are obsessed with the sensoria of car culture. Parasitic superheroes survive by feeding off of each other—by eating, walking, and talking next to someone else. These relations of adjacency lead individual persons to hide themselves on a collective host body. Lu's ambient artists, meanwhile, operate as an aggregate "we." Their incapacity to be intelligible as individuals is a symptom of their immersion in their artistic project. Unlike the self-interested parasite, this immersive tendency of the Ambient Parkers appears to be driven by grandly aesthetic aims: these musicians are always willfully losing themselves in the asphalt cacophony they seek to record. If *Dear Cyborgs* is about the disappearance of the individual into a parasitic formation of cyborgs, then we might say that *Ambient Parking Lot* is about the disappearance of the individual into an ambient environment of parking lots. Yet in both novels, a commons *is* a milieu, a collective "we" as well as an overwhelming surround.

In the early pages of *Ambient Parking Lot*, the we-narrator's descriptions of an "asphalt frontier" lampoon the spirit of pioneering discovery and heroic conquest (19): "we plotted the emergence of a new cadence of parking—not just the parking lot but the hum of engines in idle, not just the cars in action but the action without the cars, the pure gestalt of parking itself" (7). This histrionic language of exuberant exploration seems misplaced, for what enthralls the Ambient Parkers is idleness rather than action. The "gestalt of parking itself" has nothing to do with vehicles on the move (the topic of *Pamela*) and instead describes the vitality of subsisting in dormancy, of coming to an ecstatic rest. The Ambient Parkers are committed artists. But their self-sacrificing *commitment to* their art requires a wholesale *absorption by* it. This is what separates the Parkers from "the artsy go-getters with a million projects to finish, a million people to see" (143). Among art critics, absorption has typically been theorized in relation to aesthetic *reception*, often in the context of capitalism's reordering of perception. Many have characterized this absorption as simultaneously attentive and distracted, sublime and stupefying.[31] The Ambient Parkers are absorbed in all these ways, with the important distinction that they turn receptiveness into the bedrock of artistic *production*. In some respect, surrendering one's self for the purpose of amplifying one's art appears virtuous. One of the band's artistic collaborators called the Dancer observes, "It was their relation to their work that moved me, not just their overall stance but the level of intimacy they maintained with their source materials" (147). This intimacy with source materials is a distinguishing virtue that has the counterintuitive effect of radically undercutting personality, individuality, discreteness, and liveliness. Absorption enlivens the urban environment but deadens the artists themselves: "In the vast determination of this landscape novel, living things were consigned to the backdrop" (32). As a part of their aesthetic credos, Ambient Parkers collectively maintain "expressionless, pavement faces" (146).

Being engrossed in an artistic project that surrenders the self to the suburban environment is perhaps the late capitalist alternative to being engrossed in a book or lost in contemplation. The ambiguity of absorption lies in "the peculiar way it combines concentration and distraction," self-possession and self-negation.[32] We can discern this ambiguity in the Parkers' account of their compositional method: "Our few lucid hours were filled with the artistry of attentive apathy" (27). Dormancy is the precursor to creativity, to the extent that "we let our heads drop and arranged melodies from deep within the REM state" (39). To glorify an ambient aesthetic produced by soporific states is to concede that "the very notion of inspiration was bankrupt" and to "stimulate production through chance" (53). This aesthetic method is reminiscent of Surrealist artists such as André Breton who, through the combination of stupor and chance, produced "automatic" paintings and writings. For the Parkers, however, chance is coordinated with "daily fluctuations in the stock market." Like the stock market, the Ambient Parkers achieve "the illusion of prolific output" without "the risks of personal involvement" (53).

Because the Parkers' eager capitulation to ambience is mediated by the capitalist everyday, when "the economy collapsed," so too do "the lush arpeggios of grocery bags being loaded into single-driver vehicles" (21). An enlarged receptivity, the correlate of a practiced flexibility, allows the Parkers to adjust accordingly. And in time, it becomes increasingly unclear if ambience refers to a style of sonic realism derived from a doctrinaire aesthetic commitment or if ambience in fact names a haphazard mode of economic survival. In the passage below, the Dancer frames ambience as the murky realm between aesthetic orthodoxy and economic insecurity:

> They had made themselves homeless for their art, living for four months out of a borrowed station wagon which they parked in a corporate garage, bribing the parking attendants to leave them in peace as they moved the car over to the next marked stall every night, until they had systematically occupied every single space in the garage—a total of one hundred sixteen spaces, including the disabled spaces and stalls reserved for motorcycles and mopeds. (147)

This systematic method of artistic creation shares much with what we saw in *Dear Cyborgs*. Similar to the parasite's "protest art," the ambient soundtrack of parking lots shows how both artistic practice and political protest have become integrated into the quotidian everyday. In *Dear Cyborgs*, parasitism was a self-indulgent process of turning habitual activities (eating at McDonald's) into veiled political acts. The activities described above, by contrast, are not intuitively habitual. For the Parkers, an obsessive, microscopic attention to their artistic object comprehensively restructures their everyday routine—to the point that "routine" loses its comforting familiarity and literally entails an unhoming. The aesthetically motivated desire to occupy every corner of a parking garage thereby leads to the seemingly self-sacrificial act of becoming "homeless for their art." But what exactly counts as being "for their art?" The Parkers undertake an assortment of odd jobs and casual commitments, loosely related to the all-consuming artistic project of auditory harvesting. These include bussing tables, working stockrooms, greeting shoppers, and clerking for a Fortune 500 company. Most homey is the "familiar terrain" of an auto dealership where "we formed a phalanx of welcoming statues . . . , encouraging big-ticket consumerism" (55). Alongside these temp jobs, the band also cycles through an endless array of arbitrary diversions—directing Super 8 shorts starring themselves as "languid robots" (42), reading and writing poetry, collecting self-help books, and hiring interns who are as unreliable as themselves.³³ Like the superheroes who suit up Monday through Friday yet also pick up side jobs to make ends meet, the Ambient Parkers are flexible laborers whose ambient lifestyle suggests the total solubility of art, politics, and work in the capitalist mundane.³⁴

In being guided by the anti-art aesthetic of ambience, the Parkers end up doing much more than making music. Hungry and distracted, they embark on a meandering path that leads to the nagging question of whether the protagonist "we" still refers to a band of musicians. What kind of binding power does ambience afford? Parasitism, we saw earlier, is a weak relation produced by self-interest and sustained by self-diminishment. A parasitic collective comes into existence by way of a fugitive self hiding among a cluster of otherwise unrelated freeloaders. While parasitism is premised on the logic of adjacency, of one eating next to another, ambience is a function of mass gatherings, of being in the thick or in the middle of things. Compared to parasitism, ambience seems closer to the moods or atmospheres that critics have associated with political potentiality. In *Ambient Parking Lot*, however, ambience is less a "rhythmic entrainment with one's fellows" than a radical openness to the world.³⁵ This pseudo-aestheticized receptivity requires a wholesale absorption into a social environment—even one as dull as a parking lot. If there is a collectivizing force that binds the Parkers, it is a happy side effect of this absorptive process. A politically united front is not what the Ambient Parkers actively aspire to forge, but a protean commons nevertheless emerges as an unintended byproduct of their acquiescence.

The Ambient Parkers rarely reflect on their own collective identity. Instead, we best see how this unreflective "we" constitutes a group formation through the perspective of other characters, for instance the Dancer:

As individuals, they could have gone unnoticed in a room full of quirky, vivacious people chatting, gossiping, flirting, and networking at top speed.... By contrast, each member of the Ambient Parkers looked more like a sulky wallflower, crossing the floor alone to the bar or waiting silently in the restroom line. But standing next to one another, they somehow came together as a group, amassing an identity that you couldn't ignore or deny. I'm not saying that they looked particularly united in purpose—no, quite the opposite. What they shared most was an air of distraction, a sense of foreboding that came through in their restless shifting and quiet shuffling, which contrasted sharply with the frenetic energy around them. (143)

This is hardly the picture of a decisive coalition. The collective identity of the Parkers is achieved through standing indifferently next to each other. They acquire definition only when cast against the livelier personalities around them. Furthermore, like a parasite, an Ambient Parker—a pavement face and a wallflower—cannot exist in the singular. Only by "standing next to one another" can they become intelligible—though not as "an identity" but as a ground (pavement) or a background (wall). We might say something similar about the Ambient Parkers' *narrative* persona. The we-narrator is incapable of describing any of its constitutive members, nor does it ever divulge how many people make up this band at any particular moment. We do learn of different factions within the Parkers, but in a way that expands the protean "we" without personalizing it. If the "restless shifting and quiet shuffling" of this we-formation serves a cause, it is the cause of collective stupor. An absorption into the atmosphere denotes not a desire to overturn or change the known world but a desire to yield to it: "Never before had we felt so available to one another. Our softness was unguarded and our unguardedness was revealed as a sign of power.... We turned to the world" (35).

Like parasitism, ambience carries a racial tinge. If parasitism evokes the discourse of yellow peril, ambience evokes the closely related discourse of "techno-Orientalism." In techno-Orientalist productions new and old—from "future war" popular fiction of the late nineteenth century to blockbuster films such as *Blade Runner* and *Ghost in the Shell* in the late twentieth century—racial difference inheres in "Asian-influenced visions of the future" rather than in the physical attributes of a character.[36] Wendy Chun has posited "cyberspace" as one example of this Asian-influenced futurity: "In cyberspace, then, as in all Orientalist spaces, there are disembodied minds, on the one hand, and disembodied representations, on the other. There are those who can reason online and those who are reduced to information." For Chun, the distinguishing feature of "cyberspace" (which signifies differently than "internet") is its "seductive 'orientation.'"[37] A literal combination of "Orient" and "information," what Chun calls "orientation" is a technologized version of guidance, a transformation of the terms of service. Instead of an embodied racial tour guide, orientation locates racial information in "disembodied representations." Being "reduced to information"—to pictographic words in a storefront or to a corporate ad with a geisha—is what enables a user's navigation. At the same time, the informatics of "orientation" also has a deceptive element. To the extent that cold war optics cast the inscrutable Oriental as an ideological enemy whose ulterior motives cannot be seen, post–cold war suspicion—what has been called "postmodern white schizophrenia" and "a paranoid reaction to global economic and data flows"[38]—arises from a radically compromised link between visible surfaces and hidden depths. Hence, in the 1982 version of *Blade Runner*, we encounter "replicants" whose "visible exterior shows no marked difference from white humans, but whose interiorities pose an essential difference."[39] In adventure narratives of this kind, "orientation" has a worlding effect, as it conflates enemies on the horizon with the outlines of a distant rim. An update of what Mark Jerng has termed "climate-and-custom" racism, techno-Orientalism offers a futuristic rendition of "yellow flood," "yellow wave," "yellow world," and "the yellow peril in action"[40]—a racial realism of shifting referents and receding details.

Lu's production of a diffuse atmosphere likewise relies on the virtualization of characters into ambience. Her novel's actual and metaphorical parking lots are full of ambience and empty of meaning. If we are looking for the "orientation" of racial codes, we are left sorely wanting. When Lu does invoke the Orient, it is as a sign of hollowness, asceticism, alienation, and illusion. One instance involves the picaresque adventures of a radio personality named the Station Master. Like Alice burrowing down the rabbit hole or Big Bird digging a hole to China, the Station Master, who "succumbed to the inverted gaze of the Orient," feels his "very contours... contracting," as if he is "sucked down the tube of a telescope pointing doggedly in the wrong direction" (98). Other allusions to the Orient involve Brechtian tropes of masking, whether through "Butoh-inflected body movements" or "a wooden acting style" that, "devoid of all Western forms of expression," conveys "a uniquely Asiatic sensibility" (24).

Lu's ambient parking lot, like a techno-Orientalist cyberspace, renders "character" nothing more than a vanishing point. This absorption of the well-defined subject into air and asphalt may initially seem like a self-annihilating politics—a politics for which "the coupling of the terms public-private, as well as the coupling of the terms collective-individual, can no longer stand up on their own, [and] are gasping for air, burning themselves out." Paolo Virno hypothesizes that new regimes of labor have engendered "personal dependence." The opposite of *personal days*, whereby one takes time for oneself, the notion of *personal dependence* means that "one depends on this person or on that person, not on rules endowed with anonymous coercive power."[41] Lu's provisional formless "we" and Lim's loosely adjacent parasites can perhaps be viewed as manifestations of this personal dependence. These strategies of subsisting as a common "we" present the possibility of being united by a sense of collective risk, even if there isn't a specified organizing rationale or rubric. Considered thusly, personal dependence, the problem of not being able to stand up on one's own, looks something like what Myung Mi Kim calls standing in proximity.

IN, WITH, OF

In depicting contingent forms of collectivity, Myung Mi Kim, Ed Park, Eugene Lim, and Pamela Lu locate some redemptive element in a landscape of defeatism, impoverishment, and apathy. I conclude with these writers, then, because they offer us a study of "proxemics"—a style of coexistence whose politics is "distinct from the possessive attachment languages of belonging."[42] If "identity" has been an *uncommon ground*, a strategic essentialism, then the tonal environs that we have surveyed might be characterized as a *common unground*. This unground does not demand more cohesiveness from a diaspora held by dissolution, more motivation from a relation of co-incidence, or more substance from a solidarity without a solid. Rather, these writers take a barren and blighted world—a world that is not *at war* yet not *past war*—as an impetus for fashioning new modes of affiliation and allyship. The solidarities in their novels are brimming with difference, racial and otherwise, yet the indices of this difference remain unarticulated and unseized; "difference" manifests not as a trait but as a tone. Instead of presenting characters who perform the scripts of *identification*, Kim, Park, Lim, and Lu create entire moods by focusing on groups in *motion*. Admittedly, what qualifies as motion may be an embarrassment to politics. But without at all championing these writers' political experiments as political ideals, I do want to offer a reparative reading of their work. Specifically, I'd like to write down some of the questions generated by their efforts to model modes of connection that are *not* organized by a delineated identity. These questions do not demand that we dispense entirely with "identity." But they do cast "identity" as a powerful and meaningful ground from which we might depart in order to find common unground. In forging an allyship so fierce that we're willing to diminish the self—to minimize, abstract, and unmark our own presence—does it become possible to pursue a broader sense of justice? At the same time, in building around common practices rather than common identities, can we admit more informal and colloquial forms of justice into our purview? At its most radical and its most quotidian, the question is: What might it mean to conceive of solidarity as a project of thoroughgoing interdependence, one in which our support for each other is so steadfast that, in holding each other up, we are in effect holding each other in place? Described this way, an interdependent support system called "we" seems not merely collectivist, something unto ourselves, but veritably infrastructural, something that *makes* the world. "We" are not inertly submerged in, but rather dynamically constitutive of, history's temperamental turns.

I've singled out Lu and Lim not only because their novels most intentionally query what counts as and what can be legible as a commons, but also because parasitism and ambience reflect back to us, in a clarified and rarefied way, the range of techniques and tones that we have encountered in other post–cold war aesthetic texts. Lim's creation of minor characters who possess no distinguishing features beyond a code name is similar in concept to the character-system of Kazuo Ishiguro's novels. Whereas Ishiguro's rumor logic mobilizes characters who talk, Lim presents characters who monologue, a narratological structure that further embellishes the effects of character attenuation. Meanwhile, for Lu's barely sentient and routinely overextended characters, the affective and temporal suspension provoked by Theresa Hak Kyung Cha's permutational aesthetic has become a hallowed principle of artistic creation and a basic fact of everyday living. In surrendering to an immersive present, these waiting and waning, languishing and lingering characters experience duration as endurance. A perhaps surprising aspect of Lu's and Lim's novels is that they both take public performance (rather than a published book) as a standard for artistic creation. This ritualistic, procedural, and exhaustive aesthetic method is both an inversion and an intensification of Ha Jin's "documentary manner." Performance pieces that render inscriptions simultaneously embodied and ephemeral are in some sense the opposite of

CODA—THE TONE OF COMMONS

Jin's efforts to stabilize inscriptions and to simulate an archival record. Yet the blurring of everyday habit and aesthetic practice (which transforms an artist into a cyborg) is also a more extravagant sendup of the blurring of historical tract and illegitimate copy (which transforms an author into a forger). Lastly, the formal intimacy that Trinh facilitates among the various participants of a self-representational act appears in Lu's and Lim's novels as mutual dependence or standing in proximity. Dependence may not be immediately legible as a politics because it precludes articulated solidarities and direct opposition. Short on foresight, conviction, and zeal, dependence entails the "dynamism of nomadic morphing performed as a form of survival." Neferti Tadiar writes, "the convertibility of one's personhood in and out of, to and from things, pertinent existences, organic and inorganic beings; our habit and ability to make ourselves into the *verbs* of others—these are also what animate the world."[43]

Tadiar's call to "make ourselves into the *verbs* of others" underscores the power of transitivity and adjacency. This mode of power is derived from friction rather than force, from *being in relation* rather than from *rising above*. I believe that our collective embedment in "wartime" requires this frictional kind of energy. Hence, although I've often found myself wanting to see more, know more, and write more than I've been able to, *Tonal Intelligence* has ultimately been a frictive effort to feel things out at close range. Working incrementally, impressionistically, and tonally, it has lingered on the prepositional, the adverbial, the interdependent, and the processual. And so, even as this book ends, it nonetheless remains: in, with, and of.

NOTES

INTRODUCTION

1. This account of war is adapted from Mary L. Dudziak, *War Time: An Idea, Its History, Its Consequences* (New York: Oxford University Press, 2012).
2. Masuda Hajimu, *Cold War Crucible: The Korean Conflict and the Postwar World* (Cambridge, Mass.: Harvard University Press, 2015), 1.
3. Odd Arne Westad, *The Global Cold War: Third World Interventions and the Making of Our Times* (New York: Cambridge University Press, 2005), 2.
4. Heonik Kwon, *The Other Cold War* (New York: Columbia University Press, 2010). Kwon writes, "The term *cold war* is both the general reference for the global bipolar conflict and the representation of this conflict from a particular regional point of view" (18, emphasis in original).
5. Don Mee Choi, *Hardly War* (Seattle: Wave, 2016), 6. Subsequent references are cited in the text.
6. According to the *Oxford English Dictionary* (hereafter cited as *OED*), the older definition of *hardly* is "with energy, force, or strenuous exertion; vigorously; violently." In modern usage, the term means "scarcely; barely; not quite; almost not at all."
7. Memorandum of Conversation, Dean Acheson, March 24, 1950, *Foreign Relations of the United States* (hereafter cited as *FRUS), 1950, National Security Affairs; Foreign Economic Policy*, Vol. I, (Washington, D.C.: Government Printing Office, 1977), Document 74 (emphasis mine). Similar language about "a real war" would appear weeks later in NSC-68, an iconic instrument of US cold war policy.
8. Gallup Poll #557, December 6, 1955, https://institution.gallup.com/documents/questionnaire.aspx?STUDY=AIPO0557, quoted in Kenneth Alan Osgood, *Total Cold War: Eisenhower's Secret Propaganda Battle at Home and Abroad* (Lawrence: University of Kansas, 2008), 1.

INTRODUCTION

9. As Dudziak notes, wars of empire tend to consist of "small wars" that eclipse the domain of national memory and are therefore consigned to the halcyon realm of "peace time." Wars of empire also appear un-warlike because they tend to be seen as "matters of imperial governance" or, Dudziak quotes Greg Grandin, "tactics of extraterritorial administration" (*War Time*, 31, 32). I'd add that another reason "small wars" are more likely to be forgotten is that they often involved covert operations, the documentations of which may be edited, redacted, or nonexistent.
10. Dwight Eisenhower, "Chance for Peace," speech presented at the American Society of Newspaper Editors, Washington, D.C., April 16, 1953. On total war as a democratic campaign for peace, see Osgood, *Total Cold War*; Scott Lucas, *Freedom's War: The US Crusade Against the Soviet Union, 1945–56* (New York: NYU Press, 1999); Laura Belmonte, *Selling the American Way: U.S. Propaganda and the Cold War* (Philadelphia: University of Pennsylvania Press, 2010).
11. Scholars often observe a shift away from conventional warfare during the cold war. For example, in *Special Forces, Strategy and the War on Terror: Warfare By Other Means* (New York: Routledge, 2008), Alastair Finlan writes that "the Second World War witnessed conventional warfare on a massive scale in which states were forced to deploy and sustain immense armies as well as fight campaigns that lasted years rather than days, weeks or months" (26). The cold war, by contrast, was a new order in which conventional war was no longer possible or desirable, either from the perspective of the old colonial powers, or that of the new superpowers (26–28).
12. David Sarnoff, board chairman of Radio Corporation of America, once used the term "psychological peace-fare" to describe a revamped Voice of America; Charles Parmer, "Parmer from Washington," August 17, 1951, Staff Member and Office File, Psychological Strategy Files, 000.1, Rand Corporation Study, Truman Papers, Truman Library.
13. Dudziak, *War Time*, 11, 76. Dudziak's study has been foundational to my understanding of "wartime" as normal rather than exceptional. I've also benefited from: Christine Hong's formulation of the cold war as a "perceptual problematic in which wartime would be misrecognized as peacetime" in "The Unending Korean War," *Positions: Asia Critique* 23, no. 4 (Fall 2015): 600; Prasenjit Duara's discussion of the cold war's periodicity in relation to American hegemony, which forged a new type of relationship between "powers" and "partners," in "The Cold War as a Historical Period," *Journal of Global History* 6, no. 3 (November 2011): 457–80; and Crystal Baik's brilliant conceptualization of "reencounters" as a way to account for the intermingling of the Korean War's dissident, unexceptional, and unresolvable temporalities in *Reencounters: On the Korean War and Diasporic Memory Critique* (Philadelphia: Temple University Press, 2019). Also relevant is Judith Butler's meditation on modern media's administration of how we apprehend war in *Frames of War: When Is Life Grievable?* (New York: Verso, 2009).
14. A select bibliography of works whose interests range closest to my own (and which I have not yet cited) includes: Keith L. Camacho, *Cultures of Commemoration: The Politics of War, Memory, and History in the Mariana Islands* (Honolulu: University of Hawai'i Press, 2011); Cindy I-Fen Cheng, *Citizens of Asian America: Democracy and Race During the Cold War* (New York: NYU Press, 2013); Leo Ching, *Anti-Japan: The Politics of Sentiment in Postcolonial East Asia* (Durham: Duke University Press, 2019); Yến Lê Espiritu, *Body Counts: The Vietnam War*

INTRODUCTION

and Militarized Refugees (Berkeley: University of California Press, 2014); Takashi Fujitani, *Race for Empire: Koreans as Japanese and Japanese as Americans During World War II* (Berkeley: University of California Press, 2011); Takashi Fujitani, Geoffrey M. White, and Lisa Yoneyama, eds. *Perilous Memories: The Asia-Pacific War(s)* (Durham: Duke University Press, 2001); Jodi Kim, *Ends of Empire: Asian American Critique and the Cold War* (Minneapolis: University of Minnesota Press, 2010); Jodi Kim, "Settler Modernity, Debt Imperialism, and the Necropolitics of the Promise," *Social Text* 36, no. 2 (2018): 41–61; Christina Klein, *Cold War Orientalism: Asia in the Middlebrow Imagination, 1945–1961* (Berkeley: University of California Press, 2003); Simeon Man, *Soldiering Through Empire: Race and the Making of the Decolonizing Pacific* (Berkeley: University of California Press, 2018); Marguerite Nguyen, *America's Vietnam: The Longue Durée of U.S. Literature and Empire* (Philadelphia: Temple University Press, 2018); Josephine Nock-Hee Park, *Cold War Friendships: Korea, Vietnam, and Asian American Literature* (New York: Oxford University Press, 2016); Dean Itsuji Saranillio, *Unsustainable Empire: Alternative Histories of Hawai'i Statehood* (Durham: Duke University Press, 2018); Cathy J. Schlund-Vials, *War, Genocide, and Justice: Cambodian American Memory Work* (Minneapolis: University of Minnesota Press, 2012); Shuang Shen, "Empire of Information: The Asia Foundation's Network and Chinese-Language Cultural Production in Hong Kong and Southeast Asia," *American Quarterly* 63, no. 3 (September 2017): 589–610; Setsu Shigematsu and Keith L. Camacho, eds. *Militarized Currents: Toward a Decolonized Future in Asia and the Pacific* (Minneapolis: University of Minnesota Press, 2010); Rob Wilson, *Reimagining the American Pacific: From South Pacific to Bamboo Ridge and Beyond* (Durham: Duke University Press, 2000); Ellen Wu, *The Color of Success: Asian Americans and the Origins of the Model Minority* (Princeton: Princeton University Press, 2013); Lisa Yoneyama, *Cold War Ruins: Transpacific Critique of American Justice and Japanese War Crimes* (Durham: Duke University Press, 2016). I've also been inspired by the work of the Everyday Militarisms research collaborative, steered by the University of California, Davis, and the University of Sydney: https://everydaymilitarisms.squarespace.com/.

15. For an incisive and generative deliberation on the "transpacific," see Erin Suzuki and Aimee Bahng, "The Transpacific Subject in Asian American Culture," *Oxford Research Encyclopedia of Literature,* January 30, 2020, https://oxfordre.com/literature/view/10.1093/acrefore/9780190201098.001.0001/acrefore-97801902 01098-e-877. Discussions of the relation between "Asian," "Asian American," and "Pacific" can be found in J. Kehaulani Kauanui, "Asian American Studies and the 'Pacific Question,'" *Asian American Studies after Critical Mass*, ed. Kent A. Ono (Malden, Mass.: Blackwell, 2005): 123–43; Vicente M. Diaz, "To 'P' or Not to 'P': Marking the Territory between Pacific Islander and Asian American Studies," *Journal of Asian American Studies* 7, no. 3 (October 2004): 183–208; Candace Fujikane and Jonathan Y. Okamura, eds. *Asian Settler Colonialism: From Local Governance to the Habits of Everyday Life in Hawai'i* (Honolulu: University of Hawai'i Press, 2008).

16. Kwon writes, "If racial colors were ideological constructs, not biological conditions, political ideologies, in turn, took on biological and racial imagery in the history of the twentieth century" (*The Other Cold War*, 42).

INTRODUCTION

17. This perspective is developed in *Marxism and Literature* (New York: Oxford University Press, 1977) and *Culture and Society: 1780–1950* (New York: Doubleday, 1958).
18. John Eperjesi, *The Imperialist Imaginary: Visions of Asia and the Pacific in American Culture* (Hanover, N.H.: University Press of New England, 2005), 2.
19. Michael Schaller, "Securing the Great Crescent: Occupied Japan and the Origins of Containment in Southeast Asia," *Journal of American History* 69, no. 2 (September 1982): 392–93. To link the cold war "American lake" to the contemporary "Pacific Rim," Jinah Kim coins the term the "Pacific Arena" (*Postcolonial Grief: The Afterlives of the Pacific Wars in the Americas* [Durham: Duke University Press, 2019], 17–18). It is imperative to note that the "Great Crescent" and the "Pacific Rim" also map onto the "Greater East Asia Co-Prosperity Sphere" promulgated by the Japanese empire during World War II.
20. Christopher Castiglia, *The Practices of Hope: Literary Criticism in Disenchanted Times* (New York: NYU Press, 2017), 12, emphasis in original.
21. Many Asian American scholars have written on the subversive possibilities of "double agency," betrayal, and collaboration. Though not always linked to the cold war, such studies show the durability of cold war tropes and epistemologies: Tina Chen, *Double Agency: Acts of Impersonation in Asian American Literature and Culture* (Stanford: Stanford University Press, 2005); Crystal Parikh, *An Ethics of Betrayal: The Politics of Otherness in Emergent U.S. Literatures and Culture* (New York: Fordham University Press, 2009); Leslie Bow, *Betrayal and Other Acts of Subversion: Feminism, Sexual Politics, Asian American Women's Literature* (Princeton: Princeton University Press, 2001); Lan Duong, *Treacherous Subjects: Gender, Culture, and Trans-Vietnamese Feminism* (Philadelphia: Temple University Press, 2012).
22. Espiritu, *Body Counts*, 21.
23. Kim, *Ends of Empire*, 31, 9.
24. Bruce Cumings, *Parallax Visions: Making Sense of American-East Asian Relations* (Durham: Duke University Press, 2002), x.
25. Kim, *Ends of Empire*, 6.
26. Alan Liu, *The Laws of Cool: Knowledge Work and the Culture of Information* (Chicago: University of Chicago Press, 2004); Sianne Ngai, *Ugly Feelings* (Cambridge, Mass.: Harvard University Press, 2007); Kathleen Stewart, *Ordinary Affects* (Durham: Duke University Press, 2007). On underperformativity, see Lauren Berlant, "Structures of Unfeeling: Mysterious Skin," *International Journal of Politics, Culture & Society* 28, no. 3 (September 2015): 191–213. The typology of the insensate and insensitive Oriental is derived from a European discourse that took on economic ramifications in the nineteenth-century American West. See Eric Hayot, *The Hypothetical Mandarin: Sympathy, Modernity, and Chinese Pain* (New York: Oxford University Press, 2009); Colleen Lye, *America's Asia: Racial Form and American Literature, 1893–1945* (Princeton: Princeton University Press, 2005); Hsuan Hsu, *Sitting in Darkness: Mark Twain's Asia and Comparative Racialization* (New York: NYU Press, 2015).
27. Kuan-Hsing Chen, *Asia as Method: Toward Deimperialization* (Durham: Duke University Press, 2010), 120. On the cold war as an epistemological problem, see also Jodi Kim, *Ends of Empire*. I am offering my own interpretation of Chen, who may not necessarily support a rapprochement between Asian and Asian

INTRODUCTION

American Studies, at least based on his remarks in "Missile Internationalism," in *Orientations: Mapping Studies in the Asian Diaspora*, eds. Kandice Chuh and Karen Shimakawa (Durham: Duke University Press, 2001), 172.

28. Leigh Kagan, "A Statement of Directions," *Bulletin of Concerned Asian Scholars* 1, no.1 (May 1968): 1; Fabio Lanza, *The End of Concern: Maoist China, Activism, and Asian Studies* (Durham: Duke University Press, 2017).
29. Madeline Y. Hsu, "Asian Americans and the Cold War," *Oxford Research Encyclopedia of American History*, May 2015, https://oxfordre.com/americanhistory/view/10.1093/acrefore/9780199329175.001.0001/acrefore-9780199329175-e-44.
30. De–cold war scholars have been cited throughout, but see in particular footnote 14.
31. Other scholars have also pondered how a knowledge formation that knows itself as "Asian American" might include in its purview the critique not only of an American empire but also of an *Asian* empire or subempire. See Wen Jin, *Pluralist Universalism: An Asian Americanist Critique of U.S. and Chinese Multiculturalisms* (Columbus: Ohio State University Press, 2012). Colleen Lye, "Unmarked Character and the 'Rise of Asia': Ed Park's *Personal Days*," *Verge: Studies in Global Asias* 1, no.1 (Spring 2015): 230–54; Joseph Jonghyun Jeon, *Vicious Circuits: Korea's IMF Cinema and the End of the American Century* (Stanford: Stanford University Press, 2019).
32. Pheng Cheah, "Universal Areas: Asian Studies in a World of Motion," in *The Postcolonial and the Global*, ed. Revathi Khishnaswarmy and John C. Hawley (Minneapolis: University of Minnesota Press, 2008), 58–59.
33. Sylvia Yanagisako, "Asian Exclusion Acts," in *Learning Places: The Afterlives of Area Studies*, eds. Masao Miyoshi and Harry Harootunian (Durham: Duke University Press, 2002), 186, 175.
34. With regard to the United States' transpacific empire, archival studies on the Philippines have been extremely valuable to my thinking: Nerissa Balce, *Body Parts of Empire: Visual Abjection, Filipino Images, and the American Archive* (Ann Arbor, Mich.: University of Michigan Press, 2016); Cheryl Beredo, *Import of the Archive: U.S. Colonial Rule of the Philippines and the Making of American Archival History* (Sacramento, Calif.: Litwin, 2013). Broadly speaking, however, colonial/postcolonial studies and Black studies—particularly works focused on the long nineteenth and early twentieth centuries—have been more influential to my understanding of archives than scholarship more squarely in Asian American Studies, Asian Studies, or Cold War Studies. A partial bibliography of these includes: Anjali Arondekar, *For the Record: On Sexuality and the Colonial Archive in India* (Durham: Duke University Press, 2009); Brent Hayes Edwards, "The Taste of the Archive," *Callaloo* 35, no. 4 (Fall 2012): 944–72; Saidiya Hartman, "Venus in Two Acts," *Small Axe* 12, no. 2 (June 2008): 1–14; Lisa Lowe, *The Intimacies of Four Continents* (Durham: Duke University Press, 2015); Helena Michie and Robyn Warhol, *Love Among the Archives: Writing the Lives of Sir George Scharf, Victorian Bachelor* (Edinburgh: Edinburgh University Press, 2015); Ann Laura Stoler, *Along the Archival Grain: Epistemic Anxieties and Colonial Common Sense* (Princeton: Princeton University Press, 2009); Diana Taylor, *The Archive and the Repertoire: Performing Cultural Memory in the Americas* (Durham: Duke University Press, 2003); Katherine Verdery, *Secrets and Truth: Ethnography in the Archive of Romania's Secret Police* (New York: Central European University, 2014).

35. Fred Moten, *In the Break: The Aesthetics of the Black Radical Tradition* (Minneapolis: University of Minnesota Press, 2003); Tavia Nyong'o, "Racial Kitsch and Black Performance," *Yale Journal of Criticism* 15, no. 2 (2002): 371–91; W. J. T. Mitchell, *What Do Pictures Want? The Lives and Loves of Images* (Chicago: University of Chicago Press, 2005); Stephen Best, *The Fugitive's Properties: Law and the Poetics of Possession* (Chicago: University of Chicago Press, 2004); Joseph Jonghyun Jeon, *Racial Things, Racial Forms: Objecthood in Avant-Garde Asian American Poetry* (Iowa City: University of Iowa Press, 2012); Anne Cheng, *Ornamentalism* (New York: Oxford, 2019); Summer Kim Lee, "Someone Else's Object," *Post45*, December 9, 2019. My use of the term *opacity* is, of course, indebted to Édouard Glissant, *Poetics of Relation*, trans. Betsy Wing (Ann Arbor: University of Michigan Press, 1997).
36. Robyn Wiegman, *Object Lessons* (Durham: Duke University Press, 2012).
37. On hesitation as method, see Lisa Lowe, "History Hesitant," *Social Text* 33, no. 4 (December 2015): 85–107; Hentyle Yapp, *Minor China: Materialisms, Method, and Mediation on the Global Art Market* (Durham: Duke University Press, forthcoming).
38. Yoneyama, *Cold War Ruins*.
39. David Scott, *Conscripts of Modernity: The Tragedy of Colonial Enlightenment* (Durham: Duke University Press, 2004), 134.

1. THE TONE OF INTELLIGENCE

1. Arif Dirlik, *What Is in a Rim? Critical Perspectives on the Pacific Region Idea* (Lanham, M.D.: Rowman & Littlefield, 1998).
2. Brian Russell Roberts and Michelle Ann Stephens, "Archipelagic American Studies: Decontinentalizing the Study of American Culture," in *Archipelagic American Studies*, eds. Roberts and Stephens (Durham: Duke University Press, 2017), 6, 7, 8.
3. Bruce Cumings, "Rimspeak; or, The Discourse of the Pacific Rim," in *What Is in a Rim*, 29–47.
4. Dirlik, "Introduction: Pacific Contradictions," in *What Is in a Rim*, 5.
5. Wendy Hui Kyong Chun, *Control and Freedom: Power and Paranoia in the Age of Fiber Optics* (Cambridge, Mass.: MIT Press, 2006).
6. Christopher L. Connery, "Pacific Rim Discourse: The U.S. Global Imaginary in the Late Cold War Years," *boundary 2* 21, no. 1 (Spring 1994): 44.
7. Alfred W. McCoy, *Policing America's Empire: The United States, the Philippines, and the Rise of the Surveillance State* (Madison: University of Wisconsin Press, 2009). According to Nerissa Balce, the Philippine–American War also functions as an origin story for American counterinsurgency, which, as we will see in chapter 5, became popularized across Southeast Asia in the 1950s as a form of "pacification" and "civic action" (*Body Parts of Empire*, 161–63).
8. Kate Doyle, "The End of Secrecy: U.S. National Security and the Imperative for Openness," *World Policy Journal* 16, no. 1 (Spring 1999): 37.
9. A.R. Northridge, "Pearl Harbor: Estimating Then and Now," *Studies in Intelligence* 9, no. 4 (Fall 1965): 64. After bemoaning the failures of intelligence analysts,

1. THE TONE OF INTELLIGENCE

Northridge recalls how, on December 5, a political science professor, despite possessing "no formal military training nor access to classified information," was capable of predicting that "Japan would attack the United States, possibly that weekend" (71).

10. Ron Robin, *The Making of the Cold War Enemy: Culture and Politics in the Military-Intellectual Complex* (Princeton: Princeton University Press, 2001), 96.
11. Anthony Marc Lewis, "Re-examining Our Perceptions on Vietnam," *Studies in Intelligence* 17, no. 4 (Winter 1973): 1–62; Frances FitzGerald, *Fire in the Lake: The Vietnamese and the Americans in Vietnam* (New York: Little, Brown, 1972), 3–31.
12. Allen Dulles, *The Craft of Intelligence* (New York: Harper & Row, 1963), 11, 14, 181.
13. In addition to the CIA and the USIA, there were numerous intelligence organizations within the State Department, Army, Navy, and Air Force. Private organizations and foreign governments also contributed to U.S. intelligence. Overseas, the U.S. Information Agency was sometimes referred to as the U.S. Information Services (USIS). The latter was a friendlier appellation since the term "agency" was often interpreted as covert operations.
14. Klein, *Cold War Orientalism*, 23.
15. Osgood, *Total Cold War*, 97–98.
16. For an excellent reading of Kennan's Orientalism, see chapter 1 of Kim, *Ends of Empire*.
17. Kennan's efforts to give containment an Orientalist flavor extend from his earlier writings. In discussing Kennan's coverage of the Russo-Japanese war, Colleen Lye observes how "Kennan undercuts the inevitability of Orientalist designations, yet preserves Orientalism's dichotomizing logic." In the face of the unknown and the unseeable, Kennan here, too, employs racialization as "the representational form of explanation" (*America's Asia*, 24–25, 32).
18. John Lewis Gaddis, *Strategies of Containment: A Critical Appraisal of American National Security Policy During the Cold War* (New York: Oxford University Press, 2005), 34, 21. Gaddis quotes Clark Clifford.
19. "The U.N. and the New Slavery," *Life*, July 27, 1953: 28. On the cold war rhetoric of slavery in relation to "Iron Curtain" captivity, see Susan L. Carruthers, *Cold War Captives: Imprisonment, Brainwashing, Escape* (Berkeley: University of California Press, 2009).
20. Hee-wan Yang, "A Critical Edition of Major Speeches by Rhee Syngman and Park Chunghee on the Issue of Korean Unification, 1945–1979" (PhD diss., University of Wisconsin-Madison, 1985), 154; William Frank Zornow, "Lincoln and Rhee: An Historical Analogy," *Lincoln Herald* 55 no. 3 (Fall 1953): 23–46.
21. "The Position of the United States with Respect to Asia," Report by the National Security Council, NSC 48/1, December 23, 1949, Department of Defense, *United States–Vietnam Relations, 1945–1967, Book 8* (Washington, D.C.: Government Printing Office, 1971), 239.
22. Dean Acheson, "The Secretary of State to the Consulate at Hanoi," May 20, 1949, *FRUS, 1949, Vol. VII, Part 2* (Washington, D.C.: Government Printing Office, 1976), document 28.
23. Arthur Radford, Memorandum from the Chairman of the Joint Chiefs of Staff to the Secretary of Defense, March 1954, *FRUS, Foreign Aid and Economic Defense*

Policy, 1955–1957, Vol. X (Washington, D.C.: U.S. Government Printing Office, 1989), document 185.

24. Roger J. Bell, *Last Among Equals: Hawaiian Statehood and American Politics* (Honolulu: University of Hawai'i Press, 1984); Saranillio, *Unsustainable Empire*.
25. One could make the case that the Second World War was this pivot point, given the centrality of antiracism and anti-imperialism to both American and Japanese propaganda. But while central, these ideas had yet to become fully hegemonic. In fact, many critics have identified the overt white supremacy of Nazism as a key motivator for reconceiving race as malleable culture rather than fixed biology. Especially relevant accounts of the continuity between the United States' WWII and cold war policies, including the New Deal's impact on cold war liberalism, can be found in Nikhil Pal Singh, *Black Is a Country: Race and the Unfinished Struggle for Democracy* (Cambridge, Mass.: Harvard University Press, 2004); Brenda Gayle Plummer, *Rising Wind: Black Americans and U.S. Foreign Affairs, 1935–1960* (Chapel Hill: University of North Carolina Press, 1996); Madeline Y. Hsu, *The Good Immigrants: How the Yellow Peril Became the Model Minority* (Princeton: Princeton University Press, 2015); Lye, *America's Asia*; Michael Rogin, *Ronald Reagan, the Movie: And Other Episodes in Political Demonology* (Berkeley: University of California Press, 1988).
26. Andrew Rubin, *Archives of Authority: Empire, Culture, and the Cold War* (Princeton: Princeton University Press, 2012), 6–7.
27. Lowe, *Intimacies of Four Continents*, 71, 78.
28. Stoler, *Along the Archival Grain*, 32–33.
29. On the problem of archival recovery and New World slavery, see Hartman, "Venus in Two Acts"; see also the special issue "On the Archaeologies of Black Memory" in which Hartman's essay appears. On the reparative possibilities of counter-archives, see Deborah A. Thomas, "Caribbean Studies, Archive Building, and the Problem of Violence," *Small Axe: A Caribbean Journal of Criticism* 17, no. 2 (July 1, 2013): 27–42. On the policed absence of queer subjects in official archives, see Ann Cvetkovich, *An Archive of Feelings: Trauma, Sexuality, and Lesbian Public Cultures* (Durham: Duke University Press, 2003); José Esteban Muñoz, "Ephemera as Evidence: Introductory Notes to Queer Acts," *Women & Performance: A Journal of Feminist Theory* 8, no. 2 (January 1, 1996): 5–16.
30. Anjali Arondekar, "In the Absence of Reliable Ghosts: Sexuality, Historiography, South Asia," *differences* 25, no. 3 (2014): 110. Other astute analyses of documentary excess include Arondekar, *For the Record*; Beredo, *Import of the Archive*; Verdery, *Secrets and Truth*.
31. Hartman, "Venus in Two Acts," 2, 10. Dialoguing with Hartman, Stephen Best's *None Like Us: Blackness, Belonging, Aesthetic Life* (Durham: Duke University Press, 2018) also critiques "melancholic historicism." In the context of postcolonial criticism, Colleen Lye has noted that melancholic historicism is "resigned to history's arrest" in "Afterword: Realism's Futures," *Novel: A Forum on Fiction* 49, no. 2 (August 2016): 344. See also Baik's introduction in *Reencounters*.
32. Max Weber, *From Max Weber: Essays in Sociology*, trans. and ed. H.H. Gerth and C. Wright Mills (New York: Oxford University Press, 1946), 233; Wesley K. Wark, "The Intelligence Revolution and the Future," *Studies in Intelligence* 37, no. 5 (1994): 15.

1. THE TONE OF INTELLIGENCE

33. *OED*.
34. Osgood, *Total Cold War*, 115.
35. Roland Végső, *The Naked Communist: Cold War Modernism and the Politics of Popular Culture* (New York: Fordham University Press, 2013), 58.
36. Joseph Burkholder Smith, *Portrait of a Cold Warrior* (New York: Putnam, 1976), 79.
37. In these decades, Asian self-representations did not always proceed under the auspices of the cold war, but they were nonetheless products of and responses to U.S.–Asian geopolitical relations. This geopoliticized origin of Asian self-representation marks a key difference between the Asian American and African American cold war stories. Asian Americans were much more inclined to position themselves in relation to U.S. commitments in Asia, while African Americans more often drew on a civil rights framework and the history of American slavery. African Americanist scholars have been formative, however, in helping us comprehend the cold war as a war of race and empire. See Plummer, *Rising Wind*; Lawrence Jackson, *The Indignant Generation: A Narrative History of African American Writers and Critics, 1934–1960* (Princeton: Princeton University Press, 2011); Mary Dudziak, *Cold War Civil Rights: Race and the Image of American Democracy* (Princeton: Princeton University Press, 2000); Penny Von Eschen, *Race Against Empire: Black Americans and Anticolonialism, 1937–1957* (Ithaca, N.Y.: Cornell University Press, 1997); Thomas Borstelmann, *The Cold War and the Color Line: American Race Relations in the Global Arena* (Cambridge, Mass.: Harvard University Press, 2003); William Maxwell, *F. B. Eyes: How J. Edgar Hoover's Ghostreaders Framed African American Literature* (Princeton: Princeton University Press, 2015).
38. These terms belong to Klein, *Cold War Orientalism*, and Melani McAlister, *Epic Encounters: Culture, Media, and U.S. Interests in the Middle East since 1945* (Berkeley: University of California Press, 2001). McAlister argues that a "post-Orientalist model of representing the Middle East for American audiences" required "fracturing the East-West binary on which traditional Orientalism had depended" (40). Klein mostly focuses on East and Southeast Asia but makes analogous claims. In analyzing the cold war film *Anna and the King* (1956), Klein shows how, on the one hand, Anna "denies the Siamese the ability to represent themselves" (thus functioning "in the best Orientalist fashion"), but on the other, she "presents a world in which East and West can be understood as related to one another outside the coercive ties of empire" (12).
39. McAlister, *Epic Encounters*, 69.
40. Rey Chow, *The Protestant Ethnic and the Spirit of Capitalism* (New York: Columbia University Press, 2002), 107.
41. Park, *Cold War Friendships*, 16; Cheng, *Citizens of Asian America*, 12.
42. Wu, *The Color of Success*, 5.
43. Cheng, *Citizens of Asian America*, chapter 3; Ellen Wu, "'America's Chinese': Anti-Communism, Citizenship, and Cultural Diplomacy during the Cold War," *Pacific Historical Review* 77, no. 3 (2008): 391–422; Mary Lui, "Rehabilitating Chinatown at Mid-Century: Chinese Americans, Race, and U.S. Cultural Diplomacy," in *Chinatowns in a Transnational World: Myths and Realities of an Urban Phenomenon*, eds. Vanessa Künnemann and Ruth Mayer (New York: Routledge, 2011).

1. THE TONE OF INTELLIGENCE

44. Or, put differently, the overlap of the aesthetic and the anthropological in U.S. discourse on Asia—for instance, through the ethnic autobiography—established a cold war "cultural hegemony." As Raymond Williams has shown, a cultural hegemony means that both anthropological and aesthetic forms not only held as much determinative force as social and economic structures but also "related to *a much wider area of reality*" than the abstractions of 'social' and 'economic' experience" (*Marxism and Literature*, 111, emphasis in original).
45. Mark Seltzer, *Bodies and Machines* (New York: Routledge, 1992), 75, emphasis in original.
46. My focus on *intelligence* complements Shuang Shen's use of *information* in "Empire of Information" to categorize Chinese-language materials sponsored by U.S. cold war institutions. However, I prefer the term intelligence because it is more overtly geopoliticized.
47. Park, *Cold War Friendships*, 8.
48. Visit of Major Sammy Lee to Hong Kong, From Hong Kong to the Dept. of State, November 3, 1954, Educational Exchange: Visiting U.S. Grantees, Classified General Records of the USIS, 1955, Records of Foreign Service Posts of the Department of State, Record Group (RG) 84, National Archives at College Park, M.D. (hereafter cited as NACP). On Wong's failure to demonstrate cultural authority, see Wu, "'America's Chinese,'" 410–12.
49. Stanley Karnow, "Western Ignorance of Asians Produces Policies of Delusion," *Washington Post*, July 20, 1970, A23.
50. On the unacknowledged labors of native informants, see Nicholas Dirks, "Colonial Histories and Native Informants: Biography of an Archive," in *Orientalism and the Postcolonial Predicament*, ed. Carol A. Breckenridge and Peter van der Veer (Philadelphia: University of Pennsylvania Press, 1993), 279–313. Contrary to popular usage, an "agent," or a "proxy," is a foreign national, someone with local sources or expertise who reports to an "officer." "Officers" are (white) American employees of the CIA who evaluate intelligence. Because agents work in the field, they risk losing cover, whereas officers do not.
51. Meredith Oyen's *The Diplomacy of Migration: Transnational Lives and the Making of U.S.-Chinese Relations in the Cold War* (Ithaca, N.Y.: Cornell University Press, 2015) discusses how Chinese migrants both voluntarily and involuntarily served as "cold warriors." The overlap between the ambassadorial and quotidian exemplifies what Ju Yon Kim calls "the racial mundane" in *The Racial Mundane: Asian American Performance and the Embodied Everyday* (New York: NYU Press, 2015).
52. Memorandum, Eisenhower to John Foster Dulles, October 24, 1953, *FRUS, 1952–1954, Western Europe and Canada, Vol. VI, Part 1* (Washington, D.C.: Government Printing Office, 1986), document 307.
53. Mark Jerng, *Racial Worldmaking: The Power of Popular Fiction* (New York: Fordham University Press, 2017), 5.
54. Lye, *America's Asia*, 55.
55. Jerng, *Racial Worldmaking*, 43. Jerng discusses this imagery in chapter 1. The imagery of wheat is from Lye, *America's Asia*, chapter 2. In addition to the falling dominos, the other relevant cold war trope is the "human wave" as applied to Chinese troops during the Korean War: "A mythology was broad in 8th Army that it

1. THE TONE OF INTELLIGENCE

faced hundreds of thousands of drug-crazed men who attacked in suicidal human waves"; see Michael Hickey, *The Korean War: The West Confronts Communism* (Woodstock, N.Y.: Overlook, 2000), 179.

56. Frances Dyson, *The Tone of Our Times: Sound, Sense, Economy, and Ecology* (Cambridge, Mass.: MIT Press, 2014), 5.
57. Many of these ambiguities appear in Hermann von Helmholtz, *Sensations of Tone*, trans. Alexander J. Ellis (New York: Longmans, Green, 1895). On tone as noise, see Luigi Russolo, *The Art of Noises*, trans. Barclay Brown (Hillsdale, N.Y.: Pendragon, 1986), 29; Friedrich Kittler, *Discourse Networks 1800/1900*, trans. Michael Metteer (Stanford: Stanford University Press, 1990), 183.
58. For both variations, see Mladen Dolar, *A Voice and Nothing More* (Cambridge, Mass.: MIT Press, 2006), 21–22.
59. I.A. Richards, *Practical Criticism: A Study of Literary Judgement* (London: Kegan Paul, 1929), 185.
60. Monroe C. Beardsley, *Aesthetics: Problems in the Philosophy of Criticism* (Indianapolis, Ind.: Hackett, 1981), 242.
61. Ngai, *Ugly Feelings*, 28.
62. Nina Sun Eidsheim, "Voice as Action: Towards a Model for Analyzing the Dynamic Construction of Racialized Voice," *Current Musicology* 93, no. 1 (2012): 19, emphasis in original. See also Nina Sun Eidsheim, *The Race of Sound: Listening, Timbre, and Vocality in African American Music* (Durham: Duke University Press, 2019).
63. Anne Anlin Cheng, *Second Skin: Josephine Baker and the Modern Surface* (New York: Oxford University Press, 2011); Cheng, *Ornamentalism*; Michelle Ann Stephens, *Skin Acts: Race, Psychoanalysis, and the Black Male Performer* (Durham: Duke University Press, 2014); Krista Thompson, *The Visual Economy of Light in African Diasporic Aesthetic Practice* (Durham: Duke University Press, 2015).
64. Rey Chow, *Not Like a Native Speaker: Languaging as a Postcolonial Experience* (New York: Columbia University Press, 2014), 8, 41, emphasis in original.
65. According to the *OED*, both the Latin *tonus* and the Greek τόνος signify stretching. Definitions such as "pitch of voice" and "exertion of physical or mental energy" evoke the vibration of vocal cords or the stretching of ligaments. From both a physiological and an affective standpoint (or, from both a "racial" and an "aesthetic" standpoint), tone has been understood as a habituation to tension. For example, in Johann Caspar Rüegg's analysis of smooth muscles, tone has a homeopathic element insofar as a "tonic contraction" is a holding position, or "holding tension," that "can be maintained for prolonged periods without apparent fatigue." Muscles that are "slower" and "more economical" are also "more 'tonic'" ("Smooth Muscle Tone," *Psychological Reviews* 51, no.1 [January 1971], 201). We find a similar relation between tone and tension in C.W. Anderson and G.E. McMaster's discussion of how "emotional tone" can be a measure of "tension profile" and "tension level." In this account, a reader's "emotional tone scores" are partially derived from "the overall tone of the story" ("Modeling Emotional Tone in Stories Using Tension Levels and Categorical States," *Computers and the Humanities* 20, no. 1 [January–March 1986], 6, 7).
66. Rejecting the bifurcation of tone's double meaning, recent studies on tone often address both racial and aesthetic concerns: Ellen McLarney, "James Baldwin and the Power of Black Muslim Language," *Social Text* 37, no. 1 (2019): 51–84; David

1. THE TONE OF INTELLIGENCE

Humphrey, "The Tone of Laughter and the Strangely Warm Comedy of Hagimoto Kin'ichi," *Japan Forum* 26, no.4 (2014): 530–50; Kai Hang Cheang, "Family Discord/ance: Tone and Counter-Mood in Gish Jen's *Mona in the Promised Land*," *Pacific Coast Philology* 53, no. 2 (2018): 217–38.

67. On the classification system for intelligence, see Peter Galison, "Removing Knowledge," *Critical Inquiry* 31, no. 1 (2004): 235. Apart from classifications, the State Department also attempted to limit distribution through designations such as "NoDis," "ExDis," and "LimDis." These layers of secrecy can modulate the affective tenor of a file. Daniel Ellsberg recalls seeing "rather desperate warnings" of "Literally Eyes Only of the Secretary" and "the President" in his perusal of "Vietnam" files (*Secrets: A Memoir of Vietnam and the Pentagon Papers* [New York: Penguin, 2003], 38–39).
68. Gaddis, *Strategies of Containment*, 104, 105.
69. U.S. President's Committee on International Information Activities (the Jackson Committee), "The President's Committee on International Information Activities: Report to the President," June 30, 1953, Central Intelligence Agency, 61, 62, 77, 78.
70. Jackson Committee, "The President's Committee on International Information Activities," 55. For a fuller account of the Jackson Committee's recommendations in relation to Eisenhower's expansion of intelligence operations, see Shawn J. Parry-Giles, *The Rhetorical Presidency, Propaganda, and the Cold War, 1945–1955* (Westport, Conn.: Praeger, 2002).
71. Sherman Kent, *Strategic Intelligence for American World Policy* (Princeton: Princeton University Press, 2016), 7–9.
72. Sherman Kent, *Strategic Intelligence*, 61.
73. Sherman Kent, "Valediction," *Studies in Intelligence* 12, no. 1 (Winter 1968): 3.
74. Sherman Kent, "The Need for an Intelligence Literature," *Studies in Intelligence* 1, no. 1 (Fall 1955): 5–7, emphasis in original.
75. Sherman Kent, "Estimates and Influence," *Studies in Intelligence* 12, no. 3 (Summer 1968): 155; Sherman Kent, "Words of Estimative Probability," *Studies in Intelligence* 8, no. 4 (Fall 1964): 56.
76. Kent, "Words of Estimative Probability," 57, 54, emphases in original.
77. For example, Burney B. Bennett rails against "the Literary Bent," which renders communication secondary to "the elegant phrase and the meaningful metaphor" ("The Great Barrier," *Studies in Intelligence* 2, no. 4 [Fall 1958]: 110). George Berkeley dubs "poets" the writers who spout abstractions such as "democracy," "nationalism," "insurgency," "the right," and "the left" ("For a Board of Definitions," *Studies in Intelligence* 9, no. 3 [Summer 1965]: 13). The most elaborate takedown comes from Richard Puderbaugh's satire on "elegant writing" in "Elegant Writing in the Clandestine Services," *Studies in Intelligence* 16, no. 1 (1972): 1–7 and "Elegant Writing—Report Number Two," *Studies in Intelligence* 17, no. 2 (Summer 1973): 61–69.
78. Bennett, "The Greater Barrier," 106, 107.
79. Kent, "Words of Estimative Probability," 55, 57; Wayne Jackson, "Scientific Estimating," *Studies in Intelligence* 9, no. 3 (Summer 1965): 8; Abbot E. Smith, "On the Accuracy of National Intelligence Estimates," *Studies in Intelligence* 13, no. 4 (Fall 1969): 35.
80. Jackson, "Scientific Estimating," 8, 10.

1. THE TONE OF INTELLIGENCE

81. Smith, "On the Accuracy of National Intelligence Estimates," 29.
82. Lewis, "Re-examining Our Perceptions on Vietnam," 13, 29, 35.
83. Sherman Kent, "Death of a Hypothesis," *Studies in Intelligence* 9, no. 2 (Spring 1965): 22. Kent's first object: "It was sculpted stone; its subject was clearly anatomical (some sort of organ from some sort of animal; and it was embellished with a good amount of cuneiform script)" (21). The second concerns the hypothesis that "if the Chinese Communist government finds itself really pressed for hard currency, it might turn to selling its national art treasures" (23).
84. Interestingly, while Kent's first two books outline the ideal traits and sensibilities of a historian and/or analyst, his later writings in *Studies in Intelligence* pit the imperfect intelligence analyst (who possesses "normal human fallibilities") against the unpredictable enemy (who "zigs violently out of the track of 'normal' behavior"). Implied is that the normally fallible analyst will "probably misestimate" the abnormally aberrant enemy ("A Crucial Estimate Relived," *Studies in Intelligence* 36, no.5 [Spring 1964]: 114).
85. Kent, "Estimates and Influence," 13.
86. Kent, *Strategic Intelligence*, 39.
87. Castiglia, *The Practices of Hope*, 13, emphasis mine. See also Tobin Siebers, *Cold War Criticism and the Politics of Skepticism* (New York: Oxford University Press, 1993); William H. Epstein, "Counter-Intelligence: Cold-War Criticism and Eighteenth-Century Studies," *ELH* 57, no.1 (Spring 1990): 63–99; Sharon Achinstein, "Cold War Milton," *University of Toronto Quarterly* 77 no. 3 (2008): 801–36.
88. Edward Thompson, "The Long Revolution," *New Left Review* 1, no. 9 (May–June 1961), 27, 23. Still more interesting, Williams offers an identical assessment of Thompson's review: "The onslaught from the right was so strong that I felt at certain critical moments an inability on the left to sustain theoretical differences and yet present a common front. *I am not referring here to the main argument of Edward's article, but to certain asides and tones*" (*Politics and Letters: Interviews with New Left Review* [New York: Verso, 1979], 134, emphasis mine).
89. Williams, *Marxism and Literature*, 132.
90. In this regard, tone is akin to what Jonathan Flatley calls an "affective map": "Our affective maps are likely to be especially in need of revision, repair, or invention at moments of rapid social change or upheaval" (79); see *Melancholia and the Politics of Modernism* (Cambridge, Mass.: Harvard University Press, 2008).
91. Donna V. Jones, *The Racial Discourses of Life Philosophy: Négritude, Vitalism, and Modernity* (New York: Columbia University Press, 2010); Clare Hemmings, "Invoking Affect: Cultural Theory and the Ontological Turn," *Cultural Studies* 19, no. 5 (2005): 548–67.
92. Catherine Gallagher, "Raymond Williams and Cultural Studies," *Social Text* no. 30 (1992): 85.
93. David D. Gries, "Openness and Secrecy," *Studies in Intelligence* 37, no. 5 (1994): 33.
94. Nick Cullather, *Secret History, The CIA's Classified Account of its Operations in Guatemala, 1952–1954* (Stanford: Stanford University Press, 2006), xviii; Peter Galison, "Removing Knowledge," 233.
95. Cullather, *Secret History*, xi.
96. Kim, *Ends of Empire*, 3. As my introduction discusses, Kuan-Hsing Chen's notion of "de-cold war" offers one such model. Another is Heonik Kwon's metaphor of

"decomposition," which frames the cold war's end as "a participatory, ethnographic question" (*The Other Cold War*, 8).
97. Kwon, *The Other Cold War*, 54.
98. Yoneyama, *Cold War Ruins*, 5. Redress culture largely targeted Japan and depended on U.S.-centric institutions and apparatuses. For these reasons, Yoneyama is skeptical about the forms of justice that have been available to redress movements of the 1990s.
99. Rob Wilson, *Reimagining the American Pacific*, 108.
100. Nonetheless, my thinking has been indelibly shaped by works such as McAlister, *Epic Encounters*; Inderpal Grewal, *Saving the Security State: Exceptional Citizens in Twenty-First-Century America* (Durham: Duke University Press, 2017); Ronak Kapadia, *Insurgent Aesthetics: Security and the Queer Life of the Forever War* (Durham: Duke University Press, 2019); Darryl Li, *The Universal Enemy: Jihad, Empire, and the Challenge of Solidarity* (Stanford: Stanford University Press, 2019); Stuart Schrader, *Badges without Borders: How Global Counterinsurgency Transformed American Policing* (Berkeley: University of California Press, 2019).
101. Giovanni Arrighi, *Adam Smith in Beijing: Lineages of the Twenty-First Century* (New York: Verso, 2009), 301.
102. Arlie Hochschild, *The Managed Heart: Commercialization of Human Feeling* (Berkeley: University of California Press, 2012); Eva Illouz, *Cold Intimacies: The Making of Emotional Capitalism* (Malden, Mass.: Polity, 2007); Dierdra Reber, *Coming to Our Senses: Affect and An Order of Things For Global Culture* (New York: Columbia University Press, 2016); Paolo Virno, *A Grammar of the Multitude: For an Analysis of Contemporary Forms of Life*, trans. Isabella Bertoletti, James Cascaito, and Andrea Casson (New York: Semiotext[e], 2004).

2. THE TONE OF RUMORS

1. Robert H. Knapp, "A Psychology of Rumor," *Public Opinion Quarterly* 8, no. 1 (Spring 1944): 22, 28; Gordon W. Allport and Leo Postman, *The Psychology of Rumor* (New York: Henry Holt, 1947), 179, 195, emphasis in original; Floyd Allport and Milton Lepkin, "Wartime Rumors of Waste and Special Privilege: Why Some People Believe Them," *Journal of Abnormal and Social Psychology* 40 (1945): 3.
2. Allport and Lepkin, "Wartime Rumors," 12.
3. Allport and Postman write, "this formula means that the amount of rumor in circulation will vary with the importance of the subject to the individuals concerned *times* the ambiguity of the evidence pertaining to the topic at issue" (*Psychology of Rumor*, 34).
4. Knapp, "A Psychology of Rumor," 23–24.
5. Knapp, "A Psychology of Rumor," 24.
6. Rumor studies climaxed at mid-century and all but petered out by the 1970s, when folklore and urban legends came to draw the bulk of scholarly attention; see Pamela Donovan, "How Idle Is Idle Talk? One Hundred Years of Rumor Research," *Diogenes* 213 (2007): 59–82.
7. Jessica Wang, "A State of Rumor: Low Knowledge, Nuclear Fear, and the Scientist as Security Risk," *Journal of Policy History* 28, no. 3 (2016): 408.

2. THE TONE OF RUMORS

8. Robin, *The Making of the Cold War Enemy*, 3, 4.
9. Alan Nadel, *Containment Culture: American Narrative, Postmodernism, and the Atomic Age* (Durham: Duke University Press, 1995), 3–4.
10. Knapp, "A Psychology of Rumor," 31.
11. Ann Laura Stoler, "'In Cold Blood': Hierarchies of Credibility and the Politics of Colonial Narratives," *Representations* 37 (Winter 1992): 151–89; Ranajit Guha, *Elementary Aspects of Peasant Insurgency in Colonial India* (Durham: Duke University Press, 1999); Best, *None Like Us*, chapter 4. I discuss the role of rumor in US counterinsurgency campaigns in chapter 5.
12. Fred Turner, *The Democratic Surround: Multimedia and American Liberalism from World War II to the Psychedelic Sixties* (Chicago: University of Chicago Press, 2013), 9.
13. Ruth Benedict, *The Chrysanthemum and the Sword* (Cleveland: Meridian, 1989).
14. John Dower, *War Without Mercy: Race and Power in the Pacific War* (New York: Pantheon, 1987), 18. Dower extensively discusses the figure of the Japanese enemy.
15. Wallace quoted in William Blakefield, "A War Within: The Making of Know Your Enemy," *Sight and Sound: International Film Quarterly* 52, no.2 (Spring 1983): 130.
16. Blakefield, "A War Within," 131.
17. Yoneyama, *Cold War Ruins*, ix.
18. The above quotes come from: "The Tenno—Japan's Symbol"; "Imperial Family to Directives," Civil Information & Education Section (CIE), Supreme Commander for the Allied Powers (SCAP), Military Agency Records, Records of the Allied Operational and Occupation Headquarters, World War II, RG 331, NACP.
19. Kazuo Ishiguro, *An Artist of the Floating World* (New York: Vintage, 1986): 77. Subsequent references are cited in the text.
20. Bill Bryson, "Between Two Worlds," *New York Times*, April 29, 1990; Kazuo Ishiguro, *A Pale View of Hills* (New York: Vintage, 1982); Kazuo Ishiguro, *The Remains of the Day* (New York: Vintage, 1988). Subsequent references of *Pale View* and *Remains* are cited in the text.
21. Mark McGurl, *The Program Era: Postwar Fiction and the Rise of Creative Writing* (Cambridge, Mass.: Harvard University Press, 2009), 14–15.
22. The metaphor of tutelage for national rebuilding under occupation reflects the common American view of postwar Japan as a paradoxical blend of feudalist antiquity and childlike innocence. Naoko Shibusawa writes, "The Americans were not necessarily mixing metaphors: both terms connoted underdevelopment, and the combination of feudalism and childishness would not have seemed contradictory to older Americans still informed by recapitulation theory to explain human history" (*America's Geisha Ally: Reimagining the Japanese Enemy* [Cambridge, Mass.: Harvard University Press, 2006], 60).
23. Barton J. Bernstein, "The Perils and Politics of Surrender: Ending the War with Japan and Avoiding the Third Atomic Bomb," *Pacific Historical Review* 46, no. 1 (February 1977): 1–27.
24. Roger J. Bell levels a strongly worded accusation: "Increasingly, the U.S. desired to monopolize Allied military and political policy in the Far East so as to limit possible Soviet penetration of the Pacific" (*Unequal Allies: Australian–American Relations and the Pacific War* [Carlton, Vic.: Melbourne University Press, 1977], 186).

2. THE TONE OF RUMORS

25. Takashi Fujitani, "The Reischauer Memo: Mr. Moto, Hirohito, and Japanese American Soldiers," *Critical Asian Studies* 33, no. 3 (2001): 386–87. Robert J. C. Butow's 1954 study *Japan's Decision to Surrender* (Stanford: Stanford University Press, 1954) was influential during its time for pinning the prolongation of the war to the "invisible technique" of *haragei* perpetuated by the emperor's militaristic advisers (70–75). Butow also suggests that Japan might have capitulated earlier had the United States given clearer indications of its willingness to retain the emperor.
26. Tellingly, the memo's name changed from "The True Story of Japan's Surrender" to "Hirohito's Struggle to Surrender." "Hirohito's Struggle to Surrender," undated draft, Writings, 1934–1958, Bonner F. Fellers Papers, Hoover Institution Archive (hereafter cited as HIA). The memo was later published in *Readers Digest* in July 1947.
27. John Dower, *Embracing Defeat: Japan in the Wake of World War II* (New York: Norton, 1999), 284.
28. Memorandum, Joint Chiefs of Staff, "Unconditional Surrender of Japan," 20 April, 1945, Geographic File 1942–45, 386.2 Japan (4-9-45) sec. 4 to 387 Japan (2-7-45) sec. 1, Records of the U.S. Joint Chiefs of Staff, Military Agency Records, Records of the U.S. Joint Chiefs of Staff, RG 218.
29. Douglas MacArthur, *Reminiscences* (Annapolis, M.D.: Naval Institute Press, 1964), 288.
30. Marilyn Ivy, "Formations of Mass Culture," in *Postwar Japan as History*, ed. Andrew Gordon (Berkeley: University of California Press, 1993), 244. On the multiple layers of mediation that Hirohito's broadcast entailed, as well as its consequences, see Herbert Bix "The Showa Emperor's 'Monologue' and the Problem of War Responsibility," *Journal of Japanese Studies* 18 no. 2 (1992): 295–363.
31. "Emperor System Must be Abolished," *Geijutsu*, Oct. 1948, Press Translations and Summaries: Japan. No: 707, trans. K. Osawa, November 10, 1948, Central Files Branch, Miscellaneous File, 1945–1951, SCAP Government Section, RG 331.
32. Quoted in Richard B. Finn, *Winners in Peace: MacArthur, Yoshida, and Postwar Japan* (Berkeley: University of California Press, 1992), 64.
33. Dower, *Embracing Defeat*, 278.
34. Nancy Ruttenburg, *Democratic Personality: Popular Voice and the Trial of American Authorship* (Stanford: Stanford University Press, 1998), 7.
35. Herbert Bix, "Inventing the 'Symbol Monarchy' in Japan, 1945–52," *Journal of Japanese Studies* 21, no. 2 (Summer 1995): 327.
36. Dower, *Embracing Defeat*, 336.
37. "Emperor Braves Heat in Coal Mine Tour," *Stars and Stripes*, Aug. 7, 1947, Central Files Branch, Misc. Files, SCAP Government Section, RG 331.
38. News report summary, untitled, undated, *Jiji Shimpo*, Central Files Branch, Misc. Files, SCAP Government Section, RG 331; "Low Bows Venerate 'Felt Hat,'" *Christian Science Monitor*, March 31, 1950, Central Files Branch, Misc. Files, SCAP Government Section, RG 331.
39. "'Emperor Articles' Rampant," *Asahi Shimbun*, February 23, 1950, Central Files Branch, Misc. Files, SCAP Government Section, RG 331.
40. Takeshi Ito, "Emperor Still Held in Great Respect," *Mainichi*, May 21, 1949, Central Files Branch, Misc. Files, SCAP Government Section, RG 331.

2. THE TONE OF RUMORS

41. Guy Swope, Untitled, Undated, Central Files Branch, Misc. Files, SCAP Government Section, RG 331.
42. "On Emperor's Tour," *Yomiuri Shimbun*, March 30, 1950, Central Files Branch, Misc. Files, SCAP Government Section, RG 331.
43. "A Call for Abdication of the Emperor," *Shinso*, October 1948, Press Translation and Summaries, trans. K. Osawa, 6, Nov 1948, Central Files Branch, Misc. Files, SCAP Government Section, RG 331. Dower says that Communist Party leader Tokuda Kyuichi is responsible for popularizing jokes about Hirohito's "ah so" (*Embracing Defeat*, 263–64).
44. Shibusawa, *Geisha Ally*, 106.
45. Bix, "Inventing," 362.
46. Sara Ahmed, *The Cultural Politics of Emotion* (New York: Routledge, 2004), 10, 11.
47. Contagion is also a common metaphor for affect. See, for instance, Teresa Brennan's discussion of "the transmission of affect" within crowds. Interestingly, it was respected rumor researcher Floyd Allport, cited at the start of this chapter, who would challenge the pathological characterization of crowds as "a contagious power as intense as that of microbes" (*The Transmission of Affect* [Ithaca, N.Y.: Cornell University Press, 2004], 53).
48. Quoted in Dower, *Embracing Defeat*, 214.
49. "The Attitude of the Imperial Household," December 16, 1947, Central Files Branch, Misc. Files, SCAP Government Section, RG 331. Part of the reason the tours enhanced the imperial tradition is that they in fact resuscitated a prewar ritual. In the late nineteenth century, a kind of imperial tour, or "progress" (*junko*), had been central to securing Emperor Meiji's legitimacy and power. Although Americans often assumed that the chrysanthemum crest, the sacred sword, the curved jewel, and the rising sun were relic symbols as ancient as the imperial institution itself, Takashi Fujitani writes that such emblems were in fact inventions of the Meiji period, their ritual meaning unknown to Japanese commoners until the "Six Great Imperial Tours" (*roku daijunko*) during the 1870s and 1880s. These tours were the means by which the emperor's advisers brought him "down from a godly presence somewhere 'above the clouds' in Kyoto to become an active and visible agent in politics," especially during a time when "the threat of the Western powers" redoubled the need to "unify the nation" (*Splendid Monarchy: Power and Pageantry in Modern Japan* [Berkeley: University of California Press, 1998], 52, 44). Like his grandfather's imperial progresses, Hirohito's outings were part of a *political* strategy. The difference is that Hirohito's tours aimed to undercut, not foster, the impression of exceptional power and paternalistic rule. The Meiji tours had heightened the drama of the imperial spectacle, compelling the people to view the emperor in all his symbolic pomp. By contrast, the postwar emperor tours, at least in theory, served to diminish the separation between emperor and citizen, spectator and spectacle.
50. Dower, *Embracing Defeat*, 299; Shibusawa, *Geisha Ally*, 106, 110.
51. Dower, *Embracing Defeat*, 337, 338.
52. Bix, "Inventing," 345. The tours were in fact organized by the Imperial Household Ministry with the assistance of SCAP.
53. Instead of projecting a classically cold war cult of personality, Hirohito's political affect is more reminiscent of how Lauren Berlant and Brian Massumi have

2. THE TONE OF RUMORS

portrayed U.S. Republican presidents. Massumi has claimed that the fumbling and incoherent Ronald Reagan "was more famous for his polyps than his poise" (*Parables for the Virtual: Movement, Affect, Sensation* [Durham: Duke University Press, 2002], 40). Similarly, Berlant shows how George W. Bush spurned the high polish of American politics and instead urged "the public to feel the funk, the live intensities and desires" (*Cruel Optimism* [Durham: Duke University Press, 2011], 226). Arguably, one could say that it was a similar kind of "funk"—boxy suits, social gaffes, bumbling tweets, Scotch tape in lieu of a tie clip—that helped animate Donald Trump's persona as a plebeian during his presidency. In all these cases, it is transmitting "not the message but the noise" that enables an intimate national public (226).

54. Naoki Sakai, "'You Asians': On the Historical Role of the West and Asia Binary," *The South Atlantic Quarterly* 99, no. 4 (2000): 789–817. Sakai writes that an Americanist strain of culturalism (propelled by the likes of Ruth Benedict) and a Japanese strain of culturalism (represented by conservative intellectuals such as Watsuji Tetsuro) "reached a remarkably effective synthesis in the legitimization of the new emperor system. The effects of such a culturalist endorsement of the new emperor system are surprisingly lasting" (801). Sakai goes on to say, "Japanese cultural identity was produced with a view to some imaginary observer who is positioned outside the organic whole of the Japanese nation. And this imaginary observer is habitually referred to as the West, often symbolizing U.S. hegemony" (810).

55. "Japs Seen Liking Puppet Emperor," April 26, 1946, Central Files Branch, Misc. Files, SCAP Government Section, RG 331.

56. Press Translations and Summaries, Item 10: Loyalty to Emperor a Check to Communism, June 15, 1949, Central Files Branch, Misc. Files, SCAP Government Section, RG 331.

57. Anna M. Parkinson, *An Emotional State: The Politics of Emotion in Postwar West German Culture* (Ann Arbor, Mich.: University of Michigan Press, 2015), 16.

58. I'm influenced here by Berlant's claim that "feeling political together" requires "noise" as the crucial sticking (and sticky) point, which makes political messages "affectively immediate, seductive, and binding" (*Cruel Optimism*, 230).

59. Lisa Yoneyama, *Hiroshima Traces: Time, Space, and the Dialectics of Memory* (Berkeley: University of California Press, 1999), 20.

60. Carol Gluck, "The 'End' of the Postwar: Japan at the Turn of the Millennium," *Public Culture* 10, no. 1 (1997): 5.

61. Roland Barthes, *The Empire of Signs*, trans. Richard Howard (New York: Hill and Wang, 1982), 30–31. See also John Whittier Treat, "Beheaded Emperors and the Absent Figure in Contemporary Japanese Literature," *PMLA* 109, no. 1 (Jan. 1994): 100–15.

62. Robert Meister, *After Evil: A Politics of Human Rights* (New York: Columbia University Press, 2012).

63. Bruce Cumings, *Origins of the Korean War, Vol. 1: Liberation and the Emergence of Separate Regimes, 1945–1947* (Princeton: Princeton University Press, 1981), 128.

64. Yoneyama, *Cold War Ruins*, 16.

65. "But after *Remains of the Day* I felt I had almost written myself into a corner," Ishiguro is quoted as saying. "You could say I'd rewritten the same novel three times

2. THE TONE OF RUMORS

and I thought I had to move on" (Nicholas Wroe, "Living Memories," *The Guardian*, February 18, 2005).

66. Kazuo Ishiguro, "My Twentieth Century Evening—and Other Small Breakthroughs," *The Nobel Prize*, December 7, 2017, https://www.nobelprize.org/prizes/literature/2017/ishiguro/25124-kazuo-ishiguro-nobel-lecture-2017.
67. These early novels were an "act of preservation," Ishiguro says in his Nobel lecture. He continues: "as I was growing up, . . . I was busily constructing in my mind a richly detailed place called 'Japan'—a place to which I in some way belonged, and from which I drew a certain sense of my identity and my confidence. The fact that I'd never physically returned to Japan during that time only served to make my own vision of the country more vivid and personal" (Ishiguro, "My Twentieth Century Evening").
68. The indirect effects of the emperor policy on the Japanese diaspora are also apparent in the title of Julie Otsuka's 2002 novel *When the Emperor Was Divine*. On the emperor's oblique role in this novel, see Josephine Nock-Hee Park, "Alien Enemies in Julie Otsuka's *When the Emperor Was Divine*," *MFS Modern Fiction Studies* 59, no. 1 (Spring 2013): 135–55.
69. Dower, *Embracing Defeat*, 278.
70. Hajimu, *Cold War Crucible*, 36.
71. Parkinson, *An Emotional State*, 122.
72. Ezra Vogel, "Foreword," in *The Chrysanthemum and the Sword*, xii.
73. Douglas H. Mendel, "Perspectives on Japanese Foreign Policy," *Monumenta Nipponica* 21 no. 3/4 (1966): 346.
74. Peter Drucker, "Japan and Adversarial Trade," *Wall Street Journal*, April 1, 1986: 32, emphasis in original.
75. Karel van Wolferen, *The Enigma of Japanese Power: People and Politics in a Stateless Nation* (New York: Vintage, 1989), 6, 4.
76. For a history of how such publications touted the compatibility between Confucianism and Protestantism and promoted the "model minority myth," see David Palumbo-Liu, *Asian/America Historical Crossings of a Racial Frontier* (Stanford: Stanford University Press, 1999), 195–207.
77. Pico Iyer, "Waiting Upon History: *The Remains of the Day*," *Partisan Review* 58 (September 1991): 585–86.
78. Bryson, "Between Two Worlds."
79. Kazuo Ishiguro and Malcolm Bradbury, "Kazuo Ishiguro and Malcolm Bradbury," ICA Talks, Institute of Contemporary Arts, March 17, 1982, https://sounds.bl.uk/Arts-literature-and-performance/ICA-talks/024M-C0095X0015XX-0200V0.
80. Zoe Heller, "A Tissue of Truths," *Independent*, October 28, 1989: 36.
81. Amit Chaudhuri, "Unlike Kafka," *London Review of Books* 17, no. 11, June 8, 1995; Philip Hensher, "It's the Way He Tells It," *Guardian*, September 19, 2000; Kazuo Ishiguro, *The Unconsoled* (New York: Vintage, 1995); Kazuo Ishiguro, *When We Were Orphans* (New York: Vintage, 2000). Subsequent references to Ishiguro's novels are cited in the text.
82. Rebecca Walkowitz, *Cosmopolitan Style: Modernism Beyond the Nation* (New York: Columbia University Press, 2006), 122; Rebecca Walkowitz, *Born Translated: The Contemporary Novel in an Age of World Literature* (New York: Columbia University Press, 2015), 120.

2. THE TONE OF RUMORS

83. Tim Adams, "For Me, England Is a Mythical Place," *Guardian*, February 19, 2005.
84. Kazuo Ishiguro, *Never Let Me Go* (New York: Vintage, 2006).
85. Deidre Lynch, *The Economy of Character: Novels, Market Culture, and the Business of Inner Meaning* (Chicago: University of Chicago Press, 1998), 103.
86. Yoneyama, *Cold War Ruins*, 3.
87. In *The Rhetoric of Fiction* (Chicago: The University of Chicago Press, 1983), Wayne Booth writes, "we travel with the silent author, observing as from a rear seat the humorous or disgraceful or ridiculous or vicious driving behavior of the narrator seated in front. The author may wink and nudge, but he may not speak. The reader may sympathize or deplore, but he never accepts the narrator as a reliable guide" (300).
88. For a historical account of this shift in the context of human rights, see Susan Koshy, "From Cold War to Trade War: Neocolonialism and Human Rights." *Social Text* no. 58 (Spring 1999): 1–32.
89. Ryan S. Trimm, "Inside Job: Professionalism and Postimperial Communities in *The Remains of the Day*," *Lit: Literature Interpretation Theory* 16 no. 2 (2005): 136; Bruce Robbins, "Very Busy Just Now: Globalization and Harriedness in Kazuo Ishiguro's *The Unconsoled*," in *Globalization and the Humanities*, ed. David Leiwei Li (Hong Kong: Hong Kong University Press, 2004), 239, 232; Bruce Robbins, "Cruelty Is Bad: Banality and Proximity in *Never Let Me Go*," *Novel* 40, no. 3 (Spring 2007): 295; Lisa Fluet, "Immaterial Labors: Ishiguro, Class, and Affect," *Novel* 40, no. 3 (Summer 2007): 269, 279.
90. Manuel Castells, *The Rise of the Network Society* (Malden, Mass.: Blackwell, 2000), 180.
91. Michael Hardt and Antonio Negri, *Empire* (Cambridge, Mass.: Harvard University Press, 2000), 290; Luc Boltanski and Eve Chiapello, *The New Spirit of Capitalism*, trans. Gregory Elliott (London: Verso, 2007), 81.
92. Stephen Wood, "The Japanization of Fordism," *Economic and Industrial Democracy* 14, no. 4 (November 1993): 535; Martin Kenney and Richard Florida, "Japan's Role in a Post-Fordist Age," *Futures* 21, no. 2 (April 1989): 143.
93. Benjamin Coriat, "The 'Abominable Ohno Production System': Competences, Monitoring, and Routines in Japanese Production Systems," in *The Nature and Dynamics of Organizational Capabilities*, eds. Giovanni Dosi, Richard R. Nelson, and Sidney G. Winter (New York: Oxford University Press, 2000), 220.
94. Sianne Ngai, *Our Aesthetic Categories: Zany, Cute, Interesting* (Cambridge, Mass.: Harvard University Press, 2012), 174.
95. Viet Thanh Nguyen, *Nothing Ever Dies: Vietnam and the Memory of War* (Cambridge, Mass.: Harvard University Press, 2016), 202.
96. Hardt and Negri, *Empire*, 290–91, 292–93.
97. Liu, *The Laws of Cool*, 76, 67, emphasis in original.
98. Liu, *The Laws of Cool*, 67–68, 76.
99. According to the *OED*, *coolie*, the variants of which include *coule*, is a term likely derived from Gujarati, Hindi, Bengali, Tamil, Telugu, Chinese, and/or Portuguese. On the relation between physical laborers and "high tech coolies," see Iyko Day, *Alien Capital: Asian Racialization and the Logic of Settler Colonial Capitalism* (Durham: Duke University Press, 2016), 155–89; L. Ling-chi Wang, "Model Minority, High-Tech Coolies, and Foreign Spies," *Amerasia* 33, no. 1 (2007): 49–62. On

the Chinese male laborer's indifference to pain, see Hayot, *The Hypothetical Mandarin*.
100. Eve Kosofsky Sedgwick, *Epistemology of the Closet* (Berkeley: University of California Press, 1990), 3, 23, emphasis in original.
101. Some critics make a hard distinction between rumors and gossip, often associating gossip with intimacy, relaxation, small talk, personal affairs and rumors with events, magnitude, belief, and fear. Stoler, for example, contrasts "the tension of rumor" with the "'coziness' of gossip" ("In Cold Blood," 179, 189). I prefer to avoid such differentiations because what gossip and rumor share is a preoccupation with typologies of identity. For more on distinctions between gossip and rumor, see Ralph L. Rosnow and Gary Alan Fine, *Rumor and Gossip: The Social Psychology of Hearsay* (New York: Elsevier, 1976).
102. Fredric Jameson, *The Antinomies of Realism* (New York: Verso, 2013), 98.
103. Rachel C. Lee's reading of Ishiguro's *Never Let Me Go* locates "race" in organs rather than epidermis—in a "minoritized bioavailable subject, even as that subject appears to not correspond to a visibly racial other" (*The Exquisite Corpse of Asian America: Biopolitics, Biosociality, and Posthuman Ecologies* [New York: NYU Press, 2014], 59–60).
104. Kazuo Ishiguro, *The Buried Giant* (New York: Vintage, 2015), 163.
105. I'm grateful to Mieko Kurata Anders for telling me about Ishiguro's early drafts of *Artist*, which were set in England of the 1980s and featured Ono's grandson Ichiro working at a corporate firm.

3. THE TONE OF THE TIMES

1. In this chapter, I will use "Republic of Korea" (ROK) and "Korea" interchangeably with "South Korea."
2. Choong Soon Kim, *The Culture of Korean Industry: An Ethnography of Poongsan Corporation* (Tucson: University of Arizona, Press, 1992), xiv. Kim refers to Alvin and Heidi Toffler's 1970 book *Future Shock*.
3. John Lie, *Han Unbound: The Political Economy of South Korea* (Stanford: Stanford University Press, 1998), 1, 4.
4. Seung-kyung Kim, *Class Struggle or Family Struggle? The Lives of Women Factory Workers in South Korea* (New York: Cambridge University Press, 1997), xx.
5. Christopher T. Fan would describe Chang's *Bad Samaritans* as "*science fictional* rather than science fiction, which is an adjectival way to index the entire social context in which science fiction aesthetics are generated and received"; see "Andrew Yang and Post-'65 Asian America," American Literary History, March 3, 2020, https://doi.org/10.1093/alh/ajaa005, emphasis in original.
6. Ha-Joon Chang, *Bad Samaritans: The Myth of Free Trade and the Secret History of Capitalism* (New York: Bloomsbury, 2008), 3–12.
7. Reinhart Koselleck, *Futures Past: On the Semantics of Historical Time*, trans. Keith Tribe (New York: Columbia University Press, 2004), 241, 246.
8. Koselleck, *Futures Past*, 252.
9. Cha's family immigrated to the United States in 1963. Her first return journey to Korea was in 1979.

3. THE TONE OF THE TIMES

10. Cha's brother James recalls intense police surveillance and ongoing demonstrations during their visit. Theresa ultimately approached this scene, he says, from "an artist's point of view" (James Cha, phone conversation with author, October 26, 2019). Cha's sister Bernadette offers the following observation of *White Dust*: "Modern Korea vs old Korea of her youth. Contrast old vs new" (Theresa Hak Kyung Cha, "White Dust from Mongolia (film)," Online Archive of California, https://oac.cdlib.org/ark:/13030/tf7g50056f/?brand=oac4). This "modern" versus "old" dichotomy acknowledges change but also banalizes it.
11. Ed Park, "This is the Writing You Have Been Waiting For," in *Exilée and Temps Morts*, ed. Constance Lewallen (Berkeley: University of California Press, 2009), 14.
12. Induk Pahk, *The Cock Still Crows* (New York: Vantage, 1977), 90. Subsequent references are cited in the text.
13. Thomas Laqueur, *The Work of the Dead: A Cultural History of Mortal Remains* (Princeton: Princeton University Press, 2016), 4. Laqueur writes, "To treat a dead body as if it were ordinary organic matter . . . is to erase it from culture and from the human community" (4).
14. Koselleck, *Futures Past*, xxiii.
15. "Induk Pahk," Report to accompany H.R. 2054, 84th Cong., 2nd sess., February 22, 1956, 3. In a bill seeking permanent residency during the era of immigration quotas, Pahk's insistence on her "unofficial" status serves to emphasize the voluntariness of her lectures.
16. Induk Pahk, *September Monkey* (New York: Harper, 1954); *The Hour of the Tiger* (New York: Harper, 1965). Subsequent references are cited in the text.
17. Pahk, Kim, and Yim were born within three years of each other. They are also exact contemporaries of Younghill Kang, who likewise received an American missionary education and later served the U.S. military government in the ROK. Taiwon Koh is of a younger generation, but her memoir *The Bitter Fruit of Kom-Pawi* (1959) similarly details her experiences in American mission schools during the war against Japan and her travels to the United States during the war against communism. The most famous adaptation of the Korean Christian memoir is Richard Kim's novel *The Martyred* (1964).
18. On "Cold War imperial feminism," see Mire Koikari, *Pedagogy of Democracy: Feminism and the Cold War in the U.S. Occupation of Japan* (Philadelphia: Temple University Press, 2008), 5. Christina Klein discusses "Cold War cosmopolitan feminism" in *Cold War Cosmopolitanism: Period Style in 1950s Korean Cinema* (Berkeley: University of California Press, 2020), 40.
19. My readings of Cha in this chapter would not be possible without Jeehyun Choi's insights and guidance on *Dictee* and "melancholic historicism."
20. Kang and Kim both contributed to an influential critical anthology on Cha edited by Kim and Norma Alarcón called *Writing Self, Writing Nation*, eds. (Berkeley: Third Woman, 1994). The topic of comfort women is also central to Kim's edited collection *Dangerous Women: Gender and Korean Nationalism* (New York: Routledge, 1998). See also Kang, "Conjuring 'Comfort Women': Mediated Affiliations and Disciplined Subjects in Korean/American Transnationality," *Journal of Asian American Studies* 6, no. 1 (February 2003): 25–55.

3. THE TONE OF THE TIMES

21. Grace M. Cho, *Haunting the Korean Diaspora: Shame, Secrecy, and the Forgotten War* (Minneapolis: University of Minnesota Press, 2008).
22. Michael Davidson is the rare critic who interprets Cha in the context of "containment and Pacific Rim." This chapter tries to take seriously Davidson's passing observation that a "shift in global power and international relations in Asia" can offer "a useful stratification of the postmodern as a cultural dominant under late capitalism" (*Guys Like Us: Citing Masculinity in Cold War Poetics* [Chicago: University of Chicago Press, 2004], 198).
23. Pheng Cheah, *Inhuman Conditions: On Cosmopolitanism and Human Rights* (Cambridge, Mass.: Harvard University Press, 2007), 145.
24. Scott, *Conscripts of Modernity*, 95.
25. Yoneyama, *Cold War Ruins*, 140.
26. My use of the term "postcolonial capitalism" is inspired by Cheryl Narumi Naruse.
27. For example, Amy Elias outlines admirably nuanced models of temporality with respect to postmodernism, in "Introduction" and "Past/Future" in *Time: A Vocabulary of the Present*, eds. Joel Burges and Elias (New York: NYU Press, 2016). Yet these same essays employ jarringly punctual designations such as post-1945, post-WWII, and post-1989 (Burges and Elias, "Introduction: Time Studies Today," 3, 22; "Past/Future," 41). See also Jason Gladstone, Andrew Hoberek, and Daniel Worden, eds., *Postmodern/Postwar and After: Rethinking American Literature* (Iowa City: University of Iowa Press, 2016).
28. Ewha is the first school for girls founded by U.S. missions and continues to be a pillar of higher education. All the Korean female memoirists referenced thus far either attended or taught at Ewha. See Hyaeweol Choi, *Gender and Mission Encounters in Korea: New Women, Old Ways* (Berkeley: University of California Press, 2009); Theodore Jun Yoo, *The Politics of Gender in Colonial Korea: Education, Labor, and Health, 1910–1945* (Berkeley: University of California Press, 2008).
29. "Mrs. Induk Pahk to Speak Before W. Mass Women," *Springfield Republican*, November 7, 1948: 19; "Federation of B and P Clubs Will Hear Talk on Korea," *Trenton Evening Times*, March 15, 1949: 12.
30. "Korean Broadcasts Moral Support to the Homeland," *Democrat and Chronicle*, December 14, 1951: 27.
31. On Pahk's divorce, see Choi, *Mission Encounters*, 160–61.
32. Reinhart Koselleck, *Sediments of Time: On Possible Histories*, trans. and ed. Sean Franzel and Stefan-Ludwig Hoffman (Stanford: Stanford University Press, 2018), 3.
33. Koselleck, *Sediments of Time*, 3.
34. Koselleck, *Futures Past*, 94–95.
35. More than 39 percent of Rhee's top posts were held by Protestants. Of the eleven Koreans that the U.S. military government appointed as advisers in 1945, six were of the Protestant faith. The thirteen bureau chiefs appointed by the U.S. occupation in 1946 included seven Protestants, all of whom were educated in the United States. See Timothy Lee, *Born Again: Evangelicalism in Korea* (Honolulu: University of Hawai'i Press, 2009), 66.
36. Charles K. Armstrong, "The Cultural Cold War in Korea, 1945–1950," *Journal of Asian Studies* 62, no. 1 (February 2003): 94.

37. Chung-shin Park, *Protestantism and Politics in Korea* (Seattle: University of Washington Press, 2003), 178.
38. Andre Schmid, *Korea between Empires, 1895–1919* (New York: Columbia University Press, 2002), 254. Many strands of Korean nationalism were prevalent during the pre-annexation and colonial eras, and disparities pervade northern and southern versions of nationalist history. Histories centered on the *minjung* (the people) and those that focus on Koreans in Manchuria have more often offered populist approaches to pre-division nationalist politics.
39. Michael G. Thompson, *For God and Globe: Christian Internationalism in the United States Between the Great War and the Cold War* (Ithaca, N.Y.: Cornell University Press, 2015), chapter 6.
40. Louise Yim, *My Forty Year Fight for Korea* (New York: A. A. Wyn, 1951), 55.
41. Helen Kim, *Grace Sufficient* (Nashville, Tenn.: Upper Room, 1964), 30.
42. Mary Poovey, *A History of the Modern Fact: Problems of Knowledge in the Sciences of Wealth and Society* (Chicago: University of Chicago Press, 1998), xii.
43. Yoon Sun Lee, *Modern Minority: Asian American Literature and Everyday Life* (New York: Oxford University Press, 2013), 4, 13.
44. Occurring just before the Paris Peace Conference, the March 1 movement introduced Korean independence into the international consciousness. March 1 was also a turning point for the involvement of educated Christian women in the independence movement.
45. Andrew Hui, *A Theory of the Aphorism: From Confucius to Twitter* (Princeton: Princeton University Press, 2019), 6, 16.
46. "Idea Born in Japanese Jail May Bring Korean College," *Sunday Press*, September 22, 1957: 3-C.
47. Carlene Stephens, "'The Most Reliable Time': William Bond, the New England Railroads, and Time Awareness in 19th-Century America," *Technology and Culture* 30, no. 1 (January 1989): 23.
48. Gerhad Dohrn-van Rossum, *History of the Hour: Clocks and Modern Temporal Orders*, trans. Thomas Dunlap (Chicago: University of Chicago Press, 1996), 347.
49. Naofumi Nakamura, "Railway Systems and Time Consciousness in Modern Japan," *Japan Review* no. 14 (2002): 31.
50. Cumings writes, "by 1945 Korea had a much better-developed transport and communications infrastructure than any other East Asian country save Japan" (*Korea's Place in the Sun* [New York: W.W. Norton, 2005], 167).
51. Y. Tak Matsusaka, "Japan's South Manchuria Railway Company in Northeast China, 1906–34," in *Manchurian Railways and the Opening of China*, eds. Bruce Elleman and Stephen Kotkin (Armonk, N.Y.: M. E. Sharpe, 2010), 37.
52. Leo Marx, *The Machine in the Garden* (New York: Oxford University Press, 1964), 31, 197, 224, 225.
53. Yu's name has been transliterated in different ways. To minimize confusion, I'll follow Cha in using Yu Guan Soon.
54. Lee, *Born Again*, 44; Sadie Maude Moore, "A Torch in Her Hand," *Korea Calling* 5, no. 9 (October 1966): 3–4.
55. Lee, *Born Again*, 44.

3. THE TONE OF THE TIMES

56. Pahk also makes it a point to describe her encounters with other nationalist luminaries, including Maria Kim and the daughter of a signee of the Korean Declaration of Independence (*Monkey*, 63, 67).
57. Georg Lukács, *The Historical Novel*, trans. Hannah Mitchell and Stanley Mitchell (London: Merlin, 1962).
58. Theresa Hak Kyung Cha, *Dictee* (New York: Tanam, 1982). Subsequent references are cited in the text.
59. Anne Anlin Cheng, *Melancholy of Race: Psychoanalysis, Assimilation, and Hidden Grief* (New York: Oxford University Press, 2000), 248–49.
60. Thy Phu, "Decapitated Forms: Theresa Hak Kyung Cha's Visual Text and the Politics of Visibility," *Mosaic* 38, no. 1 (March 2005): 18.
61. Kia Lindroos, *Now-Time/Image-Space: Temporalization of Politics in Walter Benjamin's Philosophy of History and Art* (Jyväskylä: University of Jyväskylä, 1998), 126.
62. I'm referring here to the 1982 Tanam Press edition of *Dictee*. The University of California Press editions have a different cover.
63. Roland Barthes, *Camera Lucida: Reflections on Photography*, trans. Richard Howard (New York: Hill and Wang, 1980), 94.
64. Barthes, *Camera Lucida*, 49. Barthes uses "studium" to describe photographs that capture historical eventfulness. The more frequently cited "punctum" refers to a detail that overwhelms the viewing experience.
65. Peter D. Fenves, "An Idea in Combat with Itself: Benjamin, Hölderlin, and Temporal Plasticity," *PMLA* 124, no. 3 (May 2009): 280.
66. Barthes, *Camera Lucida*, 89.
67. Barthes, *Camera Lucida*, 99.
68. On slow aesthetics, see Lutz Koepnick, *On Slowness: Toward an Aesthetic of the Contemporary* (New York: Columbia University Press, 2014); Christine Ross, *The Past is the Present; It's the Future Too: The Temporal Turn in Contemporary Art* (New York: Bloomsbury, 2012).
69. This political and economic disjuncture partially accounts for Park Chung-hee's mixed legacy. On the one hand, Park was so deeply influenced by Meiji Japan that diplomat Okazaki Hisahiko christened him "the last soldier of Imperial Japan." On the other hand, "the identification of Japan as a valuable source to learn from and imitate also meant that it was the target to catch up with and even surpass. The respect for Japan's accomplishments coexisted with Park's distrust of and enmity toward Japan"; see Chung-in Moon and Byung-joon Jun, "Modernization Strategy: Ideas and Influences," in *The Park Chung Hee Era*, eds. Byung-Kook Kim and Ezra Vogel (Cambridge, Mass.: Harvard University Press, 2011): 117, 120.
70. It is more common to view U.S. aid as a source of economic modernization. While Korea was indeed one of the largest aid recipients, Park often defied US advice in order to pursue his own vision of development. It was also Park who volunteered Korean troops for the war in Vietnam and not, as sometimes suggested, the United States who demanded contributions. See Gregg Andrew Brazinsky, "From Pupil to Model: South Korea and American Development Policy during the Early Park Chung Hee Era," *Diplomatic History* 29, no. 1 (January 2005): 83–115; Byung-Kook Kim, "The Leviathan: Economic Bureaucracy under Park," in *The Park Chung Hee Era*, 200–32.

3. THE TONE OF THE TIMES

71. Joo-Hong Kim, "The Armed Forces," *The Park Chung Hee Era*, 173.
72. Cumings, *Korea's Place in the Sun*, 322.
73. Kim, "The Leviathan," 211.
74. Moon and Joon, "Modernization Strategy," 115. See also Seungsook Moon, *Militarized Modernity and Gendered Citizenship in South Korea* (Durham: Duke University Press, 2005); Gi-Wook Shin, *Ethnic Nationalism in Korea: Genealogy, Politics, and Legacy* (Stanford: Stanford University Press, 2006).
75. Lie, *Han Unbound*, 101.
76. Masao Miyoshi, *Off Center: Power and Culture Relations Between Japan and the United States* (Cambridge, Mass.: Harvard University Press, 1991), 2.
77. Barthes, *Camera Lucida*, 99.
78. Theresa Hak Kyung Cha, *Mouth to Mouth* (New York: Electronic Arts Intermix, 1975).
79. On the "articulatory organ" theory, see Ross King, "Western Protestant Missionaries and the Origins of Korean Language Modernization," *Journal of International and Area Studies*, 11, no. 3 (2004): 17. Pahk, Kim, and Yim all note the quasi-feminist and nationalist aspects of the Korean language.
80. Jeon, *Racial Things*, 47.
81. Trinh T. Minh-ha, "White Spring," in *The Dream of the Audience*, ed. Constance Lewallen (Berkeley: University of California Press, 2001), 42.
82. Fredric Jameson, *Postmodernism, Or, The Cultural Logic of Late Capitalism* (Durham: Duke University Press, 1991), 286.
83. Jameson, *Antinomies of Realism*, 28.
84. Jameson, *Postmodernism*, 72.
85. Jameson, *Postmodernism*, 67.
86. Ngai, *Ugly Feelings*, 278.
87. Jameson, *Antinomies of Realism*, 25.
88. Jameson is likely referencing Vito Acconci's *Centers* (1971), in which Acconci holds a finger at the camera for twenty-one minutes.
89. Jameson, *Postmodernism*, 29–30.
90. "The military regimes sought legitimation via nationalism from above; the culture of dissent championed *minjung* and promoted nationalism from below. These conflicting nationalisms nonetheless converged in drawing a heroic lineage of colonial-period independence struggles and projecting a triumphant view of a future Korean nation" (Lie, *Han Unbound*, 161).
91. Hong Kal, *Aesthetic Constructions of Korean Nationalism: Spectacle, Politics and History* (New York: Routledge, 2011), 89, 99.
92. Lucy Lippard, *Six Years: The Dematerialization of the Art Object from 1966 to 1972* (Berkeley: University of California Press, 1997), xv–xvi.
93. Hardt and Negri, *Empire*, 108.
94. Boltanski and Chiapello, *The New Spirit of Capitalism*. Feminist Marxist scholars have shown how the new organizational practices deemed "flexible" have been enabled by the "exploitation and expropriation" of workers "across lines of color and culture, and between North and South" (Anna Tsing, "Supply Chains and the Human Condition," *Rethinking Marxism* 21, no. 2 [2009]: 150). See, for instance, Aihwa Ong, *Spirits of Resistance and Capitalist Discipline: Factory Women in*

Malaysia (New York: State University of New York Press, 2010); Kim, *Class Struggle or Family Struggle*.
95. Theresa Hak Kyung Cha, *Exilée and Temps Morts*, ed. Constance Lewallen (Berkeley: University of California Press, 2009). Subsequent references are cited in the text. *Exilée* was also a film and video installation.
96. Park, "This is the Writing You Have Been Waiting For," 11.
97. Park, "This is the Writing You Have Been Waiting For," 11.
98. Park, "This is the Writing You Have Been Waiting For," 9.
99. The term "difference" has a storied critical history in relation to Cha, beginning with Lisa Lowe's dazzling reading of *Dictee* in *Immigrant Acts: On Asian American Cultural Politics* (Durham: Duke University Press, 1996). For Lowe, "difference" encompasses demographic heterogeneity, anti-mimetic literary techniques, and poststructural theory. Inspired by Lowe, scholars have repeatedly turned to *Dictee* as a critical model for post-identity approaches, an aesthetic model for anti-mimetic techniques, and an anti-colonial model for a non-recuperative mode of redress.
100. Ngai, *Our Aesthetic Categories*, 120, 124, emphasis mine.
101. Lowe, *Immigrant Acts*, 152. See also Shelley Sun Wong, "Unnaming the Same: Theresa Hak Kyung Cha's *Dictee*," in *Writing Self, Writing Nation*, 103–40; Laura Hyun-Yi Kang, "The 'Liberatory Voice' of Theresa Hak Kyung Cha's *Dictee*," in *Writing Self, Writing Nation*, 73–99.
102. Mark Chiang, *Cultural Capital of Asian American Studies: Autonomy and Representation in the University* (New York: NYU Press, 2009), chapter 3; Jinqi Ling, *Narrating Nationalisms: Ideology and Form in Asian American Literature* (New York: Oxford University Press, 1998), 9.
103. Scott, *Conscripts of Modernity*, 12.
104. Jameson, *Postmodernism*, ix.

4. THE TONE OF DOCUMENTATION

Epigraph. Ha Jin as quoted in Te-hsing Shan, "Sublimating History Into Literature: Reading Ha Jin's *Nanjing Requiem*," *Amerasia Journal* 38, no. 2 (2012): 27.

1. Heidi Benson, "Profile: C.Y. Lee," *San Francisco Chronicle*, September 18, 2002; C.Y. Lee, *The Flower Drum Song* (New York: Penguin, 2002), x.
2. Hsu, *The Good Immigrants*, 104.
3. In this chapter, I capitalize the term *Communist* when referring to the *Communist* Party of the China or the *Communist* Chinese military forces. I use the lowercase term *communism* when referring to the political ideology.
4. L. Ling-chi Wang, "Roots and Changing Identity of the Chinese in the United States," *Daedalus* 120, no. 2 (Spring 1991): 191.
5. Belinda Kong, *Tiananmen Fictions Outside the Square: The Chinese Literary Diaspora and the Politics of Global Culture* (Philadelphia: Temple University Press, 2012), 4. To be sure, U.S. immigration policy toward citizens of China was complicated and contradictory in the 1940s and 1950s. The relaxation of immigrant

4. THE TONE OF DOCUMENTATION

restrictions (despite the persistence of quotas) during these decades served various ends: ameliorating Sino-American relations during the war against Japan, countering accusations of American racism from enemy nations, and promoting an ideal of free world refuge from communist slavery. My language of "stranded" students speaks to the American sentiment of embracing political refugees (there was an outpouring of public support for Chinese students in the United States after 1949). Even so, the 1950s also saw increased worry about immigration fraud and double agents. As Samuel Kung finds in "Personal and Professional Problems of Chinese Students" (PhD diss., Columbia University, 1955), some students who sought return to China, especially those specializing in the sciences, were detained by the U.S. government. The Chinese confession program was instituted in 1956 to root out potential communist spies among Chinese Americans. Hsu discusses the geopolitics of immigration in detail in *The Good Immigrants*. See also Him Mark Lai, *Becoming Chinese American: A History of Communities and Institutions* (Walnut Creek, Calif.: AltaMira, 2004).

6. Other commonalities: Both Lee and Jin have been belatedly received in Asian American literature. Both depict a divide between intellectuals and commoners among Chinese Americans. Like Lee's protagonist Wang Ta, many of Jin's male heroes make the gesture of abstaining from politics. Both Lee's and Jin's characters suggest that the Chinese language inhibits individuality.
7. Belinda Kong, "Theorizing the Hyphen's Afterlife in Post-Tiananmen Asian-America," *MFS Modern Fiction Studies* 56, no. 1 (2010): 141.
8. Jing Tsu, *Sound and Script in the Chinese Diaspora* (Cambridge, Mass.: Harvard University Press, 2010), 80–111.
9. A growing number of PRC literary writers who choose to employ English makes Jin less exceptional than he was twenty years ago. Such writers include Liyun Li, Anchee Min, Wang Ping, Xiaolu Guo, and Weike Wang.
10. Jin has often described his books as charting a path away from China and toward the United States. He names *The Free Life* (2007) as a definitive shift in his fiction: "my subject matter is not about China anymore; it's about the American experience." See Wendy Smith, "Coming to America," *Publishers Weekly*, September 10, 2007.
11. Steven G. Yao, *Foreign Accents: Chinese American Verse from Exclusion to Postethnicity* (New York: Oxford University Press, 2010), 114.
12. Ha Jin and Cynthia W. Liu, "Writing in Solitude," *International Examiner*, November 2, 1999: 18.
13. Wang Tsun-ming, *Wang Tsun-ming, Anti-Communist: An Autobiographical Account of Chinese Communist Thought Reform*, ed. William C. Bradbury (Washington, D.C.: Psychological Warfare Division, George Washington University, 1954). Subsequent references are cited in the text.
14. Ha Jin, *War Trash* (New York: Vintage, 2004). Subsequent references are cited in the text.
15. I use the term "Nationalists" to maintain consistency with Jin's novel. Some U.S. officials, however, preferred the term Kuomingtang (KMT) or Chinese Nationalist Party, which was seen as less ideologically loaded.
16. On the practical limitations of foreign relations research in China before the 1970s, especially regarding the Chinese Communist Party, see Michael Hunt,

4. THE TONE OF DOCUMENTATION

"Constructing a History of Chinese Communist Party Foreign Relations," *Cold War International History Project Bulletin* 6–7 (Winter 1995/1996): 126–46. Hunt largely commends historians based in China but notes the "neglect" on "this side of the Pacific" (128).

17. Lisa Gitelman, *Always Already New: Media, History, and the Data of Culture* (Cambridge, Mass.: MIT Press, 2006), xii.
18. Bruce Cumings's *The Korean War: A History* (New York: Random House, 2010) praises *War Trash* as a work that "rings true on every page" (75). Tal Tovy writes, "Ha Jin's wonderful book describes the adventures of a young Chinese officer" ("Manifest Destiny in POW Camps: The U.S. Army Reeducation Program during the Korean War." *Historian* 73, no. 3 [Fall 2011]: 503). Charles S. Young acknowledges that Jin's "extensively researched" novel is fiction but notes that "the author stated that 'most of the events and details' were factual" (*Name, Rank, and Serial Number: Exploiting Korean War POWs at Home and Abroad* [New York: Oxford University Press, 2014], 41).
19. Walter Kirn, "Pleased to Be Here," *New York Times*, November 25, 2007.
20. On the hypervisibility of the post-Tiananmen artist, see Yapp, *Minor China*.
21. Wen Jin notes the dangers of "criticiz[ing] one nation without reflecting on the other, thus implicitly holding up the latter as a standard." With respect to the Untied States and China, "it is these implicit comparisons that, in most cases, more powerfully shape the cultural unconscious of the two nations" (*Pluralist Universalism*, 74).
22. Jin and Liu, "Writing in Solitude," 18.
23. Ha Jin, *Between Silences: A Voice from China* (Chicago: University of Chicago Press, 1990), 2.
24. Ha Jin, *The Writer as Migrant* (Chicago: University of Chicago Press, 2008), 30.
25. King-Kok Cheung, "The Chinese American Writer as Migrant: Ha Jin's Restive Manifesto," *Amerasia* 38, no. 2 (2012): 4, 11.
26. Jin, *The Writer as Migrant*, 28–29.
27. Ha Jin, *The Boat Rocker* (New York: Pantheon, 2016), 118. Subsequent references are cited in the text.
28. Shan, "Sublimating History into Literature," 25.
29. Joseph Darda, "The Literary Afterlife of the Korean War." *American Literature* 87, no. 1 (March 2015): 89; Charles S. Young, "Voluntary Repatriation and Involuntary Tattooing of Korean War POWs," *Northeast Asia and the Legacy of Harry S. Truman: Japan, China, and the Two Koreas*, ed. James I. Matray (Kirksville, Mo.: Truman State University Press, 2012), 159. According to Daying Jin, of the 8,000 POWs at Compound 72, about 6,000 were branded with Nationalist slogans or symbols ("Accounts of the Chinese People's Volunteer Army's Prisoners of War" [Master's thesis, University of Montana, 1993], 190).
30. The Nationalist officer tearing out a man's heart is a true story (Young, "Voluntary Repatriation," 158). In Daying Jin's study, reactions to enforced tattooing are similarly gruesome: "Some POWs ... tried to scrape the tattooed words from their arms by using razor blades.... Others even hung [sic] themselves.... [Q]uite a few ... committed suicide by swallowing broken pieces of glass or razor blades" (185).
31. Andrea Bachner, *Beyond Sinology: Chinese Writing and the Scripts of Culture* (New York: Columbia University Press, 2014), 39. Bachner is writing about Chinese performance artists who "tattoo" their bodies with calligraphic script.

4. THE TONE OF DOCUMENTATION

32. Carolyn Marvin, "The Body of the Text: Literacy's Corporeal Constant," *Quarterly Journal of Speech* 80, no. 2 (May 1994): 129, 131.
33. For a reading of Ha Jin's instantiation of the cold war family, see A. J. Yumi Lee, "Cold War Erasures and the Asian American Immigrant Family in Ha Jin's *War Trash*," *Verge: Studies in Global Asias* 5, no. 2 (Fall 2019): 114–31.
34. William E. Daugherty, *A Psychological Warfare Casebook* (Baltimore, M.D.: Operations Research Office, Johns Hopkins University Press, 1958), 5.
35. Lisa Gitelman, *Scripts, Grooves, and Writing Machines: Representing Technology in the Edison Era* (Stanford: Stanford University Press, 1999), 3.
36. Matthew S. Hull, "Documents and Bureaucracy." *Annual Review of Anthropology* 41, no. 1 (2012): 256.
37. Cumings, *Parallax Visions*, 48, 55.
38. Cumings, *Origins of the Korean War, Vol. 1*, xxi. On the logic of self-defense in American militaristic engagements, see Joseph Darda, *Empire of Defense: Race and the Cultural Politics of Permanent War* (Chicago: University of Chicago Press, 2019).
39. Though global in name, the UNC was led by the United States and mostly consisted of ROK forces.
40. Barton J. Bernstein, "The Struggle over the Korean Armistice: Prisoners of Repatriation?" in *Child of Conflict: The Korean–American Relationship, 1943–1953*, ed. Bruce Cumings (Seattle: University of Washington Press, 1983), 266. The talks concluded in Panmunjom on July 27, 1953.
41. Rosemary Foot, *A Substitute For Victory: The Politics of Peacemaking at the Korean Armistice Talks* (Ithaca, N.Y.: Cornell University Press, 1990), ix.
42. Foot, *Substitute For Victory*, x.
43. Memorandum, Department of State, "Legal Considerations Underlying the Position of the United Nations Command Regarding the Issue of Forced Repatriation of Prisoners of War," October 24, 1952, part I, p. 3, Records of the Enemy Prisoner of War Information Bureau, Enemy Prisoner of War / Civilian Internee Information Center, Unclassified Records, Military Agency Records, RG 389, NACP.
44. "The Oriental Communist Prisoner of War," Office of the Provost Marshall; Office of the Assistant Chief of Staff, G-1; Headquarter, U.S. Army Forces, Far East, 1952–1957, Records of General Headquarters (GH), Far East Command, Supreme Commander Allied Powers (SCAP), and United Nations Command (UNC), RG 554.
45. "Communist Utilization of Prisoners of War," U.S. Army Forces, Far East Command, Office of the Assistant Chief of Staff G-2, Intelligence, 1953, RG 389.
46. "Indoctrination of U.S. POW's by Chinese Communist Forces," Memo, November 13, 1952, Records of the Office of the Chief of Special Warfare, 1951–58, Records of the Army Staff, RG 319. There was much speculation about the origins of "brainwashing." Edward Hunter's *Brainwashing in Red China* (New York: Vanguard, 1953) and J. A. M. Meerloo's *The Rape of the Mind: The Psychology of Thought Control, Menticide, and Brainwashing* (Cleveland: World, 1956) trace the practice to the Soviets' Pavlovian methods. By contrast, Hunter's *Brainwashing: The Story of Men Who Defied It* (New York: Farrar, Straus & Cudahy, 1956) presents Korean War brainwashing as indigenously Chinese, for example, beginning with Mencius (4). William Lindsay White's *The Captives of Korea: An Unofficial White Paper On the Treatment of War Prisoners* (New York: Scribner's, 1957) dates brainwashing

4. THE TONE OF DOCUMENTATION

to Chinese warlords (35). For studies on brainwashing as a homegrown Communist institution, see Robert Jay Lifton, *Thought Reform and the Psychology of Totalism: A Study of "Brainwashing" in China* (New York: Norton, 1961), and Edgar H. Schein, *Coercive Persuasion: A Socio-psychological Analysis of the "Brainwashing" of American Civilian Prisoners by the Chinese Communists* (New York: Norton, 1961).

47. The coinage of "brainwashing" is frequently attributed to Edward Hunter's "'Brain-Washing' Tactics Force Chinese Into Ranks of Communist Party," *Miami Sunday News*, September, 24 1950: 2.
48. Quoted in Carruthers, *Cold War Captives*, 176; Rogin, *Ronald Reagan*, 236–71; Adam Zweiback, "The 21 'Turncoat GIs': Nonrepatriations and the Political Culture of the Korean War," *Historian* 60, no. 2 (Winter 1998): 347.
49. Foot, *Substitute for Victory*, 191.
50. Eugene Kinkead, *In Every War But One* (New York: Norton, 1959), 10.
51. Kinkead, *In Every War But One*, 87.
52. United States Defense Advisory Committee on Prisoners of War, *POW, the Fight Continues After the Battle: The Report of the Secretary of Defense's Advisory Committee on Prisoners of War* (Washington, D.C.: U.S. Government Printing Office, 1955), 11.
53. Transcript of a presentation by Dr. Carleton F. Scofield, Director of Research, Psychological Warfare Division, "PSYFREE Briefing Notes," October 1, 1954, Records of the Army Staff, RG 319.
54. Memo, G2 to PsyWar, "Indoctrination of U.S. POW's by Chinese Communist Forces," November 13, 1952, Records of the Office of the Chief of Special Warfare, 1951–58, Records of the Army Staff, RG 319.
55. Meerloo, *Rape of the Mind*, 15.
56. Monica Kim, *The Interrogation Rooms of the Korean War: The Untold Story* (Princeton: Princeton University Press, 2019), 24.
57. Hunter, *Brainwashing: The Story of Men Who Defied It*, 3.
58. Dwight Eisenhower, Address at the Columbia University National Bicentennial Dinner, New York City, May 31, 1954.
59. David R. McLean, "Cranks, Nuts, and Screwballs," *Studies in Intelligence* 9, no. 3 (Summer 1965): 80–81.
60. *The Manchurian Candidate*, directed by John Frankenheimer (Beverly Hills, Calif.: MGM, 1962).
61. H. H. Wubben, "American Prisoners of War in Korea: A Second Look at the 'Something New in History' Theme," *American Quarterly* 22 (Spring 1970): 3–19.
62. Wang was a KMT officer who had spent time in both CPVA and UNC captivity. This was not uncommon among soldiers whose allegiances were simultaneously sought and questioned; Jin's narrator Yu experiences a similar fate.
63. Timothy Melley, "Brainwashed! Conspiracy Theory in the Postwar United States," *New German Critique* 103 (Winter 2008): 162–63, 149.
64. Hunter, *Brainwashing in Red China*, 58; Hunter, *Brainwashing: The Story of Men Who Defied It*, 14.
65. On the dialogue between Orientalism and media studies, see Christopher Bush, *Ideographic Modernism: China, Writing, Media* (New York: Oxford University Press, 2010).

66. Meerloo, *Rape of the Mind*, 15.
67. Meerloo, *Rape of the Mind*, 30, 66.
68. Marshall McLuhan, *The Gutenberg Galaxy: The Making of Typographic Man* (Toronto: University of Toronto Press, 1962), 19, 32.
69. Carruthers, *Cold War Captives*, 18.
70. Scott Selisker traces the broader cultural impact of brainwashing discourse, especially its influence on cults, in *Human Programming: Brainwashing, Automatons, and American Unfreedom* (Minneapolis, Minn.: University of Minnesota Press, 2016), 125–50. On Korean War brainwashing as a crisis of masculinity, see Carruthers, *Cold War Captives*, 176–79; Rogin, *Ronald Reagan*, 236–71. On moral character, see William E. Mayer, "Why Did So Many GI Captives Cave In?" *U.S. News and World Report*, February 24, 1956: 65–72. On propaganda, see Priscilla Wald, "The 'Hidden Tyrant': Propaganda, Brainwashing, and Psycho-Politics in the Cold War Period," in *The Oxford Handbook of Propaganda Studies*, ed. Jonathan Auerbach and Russ Castronovo (New York: Oxford University Press, 2013): 109–30.
71. Marshall McLuhan, *Understanding Media: The Extensions of Man* (Cambridge: MIT Press, 1994), 50.
72. Robin, *Making of the Cold War Enemy*, 95–96. The behavioralists in question are Wilbur Schramm, Alex Inkeles, and David Riesman.
73. Robin, *Making of the Cold War Enemy*, 87. Robin is referring to and quoting from the 1952 "Studies in Chinese Communism," headed by Theodore H. E. Chen and Frederick T. C. Yu.
74. John A. Alexander, "An Intelligence Role for the Footnote," *Studies in Intelligence* 8, no. 3 (Summer 1964): 1–2.
75. Allan Evans, "Against Footnotes," *Studies in Intelligence* 8, no. 4 (Fall 1964): 81–84; David McConnaughey, "More Against Footnotes," *Studies in Intelligence* 8, no. 4 (Fall 1964): 85–86.
76. On animatedness, Ngai writes, "the seemingly neutral state of 'being moved' becomes twisted into the image of the overemotional racialized subject, abetting his or her construction as unusually receptive to external control" (*Ugly Feelings*, 91).
77. CIE was based on a program run by MacArthur in postwar Japan (Robin, *Making of the Cold War Enemy*, 153–55).
78. U.S. Army Pacific, "The Handling of Prisoners of War During the Korean War."
79. Robin, *Making of the Cold War Enemy*, 158.
80. U.S. Army Forces in the Far East (USAFFE), *Interviews with 24 Korean POW Leaders* (N.p.: Psychological Warfare Section, 1954), 91, 9.
81. "Interrogation Reports 1950," Translator and Intelligence Service, Records of GH, SCAP, and UNC, RG 554.
82. USAFFE, *Interviews with 24 Korean POW Leaders*, 80.
83. Jerry A. Varsava, "An Interview with Ha Jin," *Contemporary Literature* 51, no. 1 (2010): 18.
84. Ian Buruma, "Chinese Shadows," *New York Review of Books*, March 24, 2005.
85. USAFFE, *Interviews with 24 Korean POW Leaders*, 80.
86. Jin's other historical novel, *Nanjing Requiem* (New York: Pantheon, 2011), is less controversial among PRC readers since it depicts China during the Japanese

4. THE TONE OF DOCUMENTATION

occupation. Jin is also less careful about political disinterest in *Nanjing Requiem*—he portrays the Japanese as almost unilaterally evil or, at best, sympathetic but suspicious. Although this novel is also based on a memoir, that of Minnie Vautrin, a well-known U.S. missionary, it proceeds from the perspective of an invented persona and minor historical character, a Chinese assistant named Anling. *Nanjing Requiem* thematizes the importance of record-keeping (for instance, in counting bodies to submit a petition), but it does not have the same documentary feel as *War Trash*, nor has it been interpreted as an actual historical record.

87. Marie Arana, "Book Review: 'Nanjing Requiem' by Ha Jin," *Washington Post*, October 24, 2011.
88. Faith Watson, "Ha Jin's War Trash: Writing War in a 'Documentary Manner,'" *Japan Studies Association* 7 (2009): 119, emphasis mine.
89. Leo Marx, "The Idea of 'Technology' and Postmodern Pessimism," in *Does Technology Drive History? The Dilemma of Technological Determinism*, eds. Merritt Roe Smith and Leo Marx (Cambridge, Mass.: MIT Press, 1994), 248.
90. The metaphor of the "framed" evidence recurs in Lisa Gitelman, *Paper Knowledge: Toward a Media History of Documents* (Durham: Duke University Press, 2014).
91. We can find this language in Ben Kafka, *The Demon of Writing: Powers and Failures of Paperwork* (New York: Zone, 2012), 70; Hull, "Documents and Bureaucracy."
92. Claude Lévi-Strauss, *Tristes Tropiques*, trans. John Russell (London: Hutchinson, 1961), 288–90.
93. Suzanne Dupuy-Briet proposed that an antelope can be a "document" if it is framed and therefore presented as evidence. This example is taken up in several accounts, for instance Gitelman, *Paper Knowledge*, 2; Michael Buckland, "What Is a 'Document?'" *Journal of the American Society for Information Science* 48, no. 9 (1997): 804–9.
94. John Freeman, "No escape; Ha Jin's Harrowing 'War Trash' is Almost Like a Nonfiction Account of Being in a Korean Prison Camp," *Star Tribune*, October 10, 2004, 17F. Freeman also writes, "As a result of this level of detail, the first 50 pages of 'War Trash' occasionally sound like the voice-over script of a documentary about the period."
95. Julia Lovell, "Fighting for Mao," *The Guardian*, November 11, 2005; John Updike, "Nan, American Man," *New Yorker*, December 3, 2007; Michael Upchurch, "Ha Jin's New Collection of Stories Loses Something in the 'Translation,'" *Chicago Tribune*, October 8, 2000.
96. Laikwan Pang, *Creativity and Its Discontents: China's Creative Industries and Intellectual Property Rights Offenses* (Durham: Duke University Press, 2012), 94.
97. John Pomfret, "China Firm Shelves Novel's Publication; 'Waiting' a Victim of Cultural Clampdown," *Washington Post*, June 22, 2000: A19.
98. Such stigmas explain why the Chinese state has latched onto creativity as a mode of modernization. Several critics have taken issue with this tactic. See Lily Chumley, *Art School and Culture Work in Postsocialist China* (Princeton: Princeton University Press, 2016); Pang, *Creativity and Its Discontents*.
99. Quoted in Ha Jin and Sarah Fay, "The Art of Fiction, No. 202," *Paris Review* no. 191 (Winter 2009), https://www.theparisreview.org/interviews/5991/ha-jin-the-art-of-fiction-no-202-ha-jin.

4. THE TONE OF DOCUMENTATION

100. Ha Jin and Te-hsing Shan, "In the Ocean of Words: An Interview with Ha Jin," *Tamkang Review* 38, no.2 (June 2008): 135–57," 152. Pirated copies of Jin's works are in fact easy to find in China. With the publication of *A Map of Betrayal* (2014), Jin says in one interview that "in [the] mainland, in recent years, it was very hard to get [my books] published." In another interview, he acknowledges that pirated editions of his books are available in China and that "even *A Map of Betrayal* has a published edition"; see National Public Radio, "An Ambivalent Double Agent," *NPR*, November 1, 2014; Ha Jin and Yongxi Wu, "Q. and A.: Ha Jin on Patriotism, Exile and *A Map of Betrayal*," *New York Times*, April 3, 2015.
101. Joseph A. Massey, "The Emperor is Far Away: China's Enforcement of Intellectual Property Rights Protection, 1986–2006," *Chicago Journal of International Law* 7, no. 231 (2006): 234; Andrew C. Mertha, *The Politics of Piracy: Intellectual Property in Contemporary China* (Ithaca, N.Y.: Cornell University Press, 2005), 11.
102. Office of the United States Trade Representative, "Fact Sheet: 'Special 301' on Intellectual Property," May 25, 1989. China appeared on the "priority watch list" in 1989 and was bumped up to the "priority foreign list" in 1991 (the latter requires a six-month investigation).
103. The "Agreement on Trade Relations Between the United States of America and the People's Republic of China" of 1978 is seen as marking the beginning of Western intellectual property protection in the post-Mao era. See Peter K. Yu, "Piracy, Prejudice, and Perspectives: An Attempt to Use Shakespeare to Reconfigure the U.S.-China Intellectual Property Debate," *Boston University International Law Journal* 19, no.1 (2001): 17.
104. Adrian Johns, *Piracy: The Intellectual Property Wars from Gutenberg to Gates* (Chicago: University of Chicago Press, 2009), 13–14.
105. Without recommending that Jin should distribute his works on the black market or in the public domain rather than take the buttoned-up route of publication, I do want to note the significance of counterfeit culture as a political strategy for contesting the Chinese state. On the critical possibilities of counterfeit culture, see Fan Yang, *Faked in China: Nation Branding, Counterfeit Culture, and Globalization* (Bloomington: Indiana University Press, 2015). In Bruce Sterling's novel *Distraction* (New York: Bantam, 1998), the United States loses "a major trade war" to China over intellectual property, leading China to make "all English-language intellectual property freely available on their satellite networks to anybody in the world" (104).
106. For a more measured study of Chinese counterfeit culture that critiques the creativity prerogatives of the IPR regime, see Pang, *Creativity and Its Discontents*. On the dissonances between intellectual property and the history of Chinese thought, including with respect to the nation's Confucian and socialist histories, see William P. Alford, *To Steal a Book Is an Elegant Offense* (Stanford: Stanford University Press, 1995).
107. Joseph R. Slaughter, "World Literature as Property," *Alif: Journal of Comparative Poetics* no. 34 (2014): 41.
108. Both Tsu's *Script and Sound* and Kong's *Tiananmen Fictions* discuss this reception history. For an instructive account of *War Trash*'s relation to its source texts, see Xie Xinqiu, "War Trash: War Memoir as 'False Document,'" *Amerasia* 38, no. 2 (2012): 35–42.

5. THE TONE OF INTIMACY

109. Tsu, *Sound and Script*, 108.
110. Russell Banks, "*War Trash*: View From the Prison Camp," *New York Times*, October 10, 2004.
111. Tsu, *Sound and Script*, 108.
112. Banks, "War Trash"; Freeman, "No escape."
113. Lawrence Venuti, *The Translator's Invisibility: A History of Translation* (New York: Routledge, 2008), 6.
114. Roger K. Miller, "Remembering The Forgotten War: A Chinese Soldier Recounts His Travails as a Captured Prisoner in the Korean War," *Sun Sentinel*, November 14, 2004.
115. Ha Jin, *Map of Betrayal* (New York: Pantheon, 2014), 98.
116. Ha Jin, *A Free Life* (New York: Pantheon, 2007), 32.
117. Haun Saussy, *Great Walls of Discourse and Other Adventures in Cultural China* (Cambridge, Mass.: Harvard University Press, 2001), 77.
118. Randy Boyagoda denounces *A Free Life* as "a plodding and univocal miscellany of cliché and cloying sentiment" ("Free and Too Easy," *Globe and Mail*, January 5, 2008). An anonymous reviewer uses the phrase "obvious, tardy epiphanies" ("The Lonely Language: A Chinese Immigrant Is Determined to Write Poetry in English," *Washington Post*, November 11, 2007, WBK). Tom Cooper writes: "Jin's English prose is workmanlike at best and at times descends into cliché and archaism" ("Well-Drawn Characters, but Little Drama," *St. Louis Post-Dispatch*, November 18, 2007, F8).
119. Upchurch, "Ha Jin's New Collection."
120. Jin, *Writer as Migrant*, 17.
121. Shan and Jin, "In the Ocean of Words," 152.

5. THE TONE OF INTIMACY

Epigraph. Thomas Powers, "The Truth About the CIA," *New York Review of Books*, May 13, 1993.

1. For specific references to Lansdale's dual identity, see Jonathan Nashel, *Edward Lansdale's Cold War* (Amherst, Mass.: University of Massachusetts Press, 2005), 17; Colleen Woods, "Bombs, Bureaucrats, and Rosary Beads: The United States, the Philippines, and the Making of Global Anti-Communism, 1945–1960," PhD diss., University of Michigan, 2012), 159; Richard Drinnon, *Facing West: The Metaphysics of Indian-Hating and Empire-Building* (Minneapolis: University of Minnesota Press. 1980), 387, 392.
2. This democratic phraseology of "voting" was applied to diverse waves of global migration during the 1940s and 1950s. These were the decades when, through legal and popular channels, the term "refugee" was being actively shaped. Many studies have explored cold war refugees hailing from Hungary, Poland, Yugoslavia, and other parts of Eastern Europe. Other sites of mass displacement include the partitioning of the subcontinent into India, Pakistan, and Bangladesh, and the aftermath of the 1948 Palestine War. Hong Kong played host to refugees from China. See Espiritu, *Body Counts*; Carl J. Bon Tempo, *Americans at the Gate: The United*

5. THE TONE OF INTIMACY

States and Refugees during the Cold War (Princeton: Princeton University Press, 2008); Tara Zahra, *The Great Departure: Mass Migration from Eastern Europe and the Making of the Free World* (New York: Norton, 2016); Laura Madokoro, *Elusive Refuge: Chinese Migrants in the Cold War* (Cambridge: Harvard University Press, 2016).

3. "Excerpts from Lansdale Team's Report," *New York Times*, July 5, 1971: 11; Neil Sheehan, *A Bright Shining Lie: John Paul Vann and America in Vietnam* (New York: Random House, 1988), 136–37; Nashel, *Edward Lansdale's Cold War*, 44.
4. "Excerpts From Lansdale Team's Report," 11. This accidental kidnapping augurs the transporting of Vietnamese "orphans" in Operation Babylift in 1975 (Espiritu, *Body Counts*, 41–43).
5. Espiritu, *Body Counts*, 36.
6. Chandan Reddy, *Freedom with Violence: Race, Sexuality, and the US State* (Durham: Duke University Press, 2011). See also Espiritu, *Body Counts*; Mimi Thi Nguyen, *The Gift of Freedom: War, Debt, and Other Refugee Passages* (Durham: Duke University Press, 2012); Kim, *Ends of Empire*; Schlund-Vials, *War, Genocide, and Justice*.
7. Laleh Khalili, *Time in the Shadows: Confinement in Counterinsurgencies* (Stanford: Stanford University Press, 2012), 45–46, 48.
8. Edward Lansdale, "'Pacification' in Vietnam," July 16, 1958, U.S. Dept of Defense, Office of the Secretary of Defense, Memoranda, 1958–1961, Edward G. Lansdale Papers (hereafter cited as EL), HIA. Khalili traces the philosophy of counterinsurgency manuals to the Maoist doctrine that "the relationship that should exist between the people and the troops. The former may be likened to water, the latter to the fish who inhabit it" (48).
9. On the protracted temporality of "refugee," see Vinh Nguyen, "Refugeetude: When Does a Refugee Stop Being a Refugee," *Social Text* 37, no. 2 (2019): 109–31.
10. Memo, "Operation Brotherhood," from Milton J. Evans to Mr. Alfred Cardineaux/Resettlement, September 27, 1955, Records of U.S. Foreign Assistance Agencies, 1948–1961, Mission to Vietnam, Resettlement & Rehabilitation Division, Subject Files, 1953–58, Voluntary Agencies, Records of U.S. Foreign Assistance Agencies, RG 469, NACP.
11. Trinh T. Minh-ha, *Surname Viet Given Name Nam* (New York: Women Make Movies, 1989).
12. Trinh describes "cinematic tricks" as: "the long take, hand-held camera, sync-sound (authentic sound) overlaid with omniscient commentary (the human science rationale), wide-angle lens, and anti-aestheticism (the natural versus the beautiful, or the real/native versus the fictional/foreign)"; see "Mechanical Eye, Electronic Ear, and the Lure of Authenticity," *When the Moon Waxes Red: Representation, Gender, and Cultural Politics* (New York: Routledge, 1991), 57.
13. Drinnon, *Facing West*, xv.
14. Lansdale, "Our Battleground in Asia," Reunion of Nieman Fellows, June 19, 1957, Harvard University, EL.
15. Vicente L. Rafael, *White Love and Other Events in Filipino History* (Durham: Duke University Press, 2000); Paul Kramer, *The Blood of Government: Race, Empire, the United States, & the Philippines* (Chapel Hill: University of North Carolina Press, 2006).

5. THE TONE OF INTIMACY

16. Freedom Company Philippines, Inc., "Freedom in Asia," January 1955, ECCOI/ Freedom Co. Prospectus, Charles T. R. Bohannan Papers (CB), HIA.
17. Smith, *Portrait of a Cold Warrior*, 90. While Greg Grandin's *Empire's Workshop: Latin America, the United States, and the Rise of the New Imperialism* (New York: Metropolitan, 2006) uses the phrase "workshop of empire" to portray the United States' imperial projects in Latin America as a precursor to its interventions in the Middle East, Lansdale saw the Philippines as a more programmatic model of the "workshop" and rationalized the portability of this model through the supposed kinship between the Philippines and South Vietnam.
18. Freedom Company, "Freedom in Asia."
19. D. C. Lavergne, "Continuation of Operation Brotherhood," April 8, 1959, Department of State, Bureau of Far Eastern Affairs/Office of Southeast Asian Affairs, Laos Files, 1954–1961, Department of State Central Files, RG 59.
20. Laura Wexler, *Tender Violence: Domestic Visions in an Age of U.S. Imperialism* (Chapel Hill: University of North Carolina Press, 2000).
21. Belmonte, *Selling the American Way*, 136–37.
22. Klein, *Cold War Orientalism*, 145.
23. "Remarks of Senator John F. Kennedy at the Conference on Vietnam Luncheon in the Hotel Willard," Washington, D.C., June 1, 1956.
24. *The Family of Man*, which opened in the New York Museum of Modern Art in 1955 before traveling worldwide, was among the best known USIA exhibitions. Beginning with Roland Barthes's seminal essay "The Great Family of Man" (1956), it has accrued significant critical attention.
25. Peggy Durdin, "Behind the Façade of Asian Unity," *New York Times*, April 17, 1955: SM9.
26. Oscar J. Arellano, "How Operation Brotherhood Got to Viet Nam," *Philippine Studies* 14, no. 3 (July 1996): 400, emphasis mine.
27. "Operation Brotherhood," Vietnam 1954–56, EL; Miguel A. Bernard, *Adventure in Viet-Nam: The Story of Operation Brotherhood 1954–1957* (Manila: Operation Brotherhood International, 1974), 81.
28. Eva-Lotta E. Hedman, *In the Name of Civil Society: From Free Election Movements to People Power in the Philippines* (Honolulu: University of Hawai'i Press, 2006).
29. Eva-Lotta E. Hedman, "Global Civil Society in One Country? Class Formation and Business Activism in the Philippines," in *Southeast Asian Responses to Globalization: Restructuring Governance and Deepening Democracy*, eds. Francis Kok Wah Loh and Joakim Öjendal (Copenhagen: Nordic Institute of Asian Studies, 2005), 139.
30. Jim Glassman, "On the Borders of Southeast Asia: Cold War geography and the Construction of the Other," *Political Geography* 24 (2005): 796.
31. Edward Lansdale, "Lessons Learned: The Philippines, 1946–1953," Foreign Service Institute, Washington, D.C., September 26, 1962, Speeches by Edward Lansdale, EL.
32. Lansdale, "Lessons Learned."
33. Lansdale, "Pacification," emphasis mine.
34. Nadel, *Containment Culture*, 197.
35. Richard Slotkin, *Gunfighter Nation: The Myth of the Frontier in Twentieth-century America* (Norman: University of Oklahoma Press, 1998), 447–48. On the idiom of

5. THE TONE OF INTIMACY

"Indian wars" and the role of the frontier in pre-Vietnam War foreign policy, especially in relation to the Philippine–American War, see Walter L. Williams, "United States Indian Policy and the Debate over Philippine Annexation: Implications for the Origins of American Imperialism," *Journal of American History* (1980): 810–31; William Appleman Williams, "The Frontier Thesis and American Foreign Policy," *Pacific Historical Review* 24 (November 1955): 379–95.

36. Smith, *Portrait of a Cold Warrior*, 147.
37. Rose Kushner, "The Quiet American Comes Home," Biographical File, EL.
38. Edward Lansdale, *In the Midst of Wars: An American's Mission to Southeast Asia* (New York: Harper and Row, 1972), xxiv.
39. Amy Kaplan, "Manifest Domesticity," *American Literature* 70, no. 3 (September 1998): 581–606.
40. Quoted in Nashel, *Edward Lansdale's Cold War*, 78.
41. C. T. R. Bohannan, "Unconventional Operations," in *Counter-Guerrilla Operations in the Philippines, 1946–1953: A Seminar on the Huk Campaign Held at Ft. Bragg by U.S. Army* (Saigon: USOM's Graphics Section, 1961), 51. Bohannan attributes "the use of improvised gadgets and gimmicks" in "the art of warfare" to the Filipinos: "Frankly, I've never heard of anybody more ingenious than some of my Philippine friends in dreaming up things which would have a significant effect" (51–52).
42. Max Boot, *The Road Not Taken: Edward Lansdale and the American Tragedy in Vietnam* (New York: Liveright, 2018), 229.
43. Nashel, *Edward Lansdale's Cold War*, 74.
44. Ellsberg, *Secrets*, 41. Ellsberg is speaking of both Lansdale and John McNaughton, Robert McNamara's security adviser. Ellsberg worked under Lansdale in the mid-1960s, when the war was going south, not during the idealistic days of the mid-1950s.
45. Nashel, *Edward Lansdale's Cold War*, 105.
46. William Gibbons's interview with Lansdale, November 19, 1982, Speeches and Writings 1954–1984, EL. This anecdote discloses the differences that, according to Lansdale, eventually led McNamara to push Lansdale out of Vietnam.
47. Psychological warfare specialist Paul Linebarger called Lansdale a "black mind" (Smith, *Portrait of a Cold Warrior*, 84).
48. O. J. Magee to Lansdale, October 7, 1972, Speeches and Writings 1954–1984, EL.
49. Sherwood Dickerman, "Cold War Condottiere," *Washington Post*, March 19, 1972: BW4.
50. David P. Chandler, "In the Midst of Wars: An American's Mission to Southeast Asia," *The Journal of Asian Studies* 34, no. 3 (1975): 857.
51. Dickerman, "Cold War Condottiere," BW4.
52. Nashel, *Edward Lansdale's Cold War*, 2.
53. Drinnon, *Facing West*, 380. The declassified report is attributed to "an American Officer." It became a documentary called *The Village That Refused to Die* and later appeared in the comic strip *Buz Sawyer*. The *Saturday Evening Post* was one of the most popular mid-century American publications. It also serialized *The Ugly American*, the novel that turned Kennedy into a Lansdale acolyte.
54. An American Officer (Edward Lansdale), "The Report the President Wanted Published," *Saturday Evening Post*, May 20, 1961, 69, 70.

5. THE TONE OF INTIMACY

55. Nashel, *Edward Lansdale's Cold War*, 67-68.
56. Nashel, *Edward Lansdale's Cold War*, 84.
57. Smith, *Portrait of a Cold Warrior*, 78.
58. Lansdale, "Operation Brotherhood," undated, Vietnam 1954-56, EL.
59. James. R. Schlesinger, "An Appraisal of the Foreign Aid Program," undated, Office of the Secretary of Defense, Draper Committee, Anderson Subcommittee, EL.
60. Lansdale, "Operation Brotherhood."
61. Lansdale, "Eulogy for Oscar Arellano," Speeches and Writings 1954-1984, November 9, 1974, EL.
62. Lansdale was also involved in a Civic Action program that brought Vietnamese civil servants and college-educated Americans to rebuild village communities. The tasks that the program took up were very similar to what we see from OB. See U.S. Department of Defense, "Rebellion Against My-Diem," *United States-Vietnam Relations, 1945-1967, Book 4* (Washington, D.C.: Government Printing Office, 1971), 21-24.
63. Lansdale, "Pacification."
64. OB was indeed a fundraising fixture in American cultural life, receiving sponsorship from the likes of Lane Bryant and New York's Museum of Modern Art. John D. Rockefeller III was also among the organization's renowned donors.
65. Lansdale handpicked many of the Filipinos who had helped him mastermind the campaign against the Huks to serve in an advisory capacity in Vietnam.
66. Drinnon, *Facing West*, 420; Smith, *Portrait of a Cold Warrior*, 244; Sheehan, *A Bright Shining Lie*, 142.
67. Drinnon, *Facing West*, 414-15; Nashel, *Edward Lansdale's Cold War*, 62.
68. On U.S.-Vietnam relations as melodrama, see chapter 1 of Nguyen, *America's Vietnam*.
69. Nick Cullather, "America's Boy? Ramon Magsaysay and the Illusion of Influence," *Pacific Historical Review* 62, no. 3 (August 1993): 305-38.
70. Man, *Soldiering through Empire*, 59.
71. Andrew Friedman, *Covert Capital: Landscapes of Denial and the Making of U.S. Empire in the Suburbs of Northern Virginia* (Berkeley: University of California Press, 2013), 152, 167.
72. James T. Fisher, *Dr. America: The Lives of Thomas A. Dooley, 1927-1961* (Amherst, Mass.: University of Massachusetts Press, 1997), 136.
73. Gloria Emerson, *Winners and Losers: Battles, Retreats, Gains, Losses, and Ruins from the Vietnam War* (New York: Norton, 1976), 293-94.
74. Cynthia Enloe, *Bananas, Beaches and Bases: Making Feminist Sense of International Politics* (Berkeley: University of California Press, 2014), 81.
75. The homosocial bonds that sustain an imperial and patriarchal "brotherhood" call to mind Eve Sedgwick's reinterpretation of René Girard's "erotic triangles." Sedgwick proposes that "in any male-dominated society, there is a special relationship between male homosocial (*including* homosexual) desire and the structures for maintaining and transmitting patriarchal power." This brotherly relation between men, she goes on to argue, is actively triangulated by a female object of desire (*Between Men: English Literature and Male Homosocial Desire* [New York: Columbia University Press, 1985], 25, emphasis in original).

5. THE TONE OF INTIMACY

76. Neferti X. M. Tadiar, *Things Fall Away: Philippine Historical Experience and the Makings of Globalization* (Durham: Duke University Press, 2009), 19.
77. A 1955 Operational Report notes that during a conflict between the Binh-Xuyen and the Vietnamese Nationalist army, "all lady personnel... had been recalled from the field," while male medical staff answered "a call for volunteers" to join the scuffle. As "male personnel" abandoned their humanitarian post to fight a skirmish, the remaining women contributed to "in-quarter entertainments... to relieve strained nerves and give the volunteers wholesome relaxation"; see Junior Chamber International, "Operation Brotherhood," Operational Report, March–June 1955, Mission to Vietnam, Resettlement & Rehabilitation Division, 1953–58, Records of U.S. Foreign Assistance Agencies, RG 469. Darrell Berrigan writes, "none of the Filipino volunteers are longhairs," and "the girls among them are not wallflowers escaping old-maidhood in adventure, but beautiful young women who could hold their own in any salon"; see "Operation Brotherhood," *Saturday Evening Post*, November 12, 1955: 147. Miguel Bernard's hagiographic histories of Operation Brotherhood offer the most numerous examples. In *Adventure in Viet-Nam*, Bernard writes: "It was small incidents such as this that illustrated a well-known fact: in moments of personal danger, it is often the woman doctor or the female nurse or social worker, that one can most depend on" (76). To quote from *Filipinos in Laos: A Sequel to Adventure in Vietnam* (Manila: Operation Brotherhood International, 1974): "All the nurses—Marinas, Munar, Tabuga, and Tolentino—are kind, charming, and have a sense of humor" (62).
78. Like the Peace Corps and other kindred organizations, OB stationed women in roles presumably in keeping with their sex: nurses, nutritionists, social workers, house managers, public health educators, and handicraft experts. See Bernard's *Adventures in Viet-Nam* and *Filipinos in Laos*.
79. Lansdale, *In the Midst of Wars*, 234–35.
80. U.S. Department of Defense, *United States–Vietnam Relations, 1945–1967*, Book 4, 16.
81. Lansdale to Robert A. Brand, April 3, 1958, Bureau of Far Eastern Affairs/Office of Southeast Asian Affairs, Laos Files, 1954–1961, Department of State Central Files, RG 59.
82. Saidiya Hartman's work has been especially influential in theorizing the archive in this way. For example, on the lost subject in the archives of transatlantic slavery, Hartman writes, "An act of chance or disaster produced a divergence or an aberration from the expected and usual course of invisibility and catapulted her from the underground to the surface of discourse" ("Venus in Two Acts," 2).
83. I borrow the term "imperial brotherhood" from Robert D. Dean, who argues that "U.S. hegemony over the 'free world' required the cultivation of imperial masculinity" (*Imperial Brotherhood: Gender and the Making of Cold War Foreign Policy* [Amherst, Mass.: University of Massachusetts Press, 2001], 12). Dean's account of Kennedy's valorization of heroic volunteerism (for which Lansdale was a key inspiration) is particularly relevant to Operation Brotherhood.
84. Boot, *Road Not Taken*, 67, 72–73, 47.
85. Friedman, *Covert Capital*, 150.
86. Boot, *Road Not Taken*, 114.
87. Boot, *Road Not Taken*, 222, 240.

5. THE TONE OF INTIMACY

88. Cecil B. Currey, *Edward Lansdale: The Unquiet American* (Boston: Houghton Mifflin, 1988), 142.
89. Lansdale, *In the Midst of War*, 311.
90. Joseph Alsop, *I've Seen the Best of It* (Mount Jackson, Va.: Axios, 1992), 412.
91. Bruce Robbins, *The Servant's Hand: English Fiction from Below* (New York: Columbia University Press, 1986), x, xi.
92. Lansdale, *In the Midst of Wars*, 127.
93. Long T. Bui, *Returns of War: South Vietnam and the Price of Refugee Memory* (New York: NYU Press, 2018), 12.
94. FitzGerald, *Fire in the Lake*, 78.
95. Nguyen, *The Gift of Freedom*, xii, 23.
96. Marguerite Nguyen writes, "The assertion that refugee bodies and camps were unprecedented ... erased from view a long history of racially mapping America through policies of relocation, concentration, dispersal, or extermination" (*America's Vietnam*, 135). In "Refugeetude," Vinh Nguyen offers the term "refugeetude" to reimagine the assumed temporariness of the refugee as a legal entity.
97. Edward Lansdale, "Give Me Your Tired, Your Poor," *New York Times*, April 12, 1975.
98. Lansdale, "Letter With Corrections to William C. Gibbons, June 23, 1983," Speeches and Writings 1954–1984, Interviews, EL, emphasis mine.
99. Friedman, *Covert Capital*, 188–221.
100. Espiritu, *Body Counts*, 40.
101. Espiritu, *Body Counts*, 82–83.
102. Scholarship on the Vietnam War film includes Sylvia Shin Huey Chong, *The Oriental Obscene: Violence and Racial Fantasies in the Vietnam Era* (Durham: Duke University Press, 2011); Marita Sturken, *Tangled Memories: The Vietnam War, the AIDS Epidemic, and the Politics of Remembering* (Berkeley: University of California Press, 1997); Katherine Kinney, *Friendly Fire: American Images of the Vietnam War* (New York: Oxford University Press, 2000); Susan Jeffords, *The Remasculinization of America: Gender and the Vietnam War* (Bloomington: Indiana University Press, 1989); Nguyen, *Nothing Ever Dies*. Artists who have parodied the Vietnam war/film include Jessica Hagedorn, R. Zamora Linmark, Cathy Linh Che, Viet Thanh Nguyen, Gina Apostol, and Dinh Q. Lê.
103. William Liu, *Transition to Nowhere: Vietnamese Refugees in America* (Nashville, Tenn.: Charter House, 1979), 119. The refugees Liu encountered did not in fact express gratitude toward their "sponsors." He writes, "whatever the disadvantages and unpleasantness of camp life, the camp gave a sense of security and met some of the basic physical needs. Even more it afforded the security of familiar people from the 'Vietnamese village.'" Quoting a *New York Times* article, Liu also notes, "in extreme cases, 'they keep hiding when you try to match them with a sponsor'" (153). Marguerite Nguyen's reading of Võ Phiến's *Letters to a Friend* (1976) recounts similar refusals of sponsorship (*America's Vietnam*, 137). On gratitude, see Nguyen, *The Gift of Freedom*.
104. Viet Thanh Nguyen, "Representing Reconciliation: Le Ly Hayslip and the Victimized Body," *Positions* 5, no. 2 (1997): 608.
105. Trinh, "Mechanical Eye," 66, 67.

5. THE TONE OF INTIMACY

106. See also Nguyen Van Vu's *At Home in America* (1979), Nguyen Ngoc Nga's *The Will of Heaven* (1982), Doan Van Toai, *The Vietnamese Gulag* (1986), Tran Thi Nga's *Shallow Graves* (1986), Truong Nhu Tang's *A Vietcong Memoir* (1986), Mai Holter's *While I Am Here* (1994), and Bui Diem's *In the Jaws of History* (1999). Y.-Dang Troeng uses the term "postcolonial collaborative autobiographies" to describe Vietnamese memoirs that are co-written with or ghostwritten by someone else; see "'A Gift or a Theft Depends on Who Is Holding the Pen': Postcolonial Collaborative Autobiography and Monique Truong's *The Book of Salt*," *MFS Modern Fiction Studies* 56 no. 1 (2010): 113–35. For other critiques of collaborative autobiographies, see Monique Truong, "Vietnamese American Literature," in *An Interethnic Companion to Asian American Literature*, ed. King-Kok Cheung (New York: Cambridge University Press, 1997): 219–48; George Uba, "Friend and Foe: De-Collaborating Wendy Wilder Larsen and Tran Thi Nga's *Shallow Graves*," *Journal of American Culture* 16, no. 3 (Fall 1993): 63–70; Leslie Bow, *Betrayal and Other Acts of Subversion*. Lan Duong offers a redemptive reading of "collaboration" in *Treacherous Subjects*.
107. John Tenhula, *Voices from Southeast Asia: The Refugee Experience in the United States* (New York: Holmes and Meier, 1991), 9.
108. Joanna C. Scott, *Indochina's Refugees: Oral Histories from Laos, Cambodia, and Vietnam* (Jefferson, N.C.: McFarland, 1989), xii.
109. James M. Freeman, *Hearts of Sorrow: Vietnamese-American Lives* (Stanford: Stanford University Press, 1989), 4.
110. Interestingly, the highpoint of ASEAN's visibility may have been its unified resistance to Vietnamese "boat people," whom the organization viewed not as victims of an American war but as portents of Vietnamese regional hegemony. In 1979, Philippine Foreign Minister Carlos Romulo compared Vietnam's treatment of its refugees to Nazi war crimes during World War II. Singaporean Foreign Minister S. Rajaratnam declared: "each junkload of men, women and children sent to our shores is a bomb to destabilise, disrupt, and cause turmoil and dissension in ASEAN states"; see Frank Frost, "Vietnam, ASEAN and the Indochina Refugee Crisis," *Southeast Asian Affairs* (1980): 361.
111. Simon J. Hay, "The 1995 ASEAN Summit: Scaling a Higher Peak," *Contemporary Southeast Asia* 18, no. 3 (December 1996): 256–57.
112. Anh Tuan Hoang, "Why Hasn't Vietnam Gained ASEAN Membership?" *Contemporary Southeast Asia* 15, no. 3 (December 1993): 280–91; Balazs Szalontai, "From Battlefield to Marketplace: The End of the Cold War in Indochina, 1985–1989," in *The End of the Cold War and the Third World: New Perspectives on Regional Conflict*, eds. Artemy M. Kalinovsky and Sergey Radchenko (New York: Routledge, 2011): 155–72.
113. Minh T. N. Nguyen, *Vietnam's Socialist Servants: Domesticity, Class, Gender, and Identity* (New York: Routledge, 2015); Danièle Bélanger and Magali Barbieri, eds. *Reconfiguring Families in Contemporary Vietnam* (Stanford: Stanford University Press, 2009); Jayne Werner, *Gender, Household and State in Post-Revolutionary Vietnam* (New York: Routledge, 2009).
114. Trinh T. Minh-ha with Scott MacDonald, "Film as Translation: A Net with No Fisherman," in *Framer Framed*, 132.
115. Trinh and MacDonald, "Film as Translation," 145.

5. THE TONE OF INTIMACY

116. For a comparative reading of Trinh and Mai, see Duong, *Treacherous Subjects*, 129–33.
117. Trinh, "All-Owning Spectatorship," *When the Moon Waxes Red*, 93, 97, ellipses in original.
118. Bill Nichols, *Representing Reality: Issues and Concepts in Documentary* (Bloomington: University of Indiana Press, 1991), 52.
119. Peter X. Feng, *Identities in Motion: Asian American Film and Video* (Durham: Duke University Press, 2002), 198.
120. Trinh T. Minh-ha, *Elsewhere, Within Here: Immigration, Refugeeism and the Boundary Event* (New York: Routledge, 2011), 2–3.
121. *OED*.
122. Nichols, *Representing Reality*, 53–54.
123. Trinh with Laleen Jayamane and Anne Rutherford, "Why a Fish Pond," *Framer Framed*, 164.
124. Eugenie Brinkema, *The Forms of the Affects* (Durham: Duke University Press, 2014), 23, 25.
125. P. Adams Sitney, *Visionary Film: The American Avant-Garde, 1943–2000* (New York: Oxford University Press, 2002), 348, 351.
126. Catherine Russell, *Experimental Ethnography: The Work of Film in the Age of Video* (Durham: Duke University Press, 1999), 190.
127. Trinh with MacDonald, "Film as Translation," 130.
128. Trinh with Fukuko Kobayashi, "Is Feminism Dead," *The Digital Film Event* (New York: Routledge, 2012), 165, emphasis mine.
129. Trinh, "Yellow Sprouts," *When the Moon Waxes Red*, 4; Trinh, *Elsewhere, Within Here*, 3. On tactility in film, see Laura U. Marks, *The Skin of Film: Intercultural Cinema, Embodiment, and the Senses* (Durham: Duke University Press, 2000).
130. Trinh with Harriet Hirshorn, "Questioning Truth and Fact," *Framer Framed*, 182.
131. *Framer Framed* is the title of a compilation of interviews with Trinh.
132. Susan Pui San Lok, "Staging/Translating," *Third Text* 13, no. 46 (Spring 1999): 64–65.
133. Russell, *Experimental Ethnography*, 165. Russell is describing the structural film aesthetics of Chantal Ackerman's *D'Est* (1993).
134. Lok, "Staging/Translating," 65.
135. J. "Pete" Fuentecilla, "Where Have All Our Nurses Gone?" in Bernard, *Filipinos in Laos*, 170.
136. Friedman, *Covert Capital*, 188, 220. Friedman quotes from Currey, *Edward Lansdale*.
137. Lucien Conein, Lansdale's co-conspirator from the Saigon Military Mission, met his wife Elyette Bruchot in Hanoi. Friedman writes, "[Bruchot's] Vietnamese citizenship legitimized Conein's place in the country as he infiltrated the Saigon government to monitor its coup plots" (*Covert Capital*, 154). According to Boot, William J. Lederer, the former Navy Captain who co-authored *The Ugly American*, also had a Filipina wife (*The Road Not Taken*, 323).
138. Lansdale, "Pacification."
139. Trinh with Jayamane and Rutherford, "Why A Fish Pond," 168–69.
140. Trinh with Valentina Vitali, "The Cyborg's Hand," *The Digital Film Event*, 28.

CODA—THE TONE OF COMMONS

1. Siebers, *Cold War Criticism*, 29–30.
2. Ahmed, *Cultural Politics of Emotion*, 9; Flatley, *Affective Mapping*, 79; Dora Zhang, "Notes on Atmosphere," *Qui Parle: Critical Humanities and Social Sciences* 27, no. 1 (June 2018): 132.
3. Myung Mi Kim, *Commons* (Berkeley: University of California Press, 2002), 7.
4. Kim, *Commons*, 62, 109.
5. Sau-ling C. Wong, "Denationalization Reconsidered: Asian American Cultural Criticism at a Theoretical Crossroads," *Amerasia* 21, nos. 1–2 (1995): 4, 17, 18, emphasis mine.
6. My understanding of the term "commons" most closely follows what Kim theorizes in her poetry, although it is inflected by scholarly work such as Lauren Berlant, "The Commons: Infrastructures for Troubling Times," *Society and Space* 34, no. 3 (2016): 393–419; Fred Moten and Stefano Harney, *The Undercommons: Fugitive Planning and Black Study* (London: Minor Compositions, 2013); José Esteban Muñoz, " 'Gimme Gimme This . . . Gimme Gimme That': Annihilation and Innovation in the Punk Rock Commons, *Social Text* 31 no. 3 (2013): 95–110; Dana D. Nelson, *Commons Democracy: Reading the Politics of Participation in the Early United States* (New York: Fordham University Press, 2015); Derrick R. Spires, *The Practice of Citizenship: Black Politics and Print Culture in the Early United States* (Philadelphia: University of Pennsylvania Press, 2019).
7. Nadia Ellis, *Territories of the Soul: Queered Belonging in the Black Diaspora* (Durham: Duke University Press, 2015), 80.
8. Ed Park, *Personal Days* (New York: Random House, 2008). Subsequent references are cited in the text.
9. Virno, *Grammar of the Multitude*, 33.
10. In some sense, minor characters are by definition formally incapable of distinguishing themselves from their social or novelistic background; see Alex Woloch, *The One vs. the Many: Minor Characters and the Space of the Protagonist in the Novel* (Princeton: Princeton University Press, 2003).
11. Min Hyoung Song, *The Children of 1965: On Writing, and Not Writing, as an Asian American* (Durham: Duke University Press, 2013), 82.
12. Lye, "Unmarked Character," 243, 241.
13. Lye, "Unmarked Character," 235.
14. Erica R. Edwards, *Charisma and the Fictions of Black Leadership* (Minneapolis: University of Minnesota Press, 2012).
15. Lynch, *The Economy of Character*, 5–6.
16. On the Orientalism of the ideograph, or perhaps the inscrutable face of typeface, see Bush, *Ideographic Modernism*; Rey Chow, "How (the) Inscrutable Chinese Led to Globalized Theory," *PMLA* 116, no. 1 (January 2001): 69–74.
17. Lye, "Unmarked Character," 235.
18. Eugene Lim, *Dear Cyborgs* (New York: Farrar, Straus and Giroux, 2017); Pamela Lu, *Ambient Parking Lot* (Berkeley: Kenning Editions, 2011). Subsequent references are cited in the text.
19. For other Asian Americanist accounts of literary worlds that abstract or marginalize racial markers, see Song, *Children of 1965*; Stephen Hong Song, *Racial*

Asymmetries: Asian American Fictional Worlds (New York: NYU Press, 2014); Christopher T. Fan, "Melancholy Transcendence: Ted Chiang and Asian American Postracial Form," *Post45*, November 5, 2014; Yoonmee Chang, *Writing the Ghetto: Class, Authorship, and the Asian American Ethnic Enclave* (New Brunswick, N.J.: Rutgers University Press, 2010), 201–212.
20. Stewart, *Ordinary Affects*, 28.
21. Michel Serres, *The Parasite*, trans. Lawrence R. Schehr (Minneapolis: University of Minnesota Press, 2007), 7, 10.
22. Serres, *Parasite*, 65.
23. Hsieh is a performance artist whose "one year performances" dramatically upset the conventional boundaries of life, art, and work. For example, in *Time Clock Piece* (1980–1981), Hsieh punched a timecard every hour.
24. Lye, *America's Asia*, 55.
25. Robert Taber, *The War of the Flea: Guerrilla Warfare in Theory and Practice* (New York: Brassey's, 2002); Robert M. Cassidy, "Winning the War of the Flea: Lessons from Guerrilla Warfare," *Military Review* 84, no. 5 (September–October 2004): 41–46.
26. William Pfaff, "The Strategy of the Weak," *Commonweal* 84, no. 17 (July 22, 1966): 456.
27. Lee, *Exquisite Corpse*, 216, 231, 237.
28. On the ethics of adjacency, see chapter 3 of Namwali Serpell, *Seven Modes of Uncertainty* (Cambridge, Mass.: Harvard University Press, 2014).
29. Pamela Lu, *Pamela* (Berkeley: Atelos, 1998). Subsequent references are cited in the text.
30. The specific path *Ambient Parking Lot* traces is from liberal arts student to precarious artist. To quote from a piece of fan mail that the band receives: "After graduating with honors in English, I took my essays on Blake and Derrida as writing samples to Career Day. . . . Two tables were set up outside for recruiters of liberal arts students: one for a coffee chain hiring baristas and another for an office complex hiring receptionists and stock boys. . . . How can I explain what the Ambient Parkers and their music have done for me? I now work at the Caffeine Nation in the mall, which has a multilevel garage for parking" (16–17).
31. Walter Benjamin, "The Work of Art in the Age of Mechanical Reproduction," in *Illuminations*, ed. Hannah Arendt, trans. Harry Zohn (New York: Schocken, 1969), 217–51; Michael Fried, *Absorption and Theatricality: Painting and Beholder in the Age of Diderot* (Chicago: University of Chicago Press, 1988); Jonathan Crary, *Suspensions of Perception* (Cambridge, Mass.: MIT Press, 1999); Ngai, *Ugly Feelings*, 247–97.
32. Anna Jones Abramson, "Beyond Modernist Shock: Virginia Woolf's Absorbing Atmosphere," *Journal of Modern Literature* 38, no. 4 (Summer 2015): 42.
33. Amidst all this, they even become "popular," "mainstream," and "academic"—achievements indicated through reviews by senior critics; radio time; art gallery gigs; an anthologized manifesto in course readers; a festival founded on ambient noise; and a scholarship for ambient composition.
34. If Lu's and Lim's novels seem plotless and boring, this may be the point. Theodore Martin argues, "There is a fundamental tension between the grind of work and the grip of narrative, between what novels strive to be (interesting and eventful)

and what work is—plotless and monotonous." Lacking a *vocation*—a work identity—the characters of these novels can lay claim only to an *occupation*. Martin writes, "Occupation does not concern our character; it concerns the literal structuring of our time" (*Contemporary Drift: Genre, Historicism, and the Problem of the Present* [New York: Columbia University Press, 2017], 163).
35. Brennan, *Transmission of Affect*, 70.
36. David S. Roh, Betsy Huang, and Greta A. Niu, eds., *Techno-Orientalism: Imagining Asia in Speculative Fiction, History, and Media* (New Brunswick, N.J.: Rutgers University Press, 2015), 2. Jerng discusses "future war" fictions in chapter 2 of *Racial Worldmaking*.
37. Chun, *Control and Freedom*, 42.
38. Palumbo-Liu, *Asian/America*, 326; Wendy Hui Kyong Chun, "Race and/as Technology, or How to Do Things to Race," in *Race After the Internet*, eds. Lisa Nakamura and Peter Chow-White (New York: Routledge, 2012), 51.
39. Palumbo-Liu, *Asian/American*, 327.
40. Jerng, *Racial Worldmaking*, 43. For a critical and reparative reading of speculative fiction over and against techno-capitalist futures, see Aimee Bahng, *Migrant Futures: Decolonizing Speculation in Financial Times* (Durham: Duke University Press, 2018).
41. Virno, *Grammar of the Multitude*, 24, 41. Virno goes on to propose that in a post-Fordist society of personal dependence, "all wage labor has something in common with the 'performing artist,'" so as to call "into question the personhood of the one who performs the work" (68).
42. Berlant, "The Commons," 395.
43. Neferti X. M. Tadiar, "Ground Zero," *GLQ: A Journal of Lesbian and Gay Studies* 22, no. 2 (2016): 178–79, emphasis in original.

BIBLIOGRAPHY

ARCHIVAL SOURCES

Harry S. Truman Library & Museum

Staff Member and Office File

Hoover Institution Library & Archives

Edward G. Lansdale Papers
Bonner F. Fellers
Charles T.R. Bohannan Papers

National Archives and Records Administration at College Park

Record Group 59—Department of State Central Files
Record Group 84—Records of Foreign Service Posts of the Department of State
Record Group 218—Records of the U.S. Joint Chiefs of Staff
Record Group 319—Records of the Army Staff
Record Group 331—Records of Allied Operational and Occupation Headquarters, World War II
Record Group 389—Military Agency Records
Record Group 469—Records of U.S. Foreign Assistance Agencies
Record Group 554—Records of General Headquarters, Far East Command, Supreme Commander Allied Powers, and United Nations Command

BIBLIOGRAPHY

PUBLISHED SOURCES

Abramson, Anna Jones. "Beyond Modernist Shock: Virginia Woolf's Absorbing Atmosphere." *Journal of Modern Literature* 38, no. 4 (Summer 2015): 39–56.

Achinstein, Sharon. "Cold War Milton." *University of Toronto Quarterly* 77, no. 3 (November 19, 2008): 801–36.

Adams, Tim. "For Me, England Is a Mythical Place." *Guardian*, February 19, 2005.

Ahmed, Sara. *The Cultural Politics of Emotion*. New York: Routledge, 2004.

Alarcón, Norma, and Elaine H. Kim, eds. *Writing Self, Writing Nation: A Collection of Essays on Dictee by Theresa Hak Kyung Cha*. Berkeley: Third Woman, 1994.

Alexander, John A. "An Intelligence Role for the Footnote." *Studies in Intelligence* 8, no. 3 (Summer 1964): 1–2.

Alford, William P. *To Steal a Book Is an Elegant Offense: Intellectual Property Law in Chinese Civilization*. Stanford: Stanford University Press, 1995.

Allport, Floyd H., and Milton Lepkin. "Wartime Rumors of Waste and Special Privilege: Why Some People Believe Them." *Journal of Abnormal and Social Psychology* 40, no. 1 (1945): 3–36.

Allport, Gordon W., and Leo Postman. *The Psychology of Rumor*. New York: Henry Holt, 1947.

Alsop, Joseph. *I've Seen the Best of It*. Mount Jackson, Va.: Axios, 1992.

National Public Radio. "An Ambivalent Double Agent, Torn Between Two Countries." *NPR*, November 1, 2014. https://www.npr.org/2014/11/01/360183881/an-ambivalent-double-agent-torn-between-two-countries.

An American Officer (Edward Lansdale). "The Report the President Wanted Published." *Saturday Evening Post*, May 20, 1961.

Anderson, C. W., and G. E. McMaster. "Modeling Emotional Tone in Stories Using Tension Levels and Categorical States." *Computers and the Humanities* 20, no. 1 (March 1986): 3–9.

Arana, Marie. "Book Review: 'Nanjing Requiem,' by Ha Jin." *Washington Post*, October 24, 2011.

Arellano, Oscar J. "How Operation Brotherhood Got to Viet Nam." *Philippine Studies* 14, no. 3 (1966): 396–409.

Armstrong, Charles K. "The Cultural Cold War in Korea, 1945–1950." *Journal of Asian Studies* 62, no. 1 (February 2003): 71–99.

Arondekar, Anjali. "In the Absence of Reliable Ghosts: Sexuality, Historiography, South Asia." *differences* 25, no. 3 (December 1, 2014): 98–122.

———. *For the Record: On Sexuality and the Colonial Archive in India*. Durham: Duke University Press, 2009.

Arrighi, Giovanni. *Adam Smith in Beijing: Lineages of the Twenty-First Century*. New York: Verso, 2009.

Bachner, Andrea. *Beyond Sinology: Chinese Writing and the Scripts of Culture*. New York: Columbia University Press, 2014.

Bahng, Aimee. *Migrant Futures: Decolonizing Speculation in Financial Times*. Durham: Duke University Press, 2018.

Baik, Crystal Mun-hye. *Reencounters: On the Korean War and Diasporic Memory Critique*. Philadelphia: Temple University Press, 2020.

BIBLIOGRAPHY

Balce, Nerissa. *Body Parts of Empire: Visual Abjection, Filipino Images, and the American Archive.* Ann Arbor, Mich.: University of Michigan Press, 2016.
Banks, Russell. "View From the Prison Camp." *New York Times*, October 10, 2004.
Barthes, Roland. *Camera Lucida: Reflections on Photography.* Translated by Richard Howard. New York: Hill and Wang, 1980.
———. *The Empire of Signs.* Translated by Richard Howard. New York: Hill and Wang, 1982.
Beardsley, Monroe C. *Aesthetics: Problems in the Philosophy of Criticism.* Indianapolis: Hackett, 1981.
Bélanger, Danièle, and Magali Barbieri, eds. *Reconfiguring Families in Contemporary Vietnam.* Stanford: Stanford University Press, 2009.
Bell, Roger J. *Last Among Equals: Hawaiian Statehood and American Politics.* Honolulu: University of Hawaii Press, 1984.
———. *Unequal Allies: Australian-American Relations and the Pacific War.* Carlton, Vic: Melbourne University Press, 1977.
Belmonte, Laura. *Selling the American Way: U.S. Propaganda and the Cold War.* Philadelphia: University of Pennsylvania Press, 2010.
Benedict, Ruth. *The Chrysanthemum and the Sword.* Cleveland: Meridian, 1989.
Benjamin, Walter. "The Work of Art in the Age of Mechanical Reproduction." In *Illuminations*, edited by Hannah Arendt and Harry Zohn, 217–51. New York: Schocken, 1969.
Bennett, Burney B. "The Greater Barrier." *Studies in Intelligence* 2, no. 4 (Fall 1958): 105–12.
Benson, Heidi. "Profile: C.Y. Lee." *San Francisco Chronicle*, September 18, 2002.
Beredo, Cheryl. *Import of the Archive: U.S. Colonial Rule of the Philippines and the Making of American Archival History.* Sacramento, Calif.: Litwin, 2013.
Berkeley, George. "For a Board of Definitions." *Studies in Intelligence* 9, no. 3 (Summer 1965): 13–14.
Berlant, Lauren. *Cruel Optimism.* Durham: Duke University Press, 2011.
———. "Structures of Unfeeling: Mysterious Skin." *International Journal of Politics, Culture, and Society* 28, no. 3 (September 2015): 191–213.
Bernard, Miguel A. *Adventures in Viet-nam: The Story of Operation Brotherhood, 1954–1957.* Manila: Operation Brotherhood International, 1974.
———. *Filipinos in Laos: A Sequel to Adventure in Vietnam: The Story of Operation Brotherhood.* Manila: Operation Brotherhood International, 1974.
Bernstein, Barton J. "The Perils and Politics of Surrender: Ending the War with Japan and Avoiding the Third Atomic Bomb." *Pacific Historical Review* 46, no. 1 (February 1977): 1–27.
———. "The Struggle over the Korean Armistice: Prisoners of Repatriation?" In *Child of Conflict: The Korean–American Relationship, 1943–1953*, edited by Bruce Cumings, 261–307. Seattle: University of Washington Press, 1983.
Berrigan, Darrell. "Operation Brotherhood." *Saturday Evening Post*, November 12, 1955: 147.
Best, Stephen. *The Fugitive's Properties: Law and the Poetics of Possession.* Chicago: University of Chicago Press, 2004.
———. *None Like Us: Blackness, Belonging, Aesthetic Life.* Durham: Duke University Press, 2018.

Bix, Herbert P. "Inventing the 'Symbol Monarchy' in Japan, 1945–52." *Journal of Japanese Studies* 21, no. 2 (1995): 319–63.

———. "The Showa Emperor's 'Monologue' and the Problem of War Responsibility." *Journal of Japanese Studies* 18, no. 2 (1992): 295–363.

Blakefield, William. "A War Within: The Making of Know Your Enemy." *Sight and Sound: International Film Quarterly* 52, no. 2 (Spring 1983): 128–33.

Bohannan, C. T. R.. "Unconventional Operations." In *Counter-Guerrilla Operations in the Philippines, 1946–1953: A Seminar on the Huk Campaign Held at Ft. Bragg* by U.S. Army. Saigon: USOM's Graphics Section, 1961.

Boltanski, Luc, and Eve Chiapello. *The New Spirit of Capitalism*. Translated by Gregory Elliott. London: Verso, 2007.

Boot, Max. *The Road Not Taken: Edward Lansdale and the American Tragedy in Vietnam*. New York: Liveright, 2018.

Booth, Wayne C. *The Rhetoric of Fiction*. Chicago: University of Chicago Press, 1983.

Borstelmann, Thomas. *The Cold War and the Color Line: American Race Relations in the Global Arena*. Cambridge, Mass.: Harvard University Press, 2003.

Bow, Leslie. *Betrayal and Other Acts of Subversion: Feminism, Sexual Politics, Asian American Women's Literature*. Princeton: Princeton University Press, 2001.

Boyagoda, Randy. "Free and Too Easy." *Globe and Mail*, January 5, 2008.

Brazinsky, Gregg Andrew. "From Pupil to Model: South Korea and American Development Policy During the Early Park Chung Hee Era." *Diplomatic History* 29, no. 1 (January 2005): 83–115.

Brennan, Teresa. *The Transmission of Affect*. Ithaca, N.Y.: Cornell University Press, 2004.

Brinkema, Eugenie. *The Forms of the Affects*. Durham: Duke University Press, 2014.

Bryson, Bill. "Between Two Worlds." *New York Times*, April 29, 1990.

Buckland, Michael K. "What Is a 'Document?'" *Journal of the American Society for Information Science* 48, no. 9 (1997): 804–9.

Bui, Long T. *Returns of War: South Vietnam and the Price of Refugee Memory*. New York: NYU Press, 2018.

Buruma, Ian. "Chinese Shadows." *New York Review of Books*, March 24, 2005.

Bush, Christopher. *Ideographic Modernism: China, Writing, Media*. New York: Oxford University Press, 2010.

Butler, Judith. *Frames of War: When Is Life Grievable?* New York: Verso, 2009.

Butow, Robert J. *Japan's Decision to Surrender*. Stanford: Stanford University Press, 1954.

Camacho, Keith L. *Cultures of Commemoration: The Politics of War, Memory, and History in the Mariana Islands*. Honolulu: University of Hawaii Press, 2011.

Carruthers, Susan L. *Cold War Captives: Imprisonment, Escape, and Brainwashing*. Berkeley: University of California Press, 2009.

Cassidy, Robert M. "Winning the War of the Flea: Lessons from Guerrilla Warfare." *Military Review* 84, no. 5 (September–October 2004): 41–46.

Castells, Manuel. *The Rise of the Network Society*. Oxford: Blackwell, 2000.

Castiglia, Christopher. *The Practice of Hope: Literary Criticism in Disenchanted Times*. New York: New York University Press, 2017.

Cha, Theresa Hak Kyung. *Dictee*. New York: Tanam, 1982.

———. *Exilée and Temps Morts*. Edited by Constance Lewallen. Berkeley: University of California Press, 2009.

———. *Mouth to Mouth*. New York: Electronic Arts Intermix, 1975.

———. "White Dust from Mongolia (film)." *Online Archive of California*. https://oac.cdlib.org/ark:/13030/tf7g50056f/?brand=oac4.

Chandler, David P. "In the Midst of Wars: An American's Mission to Southeast Asia." *Journal of Asian Studies* 34, no. 3 (May 1975): 856–57.

Chang, Ha-Joon. *Bad Samaritans: The Myth of Free Trade and the Secret History of Capitalism*. New York: Bloomsbury, 2008.

Chang, Yoonmee. *Writing the Ghetto: Class, Authorship, and the Asian American Ethnic Enclave*. New Brunswick, N.J.: Rutgers University Press, 2012.

Chaudhuri, Amit. "Unlike Kafka." *London Review of Books*, June 8, 1995.

Cheah, Pheng. *Inhuman Conditions: On Cosmopolitanism and Human Rights*. Cambridge, Mass.: Harvard University Press, 2007.

———. "Universal Areas: Asian Studies in a World of Motion." In *The Postcolonial and the Global*, edited by Revathi Khishnaswamy and John C. Hawley, 54–68. Minneapolis, Minn.: University of Minnesota Press, 2008.

Cheang, Kai Hang. "Family Discord/ance: Tone and Counter-Mood in Gish Jen's *Mona in the Promised Land*." *Pacific Coast Philology* 53, no. 2 (2018): 217–38.

Chen, Kuan-Hsing. *Asia as Method: Toward Deimperialization*. Durham: Duke University Press, 2010.

———. "Missile Internationalism." In *Orientations: Mapping Studies in the Asian Diaspora*, edited by Kandice Chuh and Karen Shimakawa, 172–86. Durham: Duke University Press, 2001.

Chen, Tina. *Double Agency: Acts of Impersonation in Asian American Literature and Culture*. Stanford: Stanford University Press, 2005.

Cheng, Anne Anlin. *The Melancholy of Race: Psychoanalysis, Assimilation, and Hidden Grief*. New York: Oxford University Press, 2000.

———. *Ornamentalism*. New York: Oxford University Press, 2019.

———. *Second Skin: Josephine Baker and the Modern Surface*. New York: Oxford University Press, 2011.

Cheng, Cindy I-Fen. *Citizens of Asian America: Democracy and Race during the Cold War*. New York: NYU Press, 2013.

Cheung, King-Kok. "The Chinese American Writer as Migrant: Ha Jin's Restive Manifesto." *Amerasia* 38, no. 2 (2012): 2–12.

Chiang, Mark. *The Cultural Capital of Asian American Studies: Autonomy and Representation in the University*. New York: NYU Press, 2009.

Ching, Leo T. S. *Anti-Japan: The Politics of Sentiment in Postcolonial East Asia*. Durham: Duke University Press, 2019.

Cho, Grace M. *Haunting the Korean Diaspora: Shame, Secrecy, and the Forgotten War*. Minneapolis, Minn.; University of Minnesota Press, 2008.

Choi, Don Mee. *Hardly War*. Seattle: Wave, 2016.

Choi, Hyaeweol. *Gender and Mission Encounters in Korea: New Women, Old Ways*. Berkeley: University of California Press, 2009.

Chong, Sylvia Shin Huey. *The Oriental Obscene: Violence and Racial Fantasies in the Vietnam Era*. Durham: Duke University Press, 2011.

Chow, Rey. "How (the) Inscrutable Chinese Led to Globalized Theory." *PMLA* 116, no. 1 (January 2001): 69–74.
———. *Not Like a Native Speaker: On Languaging as a Postcolonial Experience*. New York: Columbia University Press, 2014.
———. *The Protestant Ethnic and the Spirit of Capitalism*. New York: Columbia University Press, 2002.
Chumley, Lily. *Creativity Class: Art School and Culture Work in Postsocialist China*. Princeton: Princeton University Press, 2016.
Chun, Wendy Hui Kyong. *Control and Freedom: Power and Paranoia in the Age of Fiber Optics*. Cambridge, Mass.: MIT Press, 2006.
———. "Race and/as Technology, or How to Do Things to Race." In *Race After the Internet*, edited by Lisa Nakamura and Peter Chow-White, 38–60. New York: Routledge, 2012.
Connery, Christopher L. "Pacific Rim Discourse: The U. S. Global Imaginary in the Late Cold War Years." *Boundary 2* 21, no. 1 (1994): 30–56.
Cooper, Tom. "Well-Drawn Characters, but Little Drama." *St. Louis Post-Dispatch*, November 18, 2007: F8.
Coriat, Benjamin. "The 'Abominable Ohno Production System': Competences, Monitoring, and Routines in Japanese Production Systems." In *The Nature and Dynamics of Organizational Capabilities*, edited by Giovanni Dosi, Richard R. Nelson, and Sidney G. Winter, 213–43. New York: Oxford University Press, 2000.
Crary, Jonathan. *Suspensions of Perception: Attention, Spectacle, and Modern Culture*. Cambridge, Mass.: MIT Press, 1999.
Cullather, Nick. "America's Boy? Ramon Magsaysay and the Illusion of Influence." *Pacific Historical Review* 62, no. 3 (August 1993): 305–38.
———. *Secret History: The CIA's Classified Account of Its Operations in Guatemala, 1952–1954*. Stanford: Stanford University Press, 2006.
Cumings, Bruce. *The Korean War: A History*. New York: Random House, 2010.
———. *Korea's Place in the Sun: A Modern History*. New York: W. W. Norton, 2005.
———. *The Origins of the Korean War, Vol. 1: Liberation and the Emergence of Separate Regimes, 1945–1947*. Princeton: Princeton University Press, 1981.
———. *Parallax Visions: Making Sense of American–East Asian Relations*. Durham: Duke University Press, 2002.
———. "Rimspeak; or, The Discourse of the Pacific Rim." In *What Is in a Rim? Critical Perspectives on the Pacific Region Idea*, edited by Arif Dirlik, 29–47. Lanham, M.D.: Rowman and Littlefield, 1998.
Currey, Cecil B. *Edward Lansdale: The Unquiet American*. Boston: Houghton Mifflin, 1988.
Cvetkovich, Ann. *An Archive of Feelings: Trauma, Sexuality, and Lesbian Public Cultures*. Durham: Duke University Press, 2003.
Darda, Joseph. *Empire of Defense: Race and the Cultural Politics of Permanent War*. Chicago: University of Chicago Press, 2019.
———. "The Literary Afterlife of the Korean War." *American Literature* 87, no. 1 (March 2015): 79–105.
Daugherty, William E. *A Psychological Warfare Casebook*. Baltimore: Operations Research Office, Johns Hopkins Press, 1958.
Davidson, Michael. *Guys Like Us: Citing Masculinity in Cold War Poetics*. Chicago: University of Chicago Press, 2004.

BIBLIOGRAPHY

Day, Iyko. *Alien Capital: Asian Racialization and the Logic of Settler Colonial Capitalism*. Durham: Duke University Press, 2016.

Dean, Robert D. *Imperial Brotherhood: Gender and the Making of Cold War Foreign Policy*. Amherst, Mass.: University of Massachusetts Press, 2001.

Diaz, Vicente M. " 'To "P" or Not to "P"?' Marking the Territory Between Pacific Islander and Asian American Studies." *Journal of Asian American Studies* 7, no. 3 (October 2004): 183–208.

Dickerman, Sherwood. "Cold War Condottiere." *Washington Post*, March 19, 1972: BW4.

Dirks, Nicholas. "Colonial Histories and Native Informants: Biography of an Archive." In *Orientalism and the Postcolonial Predicament: Perspectives on South Asia*, edited by Carol Appadurai Breckenridge and Peter van der Veer, 279–313. Philadelphia: University of Pennsylvania Press, 1993.

Dirlik, Arif. "Introduction: Pacific Contradictions." In *What Is in a Rim? Critical Perspectives on the Pacific Region Idea*, edited by Arif Dirlik, 3–14. Lanham, M.D.: Rowman and Littlefield, 1998.

———, ed. *What Is in a Rim? Critical Perspectives on the Pacific Region Idea*. Lanham, M.D.: Rowman and Littlefield, 1998.

Dolar, Mladen. *A Voice and Nothing More*. Cambridge, Mass: MIT Press, 2006.

Donovan, Pamela. "How Idle Is Idle Talk? One Hundred Years of Rumor Research." *Diogenes* 213 (2007): 59–82.

Dower, John W. *Embracing Defeat: Japan in the Wake of World War II*. New York: Norton, 1999.

———. *War Without Mercy: Race and Power in the Pacific War*. New York: Pantheon, 1987.

Doyle, Kate. "The End of Secrecy: U.S. National Security and the Imperative for Openness." *World Policy Journal* 16, no. 1 (1999): 34–51.

Drinnon, Richard. *Facing West: The Metaphysics of Indian-Hating and Empire-Building*. Minneapolis: University of Minnesota Press, 1980.

Drucker, Peter. "Japan and Adversarial Trade." *Wall Street Journal*, April 1, 1986: 32.

Duara, Prasenjit. "The Cold War as a Historical Period: An Interpretive Essay." *Journal of Global History* 6, no. 3 (November 2011): 457–80.

Dudziak, Mary L. *Cold War Civil Rights: Race and the Image of American Democracy*. Princeton: Princeton University Press, 2000.

———. *War Time: An Idea, Its History, Its Consequences*. New York: Oxford University Press, 2012.

Dulles, Allen. *The Craft of Intelligence*. New York: Harper & Row, 1963.

Duong, Lan P. *Treacherous Subjects: Gender, Culture, and Trans-Vietnamese Feminism*. Philadelphia: Temple University Press, 2012.

Durdin, Peggy. "Behind the Façade of Asian Unity." *New York Times*, April 17, 1955: SM9.

Dyson, Frances. *The Tone of Our Times: Sound, Sense, Economy, and Ecology*. Cambridge, Mass.: MIT Press, 2014.

Edwards, Brent Hayes. "The Taste of the Archive." *Callaloo* 35, no. 4 (Fall 2012): 944–72.

Edwards, Erica R. *Charisma and the Fictions of Black Leadership*. Minneapolis: University of Minnesota Press, 2012.

Eidsheim, Nina Sun. "Voice as Action: Towards a Model for Analyzing the Dynamic Construction of Racialized Voice." *Current Musicology* 93, no. 2012 (February 6, 2020): 9–34.

———. *The Race of Sound: Listening, Timbre, and Vocality in African American Music.* Durham: Duke University Press, 2019.

Eisenhower, Dwight. "Address at the Columbia University National Bicentennial Dinner." New York City, May 31, 1954.

———. "Chance for Peace." Speech presented at the American Society of Newspaper Editors, Washington, D.C., April 16, 1953.

Elias, Amy. "Past/Future." In *Time: A Vocabulary of the Present,* edited by Joel Burges and Amy Elias, 35–50. New York: NYU Press, 2016.

Elias, Amy, and Joel Burges. "Introduction: Time Studies Today." In *Time: A Vocabulary of the Present,* edited by Joel Burges and Amy Elias, 1–32. New York: NYU Press, 2016.

Ellis, Nadia. *Territories of the Soul: Queered Belonging in the Black Diaspora.* Durham: Duke University Press, 2015.

Ellsberg, Daniel. *Secrets: A Memoir of Vietnam and the Pentagon Papers.* New York: Penguin, 2003.

Emerson, Gloria. *Winners & Losers: Battles, Retreats, Gains, Losses, and Ruins from the Vietnam War.* New York: Norton, 1976.

Enloe, Cynthia. *Bananas, Beaches and Bases: Making Feminist Sense of International Politics.* Berkeley: University of California Press, 2014.

Eperjesi, John R. *The Imperialist Imaginary: Visions of Asia and the Pacific in American Culture.* Hanover, N.H.: University Press of New England, 2005.

Epstein, William H. "Counter-Intelligence: Cold-War Criticism and Eighteenth-Century Studies." *ELH* 57, no. 1 (1990): 63–99.

Espiritu, Yến Lê. *Body Counts: The Vietnam War and Militarized Refuge(es).* Berkeley: University of California Press, 2014.

Evans, Allan. "Against Footnotes." *Studies in Intelligence* 8, no. 4 (Fall 1964): 81–84.

Fan, Christopher T. "Andrew Yang and Post-'65 Asian America." *American Literary History,* March 3, 2020. https://doi.org/10.1093/alh/ajaa005.

———. "Melancholy Transcendence: Ted Chiang and Asian American Postracial Form." *Post45: Peer-Reviewed,* November 5, 2014.

Feng, Peter X. *Identities in Motion: Asian American Film and Video.* Durham: Duke University Press, 2002.

Fenves, Peter D. "An Idea in Combat with Itself: Benjamin, Hölderlin, and Temporal Plasticity." *PMLA* 124, no. 1 (May 2009): 280–82.

Finlan, Alastair. *Special Forces, Strategy and the War on Terror: Warfare By Other Means.* New York: Routledge, 2008.

Finn, Richard B. *Winners in Peace: MacArthur, Yoshida, and Postwar Japan.* Berkeley: University of California Press, 1992.

Fisher, James T. *Dr. America: The Lives of Thomas A. Dooley, 1927–1961.* Amherst, Mass.: University of Massachusetts Press, 1997.

FitzGerald, Frances. *Fire in the Lake: The Vietnamese and the Americans in Vietnam.* New York: Little, Brown, 1972.

Flatley, Jonathan. *Affective Mapping: Melancholia and the Politics of Modernism.* Cambridge, Mass.: Harvard University Press, 2008.

Fluet, Lisa. "Immaterial Labors: Ishiguro, Class, and Affect." *Novel* 40, no. 3 (Summer 2007): 265–88.

Foot, Rosemary. *A Substitute for Victory: The Politics of Peacemaking at the Korean Armistice Talks.* Ithaca, N.Y.: Cornell University Press, 2018.

BIBLIOGRAPHY

Frankenheimer, John, dir. *The Manchurian Candidate*. Beverly Hills, Calif.: MGM, 1962.
Freeman, James M. *Hearts of Sorrow: Vietnamese-American Lives*. Stanford: Stanford University Press, 1989.
Freeman, John. "No escape; Ha Jin's Harrowing 'War Trash' is Almost Like a Nonfiction Account of Being in a Korean Prison Camp" *Star Tribune*, October 10, 2004: 17F.
Fried, Michael. *Absorption and Theatricality: Painting and Beholder in the Age of Diderot*. Chicago: University of Chicago Press, 1988.
Friedman, Andrew. *Covert Capital: Landscapes of Denial and the Making of U.S. Empire in the Suburbs of Northern Virginia*. Berkeley: University of California Press, 2013.
Frost, Frank. "Vietnam, ASEAN and the Indochina Refugee Crisis." *Southeast Asian Affairs* (1980): 347–67.
Fuentecilla, J. "Pete." "Where Have All Our Nurses Gone." In *Filipinos in Laos: A Sequel to Adventure in Vietnam: The Story of Operation Brotherhood*, edited by Miguel A. Bernard, 169–72. Manila: Operation Brotherhood International, 1974.
Fujikane, Candace, and Jonathan Y. Okamura, eds. *Asian Settler Colonialism: From Local Governance to the Habits of Everyday Life in Hawai'i*. Honolulu: University of Hawai'i Press, 2008.
Fujitani, Takashi. *Race for Empire: Koreans as Japanese and Japanese as Americans During World War II*. Berkeley: University of California Press, 2011.
———. "The Reischauer Memo: Mr. Moto, Hirohito, and Japanese American Soldiers." *Critical Asian Studies* 33, no. 3 (September 1, 2001): 379–402.
———. *Splendid Monarchy: Power and Pageantry in Modern Japan*. Berkeley: University of California Press, 1998.
Fujitani, Takashi, Geoffrey M. White, and Lisa Yoneyama, eds. *Perilous Memories: The Asia-Pacific War(s)*. Durham: Duke University Press, 2001.
Gaddis, John Lewis. *Strategies of Containment: A Critical Appraisal of American National Security Policy During the Cold War*. New York: Oxford University Press, 2005.
Galison, Peter. "Removing Knowledge." *Critical Inquiry* 31, no. 1 (2004): 229–43.
Gallagher, Catherine. "Raymond Williams and Cultural Studies." *Social Text*, no. 30 (1992): 79–89.
Gallup Poll #557. December 6, 1955. https://institution.gallup.com/documents/questionnaire.aspx?STUDY=AIPO0557.
Gitelman, Lisa. *Always Already New: Media, History and the Data of Culture*. Cambridge, Mass.: The MIT Press, 2006.
———. *Paper Knowledge: Toward a Media History of Documents*. Durham: Duke University Press, 2014.
———. *Scripts, Grooves, and Writing Machines: Representing Technology in the Edison Era*. Stanford: Stanford University Press, 1999.
Gladstone, Jason, Andrew Hoberek, and Daniel Worden, eds. *Postmodern/Postwar and After: Rethinking American Literature*. Iowa City: University of Iowa Press, 2016.
Glassman, Jim. "On the Borders of Southeast Asia: Cold War Geography and the Construction of the Other." *Political Geography* 24 (2005): 784–807.
Glissant, Édouard. *Poetics of Relation*. Translated by Betsy Wing. Ann Arbor, Mich.: University of Michigan Press, 1997.

Gluck, Carol. "The 'End' of the Postwar: Japan at the Turn of the Millennium." *Public Culture* 10, no. 1 (1997): 1–23.

Grandin, Greg. *Empire's Workshop: Latin America, the United States, and the Rise of the New Imperialism.* New York: Metropolitan, 2006.

Grewal, Inderpal. *Saving the Security State: Exceptional Citizens in Twenty-First-Century America.* Durham: Duke University Press, 2017.

Gries, David D. "Openness and Secrecy." *Studies in Intelligence* 37, no. 5 (1994): 33–35.

Guha, Ranajit. *Elementary Aspects of Peasant Insurgency in Colonial India.* Durham: Duke University Press, 1999.

Hardt, Michael, and Antonio Negri. *Empire.* Cambridge, Mass.: Harvard University Press, 2000.

Hartman, Saidiya. "Venus in Two Acts." *Small Axe* 12, no. 2 (June 2008): 1–14.

Hay, Simon J. "The 1995 ASEAN Summit: Scaling a Higher Peak." *Contemporary Southeast Asia* 18 (December 1996): 254–74.

Hayot, Eric. *The Hypothetical Mandarin: Sympathy, Modernity, and Chinese Pain.* New York: Oxford University Press, 2009.

Hedman, Eva-Lotta E. "Global Civil Society in One Country? Class Formation and Business Activism in the Philippines." In *Southeast Asian Responses to Globalization: Restructuring Governance and Deepening Democracy,* edited by Francis Kok Wah Loh and Joakim Öjendal, 138–72. Copenhagen: Nordic Institute of Asian Studies, 2005.

———. *In the Name of Civil Society: From Free Election Movements to People Power in the Philippines.* Honolulu: University of Hawai'i Press, 2006.

Heller, Zoe. "A Tissue of Truths." *Independent,* October 28, 1989: 36.

Helmholtz, Hermann von. *On the Sensations of Tone as a Physiological Basis for the Theory of Music.* Translated by Alexander John Ellis. New York: Longmans, Green, 1895.

Hemmings, Clare. "Invoking Affect: Cultural Theory and the Ontological Turn." *Cultural Studies* 19 (2005): 548–67.

Hensher, Philip. "It's the Way He Tells It." *Guardian,* March 19, 2000.

Hickey, Michael. *The Korean War: The West Confronts Communism.* Woodstock, N.Y.: Overlook, 2000.

Hochschild, Arlie Russell. *The Managed Heart: Commercialization of Human Feeling.* Berkeley: University of California Press, 2012.

Hong, Christine. "The Unending Korean War." *Positions: Asia Critique* 23, no. 4 (Fall 2015): 597–617.

Hsu, Hsuan. *Sitting in Darkness: Mark Twain's Asia and Comparative Racialization.* New York: NYU Press, 2015.

Hsu, Madeline Y. "Asian Americans and the Cold War." *Oxford Research Encyclopedia of American History,* May 4, 2015. https://oxfordre.com/americanhistory/view/10.1093/acrefore/9780199329175.001.0001/acrefore-9780199329175-e-44.

———. *The Good Immigrants: How the Yellow Peril Became the Model Minority.* Princeton: Princeton University Press, 2015.

Hui, Andrew. *A Theory of the Aphorism: From Confucius to Twitter.* Princeton: Princeton University Press, 2019.

Hull, Matthew S. "Documents and Bureaucracy." *Annual Review of Anthropology* 41, no. 1 (2012): 251–67.

BIBLIOGRAPHY

Humphrey, David. "The Tone of Laughter and the Strangely Warm Comedy of Hagimoto Kin'ichi." *Japan Forum* 26, no. 4 (October 2, 2014): 530–50.
Hunt, Michael. "Constructing a History of Chinese Communist Party Foreign Relations." *Cold War International History Project Bulletin* 6–7 (Winter 1995/1996): 126–46.
Hunter, Edward. *Brainwashing in Red China: The Calculated Destruction of Men's Minds*. New York: Vanguard, 1953.
———. " 'Brain-Washing' Tactics Force Chinese Into Ranks of Communist Party." *Miami Sunday News*, September 24, 1950: 2.
———. *Brainwashing: The Story of Men Who Defied It*. New York: Farrar, Straus & Cudahy, 1956.
Illouz, Eva. *Cold Intimacies: The Making of Emotional Capitalism*. Malden, Mass.: Polity, 2007.
Ishiguro, Kazuo. *An Artist of the Floating World*. New York: Vintage, 1986.
———. *The Buried Giant*. New York: Vintage, 2015.
———. "My Twentieth Century Evening—and Other Small Breakthroughs." The Nobel Prize, December 17, 2017. https://www.nobelprize.org/prizes/literature/2017/ishiguro/25124-kazuo-ishiguro-nobel-lecture-2017/.
———. *Never Let Me Go*. New York: Vintage, 2006.
———. *A Pale View of Hills*. New York: Vintage, 1982.
———. *The Remains of the Day*. New York: Vintage, 1988.
———. *The Unconsoled*. New York: Vintage, 1995.
———. *When We Were Orphans*. New York: Vintage, 2000.
Ishiguro, Kazuo, and Malcolm Bradbury. *Kazuo Ishiguro and Malcolm Bradbury*. ICA Talks. Institute of Contemporary Arts, 1982. https://sounds.bl.uk/Arts-literature-and-performance/ICA-talks/024M-C0095X0015XX-0200V0.
Ivy, Marilyn. "Formations of Mass Culture." In *Postwar Japan as History*, edited by Andrew Gordon, 239–58. Berkeley: University of California Press, 1993.
Iyer, Pico. "Waiting Upon History: The Remains of the Day." *Partisan Review*, no. 55 (September 1991): 582–89.
Jackson, Lawrence. *The Indignant Generation: A Narrative History of African American Writers and Critics, 1934–1960*. Princeton: Princeton University Press, 2011.
Jackson, Wayne. "Scientific Estimating." *Studies in Intelligence* 9, no. 3 (Summer 1965): 7–11.
Jameson, Fredric. *Postmodernism, Or, The Cultural Logic of Late Capitalism*. Durham: Duke University Press, 1991.
———. *The Antinomies Of Realism*. New York: Verso, 2013.
Jeffords, Susan. *The Remasculinization of America: Gender and the Vietnam War*. Bloomington: Indiana University Press, 1989.
Jeon, Joseph Jonghyun. *Racial Things, Racial Forms: Objecthood in Avant-Garde Asian American Poetry*. Iowa City: University of Iowa Press, 2012.
———. *Vicious Circuits: Korea's IMF Cinema and the End of the American Century*. Stanford: Stanford University Press, 2019.
Jerng, Mark C. *Racial Worldmaking: The Power of Popular Fiction*. New York: Fordham University Press, 2017.
Jin, Daying. "Accounts of the Chinese People's Volunteer Army's Prisoners of War." PhD dissertation, University of Montana, 1993.

Jin, Ha. *The Boat Rocker*. New York: Pantheon, 2016.
———. *Between Silences: A Voice from China*. Chicago: University of Chicago Press, 1990.
———. *A Free Life*. New York: Pantheon, 2007.
———. Interview with Sarah Fay. "Ha Jin, The Art of Fiction No. 202." *Paris Review*, Winter 2009. https://www.theparisreview.org/interviews/5991/the-art-of-fiction-no-202-ha-jin.
———. Interview with Yongxi Wu. "Q. and A.: Ha Jin on Patriotism, Exile and 'A Map of Betrayal.'" *New York Times*, April 3, 2015.
———. *Map of Betrayal*. New York: Pantheon, 2014.
———. *Nanjing Requiem*. New York: Pantheon, 2011.
———. *War Trash*. New York: Vintage, 2004.
———. *The Writer as Migrant*. Chicago: University of Chicago Press, 2008.
Jin, Ha and Cynthia W. Liu. "Writing in Solitude." *International Examiner*, November 2, 1999: 18.
Jin, Ha and Te-hsing Shan. "In the Ocean of Words: An Interview with Ha Jin." *Tamkang Review* 38, no.2 (June 2008): 135–57.
Jin, Wen. *Pluralist Universalism: An Asian Americanist Critique of U.S. and Chinese Multiculturalisms*. Columbus: Ohio State University Press, 2012.
Johns, Adrian. *Piracy: The Intellectual Property Wars from Gutenberg to Gates*. Chicago: University of Chicago Press, 2009.
Jones, Donna V. *The Racial Discourses of Life Philosophy: Negritude, Vitalism, and Modernity*. New York: Columbia University Press, 2010.
Kafka, Ben. *The Demon of Writing: Powers and Failures of Paperwork*. New York: Zone, 2012.
Kagan, Leigh. "A Statement of Directions." *Bulletin of Concerned Asian Scholars* 1, no. 1 (May 1968): 1.
Kal, Hong. *Aesthetic Constructions of Korean Nationalism: Spectacle, Politics and History*. New York: Routledge, 2011.
Kang, Laura Hyun Yi. "Conjuring 'Comfort Women': Mediated Affiliations and Disciplined Subjects in Korean/American Transnationality." *Journal of Asian American Studies* 6, no. 1 (February 2003): 25–55.
———. "The 'Liberatory Voice' of Theresa Hak Kyung Cha's *Dictee*." In *Writing Self, Writing Nation: A Collection of Essays on Dictee by Theresa Hak Kyung Cha*, edited by Norma Alarcón and Elaine H. Kim, 73–99. New York: Third Woman, 1994.
Kapadia, Ronak. *Insurgent Aesthetics: Security and the Queer Life of the Forever War*. Durham: Duke University Press, 2019.
Kaplan, Amy. "Manifest Domesticity." *American Literature* 70, no. 3 (September 1998): 581–606.
Karnow, Stanley. "Western Ignorance of Asians Produces Policies of Delusion." *Washington Post*, July 20, 1973: A23.
Kauanui, J. Kēhaulani. "Asian American Studies and the 'Pacific Question.'" In *Asian American Studies After Critical Mass*, edited by Kent A. Ono, 123–43. Malden, Mass.: Blackwell, 2005.
Kennedy, John F. "Remarks of Senator John F. Kennedy at the Conference on Vietnam Luncheon in the Hotel Willard." Washington, D.C., June 1, 1956.

BIBLIOGRAPHY

Kenney, Martin, and Richard Florida. "Japan's Role in a Post-Fordist Age." *Futures* 21, no. 2 (April 1, 1989): 136–51.
Kent, Sherman. "A Crucial Estimate Relived." *Studies in Intelligence* 36, no. 5 (Spring 1964): 111–19.
———. "Death of a Hypothesis." *Studies in Intelligence* 9, no. 2 (Spring 1965): 21–24.
———. "Estimates and Influence." *Studies in Intelligence* 12, no. 3 (Summer 1968): 11–21.
———. "The Need for an Intelligence Literature." *Studies in Intelligence* 1, no. 1 (Fall 1955): 1–11.
———. *Strategic Intelligence for American World Policy*. Princeton: Princeton University Press, 2016.
———. "Valediction." *Studies in Intelligence* 12, no. 1 (Winter 1968): 1–11.
———. "Words of Estimative Probability." *Studies in Intelligence* 8, no. 4 (Fall 1964): 49–65.
Khalili, Laleh. *Time in the Shadows: Confinement in Counterinsurgencies*. Stanford: Stanford University Press, 2012.
Kim, Byung-Kook. "The Leviathan: Economic Bureaucracy Under Park." In *The Park Chung Hee Era*, edited by Byung-Kook Kim and Ezra Vogel, 200–232. Cambridge, Mass.: Harvard University Press, 2011.
Kim, Choong Soon. *The Culture of Korean Industry: An Ethnography of Poongsan Corporation*. Tucson: University of Arizona Press, 1992.
Kim, Elaine H., and Chungmoo Choi. *Dangerous Women: Gender and Korean Nationalism*. New York: Routledge, 1998.
Kim, Helen. *Grace Sufficient: The Story of Helen Kim*. Nashville, Tenn.: Upper Room, 1964.
Kim, Jinah. *Postcolonial Grief: The Afterlives of the Pacific Wars in the Americas*. Durham: Duke University Press, 2019.
Kim, Jodi. *Ends of Empire: Asian American Critique and the Cold War*. Minneapolis, Minn.: University of Minnesota Press, 2010.
———. "Settler Modernity, Debt Imperialism, and the Necropolitics of the Promise." *Social Text* 36, no. 2 (2018): 41–61.
Kim, Joo-Hong. "The Armed Forces." In *The Park Chung Hee Era*, edited by Byung-Kook Kim and Ezra Vogel, 168–99. Cambridge, Mass.: Harvard University Press, 2011.
Kim, Ju Yon. *The Racial Mundane: Asian American Performance and the Embodied Everyday*. New York: New York University Press, 2015.
Kim, Monica. *The Interrogation Rooms of the Korean War: The Untold History*. Princeton: Princeton University Press, 2019.
Kim, Myung Mi. *Commons*. Berkeley: University of California Press, 2002.
Kim, Seung-kyung. *Class Struggle Or Family Struggle? The Lives of Women Factory Workers in South Korea*. New York: Cambridge University Press, 1997.
King, Ross. "Western Protestant Missionaries and the Origins of Korean Language Modernization." *Journal of International and Area Studies* 11, no. 3 (2004): 7–38.
Kinkead, Eugene. *In Every War But One*. New York: Norton, 1959.
Kinney, Katherine. *Friendly Fire: American Images of the Vietnam War*. New York: Oxford University Press, 2000.
Kirn, Walter. "Pleased to Be Here." *New York Times*, November 25, 2007.

Kittler, Friedrich. *Discourse Networks 1800/1900*. Translated by Michael Metteer. Stanford: Stanford University Press, 1990.

Klein, Christina. *Cold War Cosmopolitanism: Period Style in 1950s Korean Cinema*. Berkeley: University of California Press, 2020.

———. *Cold War Orientalism: Asia in the Middlebrow Imagination, 1945–1961*. Berkeley: University of California Press, 2003.

Knapp, Robert H. "A Psychology of Rumor." *Public Opinion Quarterly* 8, no. 1 (Spring, 1944): 22–37.

Koepnick, Lutz. *On Slowness: Toward an Aesthetic of the Contemporary*. New York: Columbia University Press, 2014.

Koikari, Mire. *Pedagogy of Democracy: Feminism and the Cold War in the U.S. Occupation of Japan*. Philadelphia: Temple University Press, 2008.

Kong, Belinda. *Tiananmen Fictions Outside the Square: The Chinese Literary Diaspora and the Politics of Global Culture*. Philadelphia: Temple University Press, 2012.

———. "Theorizing the Hyphen's Afterlife in Post-Tiananmen Asian-America." *MFS Modern Fiction Studies* 56 (2010): 136–59.

Koselleck, Reinhart. *Futures Past: On the Semantics of Historical Time*. Translated by Keith Tribe. New York: Columbia University Press, 2004.

———. *Sediments of Time: On Possible Histories*. Translated and edited by Sean Franzel and Stefan-Ludwig Hoffman. Stanford: Stanford University Press, 2018.

Koshy, Susan. "From Cold War to Trade War: Neocolonialism and Human Rights." *Social Text*, no. 58 (Spring 1999): 1–32.

Kramer, Paul A. *The Blood of Government: Race, Empire, the United States, and the Philippines*. Chapel Hill: University of North Carolina Press, 2006.

Kung, Samuel. "Personal and Professional Problems of Chinese Students." PhD dissertation, Columbia University, 1955.

Kwon, Heonik. *The Other Cold War*. New York: Columbia University Press, 2010.

Lai, Him Mark. *Becoming Chinese American: A History of Communities and Institutions*. Walnut Creek, Calif.: AltaMira, 2004.

Lansdale, Edward Geary. "Excerpts from Lansdale Team's Report." *New York Times*, July 5, 1971, 11.

———. "Give Me Your Tired, Your Poor." *New York Times*, April 12, 1975.

———. *In the Midst of Wars: An American's Mission to Southeast Asia*. New York: Harper & Row, 1972.

Lanza, Fabio. *The End of Concern: Maoist China, Activism, and Asian Studies*. Durham: Duke University Press, 2017.

Laqueur, Thomas W. *The Work of the Dead: A Cultural History of Mortal Remains*. Princeton: Princeton University Press, 2016.

Lee, A. J. Yumi. "Cold War Erasures and the Asian American Immigrant Family in Ha Jin's *War Trash*." *Verge: Studies in Global Asias* 5, no. 2 (Fall 2019): 114–31.

Lee, C. Y. *The Flower Drum Song*. New York: Penguin, 2002.

Lee, Rachel C. *The Exquisite Corpse of Asian America: Biopolitics, Biosociality, and Posthuman Ecologies*. New York: NYU Press, 2014.

Lee, Summer Kim. "Introduction: Someone Else's Object." *Post45*, December 9, 2019.

Lee, Timothy. *Born Again: Evangelicalism in Korea*. Honolulu: University of Hawai'i Press, 2009.

BIBLIOGRAPHY

Lee, Yoon Sun. *Modern Minority: Asian American Literature and Everyday Life.* New York: Oxford University Press, 2013.
Levi-Strauss, Claude. *Tristes Tropiques.* Translated by John Russell. London: Hutchinson, 1961.
Lewis, Anthony Marc. "Re-Examining Our Perceptions on Vietnam." *Studies in Intelligence* 17, no. 4 (Winter 1973): 1–62.
Li, Darryl. *The Universal Enemy: Jihad, Empire, and the Challenge of Solidarity.* Stanford: Stanford University Press, 2019.
Lie, John. *Han Unbound: The Political Economy of South Korea.* Stanford: Stanford University Press, 1998.
Lifton, Robert Jay. *Thought Reform and the Psychology of Totalism: A Study of "Brainwashing" in China.* New York: Norton, 1961.
Lim, Eugene. *Dear Cyborgs.* New York: Farrar, Straus and Giroux, 2017.
Lindroos, Kia. *Now-Time Image-Space: Temporalization of Politics in Walter Benjamin's Philosophy of History and Art.* Jyväskylä: University of Jyväskylä, 1998.
Ling, Jinqi. *Narrating Nationalisms: Ideology and Form in Asian American Literature.* New York: Oxford University Press, 1998.
Lippard, Lucy R. *Six Years: The Dematerialization of the Art Object from 1966 to 1972.* Berkeley: University of California Press, 1997.
Liu, Alan. *The Laws of Cool: Knowledge Work and the Culture of Information.* Chicago: University of Chicago Press, 2004.
Liu, William. *Transition to Nowhere: Vietnamese Refugees in America.* Nashville, Tenn.: Charter House, 1979.
Lok, Susan Pui San. "Staging/Translating." *Third Text* 13, no. 46 (Spring 1999): 61–72.
Lovell, Julia. "Fighting for Mao." *Guardian*, November 11, 2005.
Lowe, Lisa. "History Hesitant." *Social Text* 33, no. 4 (December 2015): 85–107.
——. *Immigrant Acts: On Asian American Cultural Politics.* Durham: Duke University Press, 1996.
——. *The Intimacies of Four Continents.* Durham: Duke University Press, 2015.
Lu, Pamela. *Ambient Parking Lot.* Berkeley: Kenning Editions, 2011.
——. *Pamela.* Berkeley: Atelos, 1998.
Lucas, Scott. *Freedom's War: The American Crusade Against the Soviet Union.* New York: New York University Press, 1999.
Lui, Mary. "Rehabilitating Chinatown at Mid-Century: Chinese Americans, Race, and US Cultural Diplomacy." In *Chinatowns in a Transnational World: Myths and Realities of an Urban Phenomenon*, edited by Vanessa Künnemann and Ruth Mayer. New York: Routledge, 2011.
Lukács, Georg. *The Historical Novel.* Translated by Hannah Mitchell and Stanley Mitchell. London: Merlin Press, 1962.
Lye, Colleen. "Afterword: Realism's Futures." *Novel* 49, no. 2 (August 1, 2016): 343–57.
——. *America's Asia: Racial Form and American Literature, 1893–1945.* Princeton: Princeton University Press, 2005.
——. "Unmarked Character and the 'Rise of Asia': Ed Park's Personal Days." *Verge: Studies in Global Asias* 1, no. 1 (Spring 2015): 230–54.
Lynch, Deidre. *The Economy of Character: Novels, Market Culture, and the Business of Inner Meaning.* Chicago: University of Chicago Press, 1998.
MacArthur, Douglas. *Reminiscences.* Annapolis, M.D.: Naval Institute Press, 1964.

Madokoro, Laura. *Elusive Refuge: Chinese Migrants in the Cold War*. Cambridge, Mass.: Harvard University Press, 2016.

Man, Simeon. *Soldiering Through Empire: Race and the Making of the Decolonizing Pacific*. Berkeley: University of California Press, 2018.

Marks, Laura U. *The Skin of the Film: Intercultural Cinema, Embodiment, and the Senses*. Durham: Duke University Press, 2000.

Martin, Theodore. *Contemporary Drift: Genre, Historicism, and the Problem of the Present*. New York: Columbia University Press, 2017.

Marvin, Carolyn. "The Body of the Text: Literacy's Corporeal Constant." *Quarterly Journal of Speech* 80, no. 2 (May 1994): 129–49.

Marx, Leo. "The Idea of 'Technology' and Postmodern Pessimism." In *Does Technology Drive History? The Dilemma of Technological Determinism*, edited by Merritt Roe Smith and Leo Marx, 237–58. Cambridge, Mass.: The MIT Press, 1994.

——. *The Machine in the Garden: Technology and the Pastoral Ideal in America*. New York: Oxford University Press, 1964.

Massey, Joseph. "The Emperor Is Far Away: China's Enforcement of Intellectual Property Rights Protection, 1986–2006." *Chicago Journal of International Law* 7, no. 1 (2006): 231–37.

Massumi, Brian. *Parables for the Virtual: Movement, Affect, Sensation*. Durham: Duke University Press, 2002.

Masuda, Hajimu. *Cold War Crucible: The Korean Conflict and the Postwar World*. Cambridge, Mass.: Harvard University Press, 2015.

Matsusaka, Y. Tak. "Japan's South Manchuria Railway Company in Northeast China, 1906–34." In *Manchurian Railways and the Opening of China: An International History*, edited by Bruce Elleman and Stephen Kotkin, 37–58. Armonk, N.Y.: M. E. Sharpe, 2010.

Maxwell, William. *F.B. Eyes: How J. Edgar Hoover's Ghostreaders Framed African American Literature*. Princeton: Princeton University Press, 2015.

Mayer, William E. "Why Did So Many GI Captives Cave In." *U.S. News and World Report*, February 24, 1956, 65–72.

McAlister, Melani. *Epic Encounters: Culture, Media, and U.S. Interests in the Middle East since 1945*. Berkeley: University of California Press, 2001.

McConnaughey, David. "More Against Footnotes." *Studies in Intelligence* 8, no. 4 (Fall 1964): 85–86.

McCoy, Alfred W. *Policing America's Empire: The United States, the Philippines, and the Rise of the Surveillance State*. Madison: University of Wisconsin Press, 2009.

McGurl, Mark. *The Program Era: Postwar Fiction and the Rise of Creative Writing*. Cambridge, Mass.: Harvard University Press, 2009.

McLarney, Ellen. "James Baldwin and the Power of Black Muslim Language." *Social Text* 37, no. 1 (March 1, 2019): 51–84.

McLean, David R. "Cranks, Nuts, and Screwballs." *Studies in Intelligence* 9, no. 3 (Summer 1965): 79–89.

McLuhan, Marshall. *The Gutenberg Galaxy*. Toronto: University of Toronto Press, 1962.

——. *Understanding Media: The Extensions of Man*. Cambridge, Mass.: MIT Press, 1994.

Meerloo, J. A. M. *The Rape of the Mind: The Psychology of Thought Control, Menticide, and Brainwashing*. Cleveland: World, 1956.

Meister, Robert. *After Evil: A Politics of Human Rights*. New York: Columbia University Press, 2012.
Melley, Timothy. "Brainwashed! Conspiracy Theory and Ideology in the Postwar United States." *New German Critique*, no. 103 (Winter 2008): 145–64.
Mendel, Douglas H. "Perspectives on Japanese Foreign Policy." *Monumenta Nipponica* 21, no. 3/4 (1966): 346–53.
Mertha, Andrew C. *The Politics of Piracy: Intellectual Property in Contemporary China*. Ithaca, N.Y.: Cornell University Press, 2005.
Michie, Helena, and Robyn R. Warhol. *Love Among the Archives: Writing the Lives of Sir George Scharf, Victorian Bachelor*. Edinburgh: Edinburgh University Press, 2015.
Miller, Roger K. "Remembering the Forgotten War: A Chinese Soldier Recounts His Travails as a Captured Prisoner in the Korean War." *Sun Sentinel*, November 14, 2004.
Minh-ha, Trinh T. *Elsewhere, Within Here: Immigration, Refugeeism and the Boundary Event*. New York: Routledge, 2010.
——. *Surname Viet, Given Name Nam*. New York: Women Make Movies, 1989.
——. "White Spring." In *The Dream of the Audience*, edited by Constance Lewallen, 33–50. Berkeley: University of California Press, 2001.
Mitchell, W. J. T. *What Do Pictures Want? The Lives and Loves of Images*. Chicago: University of Chicago Press, 2005.
Miyoshi, Masao. *Off Center: Power and Culture Relations Between Japan and the United States*. Cambridge, Mass.: Harvard University Press, 1991.
Moon, Chung-in, and Byung-joon Jun. "Modernization Strategy: Ideas and Influences." In *The Park Chung Hee Era*, edited by Byung-Kook Kim and Ezra Vogel, 115–39. Cambridge, Mass.: Harvard University Press, 2011.
Moon, Seungsook. *Militarized Modernity and Gendered Citizenship in South Korea*. Durham: Duke University Press, 2005.
Moore, Sadie Maude. "A Torch in Her Hand," *Korea Calling* 5, no. 9 (October 1966): 3–4.
Moten, Fred. *In the Break: The Aesthetics of the Black Radical Tradition*. Minneapolis: University of Minnesota Press, 2003.
Muñoz, José Esteban. "Ephemera as Evidence: Introductory Notes to Queer Acts." *Women & Performance: A Journal of Feminist Theory* 8, no. 2 (January 1, 1996): 5–16.
Nadel, Alan. *Containment Culture: American Narrative, Postmodernism, and the Atomic Age*. Durham: Duke University Press, 1995.
Nakamura, Naofumi. "Railway Systems and Time Consciousness in Modern Japan." *Japan Review*, no. 14 (2002): 13–38.
Nashel, Jonathan. *Edward Lansdale's Cold War*. Amherst: University of Massachusetts Press, 2005.
Ngai, Sianne. *Our Aesthetic Categories: Zany, Cute, Interesting*. Cambridge, Mass.: Harvard University Press, 2012.
——. *Ugly Feelings*. Cambridge, Mass.: Harvard University Press, 2007.
Nguyen, Marguerite. *America's Vietnam: The Longue Duree of U.S. Literature and Empire*. Philadelphia: Temple University Press, 2018.
Nguyen, Mimi Thi. *The Gift of Freedom: War, Debt, and Other Refugee Passages*. Duke University Press, 2012.

Nguyen, Minh T. N. *Vietnam's Socialist Servants: Domesticity, Class, Gender, and Identity*. New York: Routledge, 2015.

Nguyen, Viet Thanh. *Nothing Ever Dies: Vietnam and the Memory of War*. Cambridge, Mass.: Harvard University Press, 2016.

———. "Representing Reconciliation: Le Ly Hayslip and the Victimized Body." *Positions: Asia Critique* 5, no. 2 (1997): 605–42.

Nguyen, Vinh. "Refugeetude: When Does a Refugee Stop Being a Refugee." *Social Text* 37, no. 2 (2019): 109–31.

Nichols, Bill. *Representing Reality: Issues and Concepts in Documentary*. Bloomington: Indiana University Press, 1991.

Northridge, A.R. "Pearl Harbor: Estimating Then and Now." *Studies in Intelligence* 9, no. 4 (Fall 1965): 65–74.

Nyong'o, Tavia. "Racial Kitsch and Black Performance." *Yale Journal of Criticism* 15, no. 2 (2002): 371–91.

Office of the United States Trade Representative. "Fact Sheet: 'Special 301' on Intellectual Property." May 25, 1989.

Ong, Aihwa. *Spirits of Resistance and Capitalist Discipline: Factory Women in Malaysia*. New York: State University of New York Press, 2010.

Osgood, Kenneth Alan. *Total Cold War: Eisenhower's Secret Propaganda Battle at Home and Abroad*. Lawrence: University of Kansas, 2006.

Oyen, Meredith. *The Diplomacy of Migration: Transnational Lives and the Making of U.S.-Chinese Relations in the Cold War*. Ithaca, N.Y.: Cornell University Press, 2015.

Pahk, Induk. *The Cock Still Crows*. New York: Vantage, 1977.

———. *The Hour of the Tiger*. New York: Harper, 1965.

———. *September Monkey*. New York: Harper, 1954.

Palumbo-Liu, David. *Asian/American: Historical Crossings of a Racial Frontier*. Stanford: Stanford University Press, 1999.

Pang, Laikwan. *Creativity and Its Discontents: China's Creative Industries and Intellectual Property Rights Offenses*. Durham: Duke University Press, 2012.

Parikh, Crystal. *An Ethics of Betrayal: The Politics of Otherness in Emergent U.S. Literatures and Culture*. New York: Fordham University Press, 2009.

Park, Chung-shin. *Protestantism and Politics in Korea*. Seattle: University of Washington Press, 2003.

Park, Ed. *Personal Days*. New York: Random House, 2008.

———. "This Is the Writing You Have Been Waiting For." In *Exilée: Temps Morts: Selected Works*, edited by Constance Lewallen, 8–15. Berkeley: University of California Press, 2009.

Park, Josephine Nock-Hee. "Alien Enemies in Julie Otsuka's *When the Emperor Was Divine*." *MFS Modern Fiction Studies* 59 (Spring 2013): 135–55.

———. *Cold War Friendships: Korea, Vietnam, and Asian American Literature*. New York: Oxford University Press, 2016.

Parkinson, Anna M. *An Emotional State: The Politics of Emotion in Postwar West German Culture*. Ann Arbor: University of Michigan Press, 2015.

Parry-Giles, Shawn J. *The Rhetorical Presidency, Propaganda, and the Cold War, 1945–1955*. Westport, Conn.: Praeger, 2002.

Pfaff, William. "The Strategy of the Weak." *Commonweal* 87, no. 17 (July 22, 1966): 456–57.

Phu, Thy. "Decapitated Forms: Theresa Hak Kyung Cha's Visual Text and the Politics of Visibility." *Mosaic: An Interdisciplinary Critical Journal* 38, no. 1 (2005): 17–36.
Plummer, Brenda Gayle. *Rising Wind: Black Americans and U.S. Foreign Affairs, 1935–1960*. Chapel Hill: University of North Carolina Press, 1996.
Pomfret, John. "China Firm Shelves Novel's Publication." *Washington Post*, June 22, 2000: A19.
Poovey, Mary. *A History of the Modern Fact: Problems of Knowledge in the Sciences of Wealth and Society*. Chicago: University of Chicago Press, 1998.
Powers, Thomas. "The Truth About the CIA." *New York Review of Books*, May 13, 1993.
Puderbaugh, Richard T. "Elegant Writing—Report Number Two." *Studies in Intelligence* 17, no. 2 (1973): 61–69.
———. "Elegant Writing in the Clandestine Services." *Studies in Intelligence* 16, no. 1 (1972): 1–7.
Rafael, Vicente L. *White Love and Other Events in Filipino History*. Durham: Duke University Press, 2000.
Reber, Dierdra. *Coming to Our Senses: Affect and an Order of Things for Global Culture*. New York: Columbia University Press, 2016.
Reddy, Chandan. *Freedom with Violence: Race, Sexuality, and the US State*. Durham: Duke University Press, 2011.
Richards, I.A. *Practical Criticism: A Study of Literary Judgement*. London: Kegan Paul, 1929.
Robbins, Bruce. "Cruelty Is Bad: Banality and Proximity in *Never Let Me Go*." *NOVEL: A Forum on Fiction* 40, no. 3 (Spring 2007): 289–302.
———. *The Servant's Hand: English Fiction from Below*. New York: Columbia University Press, 1986.
———. "Very Busy Just Now: Globalization and Harriedness in Kazuo Ishiguro's *The Unconsoled*." In *Globalization and the Humanities*, edited by David Leiwei Li, 233–48. Hong Kong: Hong Kong University Press, 2004.
Roberts, Brian Russell, and Michelle Ann Stephens. "Archipelagic American Studies: Decontinentalizing the Study of American Culture." In *Archipelagic American Studies*, edited by Brian Russell Roberts and Michelle Ann Stephens, 1–54. Durham: Duke University Press, 2017.
Robin, Ron. *The Making of the Cold War Enemy: Culture and Politics in the Military-Intellectual Complex*. Princeton: Princeton University Press, 2001.
Rogin, Michael Paul. *Ronald Reagan, the Movie: And Other Episodes in Political Demonology*. Berkeley: University of California Press, 1988.
Roh, David S., Betsy Huang, and Greta A. Niu, eds. *Techno-Orientalism: Imagining Asia in Speculative Fiction, History, and Media*. New Brunswick, N.J.: Rutgers University Press, 2015.
Rosnow, Ralph L., and Gary Alan Fine. *Rumor and Gossip: The Social Psychology of Hearsay*. New York: Elsevier, 1976.
Ross, Christine. *The Past Is the Present; It's the Future Too: The Temporal Turn in Contemporary Art*. New York: Bloomsbury, 2012.
Rossum, Gerhard Dohrn-van. *History of the Hour: Clocks and Modern Temporal Orders*. Translated by Thomas Dunlap. Chicago: University of Chicago Press, 1996.

Rubin, Andrew. *Archives of Authority: Empire, Culture, and the Cold War.* Princeton: Princeton University Press, 2012.

Rüegg, Johann Caspar. "Smooth Muscle Tone." *Psychological Reviews* 51, no. 1 (January 1971): 201–48.

Russell, Catherine. *Experimental Ethnography: The Work of Film in the Age of Video.* Durham: Duke University Press, 1999.

Russolo, Luigi. *The Art of Noises.* Translated by Barclay Brown. Hillsdale, N.Y.: Pendragon, 1986.

Ruttenburg, Nancy. *Democratic Personality: Popular Voice and the Trial of American Authorship.* Stanford: Stanford University Press, 1998.

Sakai, Naoki. "'You Asians': On the Historical Role of the West and Asia Binary." *South Atlantic Quarterly* 99, no. 4 (2000): 789–817.

Saranillio, Dean Itsuji. *Unsustainable Empire: Alternative Histories of Hawai'i Statehood.* Durham: Duke University Press, 2018.

Saussy, Haun. *Great Walls of Discourse and Other Adventures in Cultural China.* Cambridge, Mass.: Harvard University Press, 2001.

Schaller, Michael. "Securing the Great Crescent: Occupied Japan and the Origins of Containment in Southeast Asia." *Journal of American History* 69, no. 2 (September 1982): 392–414.

Schein, Edgar H. *Coercive Persuasion: A Socio-Psychological Analysis of the "Brainwashing" of American Civilian Prisoners by the Chinese Communists.* New York: Norton, 1961.

Schlund-Vials, Cathy J. *War, Genocide, and Justice: Cambodian American Memory Work.* Minneapolis, Minn.: University of Minnesota Press, 2012.

Schmid, Andre. *Korea between Empires, 1895–1919.* New York: Columbia University Press, 2002.

Schrader, Stuart. *Badges without Borders: How Global Counterinsurgency Transformed American Policing.* Berkeley: University of California Press, 2019.

Scott, David. *Conscripts of Modernity: The Tragedy of Colonial Enlightenment.* Durham: Duke University Press, 2004.

Scott, Joanna C. *Indochina's Refugees: Oral Histories from Laos, Cambodia and Vietnam.* Jefferson, N.C.: McFarland, 1989.

Sedgwick, Eve Kosofsky. *Between Men: English Literature and Male Homosocial Desire.* New York: Columbia University Press, 1985.

——. *Epistemology of the Closet.* Berkeley: University of California Press, 1990.

Selisker, Scott. *Human Programming: Brainwashing, Automatons, and American Unfreedom.* Minneapolis: University of Minnesota Press, 2016.

Seltzer, Mark. *Bodies and Machines.* New York: Routledge, 1992.

Serpell, Namwali. *Seven Modes of Uncertainty.* Cambridge, Mass.: Harvard University Press, 2014.

Serres, Michel. *The Parasite.* Translated by Lawrence R. Schehr. Minneapolis, Minn.: University of Minnesota Press, 2007.

Shan, Te-hsing. "Sublimating History into Literature: Reading Ha Jin's *Nanjing Requiem.*" *Amerasia* 38, no. 2 (2012): 25–34.

Sheehan, Neil. *A Bright Shining Lie: John Paul Vann and America in Vietnam.* New York: Random House, 1988.

Shen, Shuang. "Empire of Information: The Asia Foundation's Network and Chinese-Language Cultural Production in Hong Kong and Southeast Asia." *American Quarterly* 69, no. 3 (September 2017): 589–610.
Shibusawa, Naoko. *America's Geisha Ally: Reimagining the Japanese Enemy*. Cambridge, Mass.: Harvard University Press, 2006.
Shigematsu, Setsu, and Keith L. Camacho, eds. *Militarized Currents: Toward a Decolonized Future in Asia and the Pacific*. Minneapolis: University of Minnesota Press, 2010.
Shin, Gi-Wook. *Ethnic Nationalism in Korea: Genealogy, Politics, and Legacy*. Stanford: Stanford University Press, 2006.
Siebers, Tobin. *Cold War Criticism and the Politics of Skepticism*. New York: Oxford University Press, 1993.
Singh, Nikhil Pal. *Black Is a Country: Race and the Unfinished Struggle for Democracy*. Cambridge, Mass.: Harvard University Press, 2004.
Sitney, P. Adams. *Visionary Film: The American Avant-Garde, 1943–2000*. New York: Oxford University Press, 2002.
Slaughter, Joseph R. "World Literature as Property." *Alif: Journal of Comparative Poetics*, no. 34 (2014): 39–73.
Slotkin, Richard. *Gunfighter Nation: The Myth of the Frontier in Twentieth-Century America*. Norman: University of Oklahoma Press, 1998.
Smith, Abbott E. "On the Accuracy of National Intelligence Estimates." *Studies in Intelligence* 13, no. 4 (Fall 1969): 23–35.
Smith, Joseph Burkholder. *Portrait of a Cold Warrior*. New York: Putnam, 1976.
Smith, Wendy. "Coming to America." *Publishers Weekly*, September 10, 2007.
Song, Min Hyoung. *The Children of 1965: On Writing, and Not Writing, as an Asian American*. Durham: Duke University Press, 2013.
Song, Stephen Hong. *Racial Asymmetries: Asian American Fictional Worlds*. New York: NYU Press, 2014.
Stephens, Carlene. "'The Most Reliable Time': William Bond, the New England Railroads, and Time Awareness in 19th-Century America." *Technology and Culture* 30, no. 1 (January 1989): 1–24.
Stephens, Michelle Ann. *Skin Acts: Race, Psychoanalysis, and the Black Male Performer*. Durham: Duke University Press, 2014.
Sterling, Bruce. *Distraction*. New York: Bantam, 1998.
Stewart, Kathleen. *Ordinary Affects*. Durham: Duke University Press, 2007.
Stoler, Ann Laura. *Along the Archival Grain: Epistemic Anxieties and Colonial Common Sense*. Princeton: Princeton University Press, 2009.
——. "'In Cold Blood': Hierarchies of Credibility and the Politics of Colonial Narratives." *Representations*, no. 37 (1992): 151–89.
Sturken, Marita. *Tangled Memories: The Vietnam War, the AIDS Epidemic, and the Politics of Remembering*. Berkeley: University of California Press, 1997.
Suzuki, Erin and Aimee Bahng. "The Transpacific Subject in Asian American Culture," *Oxford Research Encyclopedia of Literature*. January 30, 2020. https://oxfordre.com/literature/view/10.1093/acrefore/9780190201098.001.0001/acrefore-9780190201098-e-877.
Szalontai, Balazs. "From Battlefield to Marketplace: The End of the Cold War in Indochina, 1985–1989." In *The End of the Cold War and The Third World: New*

Perspectives on Regional Conflict, edited by Artemy Kalinovsky and Sergey Radchenko, 155–72. New York: Routledge, 2011.

Taber, Robert. *War of the Flea: The Classic Study of Guerrilla Warfare*. Washington, D.C: Brassey's, 2002.

Tadiar, Neferti X. M. "Ground Zero." *GLQ: A Journal of Lesbian and Gay Studies* 22, no. 2 (2016): 173–81.

———. *Things Fall Away: Philippine Historical Experience and the Makings of Globalization*. Durham: Duke University Press, 2009.

Taylor, Diana. *The Archive and the Repertoire: Performing Cultural Memory in the Americas*. Durham: Duke University Press, 2003.

Tempo, Carl J. Bon. *Americans at the Gate: The United States and Refugees During the Cold War*. Princeton: Princeton University Press, 2008.

Tenhula, John. *Voices from Southeast Asia: The Refugee Experience in the United States*. New York: Holmes and Meier, 1991.

Thomas, Deborah A. "Caribbean Studies, Archive Building, and the Problem of Violence." *Small Axe: A Caribbean Journal of Criticism* 17, no. 2 (July 1, 2013): 27–42.

Thompson, Edward. "The Long Revolution." *New Left Review* 1, no. 9 (June 1961): 24–33.

Thompson, Krista A. *Shine: The Visual Economy of Light in African Diasporic Aesthetic Practice*. Durham: Duke University Press, 2015.

Thompson, Michael G. *For God and Globe: Christian Internationalism in the United States Between the Great War and the Cold War*. Ithaca, N.Y.: Cornell University Press, 2015.

Tovy, Tal. "Manifest Destiny In POW Camps: The U.S. Army Reeducation Program During the Korean War." *Historian* 73, no. 3 (Fall 2011): 503–25.

Treat, John Whittier. "Beheaded Emperors and the Absent Figure in Contemporary Japanese Literature." *PMLA* 109, no. 1 (1994): 100–15.

Trimm, Ryan S. "Inside Job: Professionalism and Postimperial Communities in *The Remains of the Day*." *Lit: Literature Interpretation Theory* 16, no. 2 (2005): 135–61.

Trinh, T. Minh-ha. "All-Owning Spectatorship." In *When the Moon Waxes Red: Representation, Gender and Cultural Politics*, 81–106. New York: Routledge, 1991.

———. *Elsewhere, Within Here: Immigration, Refugeeism and the Boundary Event*. New York: Routledge, 2011.

———. "Mechanical Eye, Electronic Ear, and the Lure of Authenticity." In *When the Moon Waxes Red: Representation, Gender and Cultural Politics*, 53–64. New York: Routledge, 1991.

———. *Surname Viet Given Name Nam*. New York: Women Make Movies, 1989.

———. "White Spring." In *The Dream of the Audience*, edited by Constance Lewallen, 33–50. Berkeley: University of California Press, 2001.

———. "Yellow Sprouts." In *When the Moon Waxes Red: Representation, Gender and Cultural Politics*, 1–8. New York: Routledge, 1991.

Trinh, T. Minh-ha, and Harriet Hirshorn. "Questioning Truth and Fact." In *Framer Framed*, 181–90. New York: Routledge, 1992.

Trinh, T. Minh-ha, Laleen Jayamane, and Anne Rutherford. "'Why A Fish Pond?': Fiction at the Heart of Documentation." In *Framer Framed*, 161–80. New York: Routledge, 1992.

BIBLIOGRAPHY

Trinh, T. Minh-ha, and Fukuko Kobayashi. "Is Feminism Dead." In *The Digital Film Event*. New York: Routledge, 2012.
Trinh, T. Minh-ha, and Scott MacDonald. "Film as Translation: A Net with No Fisherman." In *Framer Framed*, 111–36. New York: Routledge, 1992.
Trinh, T. Minh-ha, and Valentina Vitali. "The Cyborg's Hand." In *The Digital Film Event*, 159–80. New York: Routledge, 2012.
Troeung, Y.-Dang. "'A Gift or a Theft Depends on Who Is Holding the Pen': Postcolonial Collaborative Autobiography and Monique Truong's *The Book of Salt*." *MFS Modern Fiction Studies* 56, no. 1 (2010): 113–35.
Truong, Monique. "Vietnamese American Literature." In *An Interethnic Companion to Asian American Literature*, edited by King-Kok Cheung, 219–48. New York: Cambridge University Press, 1997.
Tsing, Anna. "Supply Chains and the Human Condition." *Rethinking Marxism* 21, no. 2 (April 1, 2009): 148–76.
Tsu, Jing. *Sound and Script in Chinese Diaspora*. Cambridge, Mass.: Harvard University Press, 2011.
Tuan, Anh Hoang. "Why Hasn't Vietnam Gained ASEAN Membership?" *Contemporary Southeast Asia* 15, no. 3 (December 1993): 280–91.
Turner, Fred. *The Democratic Surround: Multimedia and American Liberalism from World War II to the Psychedelic Sixties*. Chicago: University of Chicago Press, 2013.
Uba, George. "Friend and Foe: De-Collaborating Wendy Wilder Larsen and Tran Thi Nga's Shallow Graves." *Journal of American Culture* 16, no. 3 (Fall 1993): 63–70.
U.S. Army Forces in the Far East. *Interviews with 24 Korean POW Leaders*. Psychological Warfare Section, 1954.
U.S. Congress. "Induk Pahk." Report to accompany H.R. 2054. 84th Cong., 2nd sess., 20 February 1956.
U.S. Defense Advisory Committee on Prisoners of War. *POW, the Fight Continues After the Battle: The Report of the Secretary of Defense's Advisory Committee on Prisoners of War*. Washington, D.C.: U.S. Government Printing Office, 1955.
U.S. Department of Defense. *United States–Vietnam Relations, 1945–1967, Book 4*. Washington D.C.: Government Printing Office, 1971.
——. *United States–Vietnam Relations, 1945–1967, Book 8*. Washington, D.C.: Government Printing Office, 1971.
U.S. Department of State. *Foreign Relations of the United States*, 1949, Vol. 7, Part 2. Washington, D.C.: Government Printing Office, 1976.
——. *Foreign Relations of the United States, 1950, National Security Affairs; Foreign Economic Policy*. Washington, D.C.: Government Printing Office, 1977.
——. *Foreign Relations of the United States, 1952–1954, Western Europe and Canada*, Vol. 6, Part 1. Washington, D.C.: Government Printing Office, 1986.
——. *Foreign Relations of the United States, Foreign Aid and Economic Defense Policy, 1955–1957*, Vol. 10. Washington, D.C.: U.S. Government Printing Office, 1989.
U.S. President's Committee on International Information Activities (Jackson Committee). "The President's Committee on International Information Activities: Report to the President." June 30, 1953.
Upchurch, Michael. "Ha Jin's New Collection of Stories Loses Something in the 'Translation.'" *Chicago Tribune*, October 8, 2000.
Updike, John. "Nan, American Man." *New Yorker*, December 3, 2007.

Varsava, Jerry A. "An Interview with Ha Jin." *Contemporary Literature* 51, no. 1 (2010): 1–26.

Végső, Roland. *The Naked Communist: Cold War Modernism and the Politics of Popular Culture*. New York: Fordham University Press, 2013.

Venuti, Lawrence. *The Translator's Invisibility: A History of Translation*. New York: Routledge, 2008.

Verdery, Katherine. *Secrets and Truths: Ethnography in the Archive of Romania's Secret Police*. New York: Central European University Press, 2014.

Virno, Paolo. *A Grammar of the Multitude: For an Analysis of Contemporary Forms of Life*. Translated by Isabella Bertoletti, James Cascaito, and Andrea Casson. New York: Semiotext(e), 2004.

Vogel, Ezra. "Foreword." In *The Chrysanthemum and the Sword*, by Ruth Benedict. Cleveland: Meridian, 1989.

Von Eschen, Penny M. *Race Against Empire: Black Americans and Anticolonialism, 1937–1957*. Ithaca, N.Y.: Cornell University Press, 1997.

Wald, Priscilla. "The 'Hidden Tyrant': Propaganda, Brainwashing, and Psycho-Politics in the Cold War Period." In *The Oxford Handbook of Propaganda Studies*, edited by Jonathan Auerbach and Russ Castronovo, 109–30. New York: Oxford University Press, 2013.

Walkowitz, Rebecca L. *Born Translated: The Contemporary Novel in an Age of World Literature*. New York: Columbia University Press, 2015.

———. *Cosmopolitan Style: Modernism Beyond the Nation*. New York: Columbia University Press, 2006.

Wang, Jessica. "A State of Rumor: Low Knowledge, Nuclear Fear, and the Scientist as Security Risk." *Journal of Policy History* 28, no. 3 (2016): 406–46.

Wang, L. Ling-chi. "Model Minority, High-Tech Coolies, and Foreign Spies: Asian Americans in Science and Technology, with Special Reference to the Case of Dr. Wen Ho Lee." *Amerasia Journal* 33, no. 1 (2007): 49–62.

———. "Roots and Changing Identity of the Chinese in the United States." *Daedalus* 120, no. 2 (1991): 181–206.

Wang, Tsun-ming. *Wang Tsun-Ming, Anti-Communist: An Autobiographical Account of Chinese Communist Thought Reform*. Washington, D.C.: Psychological Warfare Division, George Washington University, 1954.

Wark, Wesley K. "The Intelligence Revolution and the Future." *Studies in Intelligence* 37, no. 5 (1994): 9–16.

Watson, Faith. "Ha Jin's *War Trash*: Writing War in a 'Documentary Manner.'" *Japan Studies Association* 7 (2009): 115–31.

Weber, Max. *From Max Weber: Essays in Sociology*. Translated and edited by H. H. Gerth and C. Wright Mills. New York: Oxford University Press, 1946.

Werner, Jayne. *Gender, Household and State in Post-Revolutionary Vietnam*. New York: Routledge, 2009.

Westad, Odd Arne. *The Global Cold War: Third World Interventions and the Making of Our Times*. New York: Cambridge University Press, 2005.

Wexler, Laura. *Tender Violence: Domestic Visions in an Age of U.S. Imperialism*. Chapel Hill: University of North Carolina Press, 2000.

White, William Lindsay. *The Captives of Korea: An Unofficial White Paper on the Treatment of War Prisoners*. New York: Scribner's, 1957.

BIBLIOGRAPHY

Wiegman, Robyn. *Object Lessons*. Durham: Duke University Press, 2012.
Williams, Raymond. *Culture and Society 1780–1950*. New York: Doubleday, 1958.
———. *Marxism and Literature*. Oxford: Oxford University Press, 1977.
———. *Politics and Letters: Interviews with New Left Review*. New York: Verso, 1979.
Williams, Walter L. "United States Indian Policy and the Debate over Philippine Annexation: Implications for the Origins of American Imperialism." *Journal of American History* 66, no. 4 (1980): 810–31.
Williams, William Appleman. "The Frontier Thesis and American Foreign Policy." *Pacific Historical Review* 24, no. 4 (November 1955): 379–95.
Wilson, Rob. *Reimagining the American Pacific: From South Pacific to Bamboo Ridge and Beyond*. Durham: Duke University Press, 2000.
Wolferen, Karel Van. *The Enigma of Japanese Power: People and Politics in a Stateless Nation*. New York: Vintage, 1989.
Woloch, Alex. *The One vs Minor Characters and the Space of the Protagonist in the Novel*. Princeton: Princeton University Press, 2003.
Wong, Sau-Ling C. "Denationalization Reconsidered: Asian American Cultural Criticism at a Theoretical Crossroads." *Amerasia* 21, nos. 1–2 (1995): 1–27.
Wong, Shelley Sun. "Unnaming the Same: Theresa Hak Kyung Cha's *Dictee*." In *Writing Self, Writing Nation: A Collection of Essays on Dictee by Theresa Hak Kyung Cha*, edited by Norma Alarcón and Elaine H. Kim, 104–40. New York: Third Woman, 1994.
Wood, Stephen. "The Japanization of Fordism." *Economic and Industrial Democracy*, June 29, 2016: 535–55.
Woods, Colleen. "Bombs, Bureaucrats, and Rosary Beads: The United States, the Philippines, and the Making of Global Anti-Communism, 1945–1960." PhD dissertation, University of Michigan, 2012.
Wroe, Nicholas. "Living Memories." *The Guardian*, February 19, 2005.
Wu, Ellen. "'America's Chinese': Anti-Communism, Citizenship, and Cultural Diplomacy during the Cold War." *Pacific Historical Review* 77, no. 3 (2008): 391–422.
———. *The Color of Success: Asian Americans and the Origins of the Model Minority*. Princeton: Princeton University Press, 2013.
Wubben, H. H. "American Prisoners of War in Korea: A Second Look at the 'Something New in History' Theme." *American Quarterly* 22, no. 1 (1970): 3–19.
Xinqiu, Xie. "*War Trash*: War Memoir as 'False Document.'" *Amerasia* 38, no. 2 (2012): 35–42.
Yanagisako, Sylvia. "Asian Exclusion Acts." In *Learning Places: The Afterlives of Area Studies*, edited by Masao Miyoshi and Harry Harootunian. Durham: Duke University Press, 2002.
Yang, Fan. *Faked in China: Nation Branding, Counterfeit Culture, and Globalization*. Bloomington: Indiana University Press, 2015.
Yang, Hee-wan. "A Critical Edition of Major Speeches by Rhee Syngman and Park Chunghee on the Issue of Korean Unification, 1945–1979." PhD dissertation, University of Wisconsin-Madison, 1985.
Yao, Steven G. *Foreign Accents: Chinese American Verse from Exclusion to Postethnicity*. New York: Oxford University Press, 2010.
Yapp, Hentyle. *Minor China: Materialisms, Method, and Mediation on the Global Art Market*. Durham: Duke University Press, forthcoming.

Yim, Louise. *My Forty Year Fight for Korea*. New York: A. A. Wyn, 1951.
Yoneyama, Lisa. *Cold War Ruins: Transpacific Critique of American Justice and Japanese War Crimes*. Durham: Duke University Press, 2016.
——. *Hiroshima Traces: Time, Space, and the Dialectics of Memory*. Berkeley: University of California Press, 1999.
Yoo, Theodore Jun. *The Politics of Gender in Colonial Korea: Education, Labor, and Health, 1910–1945*. Berkeley: University of California Press, 2008.
Young, Charles S. "Voluntary Repatriation and Involuntary Tattooing of Korean War POWs." In *Northeast Asia and the Legacy of Harry S. Truman: Japan, China, and the Two Koreas*, edited by James I. Matray, 145–67. Kirksville, MO: Truman State University Press, 2015.
——. *Name, Rank, and Serial Number: Exploiting Korean War POWs at Home and Abroad*. New York: Oxford University Press, 2014.
Yu, Peter K. "Piracy, Prejudice, and Perspectives: An Attempt to Use Shakespeare to Reconfigure the U.S.-China Intellectual Property Debate." *Boston University International Law Journal* 19, no. 1 (2001): 1–87.
Zahra, Tara. *The Great Departure: Mass Migration from Eastern Europe and the Making of the Free World*. New York: Norton, 2016.
Zhang, Dora. "Notes on Atmosphere." *Qui Parle: Critical Humanities and Social Sciences* 27, no. 1 (June 2018): 121–55.
Zornow, William Frank. "Lincoln and Rhee: An Historical Analogy." *Lincoln Herald* 55, no. 3 (Fall 1953): 23–46.
Zweiback, Adam J. "The 21 'Turncoat GIs': Nonrepatriations and the Political Culture of the Korean War." *Historian* 60, no. 2 (Winter 1998): 345–62.

INDEX

Abegglen, James, 76
Acheson, Dean, 30
aesthetics: as intelligence, 7–8; in intelligence, 44, 274n77; and methodology, 50; post–cold war, 14; of ruination, 99, 135–36; and tone, 39–41, 273n65
affect: and capitalism, 14, 51; formal, 223; of free Asians, 70–71; and Hirohito's tours, 68, 75; and Orientalism, 14; and post-Fordism, 14; tone as, 275n90; and U.S. Republican presidents, 279–80n53; viral/contagion metaphors for, 68, 279n57; and work, 86–87
affective norming, 71–72, 94, 100, 280n58
African Americans, 7, 38, 242, 271n37. *See also* Black studies
After Evil (Meister), 73
agency: of Asian diasporans, 14–15; and brotherhood concept, 221; and commons, 238, 250; of free Asians, 14–15, 194; and historical time as progress, 101–2; and motion, 252; and parasitism, 246–47, 250; and U.S. empire, 193–94

ahistoricity, 98–99, 100, 104, 121, 132, 141
Ahmed, Sara, 68, 238
Alexander, John A., 166
Allport, Floyd, 276n3, 279n57
Alsop, Joseph, 212
Ambient Parking Lot (Lu), 252–59; on absorption, 253–54; ambient lifestyle in, 255–56, 307n33; artists in, 253–54, 307n30; capitalism in, 254–55; characterization in, 243–44, 258–59; narrative persona in, 257; quiescence in, 252–53; and suspension of historical time, 260; and techno-Orientalism, 258–59
American cold war. *See* cold war
American lake, 266n19
American Studies, 15
amputation metaphors, 106–7, 111, 113–16, 127
Anderson, C. W., 273n65
Anna and the King, 271n38
anticolonialism: and brotherhood concept, 197; and U.S. propaganda, 29–31, 110. *See also* Korean colonial history; redress movements;

anticolonialism *(continued)*
U.S. transwar policy in Japan; U.S. transwar policy in Korea
anticommunism: post–cold war, 145, 147–48, 149, 150, 182, 188, 291*n*21; in Wang Report, 146, 147, 165, 166, 168–69, 174, 188. *See also* cold war; U.S. propaganda; U.S. transwar policy in Japan; U.S. transwar policy in Korea
apocalyptic imagery, 38–39, 56, 272–73*n*55
applied knowledge approach, 16–17
archives, 31–34, 160, 302*n*82
Archives of Authority (Rubin), 31
Arellano, Oscar, 196, 205, 206
Arondekar, Anjali, 32
Arrighi, Giovanni, 51
articulatory organ theory of Korean language, 129–30, 288*n*79
Artist of the Floating World, An (Ishiguro), 79–84; blame/exoneration in, 80–83; characterization in, 89–90; early drafts of, 283*n*105; flashbacks in, 62–63; and Hirohito's tours, 60; and Japanese economic growth, 84; Japanese postwar identity in, 94; national forgetting in, 73–75; progress in, 79; quiet style in, 78–79; rumors in, 75, 79–80, 89–90, 91; self-negation in, 95; synchronization of time in, 118–19; unreliable narrator in, 61, 65, 80–81, 282*n*87; work in, 87–88
ASEAN (Association of Southeast Asian Nations), 196, 217, 304*n*110
Asian American Studies, 12, 15–16, 17, 145, 266–67*nn*27, 31
Asian Americans: vs. Asian diasporans, 12, 239–40; and commons, 239–40; self-representation of, 35, 271*n*37. *See also* Asian American Studies; free Asians
Asian capitalism, 8, 14, 50, 51, 52. *See also* Japanese economic growth; Korean economic growth
Asian diasporans: agency of, 14–15; vs. Asian Americans, 12, 239–40; and

capitalism, 52; and commons, 240; and critical juxtaposition, 13; meaning of, 12; and methodology, 50; and national forgetting, 281*n*68
Asian informants. *See* free Asians
Asian Studies, 12, 15–16, 17, 266–67*n*27
Association of Southeast Asian Nations (ASEAN), 196, 217, 304*n*110
attribution, 43

Bachner, Andrea, 154, 291*n*31
Bad Samaritans (Chang), 283*n*5
Balce, Nerissa, 268*n*7
Banks, Russell, 185, 186
Barthes, Roland, 72–73, 124–25, 129, 139, 287*n*64, 299*n*24
Beardsley, Monroe, 40
Bei Dao, 144
Bell, Roger J., 277*n*24
Benedict, Ruth, 57, 75, 280*n*54
Bennett, Burney B., 44, 274*n*77
Berkeley, George, 274*n*77
Berlant, Lauren, 279–80*nn*53, 58
Bernard, Miguel, 302*n*77
Berrigan, Darrell, 302*n*77
Besher, Alexander, 76
Best, Stephen, 270*n*31
Between Silences: A Voice from China (Jin), 150
Bitter Fruit of Kom-Pawi, The (Koh), 284*n*17
black intelligence. *See* covert operations; U.S. counterinsurgency
Black studies, 32, 267*n*34
Blade Runner, 76, 257, 258
boat people, 191, 304*n*110
Boat Rocker, The (Jin), 151, 186–87
Bohannan, C. T. R., 300*n*41
Boot, Max, 211, 395*n*137
Booth, Wayne, 282*n*87
Boyagoda, Randy, 297*n*118
Bradbury, Malcolm, 77
Bradbury, William C., 162, 165–68
brainwashing: Asians as susceptible to, 30, 158, 159, 164–65; and communication technologies, 163–64; and confessions, 162–64, 181; and

INDEX

inscriptional technology, 146–47, 156–57, 162–63, 181; origins of, 292–93nn46–47; vs. reeducation, 162, 168–69, *169*, *170*; U.S. alarm about, 159–60; U.S. propaganda on, *169*, *170*, *171*
Breton, André, 254
Bridegroom, The (Jin), 182
Brinkema, Eugenie, 223
brotherhood concept: and agency, 221; and family metaphors, 195–96, 205, 299n24; and free Asians, 192; and homosocial bonds, 301n75; and intimacy, 193, 205, 233–34; and invisible labor, 210–11; and Philippines, 194–95; and regional collective security, 196–97. *See also* Operation Brotherhood
Bui, Long, 212
Burdick, Eugene, 198
Buried Giant, The (Ishiguro), 92
Buruma, Ian, 173
Bush, George H. W., 144
Bush, George W., 280n53
Butow, Robert J. C., 278n25

Cable Guy, The, 86
capitalism: and affect, 14, 51; and ambience, 254–55; Asian, 8, 14, 50, 51, 52; and intellectual property rights, 185. *See also* Japanese economic growth; Korean economic growth; post-Fordism; work
Carruthers, Susan, 164
Castiglia, Christopher, 9, 48
censorship, 147–48, 149, 151, 182–84, 296n100
Central Intelligence Agency (CIA): and covert intelligence, 28; and estimation, 44; and gender norms, 209; openness initiative, 49; and Operation Brotherhood, 37, 206, 209; and Philippines, 195; and secrecy, 29; and Vietnam refugee operations, 190, 191. *See also* Lansdale, Edward
Cha, Bernadette, 284n10
Cha, James, 98, 284n10

Cha, Theresa Hak Kyung, 96; and aesthetic of ruination, 99, 135–36; and ahistoricity, 100, 104, 121, 141; as Asian diasporan, 12; background of, 98, 283n9; career of, 101; *Commentaire,* 134; on communication technologies, 127–28, 129–30, 134; and conjugations, 138–39; on exile, 135, 136–38, 141; *Exilée,* 135–36, 138, 140; *Faire-Part,* 134; and historical time as variation, 140–41; and immersion, 130, 132–33; *It Is Almost That,* 134; and Korean economic growth, 102–3, 133–34, 285n22; and Korean nationalism, 129–30; *Mouth to Mouth,* 129–30, *131,* 132–33, 134, 136; on old vs. modern, 284n10; and Pahk, 101; and post–cold war, 50; and postmodernism, 133–34, 141; *Repetitive Pattern,* 134; and suspension of historical time, 123–24, 127, 129, 142, 260; *Temps Morts,* 135–36, 137–39, 140; *White Dust from Mongolia,* 98–99, 284n10; on Yu Guan Soon, 122–27, *123, 124,* 129, 135. *See also Dictee*
Chandler, David, 201
Chang, Eileen, 144
Chang, Ha-Joon, 97, 98–99; *Bad Samaritans,* 283n5
characterization: and ambience, 258–59; indistinguishable characters, 241–42, 243, 306n10; and indoctrination, 156; and quiet style, 78–79; and race, 91, 95; redundancy of, 89–91; and rumors, 61, 79–80, 88–89, 91, 94, 260; and U.S. policy toward Hirohito, 63; and work, 60, 85–86, 88
Cheah, Pheng, 16–17, 103
Chen, Kuan-Hsing, 15, 266–67n27, 275n96
Chen Li, 185
Cheng, Anne, 41, 122
Cheng, Cindy, 35
Cheung, King-Kok, 151
Chiang Kai-shek, 71

Child of War, Woman of Peace (Hayslip), 216
China. *See* People's Republic of China
Chinese Nationalists, 145, 290*n*15
Cho, Grace M., 102
Choi, Don Mee, 1, 3, 4–6, 7, 8, 13, 45–46
Chow, Rey, 34, 41
Christianity: Korean memoir genre, 101, 109–10, 284*n*17, 285*n*28; political role in Korea, 109–10, 285, 285*n*35
Chrysanthemum and the Sword, The (Benedict), 57, 75
Chun, Wendy, 26, 257
CIE (Civil Information and Education Program), 171–72
Civic Action, 192, 196, 268*n*7, 301*n*62
Civil Information and Education Program (CIE), 171–72
Cock Still Crows, The (Pahk), 99–100, 101, 113, 116, 117, 118
coercive mimeticism, 34–35
cold war: apocalyptic imagery, 38–39, 272–73*n*55; and brainwashing, 160, 161, 164; and containment culture, 29–30, 55, 73, 240, 269*n*17; criticism on, 6; and culture, 35–36, 272*n*44; and disciplinarity, 15–17; and double agency, 266*n*21; end of, 49, 275–76*n*96; as expression of U.S. empire, 3, 264*n*9, 271*n*37; "hardliness" of, 1, 3, 4–6, 10, 45, 263*n*6; and intelligence origins, 28; and Korean colonial history, 103, 107; Manichaean definitions of, 2–3, 16, 271*n*38; NSC-68, 42, 263*n*7; and periodization, 2, 6, 237; plural nature of, 3; as real war, 3, 263*n*7; and redress movements, 103; and refugees, 297*n*2; and regional collective security, 196–97, 217; and suspicion, 237; term origin, 2; as total war, 3–4; typographical form for term, 3, 263*n*4; unconventional warfare in, 4, 264*n*11; and U.S. immigration policies, 289–90*n*5. *See also* free Asians; post–cold war; U.S. counterinsurgency; U.S. propaganda;

U.S. transwar policy in Japan; U.S. transwar policy in Korea
colonialism: and aesthetic of ruination, 135; and archives, 31–32; colonial/postcolonial studies, 267*n*34, 270*n*31; and communication technologies, 179, 295*n*93; and variation, 140. *See also* Korean colonial history; U.S. empire
Commentaire (Cha), 134
Committee on International Information Activities (Jackson Committee), 43
commons: and agency, 238, 250; and ambience, 244, 256; and Asian Americans, 239–40; and Asian diasporans, 240; collective, 243–44; and departure from identity, 259–60; and indistinguishable characters, 243; and motion, 259; and net metaphor, 241; parasitic, 244, 255; and rumors, 240–41; and temperament, 237–38
Commons (Kim), 236, 238–39
communication technologies: and brainwashing, 163–64; Cha on, 127–28, 129–30, 134; and colonialism, 179, 295*n*93; and Jin's documentary style, 175–76, 178–79
Communist China. *See* People's Republic of China
conceptual art, 134. *See also* Cha, Theresa Hak Kyung
Conein, Lucien, 190, 305*n*137
Connery, Christopher, 26
"Consider Japan" (Abegglen), 76
containment culture, 29–30, 55, 73, 240, 269*n*17
cool affect, 86–87
coolie, 87, 282*n*99
Cooper, Tom, 297*n*118
corpographies, 154, 291*n*31
counterfeit culture, 296*n*105
Covert Capital (Friedman), 211
covert operations, 28–29, 264*n*9. *See also* U.S. counterinsurgency
Craft of Intelligence, The (Dulles), 28

INDEX

critical juxtaposition, 13, 16
Cuba, 199–200
Cullather, Nick, 205
cultural appropriation, 186–88
cultural hegemony, 272n44
culturalism, 280n54
culture: and cold war, 35–36, 272n44; of containment, 29–30, 55, 73, 240, 269n17
Culture of Korean Industry, The (Kim), 96
Cumings, Bruce, 13, 128, 148, 157, 286n50, 291n18
cyberspace, 26, 257

Davidson, Michael, 285n22
de–cold war perspective, 15, 16, 275n96
Dean, Robert D., 302n83
Dear Cyborgs (Lim), 243–51; artists in, 249–50; characterization in, 243–44, 260; collective commons in, 243–44; habituation in, 247–48; monologues in, 248–49, 260; on parasitism, 245–48, 253; on political myths, 244–45; race in, 250–51
"Denationalization Reconsidered" (Wong), 239
Deng Xiaoping, 184
diaspora, 239. *See also* Asian diasporans
Dickerman, Sherwood, 201
Dictee (Cha): aesthetic of ruination in, 99, 135; on communication technologies, 134; conjugations in, 138; on difference, 289n99; exile in, 136; language in, 138; and redress movements, 102; on Yu Guan Soon, 122–27, *123*, *124*, 135
difference, 46, 140, 259, 289n99
Dirlik, Arif, 25, 26
Distraction (Sterling), 296n105
Dodd, Francis T., 180
Dohrn-van Rossum, Gerhard, 119
double agency, 36, 147, 266n21
Dower, John, 58, 64, 70
Drinnon, Richard, 202
Drucker, Peter, 76
Dudziak, Mary, 5, 264n9

Dulles, Allen, 28
Dupuy-Briet, Suzanne, 295n93

Edward Lansdale's Cold War (Nashel), 200
Eidsheim, Nina Sun, 40
Eisenhower, Dwight D., 3–4, 37, 43, 161
Elias, Amy, 285n27
Ellis, Nadia, 240
Ellsberg, Daniel, 200, 274n67, 300n44
Emerson, Gloria, 206
empire. *See* Japanese empire; U.S. empire
empiricism, 10, 26, 38, 39, 40
Enloe, Cynthia, 206
Espiritu, Yến Lê, 13, 191
estimation, 7, 43–45, 46–47, 275nn83–84
Even the Birds Don't Sound the Same Here (Proudfoot), 216
exile, 135, 136–38, 141, 143–44, 149, 182, 184, 187
Exilée (Cha), 135–36, 138, 140

Faire-Part (Cha), 134
Fall of South Vietnam, The: Statements by Vietnamese Military and Civilian Leaders (Rand Corporation), 216
Fallows, James, 76
Family of Man, The, 299n24
Fan, Christopher T., 97, 283n5
Far East Comes Near, The: Autobiographical Accounts of Southeast Asian Students in America (Nguyen and Halpern), 216
Fellers, Bonner, 63, 278n26
feminist Marxism, 288n94
Feng, Peter X., 221
field imaginaries, 18
Fifth Chinese Daughter (Wong), 8
Finlan, Alastair, 264n11
Fisher, James, 206
Flatley, Jonathan, 238, 275n90
Florida, Richard, 85
Flower Drum Song, The (Lee), 143
Fluet, Lisa, 84
Foot, Rosemary, 157–58
Foucault, Michel, 35, 210

framing, 219–20, 221–22, 223, 224–25, 226, 227, 235
free Asians, 34–37; affect of, 70–71; agency of, 14–15, 194; and Asian American movement, 239–40; backstage roles of, 37, 272nn50–51; and brotherhood concept, 192; and Christianity, 109–10; cold war self-representation as unprecedented, 34; and containment culture, 240; and double agency, 36, 147; exoneration of, 65; and gray intelligence, 34; Hirohito as, 11, 61, 70–71, 94–95; and national forgetting, 94; and Oriental as object of intelligence, 11–12; Pahk as, 11, 101, 105–6, 284n15; and self-Orientalization, 14; self-representation as intelligence, 36; self-representation as self-Orientalization, 34–35, 36; suspicion of, 36–37, 166; and unattributed intelligence, 43; U.S. intelligence sponsorship of, 11
Free Life, A (Jin), 187, 290n10, 297n118
free speech. *See* censorship
Freeman, James, 216–17
Freeman, John, 186, 295n94
Friedman, Andrew, 205, 211, 232, 395n137
frontier mythology, 25, 27, 189, 198
Fuentecilla, J. "Pete," 232
Fujitani, Takashi, 279n49

Gaddis, John Lewis, 29, 42
Galdós, Benito Pérez, 90
Gao Xingjian, 144
gay culture, 88–89
gender norms: and invisible labor, 210–11, 302n82; and Korean nationalism, 129–30; and Operation Brotherhood, 203, 205–10, *207*, 302nn77–78, 83; and U.S. counterinsurgency, 205–8; and U.S. empire, 302n83; and Vietnamese socialism, 218, 219–20, 233
geopolitical poetics, 4–5, 45–46. *See also* Choi, Don Mee

Germany, postwar, 72, 75
Ghost in the Shell, 257
Gibson, William, 76
Girard, René, 301n75
Glassman, Jim, 196–97
Gluck, Carol, 72
Gorbachev, Mikhail, 2
gossip, 88–89. *See also* rumors
Grace Sufficient (Kim), 101
Grandin, Greg, 264n9, 299n17
Great Crescent, 9, 266n19. *See also* Pacific Rim
Greater East Asia Co-Prosperity Sphere, 266n19
Greene, Graham, 8
Grew, Joseph, 63
Gries, David D., 49
Guo, Xiaolu, 290n9

Halpern, Joel M., 216
Han Hak Kyo, 172
Han Suyin, 144
Hardly War (Choi), 1, 3, 4–6, 7, 8, 13, 45–46
Hardt, Michael, 86
Harris, Richard P., 162
Hartman, Saidiya, 32, 302n82
Haunting the Korean Diaspora (Cho), 102
Hawai'i, 25, 30
Hayslip, Le Ly, 216
Hearts of Sorrow: Vietnamese-American Lives (Freeman), 216–17
Higgins, James, 216
Hirohito (emperor of Japan): blame/exoneration of, 59, 65, 70, 73, 82, 83, 94; Humanity Declaration, 64; as powerless, 67, 68–71, 72, 82, 94, 279–80n53; protests against, 70; surrender broadcast by, 64; as symbolic, 72–73; U.S. policy toward, 58–59, 63–65, 72–73, 278nn25–26; U.S. propaganda on, 69. *See also* Hirohito's tours
Hirohito's tours, 58–60, 64–73, *68*; and affective norming, 71–72, 280n58; democratization goal of, 58–59; and

INDEX

Hirohito as free Asian, 11, 61, 70–71, 94–95; and Hirohito as powerless, 67, 68–71, 72, 82, 94, 279–80n53; and Meiji imperial tours, 279n49; and overt vs. covert intelligence, 37; as remythologizing, 64–65; responses to, 66–68, 69; success of, 71; U.S. organization of, 71, 279n52

historical time: and ahistoricity, 98–99, 100, 104, 121, 132, 141; banishment of, 99–100, 284n13; and exile, 137–38, 141; and immersion, 130, 132–33; linear vs. cyclical, 107–8, 120; medial vs. maternal, 123; and numerousness, 112; and old vs. modern, 284n10; as ongoingness, 129; and Pacific Rim, 26; and photography, 124–25, 287n64; and railroads, 119–20, 286n50; and return narratives, 96–98, 106, 137, 283n5; suspension of, 123–24, 127, 129, 142, 260; and tone, 108; and transience, 139; as variation, 140–41; and wars, 104, 285n27. *See also* historical time as progress; melancholic historicism

historical time as progress: and agency, 101–2; and amputation metaphors, 106–7, 111; and historical transitions, 100, 108, 115–16, 129, 141–42; and numerousness, 111, 117; and photography, 124, 125; and transcendence, 117–18; and U.S. transwar policy in Korea, 102; and Yu Guan Soon, 122, 127

historical transitions: and affective maps, 275n90; and affective norming, 71–72, 100; and exile, 141; and free Asians, 71; and historical time as progress, 100, 108, 115–16, 129, 141–42; and progress, 141–42; and quiet style, 95; and race, 7; and return narratives, 98; and suspension of historical time, 142; and tone as historiographical method, 10–11, 47

historicization: of Asian diasporans, 14; of post–cold war, 50–51; and rumors, 56. *See also* wars, periodization of

Hodge, John, 105
Holocaust, 73
Hour of the Tiger, The (Pahk), 101, 110–11, 116, 118
Hsieh, Tehching, 250, 307n23
Hui, Andrew, 115
Hull, Matthew, 156
Humanity Declaration (Hirohito), 64
Hunter, Edward, 159, 163, 292n46, 293n47

I Love Lucy, 86
identity: departure from, 259–60; as illusion, 91–93; and redundant characterization, 90; and rumors, 57, 60, 61, 62, 87, 88–89, 92–93, 94. *See also* characterization; Japanese postwar identity
immersion, 130, 132–33
In the Midst of Wars (Lansdale), 200–1
Inability to Mourn, The (Mitscherlich and Mitscherlich), 75
Indian Wars, 27. *See also* frontier mythology
Indochina's Refugees: Oral Histories from Laos, Cambodia, and Vietnam (Scott), 216
informal tone, 193, 198–99, 201–2, 204, 208, 209–10, 221
inscriptional technology, 146–47, 153–57, 162–63, 175, 178–79, 181
inscrutability: and ambiguity of race, 38; and apocalyptic imagery, 38–39; and archival excess, 32, 34; and attribution, 43; and estimation, 46–47, 275nn83–84; and Japanese empire, 58; and methodology, 17–18; and Oriental as insensate, 14, 266n26; and parallax visions, 14; and rumors, 55–56; and secrecy, 33; and tone, 10
intellectual property rights (IPR): and Jin, 148–49, 174, 179–80, 182–84; and People's Republic of China, 184, 296nn102–3, 105
intelligence: and anxiety, 28; archives of, 31–34; classification of, 32–33, 42–43, 55, 274n67; covert vs. overt, 28–29, 37; and culture, 36; defined, 4, 264n12;

intelligence (*continued*)
and estimation, 7, 43–45, 46–47, 275nn83–84; footnotes in, 166–67, 169; infrastructure of, 26–27, 28–29, 269n13; and invisible labor, 210–11; and openness initiatives, 49–50; origin stories, 25–27, 28, 268–69n9; rumors in, 54–55; self-representation as, 36; term, 272n46; unattributed, 43; writing style in, 44–45, 200, 201–2, 274n77. *See also* Oriental as object of intelligence; tonal intelligence; U.S. propaganda; Wang Report

interviews: and framing, 219–20, 221–22, 223, 224–25, 226, 227, 235; and intimacy, 192, 221–23, 234; net metaphor for, 223–24, 241. *See also Surname Viet, Given Name Nam*

intimacy: and brotherhood concept, 193, 205, 233–34; and dependence, 261; and family metaphors, 199, 205, 222; and gender norms, 205–6; and informal tone, 193, 221; and interviews, 192, 221–23, 234; and tone, 193, 221, 223, 225; and U.S. counterinsurgency, 205; and volunteerism, 192

IPR. *See* intellectual property rights

Ishiguro, Kazuo: on blame/exoneration, 80–83; *The Buried Giant*, 92; and characterization, 78–79, 88–90, 94, 260; cosmopolitanism of, 77–78; on identity as illusion, 91–93; and Japanese economic growth, 60, 76–77, 84; motivation for Japanese content, 74, 281n67; and national forgetting, 73–75, 94; *Never Let Me Go*, 78, 84, 87, 283n103; *A Pale View of Hills*, 60, 73–74, 92; and post–cold war, 50; and post-Fordism, 61, 78, 84, 88; quiet style of, 61, 78–79, 86, 95; and race, 61–62, 91–92, 93–94, 95, 140, 283n103; *The Remains of the Day*, 60, 73–74, 76–77, 78, 84, 87, 92–93; and repetitive dialogue, 53, 60–61, 74; repetitive topics of, 280–81n65; on synchronization of time, 118–19; and tutelary model, 62–63; *The Unconsoled*, 77, 78; and unreliable narrators, 61, 65, 80–81, 282n87; *When We Were Orphans*, 77, 93; on work, 78, 84–85, 86, 87–88. *See also Artist of the Floating World, An*; rumors

It Is Almost That (Cha), 134

Ivy, Marilyn, 64

Iyer, Pico, 76–77

Jackson, Wayne, 45

Jackson Committee (Committee on International Information Activities), 43

Jameson, Fredric, 90, 130, 132–33

Japan: economic growth, 56, 60, 75–77, 84; Korean normalization of relations with, 103, 128, 287n69; Meiji era, 128, 279n49, 287n69; Pearl Harbor attack, 27, 268–69n9. *See also* Japanese economic growth; Japanese empire; Japanese postwar identity; Japanese war crimes, blame/exoneration for; Korean colonial history; U.S. transwar policy in Japan

Japan as Number One (Vogel), 76

Japanese economic growth, 56, 60, 75–77, 84

Japanese empire: and inscrutability, 58; and Korean economic growth, 103; occupation of China, 294–95n86; railroads as symbol of, 119, 286n50; and U.S. empire, 85; and U.S. transwar policy, 75. *See also* Japanese war crimes, blame/exoneration for; Korean colonial history

Japanese postwar identity: and affective norming, 71–72, 94, 100, 280n58; and culturalism, 71, 280n54; and national forgetting, 65, 73–75, 94; and rumors, 93–94; and U.S. policy toward Hirohito, 65, 73. *See also* Japanese war crimes, blame/exoneration for

Japanese war crimes, blame/exoneration for: and affective norming, 71–72, 94, 100; and amputation metaphors,

106–7, 111, 113–14, 115–16; Hirohito, 59, 65, 70, 73, 82, 83, 94; Ishiguro on, 80–83; and Japanese economic growth, 60, 84; and Korean collaborators, 110–11, 113–15; and national forgetting, 65, 73–75, 94; redress movements, 50, 73, 79, 84, 102–3, 276n98; and U.S. transwar policy in Japan, 59, 73, 83, 94, 100; and U.S. transwar policy in Korea, 30, 102, 109, 116, 120. *See also* Korean colonial history; U.S. transwar policy in Japan; U.S. transwar policy in Korea

Jerng, Mark, 38, 258

Jin, Daying, 291nn29–30

Jin, Ha: American subject matter of, 290n10; anticommunism of, 144, 145, 147–48, 149, 188, 291n21; as Asian diasporan, 12; *Between Silences: A Voice from China*, 150; *The Boat Rocker*, 151, 186–87; *The Bridegroom*, 182; and censorship, 147–48, 149, 151, 182–84, 296n100; *A Free Life*, 187, 290n10, 297n118; immigration history of, 143–44; and indoctrination, 155–56; and intellectual property rights, 148–49, 174, 179–80, 182–84; and C. Y. Lee, 143–44, 290n6; on literature as historical preservation, 150–51, 152–53, 173–74; *A Map of Betrayal*, 186, 296n100; *Nanjing Requiem*, 294–95n86; and post–cold war, 50; on Second World War, 294–95n86; "The Spokesman and the Tribe," 150–51, 187–88; and unobtrusive protagonists, 151–52; use of English language, 144–45, 290n9; *Waiting*, 183. *See also* Jin's documentary style; *War Trash*

Jin, Wen, 291n21

Jin's documentary style: accuracy of, 181–82, 295n94; and anticommunism, 145, 148–49, 188; and communication technologies, 175–76, 178–79; critical appreciation of, 291n18; and cultural appropriation, 186–88, 297n118; and freedom from ideology, 175; and inscriptional technology, 147–48, 156; and intellectual property rights, 182–83; and literature as historical preservation, 148, 152–53, 173–74; and performance art, 260–61; and plagiarism, 185–86; and propaganda, 179–80; and tone, 149–50, 155; and unobtrusive protagonist, 174, 180

Johns, Adrian, 184–85

Jun, Byung-joon, 128

Kal, Hong, 133
Kang, Laura Hyun-Yi, 102
Kang, Younghill, 284n17
Karnow, Stanley, 36–37
Kelly, Patrocinio Yapcinco, 211, 212, 232
Kennan, George, 29, 269n17
Kennedy, John F., 196, 201–2, 300n53, 302n83
Kenney, Martin, 85
Kent, Paul, 69, 70
Kent, Sherman, 43–44, 46, 47, 275nn83–84
Khalili, Laleh, 191, 298n8
Khien Lai, 224, 233, 234
Kim, Choong Soon, 96, 98
Kim, Elaine, 102
Kim, Helen, 101, 109–10, 284n17, 288n79
Kim, Jinah, 266n19
Kim, Jodi, 13
Kim, Ju Yon, 272n51
Kim, Maria, 287n56
Kim, Monica, 160
Kim, Myung Mi, 236, 238–39, 259
Kim, Richard, 284n17
Kim, Seung-kyung, 96
Kim Il-sung, 109
Kingman, Dong, 35
Klein, Christina, 29, 271n38
KMT (Kuomintang). *See* Chinese Nationalists
Knapp, Robert H., 53, 54, 55, 56
Know Your Enemy—Japan, 58
knowledge work, 60, 134–35, 288n94
Koh, Taiwon, 284n17
Kong, Belinda, 144

Korea: Christian memoir genre, 101, 109–10, 284*n*17, 285*n*28; collaborators in, 110–11, 114–15; language of, 129–30, 288*n*79; normalization of relations with Japan, 103, 128, 287*n*69; Park Chung-hee regime, 97, 99, 103, 128, 129, 287*nn*69–70; political role of Christianity in, 109, 285, 285*n*35; post–cold war cultural regime, 133–34; return narratives, 96–98, 106, 136–37, 283*n*5, 284*n*10; U.S. "liberation" of, 30, 105, 285*n*35; U.S. transwar policy in, 30, 102, 108, 109–10, 116, 120; and U.S. transwar policy in Japan, 73. *See also* Cha, Theresa Hak Kyung; Korean colonial history; Korean economic growth; Korean War; Pahk, Induk

Korean colonial history: and collaborators, 110–11, 114–15; and economic growth, 103, 118–19, 133–34; independence movement, 114, 116–17, 121–22, 286*n*44; Korean War POWs on, 172; overdetermination of, 133; and patriarchal marriage, 106–7; and redress movements, 102–3, 128; and synchronization of time, 118–19. *See also* Japanese war crimes, blame/exoneration for; Korean nationalism; U.S. transwar policy in Korea

Korean economic growth: and colonial history, 103, 118–19, 133–34; and Japan relations normalization, 103, 128, 287*n*69; and knowledge work, 288*n*94; and postmodernism, 285*n*22; and redress movements, 102–3; return narratives on, 96–98, 137, 284*n*10; and U.S. economic aid, 287*n*70; and Vietnam War, 103, 128, 287*n*70

Korean nationalism: independence struggles, 114, 116–17, 121–22, 286*n*44, 288*n*90; and language, 129–30; multiplicity of, 286*n*38; post–cold war, 133, 288*n*90; and U.S. transwar policy, 109–10. *See also* Korean colonial history

Korean War: apocalyptic imagery of, 272–73*n*55; and intelligence origins, 27; and Japanese economic growth, 128; and Korean colonial history, 110; and Orientalism, 158–59; and Pahk, 105; periodization of, 157; and psychological indoctrination, 146, 156–57. *See also* Korean War POWs

Korean War POWs: forcible tattoos, 153–54, 291*nn*29–30; handicrafts by, 176, *177*, *178*; repatriation dispute, 157–59, 164–65, 171; U.S. reeducation programs, 170–72. *See also* brainwashing; Wang Tsun-ming; *War Trash*

Koselleck, Reinhart, 98, 107, 108, 120

Kuomintang (KMT). *See* Chinese Nationalists

Kwangju uprising, 99

Kwon, Heonik, 3, 263*n*4, 265*n*16, 275–76*n*96

Lansdale, Edward: and brotherhood concept, 192, 197, 221; and Civic Action, 301*n*62; and family metaphors, 196, 198–99, 222; and fish pond metaphor, 234; and frontier mythology, 189, 198; and gender norms, 203, 205–6, 208, 209–10, 302*n*83; *In the Midst of Wars*, 200–1; inflated persona of, 204–5; informal tone of, 193, 198–99, 201–2, 208, 209–10, 221; and invisible labor, 211–12, 213; memoir of, 200–1; and Operation Brotherhood as U.S. counterinsurgency program, 202, 203; on psychology, 200, 300*n*46; and refugee resettlement, 214, 232, 234; and regional collective security, 197; romantic dalliances of, 211, 232; and secrecy, 189–90, 200, 300*n*47; and South Vietnam refugee migration (1950s), 190–91; and U.S. operations in the Philippines, 194–95, 204, 301*n*65; "The Village That Refuses to Die," 201–2, 300*n*53

INDEX

Laqueur, Thomas, 284n13
Lederer, William, 198, 395n137
Lee, C. Y., 143–44, 188, 290n6; *The Flower Drum Song*, 143
Lee, Rachel C., 251, 283n103
Lee, Sammy, 35
Lee, Yoon Sun, 112
Letters to a Friend (Võ), 303n103
Lévi-Strauss, Claude, 179
Lewis, Anthony Marc, 46–47
Li, Liyun, 290n9
Lie, John, 96, 98, 128
Life magazine, 202
Lim, Eugene, 241, 259. See also *Dear Cyborgs*
Lin Yutang, 144, 187–88
Lindroos, Kia, 124
Linebarger, Paul, 300n47
Lippard, Lucy, 134
Lippmann, Walter, 2
literary criticism, 40
Liu, Alan, 86–87, 95
Liu, William, 303n103
Lok, Susan, 225
"Long Telegram" (Kennan), 29
Lovell, Julia, 182
Lowe, Lisa, 31, 289n99
Lu, Pamela, 241, 243, 244, 252. See also *Ambient Parking Lot*
Lukacs, George, 121
Lye, Colleen, 38, 242–43, 269n17
Lynch, Deidre, 78, 242

Ma Jian, 144
McAlister, Melani, 34, 271n38
MacArthur, Douglas, 58, 63, 64, 71
McGurl, Mark, 60
Machine in the Garden, The (Marx), 119–20
McLean, David, 161
McLuhan, Marshall, 164
McMaster, G. E., 273n65
McNamara, Robert, 200, 300nn44, 46
McNaughton, John, 300n44
Magsaysay, Ramon, 204, 205
Mai Thu Vân, 218–19, 224

Mainland China. See People's Republic of China
Man, Simeon, 205
Manchurian Candidate, The, 4, 161
Manichaean definitions of cold war, 2–3, 16, 271n38
Maoism, 192, 298n8
Map of Betrayal, A (Jin), 186, 296n100
March 1, 1919 independence movement (Korea), 114, 121–22, 286n44
Marcos, Ferdinand, 71
Martin, Theodore, 307–8n34
Martyred, The (Kim), 284n17
Marvin, Carolyn, 154
Marx, Leo, 119–20
Massumi, Brian, 279–80n53
Meerloo, J. A.M., 163–64, 292n46
Meiji Japan: imperial tours, 279n49; and Park Chung-hee, 128, 287n69
Meister, Robert, 73
melancholic historicism, 5, 32, 99, 104, 133, 138, 270n31
Melley, Timothy, 163
Mendel, Douglas, 75–76
men's roles. See gender norms
Mertha, Andrew, 184
methodology: and aesthetics, 50; critical juxtaposition, 13, 16; and free Asians, 36; and inscrutability, 17–18; temporal and spatial arcs, 18–19; and tone, 9–11, 19
Middle East, 51
Military Information Division, 26–27
Min, Anchee, 290n9
Mitscherlich, Alexander, 75
Mitscherlich, Margarete, 75
Mo Yan, 144
Mojica, Proculo, 212
Montero, Darrel, 216
Moon, Chung-in, 128
Moon Waxes Red, The (Trinh), 220–21
More Like Us: Making America Great Again (Fallows), 76
Mouth to Mouth (Cha), 129–30, 131, 132–33, 134, 136
My Forty Year Fight for Korea (Yim), 101, 284n17

Nadel, Alan, 55
Nakamura, Naofumi, 119
Naked Communist, The (Végső), 33
Nanjing Requiem (Jin), 294–95*n*86
narrators, unreliable, 61, 65, 80–81, 282*n*87
Nashel, Jonathan, 200, 202
Nationalists. *See* Chinese Nationalists
native informants, 86. *See also* free Asians
Negri, Antonio, 86
Neuromancer (Gibson), 76
Never Let Me Go (Ishiguro), 78, 84, 87, 283*n*103
New Criticism, 40
New York Times, 202
Newly Industrialized Countries (NICs), 217
Ngai, Sianne, 40, 85–86, 132, 140–41, 294*n*76
Ngo Dinh Diem, 71, 202, 211
Nguyen, Lucy Hong Nhiem, 216
Nguyen, Marguerite, 213, 303*n*96
Nguyen, Mimi Thi, 213
Nguyen, Viet Thanh, 86
Nguyen, Vinh, 213, 303*n*96
Nichols, Bill, 221
No Chinese Stranger (Wong), 36
Northridge, A. R., 27, 268–69*n*9
NSC-68, 42, 263*n*7
numerousness, 111–13

OB. *See* Operation Brotherhood
object-subject oscillation, 18
Ohlin, Lloyd E., 162
Okazaki Hisahiko, 287*n*69
one-drop rule, 38
O'Neal, Floyd, 160
ongoingness, 129, 130, 132, 137
Operation Babylift, 298*n*4
Operation Brotherhood (OB): and agency, 221; American private funding for, 43, 204, 206, 301*n*64; and brotherhood concept, 192, 193, 195; elite participation in, 196; and fish pond metaphor, 234; and free Asians, 11; and gender norms, 203, 205–10, 207, 302*nn*77–78, 83; and informal tone, 202, 208, 221; and intimacy, 192, 193; and invisible labor, 213; Lansdale as responsible for, 204–5; and overt vs. covert intelligence, 37; as propaganda, 192–93, 195–96, 203–4; security purposes of, 196–97; as U.S. counterinsurgency program, 202–3; volunteers as refugees, 232
Operation Passage to Freedom, 190–91, 298*n*4
Oriental as object of intelligence: and free Asians, 11–12; and intelligence origins, 27; and overdetermination, 33–34; in Second World War propaganda, 69; and suspicion, 7, 8, 10, 265*n*16, 266*n*21; and U.S. empire, 26; yellow peril discourse, 38, 76, 251, 257, 258. *See also* inscrutability
Orientalism: and affect, 14; and ambience, 257–58; American, 34; and apocalyptic imagery, 39, 272–73*n*55; and archives, 31; and brainwashing, 158, 163, 164–65; and containment culture, 29–30, 269*n*17; and Korean War, 158–59; and Manichaean definitions of cold war, 16, 271*n*38; post-Orientalism, 271*n*38; techno-Orientalism, 257–59
Orwell, George, 2
Otsuka, Julie, 281*n*68
Our Town (Wilder), 201
overdetermination, 33–34, 46, 133

Pacific Rim: economic power in, 51, 52; and parallax visions, 16; and temperament, 52; terms for, 6, 9, 266*n*19; and U.S. empire, 8, 25–26
Pahk, Induk: and ahistoricity, 99, 100, 121; and amputation metaphors, 106–7, 111, 113–16, 127; and banishment of time, 99–100, 284*n*13; career of, 104–5; and Christian memoir genre, 101, 109–10, 284*n*17, 285*n*28; *The Cock Still Crows*, 99–100, 101, 113, 116, 117, 118; on communication technologies, 137; as free Asian, 11, 101, 105–6,

284*n*15; *The Hour of the Tiger,* 101, 110–11, 116, 118; and human remains, 100, 284*n*13; on Korean collaborators, 110–11, 114–15; and Korean economic growth, 113–14, 118; and Korean independence movement, 114, 116–17, 121–22, 123, 287*n*56; on Korean language, 288*n*79; and linear vs. cyclical time, 107–8; national forgetting in, 94; numerousness in, 111–13; on patriarchal marriage, 106–7; proverbs/aphorisms in, 113–14, 115; and synchronization of time, 118–19; and unattributed intelligence, 43; *The Wisdom of the Dragon,* 113. *See also* historical time as progress; *September Monkey*
Paik, Nam June, 133
Pale View of Hills, A (Ishiguro), 60, 73–74, 92
Pamela (Lu), 252, 253
Pamela (Richardson), 252
Pang, Laikwan, 183
parallax visions, 13–14, 16
paranoia. *See* suspicion
parasitism, 245–48; and agency, 246–47, 250; vs. ambience, 253; and artists, 249–50; and commons, 244, 255; and habituation, 247–48; and race, 250–51; and soliloquys, 248–49; and U.S. counterinsurgency, 251
Park, Ed, 99, 135, 259; *Personal Days,* 241–43
Park, Josephine, 35, 36
Park Chung-hee, 97, 99, 103, 128, 129, 287*nn*69–70
Parkinson, Anna, 71–72
Pax Americana, 16
Peace Corps, 302*n*78
Pearl Harbor attack, 27, 268–69*n*9
Pentagon Papers, 202
People's Republic of China (PRC): censorship by, 147–48, 149, 151, 182–84, 296*n*100; and counterinsurgency, 192, 298*n*8; and creativity, 183, 185, 295*n*98; and culture, 35; and double agency, 36; economic growth, 184; and intellectual property rights, 184–85, 296*nn*102–3, 105; Korean War entrance, 157, 160; and post-cold war anticommunism, 147–48, 149, 291*n*21; Tiananmen Square protests (1989), 144, 150, 182, 184, 188; and U.S. immigration policies, 289–90*n*5; World Trade Organization accession, 184, 188. *See also* brainwashing
Perelman, Bob, 132–33
performance art, 40–41, 260–61, 307*n*23
periodization. *See* wars, periodization of
Perry, Willis A., 160
Personal Days (Park), 241–43
Pfaff, William, 251
Philippines: and intelligence origins, 26–27; U.S. colonization of, 194–95, 299*n*17; U.S. counterinsurgency in, 199, 204, 268*n*7, 300*n*41, 301*n*65. *See also* Operation Brotherhood
photography, 122–27, *123*, *124*, 287*n*64
Phu, Thy, 122
Ping, Wang, 290*n*9
piracy, 184–85. *See also* intellectual property rights
political collectivity. *See* commons
Pomfret, John, 183
Poovey, Mary, 111–12
post-cold war: and anticommunism, 147–48, 149, 150, 182, 188, 291*n*21; and Asian capitalism, 8, 50, 52; and communication technologies, 127; and interviews, 192; Korean cultural regime, 133–34; and Korean nationalism, 133, 288*n*90; and openness initiatives, 49–50; and Pacific Rim, 8, 51; and parallax visions, 13–14; and postmodernism, 133–34, 141; scope of, 50–51; terms for, 50, 275–76*n*96; and Vietnamese reforms, 217–18. *See also* Asian diasporans
post-Fordism: and affect, 14; and artists, 308*n*41; Ishiguro on, 61, 78, 84, 88; and knowledge work, 134–35; and Korean economic growth, 103; and

post-Fordism (*continued*)
race, 242–43; and rumors, 61; and U.S. transwar policy in Japan, 12; and variation, 140–41
post-Orientalism, 271*n*38
Postman, Leo, 276*n*3
postmodernism, 104, 130, 132–34, 141, 285*n*22, 285*nn*22, 27
Postmodernism (Jameson), 130, 132–33
Powers, Thomas, 189
prognosis. *See* estimation
propaganda, 179–80. *See also* brainwashing; U.S. propaganda
Proudfoot, Robert, 216
proxemics, 259
psychological warfare. *See* U.S. counterinsurgency; U.S. propaganda
Puderbaugh, Richard, 274*n*77
punctum, 125, 142, 287*n*64

queer studies, 32
Quiet American, The (Greene), 8
Quinn, John, 160

race: ambiguity of, 38, 47; and archives, 31–32; and characterization, 91, 95; empiricization of, 10, 38, 39, 40; and hardliness, 45–46; and identity, 87; and ideology, 180–81; as illusion, 91–92; in Ishiguro's work, 61–62, 91–92, 93–94, 95, 140, 283*n*103; and Korean War POW repatriation dispute, 158–59, 164–65; and motion, 252; and overdetermination, 46; and parasitism, 250–51; and post-Fordism, 242–43; and rumors, 62, 79, 95; and suspicion, 7, 46, 265*n*16; and techno-Orientalism, 258–59; and tone, 9–10, 38, 40–42, 46–47, 88; and U.S. propaganda, 30–31, 270*n*25. *See also* inscrutability; Oriental as object of intelligence
racial intelligence, 7. *See also* Oriental as object of intelligence; race
racial mundane, 272*n*51
Radford, Arthur, 30
Rajaratnam, S., 304*n*110

Rand Corporation, 216
"Re-examining Our Perceptions on Vietnam" (Lewis), 46
Reader's Digest, 54, 202
Reagan, Ronald, 280*n*53
Reddy, Chandan, 191
redress movements, 50, 73, 79, 84, 102–3, 276*n*98
reeducation. *See* brainwashing
refugee narratives: anthologies, 216–17, 218–19; and post–cold war, 218; and spatiotemporal continuity, 231–32; and Voice/voice structure, 215–16
refugees: boat people, 191, 304*n*110; and cold war, 297*n*2; Operation Brotherhood volunteers as, 232; South Vietnam migration (1950s), 190–91, 214, 298*n*4; and U.S. empire, 213–14, 303*n*96; Vietnamese migration to West (1970s and 1980s), 214, 215, 232, 234, 303*n*103. *See also* refugee narratives
regional collective security, 196–97, 217, 304*n*110
Remains of the Day, The (Ishiguro), 60, 73–74, 76–77, 78, 84, 87, 92–93
Repetitive Pattern (Cha), 134
return narratives, 96–98, 106, 136–37, 283*n*5, 284*n*10
Rhee, Syngman, 71, 109, 110, 285*n*35
Richards, I. A., 40
Richardson, Samuel, 252
RIM (Besher), 76
Road Not Taken, The (Boot), 211
Robbins, Bruce, 84
Robin, Ron, 27, 55
Rockefeller, John D., III, 301*n*64
Rogin, Michael, 159
ROK. *See* Korea
Romulo, Carlos, 206–7, 304*n*110
Rubin, Andrew, 31
Rüegg, Johann Caspar, 273*n*65
rumors: and affective norming, 71–72; and apocalyptic imagery, 56; and characterization, 61, 79–80, 88–89, 91, 94, 260; and commons, 240–41; vs. gossip, 283*n*101; and Hirohito's tours,

59, 68–69; and identity, 57, 60, 61, 62, 87, 88–89, 92–93, 94; and inscrutability, 55–56; in intelligence, 54–55; and national forgetting, 74–75; and quiet style, 61, 79; and race, 62, 79, 95; and repetitiveness, 60–61; study of, 53–54, 276nn3, 6; and temperament, 55; and tone, 56–57, 61; viral/contagion metaphors for, 68, 279n57
Russell, Catherine, 223
Russia, 49–50
Ruttenburg, Nancy, 65

Said, Edward, 31, 34
Sakai, Naoki, 280n54
Santoli, Al, 216
Sarnoff, David, 264n12
Saturday Evening Post, 201–2, 300n53
Schwable, Frank, 160
science fiction, 97, 137, 283n5
Scott, David, 21, 103
Scott, Joanna C., 216
Scott, Ridley, 76
SEATO (Southeast Asia Treaty Organization), 196–97
Second World War: conventional warfare in, 264n11; Jin on, 294–95n86; and rumor studies, 53–54; and U.S. policy toward Hirohito, 63–64, 278nn25–26; and U.S. propaganda, 69, 270n25. *See also* U.S. transwar policy in Japan
secrecy: and CIA openness initiative, 49–50; and containment culture, 29; and intelligence classification, 32–33, 274n67; and Lansdale, 189–90, 200, 300n47; and rumors, 55; and U.S. counterinsurgency, 189–90
Sedgwick, Eve Kosofsky, 88–89, 301n75
self-representation: and agency, 14–15; and American Orientalism, 34; of Asian Americans, 35, 271n37; and Asian capitalism, 14; and gossip, 88–89; and racial Other, 34; as self-Orientalization, 14, 34–35, 36; spatial metaphors for, 231–32, 235; and

tone, 10; as unprecedented for free Asians, 34
September Monkey (Pahk): amputation metaphors in, 106–7, 111, 113–14; and Christian memoir genre, 101; Korean economic growth in, 118; on Pahk's imprisonment, 114, 116, 117, 121; on Pahk's speaking career, 104
Serres, Michael, 247
Shan, Te-hsing, 151–52
Shen, Shuang, 272n46
Shibusawa, Naoko, 70, 277n22
Siebers, Tobin, 237
Sino-U.S. Memorandum of Understanding on Intellectual Property Rights, 184
Sitney, P. Adams, 223
skin, 41
Slaughter, Joseph, 185
slavery, 30, 32, 271n37, 302n82
Slotkin, Richard, 198
Smith, Abbott, 45
Smith, Joseph B., 195
Snow Crash (Stephenson), 76
Song, Min Hyoung, 242
sound studies, 39–40, 273n65
South Korea. *See* Korea
Southeast Asia Treaty Organization (SEATO), 196–97
Southeast Asians: A New Beginning in Lowell (Higgins), 216
Soviet Union. *See* cold war
"Spokesman and the Tribe, The" (Jin), 150–51, 187–88
Standish, Burt, 201
Stephens, Michelle, 41
Stephenson, Neal, 76
Sterling, Bruce, 296n105
Stewart, Kathleen, 244
Stoler, Ann Laura, 31–32, 283n101
Strategic Intelligence (Kent), 43–44
structures of feelings, 48
Studies in Intelligence, 44, 45, 275n84
Sully, François, 216
Sun Tzu, 28

Surname Viet, Given Name Nam (Trinh), 218–22; cinematic tricks in, 193, 298*n*12; fish pond metaphor in, 234–35; framing in, 219–20, 221–22, 223, 224–25, 226, *227*, 235; on gender norms, 233; ideology in, 228–30, *228*, *229*; indiscriminateness in, 225; intimacy in, 192; movement in, 230–31, *230*; and net metaphor, 223–24, 234, 241; source for, 218–19, 224; structure of, 218, 232–33; Trinh's essay on, 220–21; and Voice/voice structure, 215, 218
suspicion: and apocalyptic imagery, 38–39; and family metaphors, 198; of free Asians, 36–37, 166; and openness initiatives, 50; and Oriental as object of intelligence, 7, 8, 10, 265*n*16, 266*n*21; and race, 7, 46, 265*n*16; and rumors, 55; and secrecy, 32; and tone, 9, 237; and Want Report, 166
Swope, Guy, 66–67

Tadiar, Neferti, 206–7, 261
techno-Orientalism, 257–59
Teilhard de Chardin, Pierre, 164
temperament: and commons, 237–38; and Pacific Rim, 52; and periodization of wars, 5–6; and political movements, 237–38; and rumors, 55; and tone, 9, 49, 108, 236–37. *See also* suspicion
temporality. *See* historical time
Temps Morts (Cha), 135–36, 137–39, 140
Tenhula, John, 216
Thompson, E. P., 48, 275*n*88
Thompson, Krista, 41
Thu Van, 224–25, 226, *227*, *228*, *229*, *230*
Ti Bah, 212
Tiananmen Square protests (1989), 144, 150, 182, 184, 188
time. *See* historical time
Time Clock Piece (Hsieh), 307*n*23
To Bear Any Burden: The Vietnam War and Its Aftermath in the Words of Americans and Southeast Asians (Santoli), 216

Tokyo War Crimes Tribunal, 59, 70
Tomkins, Silvan, 68
tonal intelligence, 42–49; and estimation, 43–45; and geopolitical poetics, 45–46; and inscrutability, 46–47; and intelligence classification, 42–43, 274*n*67; and rhetorical tone, 42; rumors as source of, 56–57; and temperament, 49; and tone vs. content, 47–48, 275*n*88; and writing style, 44–45, 274*n*77. *See also* tone
tone: aesthetic connotations of, 39–41, 273*n*65; as affective map, 275*n*90; and ahistoricity, 104; and ambiguity, 39; and brainwashing, 146, 147, 162; vs. content, 47–48, 275*n*88; and historical time, 108; as historiographical method, 9–11, 39, 47–48, 236–37; hyperbolically formal, 221–22; and indistinguishable characters, 243; informal, 193, 198–99, 201–2, 204, 208, 210, 221; and inscrutability, 10; and intimacy, 193, 221, 223, 225; and Jin's documentary style, 149–50, 155; and methodology, 9–11, 19; polyvalence of, 39; and post–cold war capitalism, 51, 52; of propaganda, 171, 294*n*76; as prosthetic, 41; and quiet style, 78, 95; and race, 9–10, 38, 40–42, 46–47, 88; and responses to Hirohito's tours, 67–68, 69; rhetorical, 42; and rumors, 56–57, 61; and temperament, 9, 49, 108, 236–37; as tension, 41, 48, 273*n*65; and transience, 139; and variation, 140, 289*n*99. *See also* historical time as progress; tonal intelligence
total war, 3–4
Tovy, Tal, 291*n*18
Toyotism, 12, 85. *See also* post-Fordism
transitional moments. *See* historical transitions
transpacific cold war. *See* cold war
transwar. *See* U.S. transwar policy in Japan; U.S. transwar policy in Korea
Trimm, Ryan, 84

INDEX

Trinh T. Minh-ha: and cinematic tricks, 193, 298*n*12; and intimacy, 192, 261; *The Moon Waxes Red,* 220–21; and post–cold war, 50; on Vietnam War memory industry, 215; on Voice/voice structure, 215–16. *See also Surname Viet, Given Name Nam*
Truman, Harry S., 50, 157
Trump, Donald, 280*n*53
Tsing, Anna, 288*n*94
Tsu, Jing, 144, 185
Twilight Zone, The, 202

Ugly American, The (Burdick and Lederer), 198, 300*n*53
unattributed intelligence, 43
Unconsoled, The (Ishiguro), 77, 78
United States. *See* cold war; intelligence; U.S. counterinsurgency; U.S. empire; U.S. Occupation of Japan; U.S. propaganda; U.S. transwar policy in Japan; U.S. transwar policy in Korea
United States Army Military Government in Korea (USAMGIK), 105, 285*n*35
Upchurch, Michael, 182, 187
Urbano, Felisa, 209–10, 211
U.S. counterinsurgency, 189–92; Civic Action, 301*n*62; and family metaphors, 198–99; and gender norms, 205–8; and informal tone, 198–201, 208, 209–10; and intelligence origins, 27; and intimacy, 205; and invisible labor, 211–13; Operation Brotherhood as, 202–3; and parasitism, 251; Philippines, 199, 204, 268*n*7, 300*n*41, 301*n*65; and secrecy, 189–90; and South Vietnam refugee migration (1950s), 190–91, 298*n*4; Vietnamese employees as refugees, 214, 232
U.S. empire: and agency, 193–94; cold war as expression of, 3, 264*n*9, 271*n*37; and family metaphors, 195–96; and gender norms, 302*n*83; and intimacy, 193–94; and Japanese empire, 85; and Korean economic growth, 103; and Pacific Rim, 8, 25–26; and Philippines, 194–95, 299*n*17; and race, 10; and refugees, 213–14, 303*n*96; and Vietnam War, 205; and volunteerism, 196
U.S. imperialism. *See* U.S. empire
U.S. Information Agency (USIA), 28–29, 109, 269*n*13, 299*n*24
U.S. intelligence. *See* intelligence
U.S.-Japan relations: postwar protests against, 70; and redress movements, 73, 276*n*98. *See also* U.S. transwar policy in Japan
U.S. Occupation of Japan: Humanity Declaration, 64; policy toward Hirohito, 72–73; and Tokyo War Crimes Tribunal, 59, 70, 73; tutelary model for, 62–63, 277*n*22. *See also* Hirohito's tours; U.S. transwar policy in Japan
U.S. propaganda: and anticolonialism, 29–31, 110; on brainwashing, *169, 170,* 171; cold war importance of, 4; and cultural hegemony, 35, 272*n*44; family metaphors in, 195–96, 299*n*24; infrastructure of, 28–29, 269*n*13; and intimacy, 233–34; and openness initiatives, 49–50; and race, 30–31, 270*n*25; and Second World War, 69, 270*n*25; unattributed, 43; on United States as benevolent, 2–3, 29–30. *See also* free Asians
U.S. Psychological Warfare Division, 145
U.S. Republican presidents, 279–80*n*53
U.S. transwar policy in Japan, 277*n*24; and affective norming, 100; and blame/exoneration, 59, 73, 83, 94, 100; and Hirohito's tours, 58–59, 72; and national forgetting, 73, 74–75; and policy toward Hirohito, 63–65; and post-Fordism, 12
U.S. transwar policy in Korea, 30, 102, 108, 109–10, 116, 120

van Wolferen, Karel, 76
variation, 104, 139–41, 289*n*99
Varsava, Jerry, 173

INDEX

Vautrin, Minnie, 295*n*86
Végső, Roland, 33
veiled enemy. *See* inscrutability
Vietnam: patriarchy in, 218, 219–20, 233; post–cold war reforms, 217–18; and regional collective security, 217, 304*n*110; U.S. efforts to retake (1980s), 232
Vietnam: Un peuple, des voix (Mai), 218–19, 224
Vietnam War: and brotherhood concept, 197; Civic Action, 301*n*62; and estimation, 46; and family metaphors, 196, 198; and intelligence classification, 274*n*67; and invisible labor, 212–13; and Korean economic growth, 103, 128, 287*n*70; Lansdale's exit from, 300*n*46; Lansdale's popular writing on, 201–2; Operation Babylift, 298*n*4; Operation Passage to Freedom, 190–91, 298*n*4; and Philippines, 195, 301*n*65; and refugee migration to West (1970s), 214, 215, 232, 234, 303*n*103; and regional collective security, 197; and romantic dalliances, 211, 232, 305*n*137; South Vietnam refugee migration (1950s), 190–91, 214, 298*n*4; U.S. memory industry, 214–15; as U.S. theatrical production, 204–5
Vietnamese Americans: Patterns of Resettlement and Socioeconomic Adaptation in the United States (Montero), 216
"Village That Refuses to Die, The" (Lansdale), 201–2, 300*n*53
Virno, Paolo, 259, 308*n*41
Võ Phiến, 303*n*103
Vogel, Ezra, 75, 76
Voice of America (VOA), 105, 264*n*12
Voice/voice structure, 215–16
Voices from Southeast Asia: The Refugee Experience (Tenhula), 216
volunteerism: and brotherhood concept, 197; and gender norms, 205–6, 208, 209, 302*n*83; impurity of, 192; and informal tone, 199, 202, 204, 208, 209; and intimacy, 192; and invisible labor, 211–12; and U.S. empire, 196. *See also* brotherhood concept

Waiting (Jin), 183
Walkowitz, Rebecca, 77–78, 79
Wallace, Irving, 58
Wang, Jessica, 54
Wang, Weike, 290*n*9
Wang Report: ambivalent tone in, 162, 166, 167; anticommunism in, 146, 147, 165, 166, 168–69, 174, 188; on brainwashing, 146–47, 161–63; editors of, 162, 165–66; embodied vocality in, 167, 173, 188, 202; emotional doubling in, 167–68; footnotes in, 166–67, 169; and repatriation dispute, 165; and Wang Tsun-ming as free Asian, 11, 149, 165, 168; and *War Trash* compared, 145–46
Wang Tsun-ming: background of, 168, 293*n*62; as free Asian, 11, 149, 165, 168. *See also* Wang Report
Wang Tsun-ming, Anti-Communist (U.S. Psychological Warfare Division), 145. *See also* Wang Tsun-ming
War Trash (Jin): anticommunism in, 147–48, 149, 150, 182, 188; communication technologies in, 175–76; and cultural appropriation, 187; frame story in, 152–53; freedom from ideology in, 172–73, 174, 175; on indoctrination, 155–56; inscriptional technology in, 153–56, 175, 178–79; intellectual property rights in, 183–84; on literature as historical preservation, 173–74; plagiarism accusation, 148–49, 174, 179–80, 185–86; unobtrusive protagonist in, 151, 152, 180; and Wang Tsun-ming compared, 145–46. *See also* Jin's documentary style
Wark, Wesley, 32
wars: and aesthetic of ruination, 135; of empire, 3, 264*n*9; and historical time, 104, 285*n*27; as temperament, 6. *See also* wars, periodization of

INDEX

wars, periodization of: and ahistoricity, 104; and cold war, 2, 6, 237; and difference, 140; and Korean War, 157; and postwar, 1; and synchronization of time, 120; and temperament, 5–6; and tone as historiographical method, 10, 39
Watson, Faith, 175
Watsuji Tetsuro, 280n54
We, The Vietnamese: Voices from Vietnam (Sully), 216
Weber, Max, 32
Wexler, Laura, 195
What Is in a Rim? Critical Perspectives on the Pacific Region Idea (Dirlik), 25
When Heaven and Earth Changed Places (Hayslip), 216
When the Emperor Was Divine (Otsuka), 281n68
When We Were Orphans (Ishiguro), 77, 93
White, William Lindsay, 292–93n46
White Dust from Mongolia (Cha), 98–99, 284n10
Wiegman, Robyn, 18
Wilder, Thornton, 201
Williams, Raymond, 7–8, 48–49, 272n44, 275n88
Wilson, Rob, 50
Wisdom of the Dragon, The (Pahk), 113
women's roles. *See* gender norms

Wong, Jade Snow, 35, 36, 240, 241; *Fifth Chinese Daughter,* 8; *No Chinese Stranger,* 36
Wong, Sau-ling, 239
Wood, Stephen, 85
work, 83–88; and ambience, 307–8n34; and artists, 308n41; and characterization, 60, 85–86, 88; and cool affect, 86–87; *coolie* trope, 87, 282n99; and Japanese economic growth, 76; knowledge, 60, 134–35, 288n94. *See also* post-Fordism
World Trade Organization (WTO), 184, 188
World War II. *See* Second World War

Yanagisako, Sylvia, 17
yanggongju, 102
Yao, Steven G., 145, 148
yellow peril discourse, 38, 76, 251, 257, 258
Yim, Louise, 101, 109–10, 284n17, 288n79
Yoneyama, Lisa, 50, 58, 103, 109, 276n98
Yoshida Shigeru, 75
"You and the Atomic Bomb" (Orwell), 2
Young, Charles S., 291n18
Yu Guan Soon, 121–27, *123, 124,* 129, 135
Yu Hua, 144

Zhang, Dora, 238
Zhang Zeshi, 148, 185, 186
Zweiback, Adam, 159

GPSR Authorized Representative: Easy Access System Europe, Mustamäe tee
50, 10621 Tallinn, Estonia, gpsr.requests@easproject.com

www.ingramcontent.com/pod-product-compliance
Lightning Source LLC
Chambersburg PA
CBHW021931290426
44108CB00012B/803